The Affect and Effect of Politics

The Affect and

4. Fotofestival
Mannheim
Ludwigshafen
Heidelberg

FF

THE EYE IS A LONELY HUNTER: IMAGES OF HUMANKIND

KEHRER

Effect of Politics

Affekt und Wirkung von Politik

ZEPHYR der Reiss-Engelhorn-Museen Mannheim

Jeder von uns wird auf die eine oder andere Weise von der Politik berührt, geht es bei dieser doch um kollektive Entscheidungen mit kollektiven Auswirkungen. Doch welche Auswirkungen hat die Politik außerhalb ihres Kernbereichs von Wahlen, Gesetzgebung und Festlegung von Richtlinien?

Wie berühren die von Politikern getroffenen (oder nicht getroffenen) Entscheidungen unser Leben ganz real und konkret? Welche Auswirkungen haben die politische Praxis oder der Missbrauch von Politik? Die sozialen Beziehungen, die mit Autorität oder Macht einhergehen – ob dies der Staat oder die Regierung, eine Religion oder ein Unternehmen ist –, sind heute womöglich einer der wichtigsten Aspekte der menschlichen Existenz. Das Wort „Politik", das auf Aristoteles' Definition der „politika" (die Sache der Stadt) zurückgeht, ruft in uns viele, häufig aber abstrakte und nur schwer greifbare Bilder hervor. Dennoch betrifft die Politik unser Leben in vielfältigerer Hinsicht, als wir uns vorstellen können und geht weit über das Wahlverfahren hinaus, das die meisten von uns mit diesem Begriff verbinden. Die Politik beeinflusst die bürgerlichen Freiheiten und die Menschenrechte wie auch wirtschaftliche, kulturelle und gesellschaftliche Rechte, Themen und Möglichkeiten. Auch vielen der umstrittensten Konflikte auf dieser Welt liegen politische Entscheidungen zugrunde. Solche Entscheidungen werden oftmals in den höheren Etagen der sozialen Hierarchie getroffen und häufig in einer nicht transparenten Weise. Die Festival-Themenkategorie „Affekt und Wirkung von Politik" richtet ihr Augenmerk auf die wirklichen und fühlbaren Auswirkungen der Politik auf den Menschen – auf die Art und Weise, wie sich diese physisch auf unsere Umgebung, auf Landschaft, Gebäude und gemeinschaftliche Orte auswirken kann, aber auch wie sie auf die Psyche des Menschen einwirkt.

Folglich wird dieser Teil der Ausstellung die Konsequenzen politischer Instabilitäten und Veränderungen erkunden, die sowohl den Menschen als auch den physischen Raum betreffen. Sie hinterlassen in uns selbst emotionale und in unserer Umwelt physische Narben oder Spuren. Ein besonderer Schwerpunkt liegt auf dem Vermächtnis des Kolonialismus und der Großmächte, auf den politischen Umbrüchen der Gegenwart und ihren Nachwirkungen wie auch auf den wirtschaftlichen Verflechtungen des Westens und der in den Entwicklungsländern entstehenden Wirtschaftsmächte. Da uns die meisten Informationen über Politik von den Medien vermittelt werden, erreichen sie uns aus einer gefühllosen Distanz. Dieses Festivalsegment hat sich deshalb zum Ziel gesetzt, wieder auf das Vermögen der Fotografie zu verweisen, Emotionen und Mitgefühl zu Ereignissen hervorzurufen, die sich häufig in sicherer Entfernung von zu Hause abzuspielen scheinen – und auch auf die Fähigkeit dieses Mediums, zu informieren und grundlegendes Wissen zu erzeugen, das im öffentlichen Diskurs der Mainstream-Medien häufig verlorengeht.

Katerina Gregos & Solvej Helweg Ovesen

The Affect and Effect of Politics

ZEPHYR of the Reiss-Engelhorn-Museen Mannheim

We are all affected by politics in one way or another since politics involves collective decisions with collective effects. But what effect does politics have outside the political arena of voting, legislation and policy making?

How do the decisions that politicians make (or don't make) affect our lives in real, tangible ways? What are the effects of political practice or malpractice? Social relations involving authority or power – whether state or governmental, religious or corporate – are key issues affecting human existence today. The word 'politics' – which originates in Aristotle's definition of 'politika' (affairs of the city) - conjures up many abstract and hard-to-grasp images. Politics affects our lives in more ways than we might ordinarily conceive – and well beyond the electoral process that most of us associate the notion with. Politics influences civil liberties and human rights, as well as economic, cultural and social rights, issues and opportunities. Political decisions also lie behind many of the world's most debated conflicts. These decisions are often made within the higher echelons of the social hierarchy, in often non-transparent ways. 'The Affect and Effect of Politics' explores the real, tangible effects of politics on human beings; how these might be imprinted on the physical environment, landscapes, buildings, and social spaces, and how they impact humans psychologically.

This part of the exhibition will thus explore the consequences of political instability and change both in human terms and in terms of the way these forces are imprinted on physical space, leaving scars or traces, emotional as well as material, on the world around us. 'The Affect and Effect of Politics' focuses on the legacy of colonialism and empires, current political upheavals and their repercussions, and the economic entanglements of the west and emerging economic powers in developing countries. Most of the information we get about politics is transmitted through mainstream media, and is often presented to us from a dispassionate distance. This category of the festival thus aims to re-emphasize photography's capacity for generating affect and empathy in relation to issues that often seem to be unfolding at a safe distance from home, as well as its capacity to inform and generate vital knowledge that often escapes the mainstream media discourse.

Katerina Gregos & Solvej Helweg Ovesen

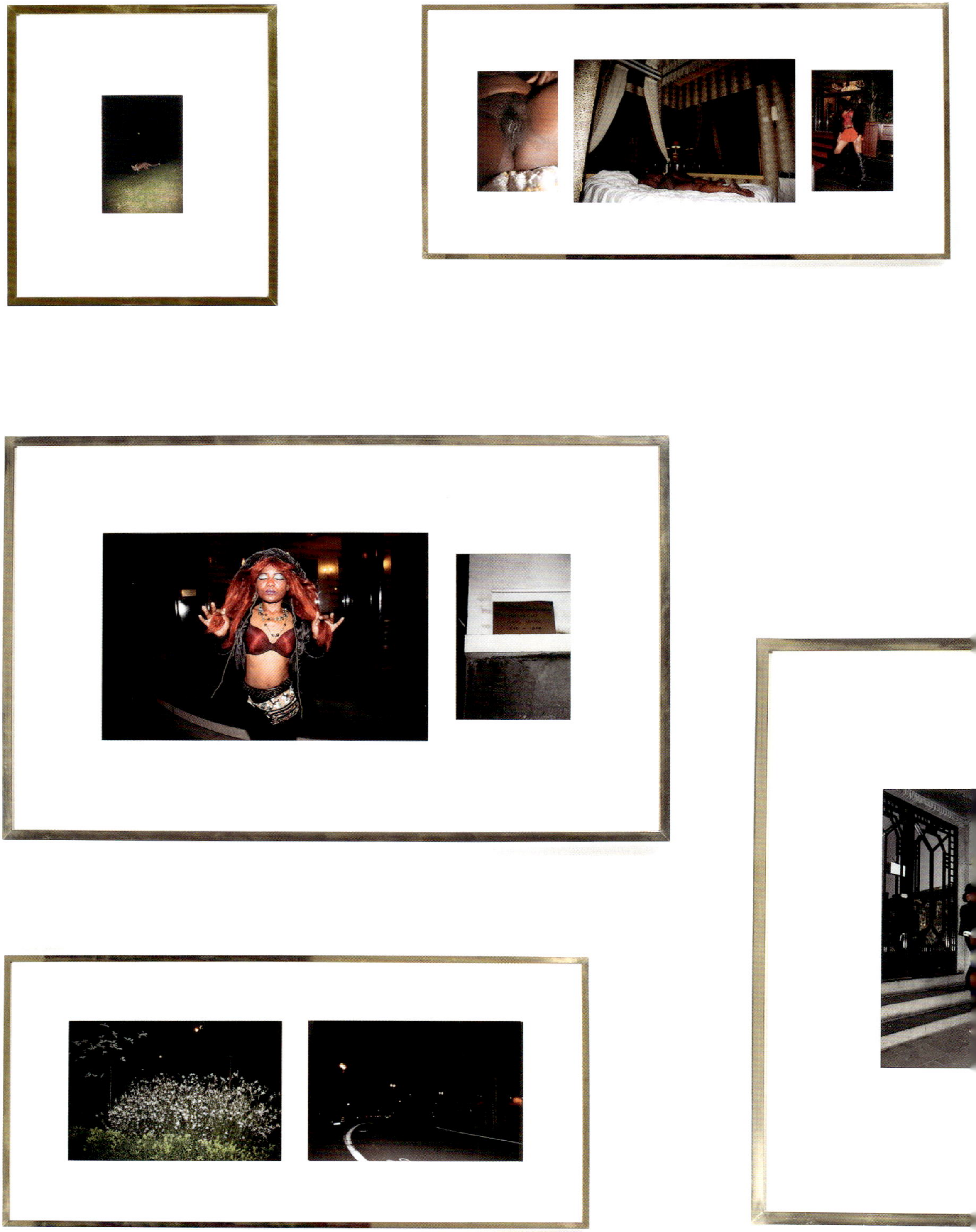

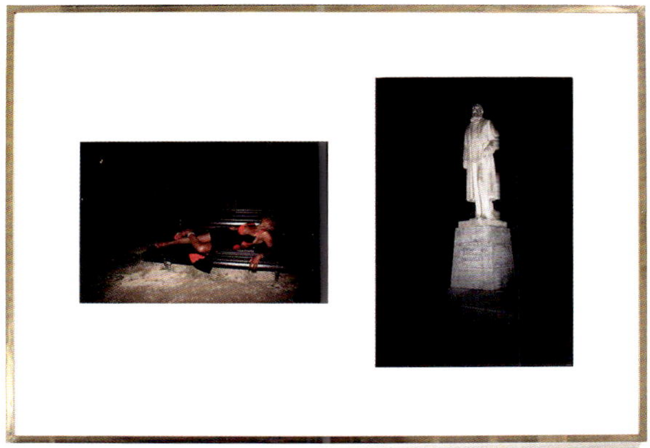

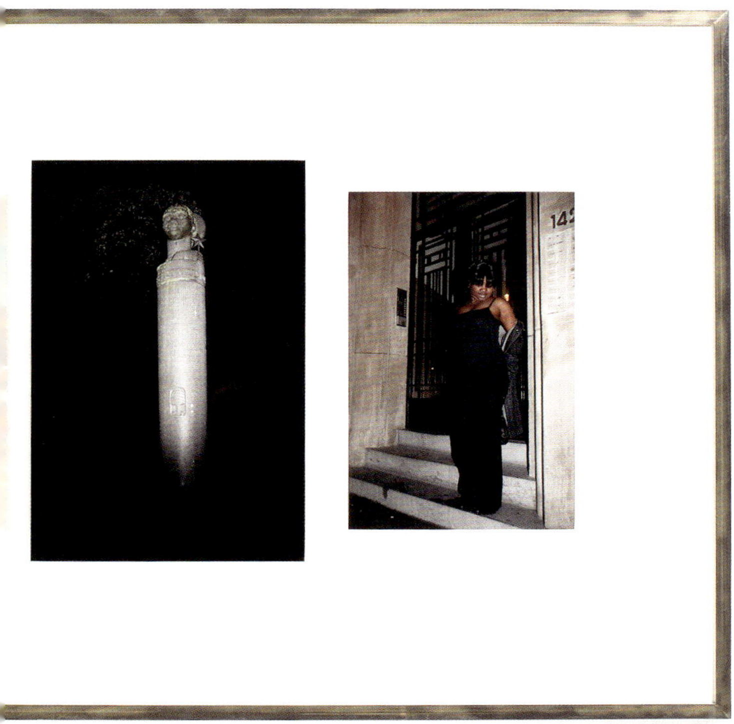

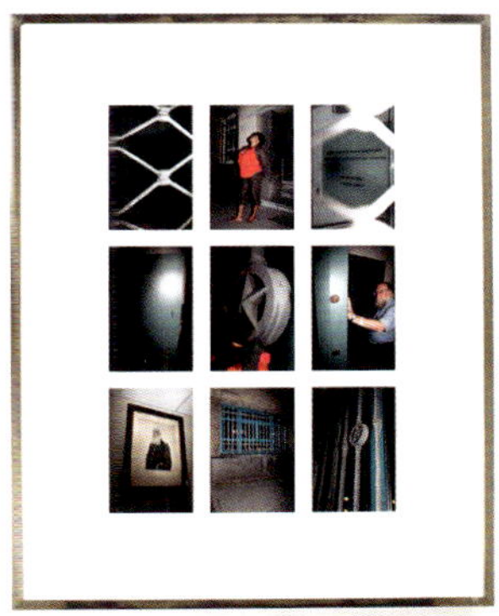

Sven Augustijnen, *Les Demoiselles de Bruxelles*, 2008

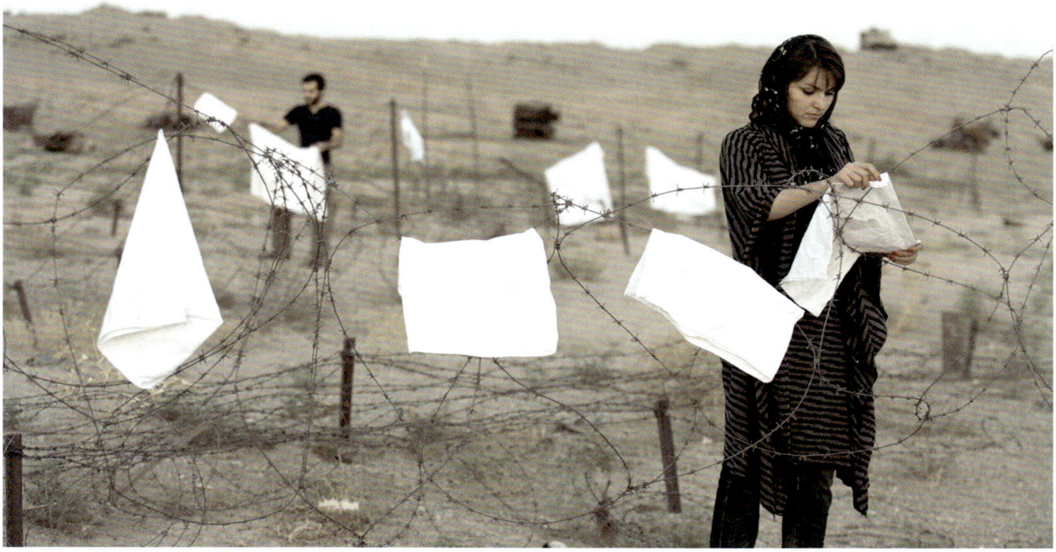

Gohar Dashti, aus der Serie / from the series *Today's life and war,* 2008

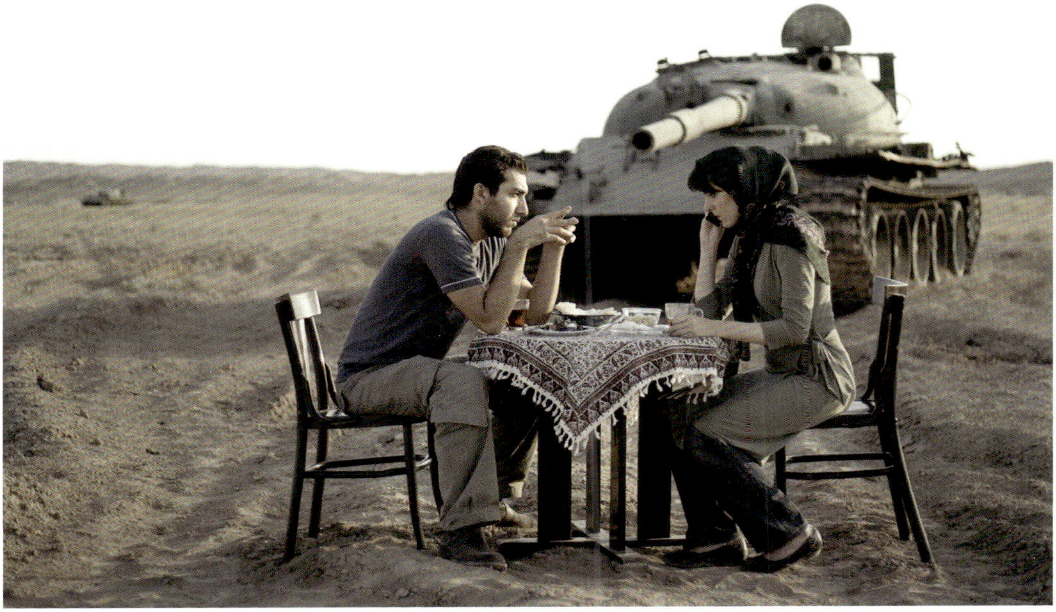

Gohar Dashti, aus der Serie / from the series *Today's life and war*, 2008

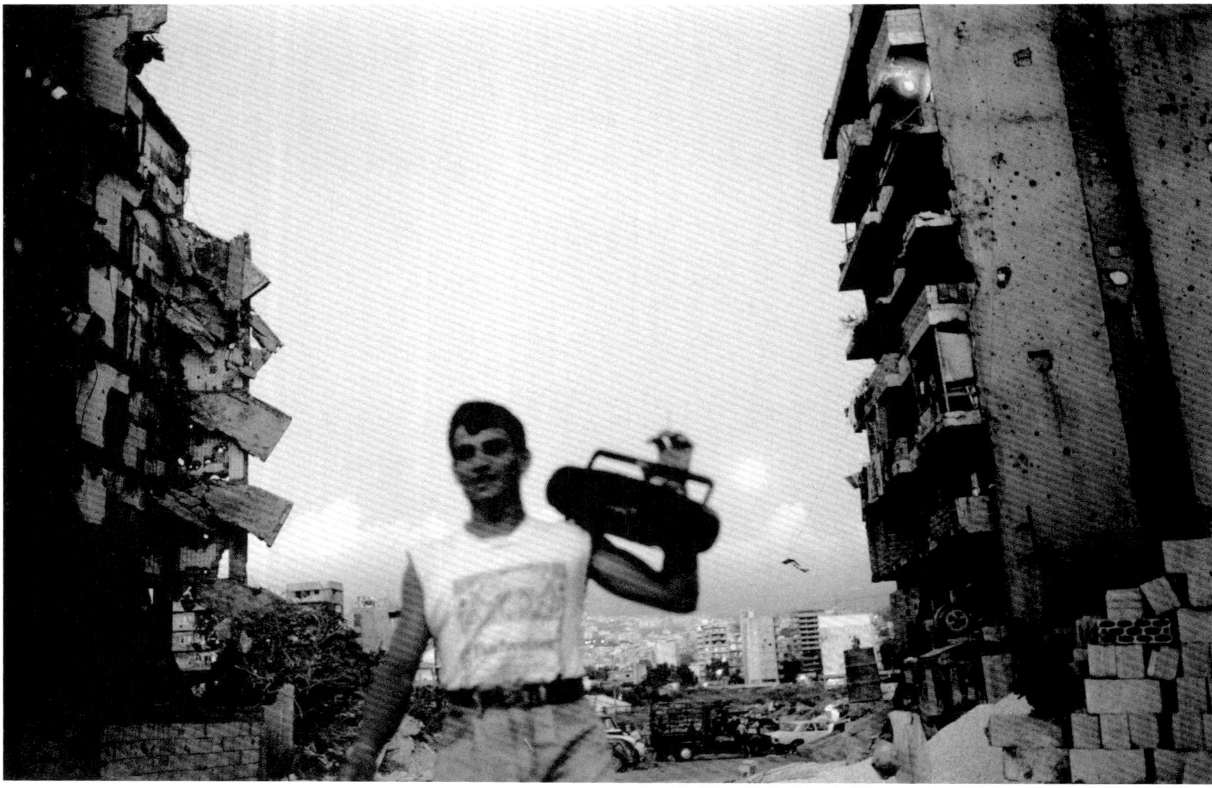

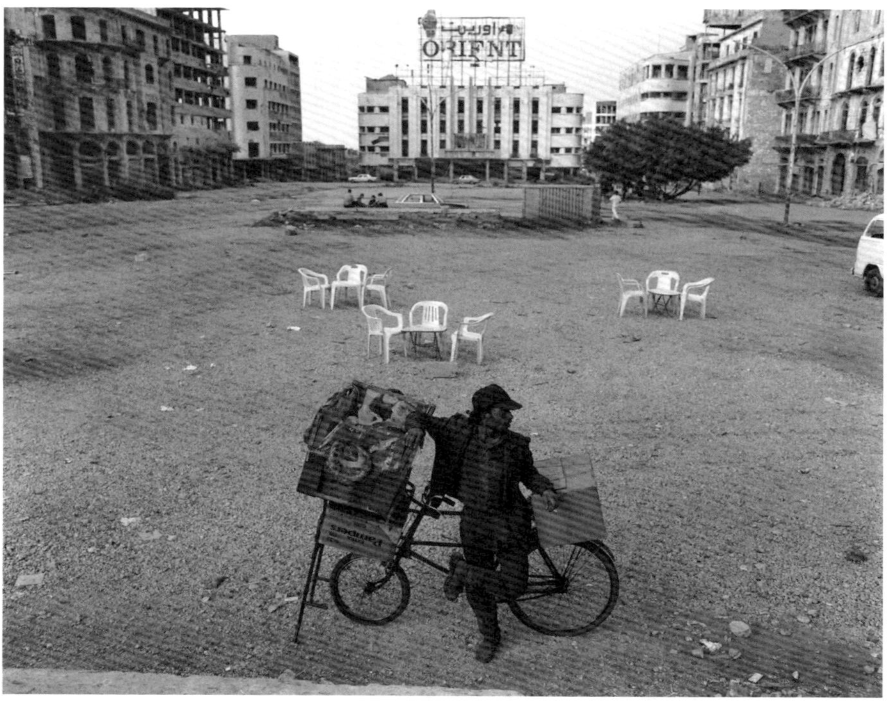

Fouad Elkoury, *Jeu de dupes / Traces of War Beirut 1995* und / and *Place des Martyrs / Beirut City Centre Beirut 1991*

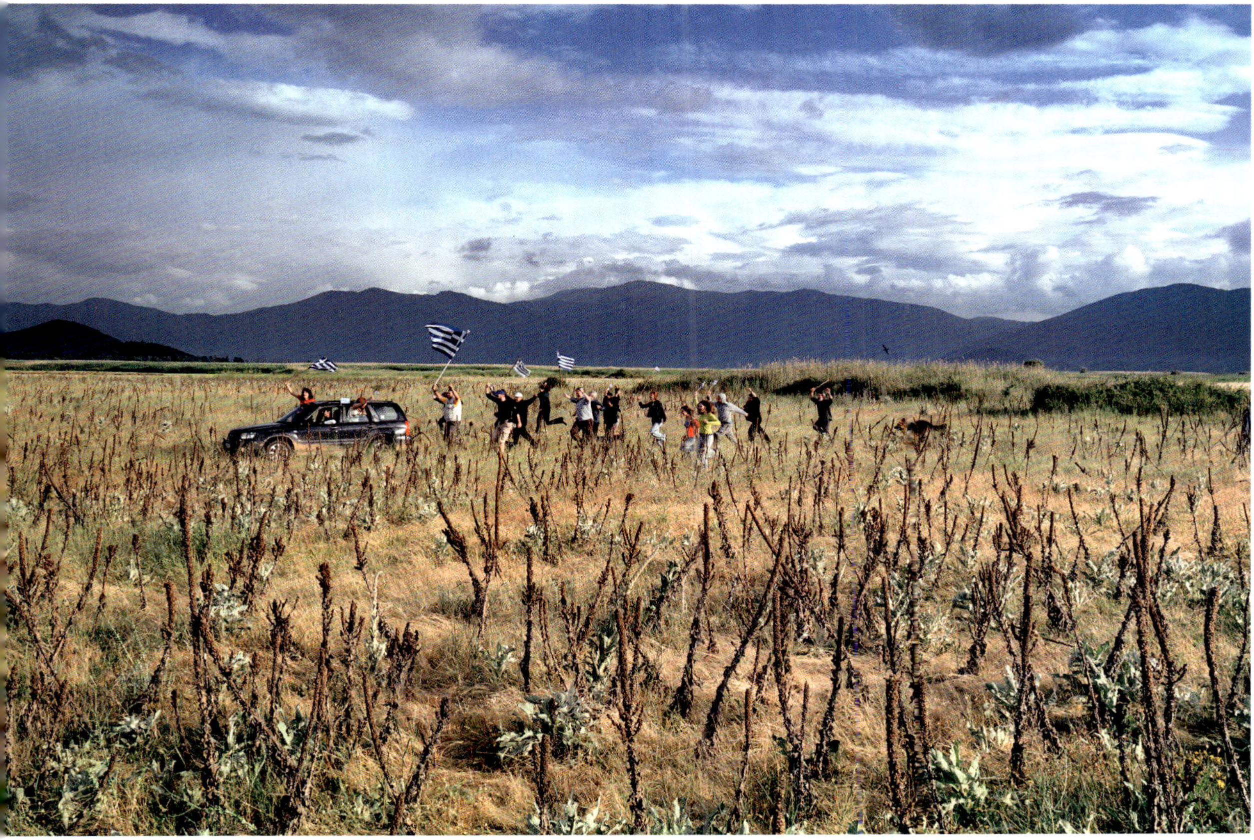

anos Kokkinias, *Prespes*, 2009
ächste Seite / next page: Boniface Mwangi, *Kenya Post Election Violence*, 2007-2008

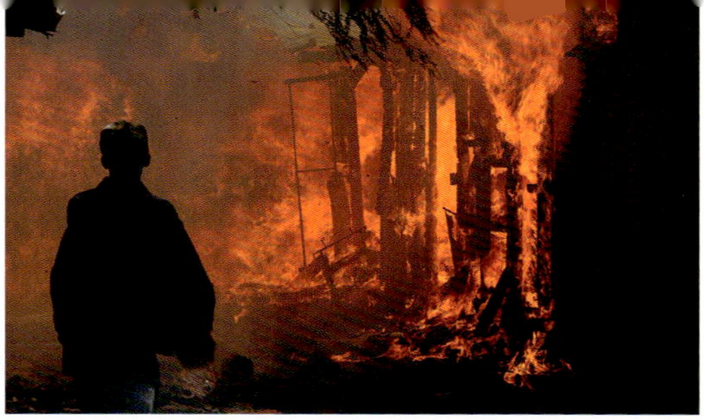

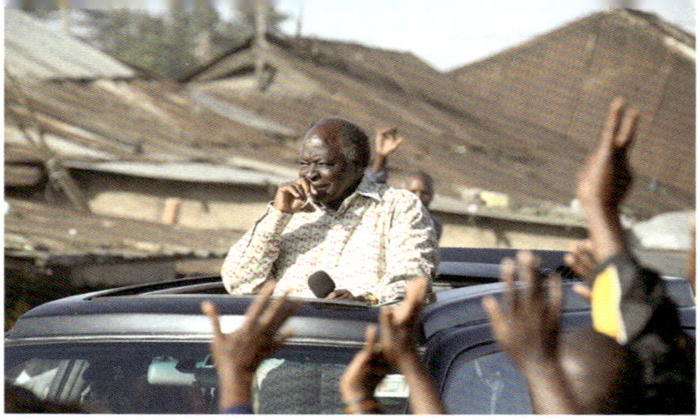

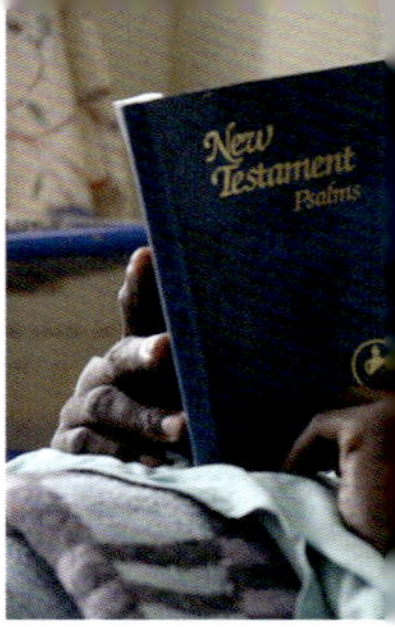
New Testament
Psalms

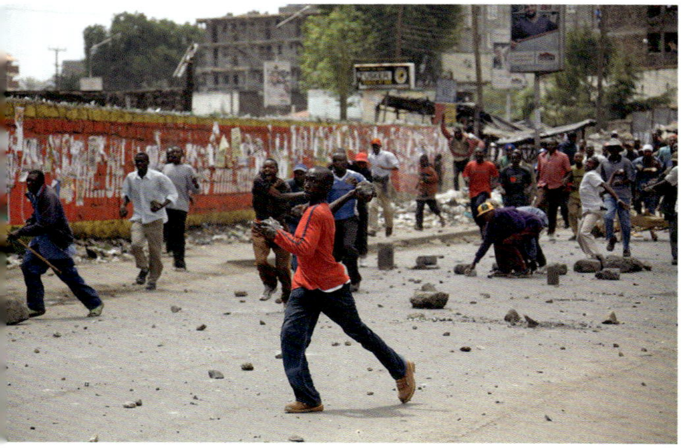

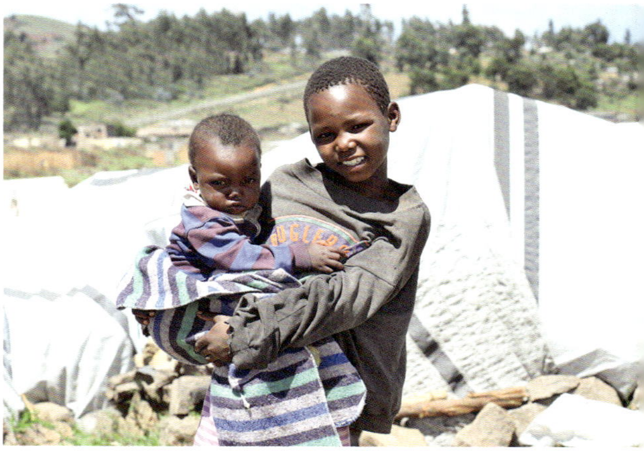

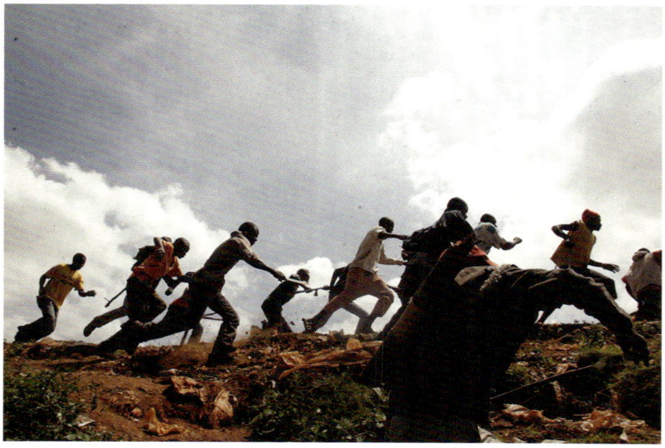

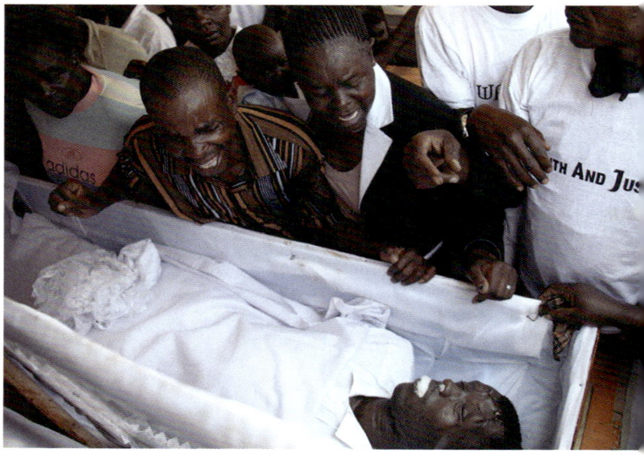
adidas
TH AND JUS

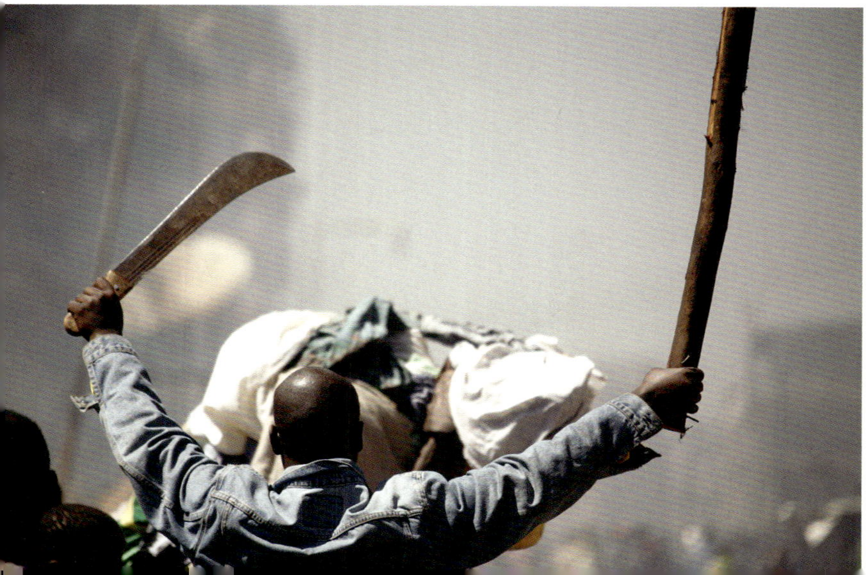

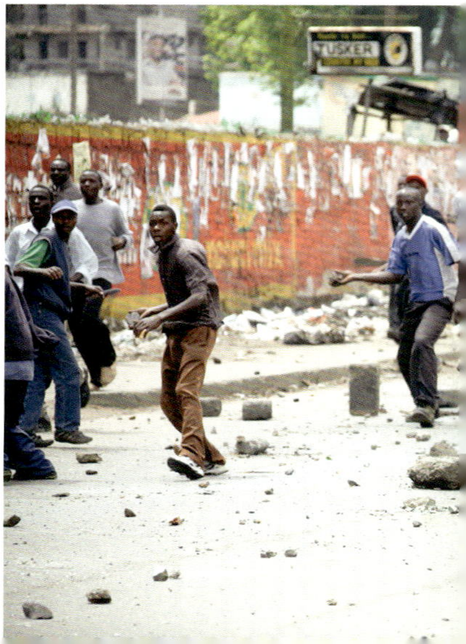
TUSKER

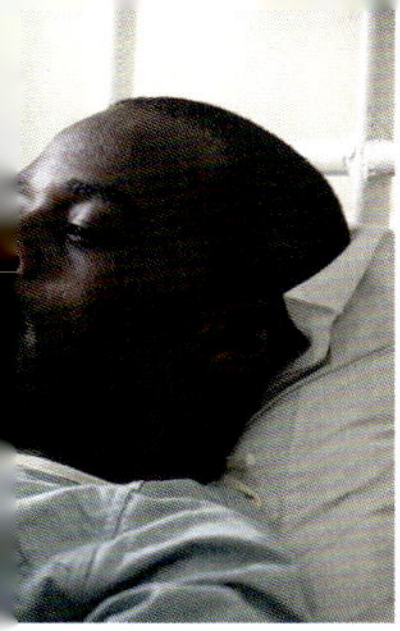

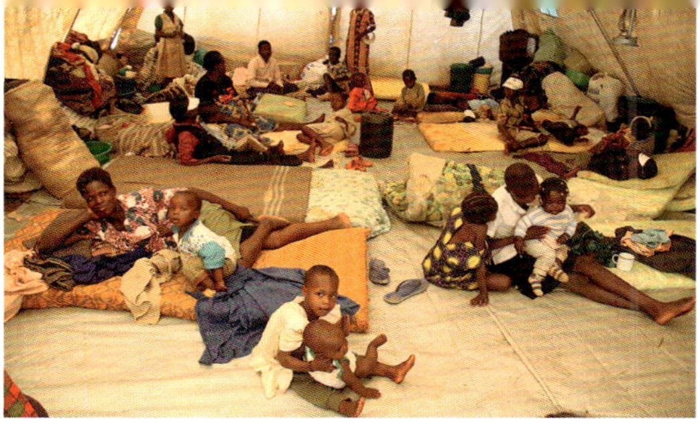

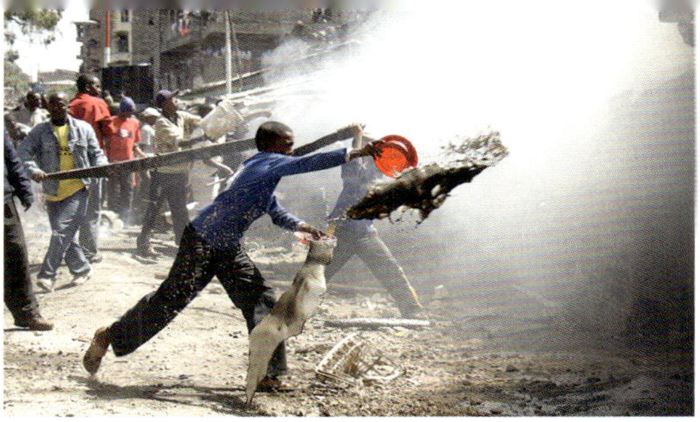

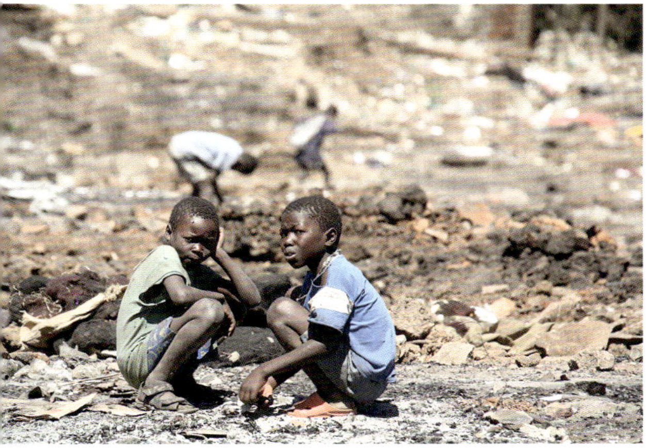

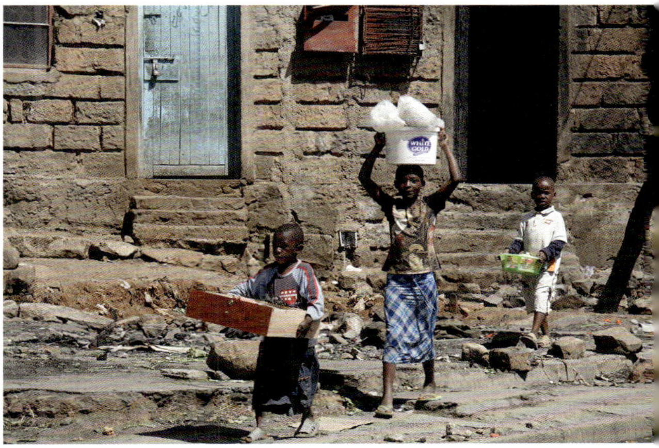

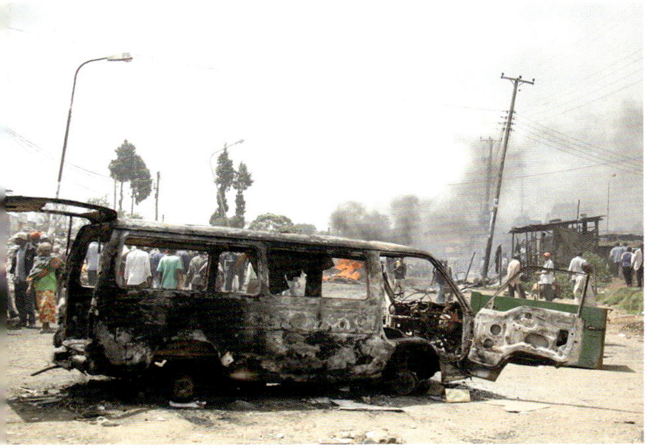

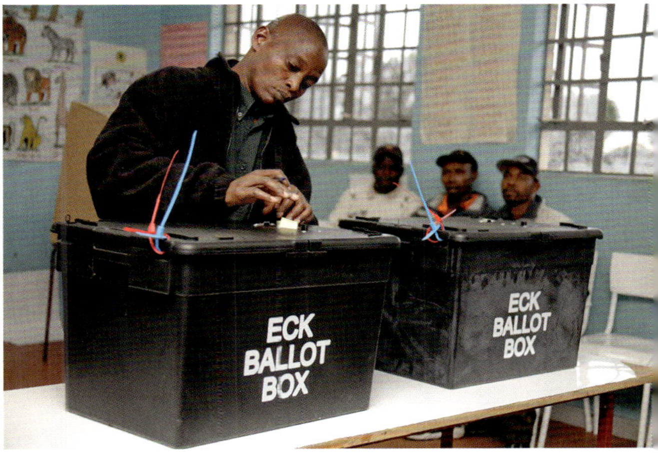
ECK
BALLOT
BOX
ECK
BALLOT
BOX

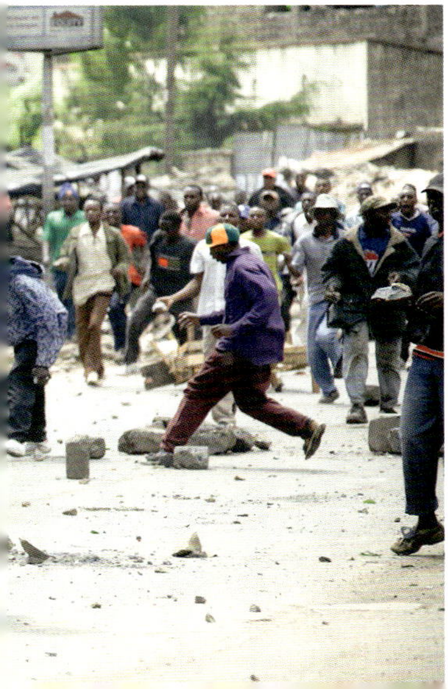

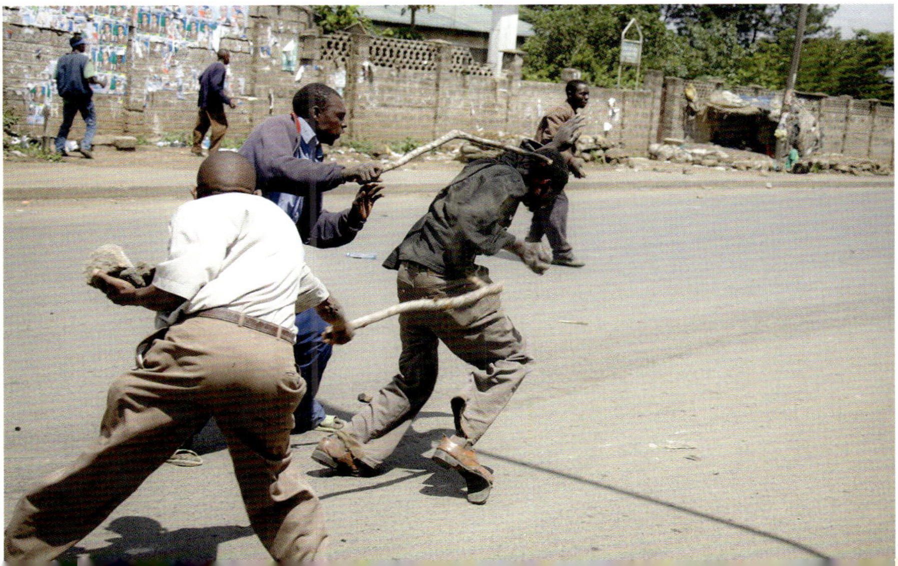

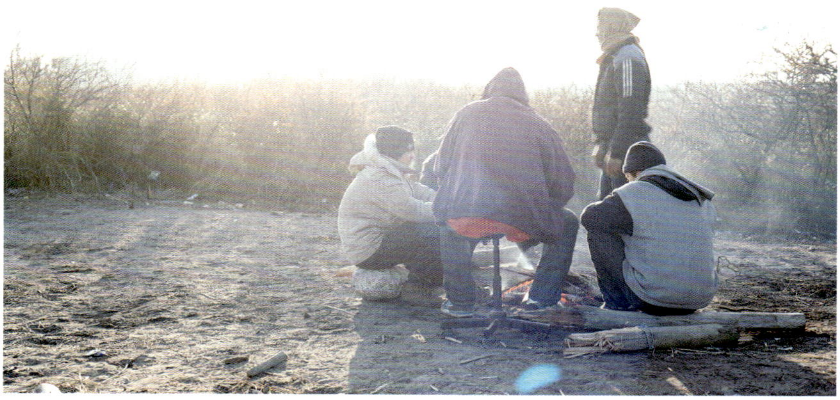

Bruno Serralongue, *Groupe d'hommes 1, Calais, décembre 2008*, aus der Serie / from the series *Calais*, 2006-2008
Rechts / right: Bruno Serralongue, *Vestige (sac de couchage), Calais, juillet 2007*, aus der Serie / from the series *Calais*, 2006-2008

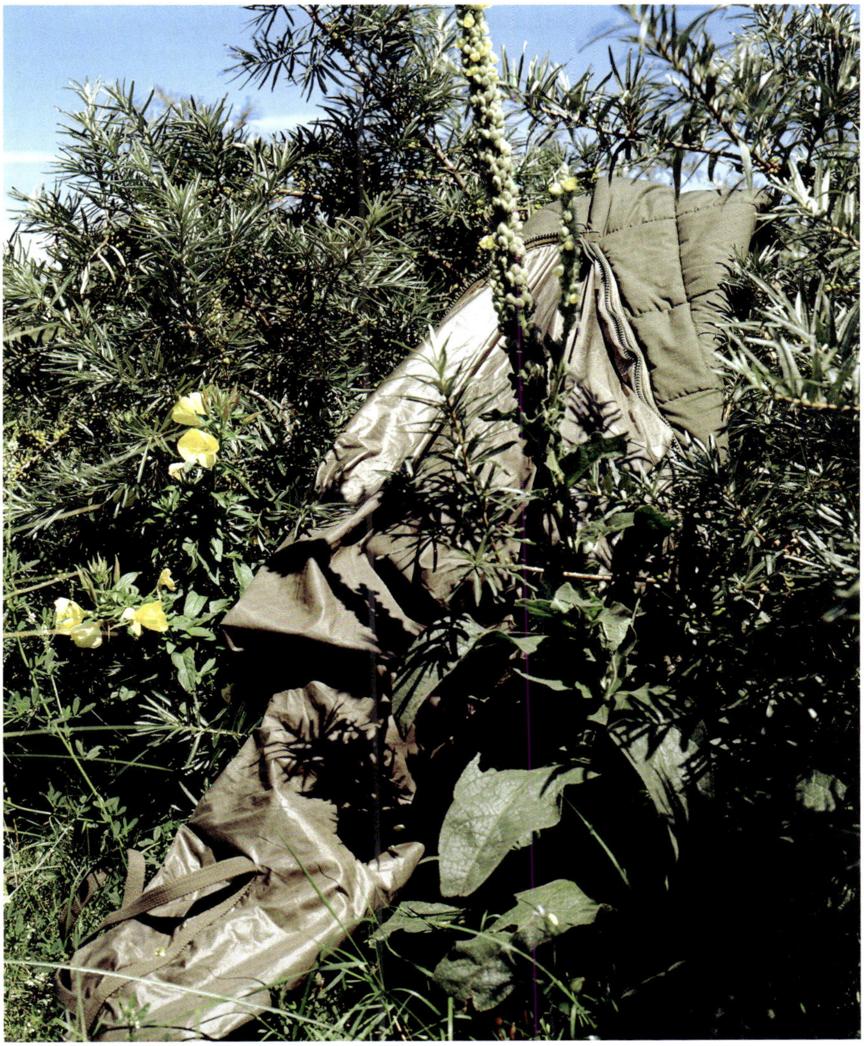

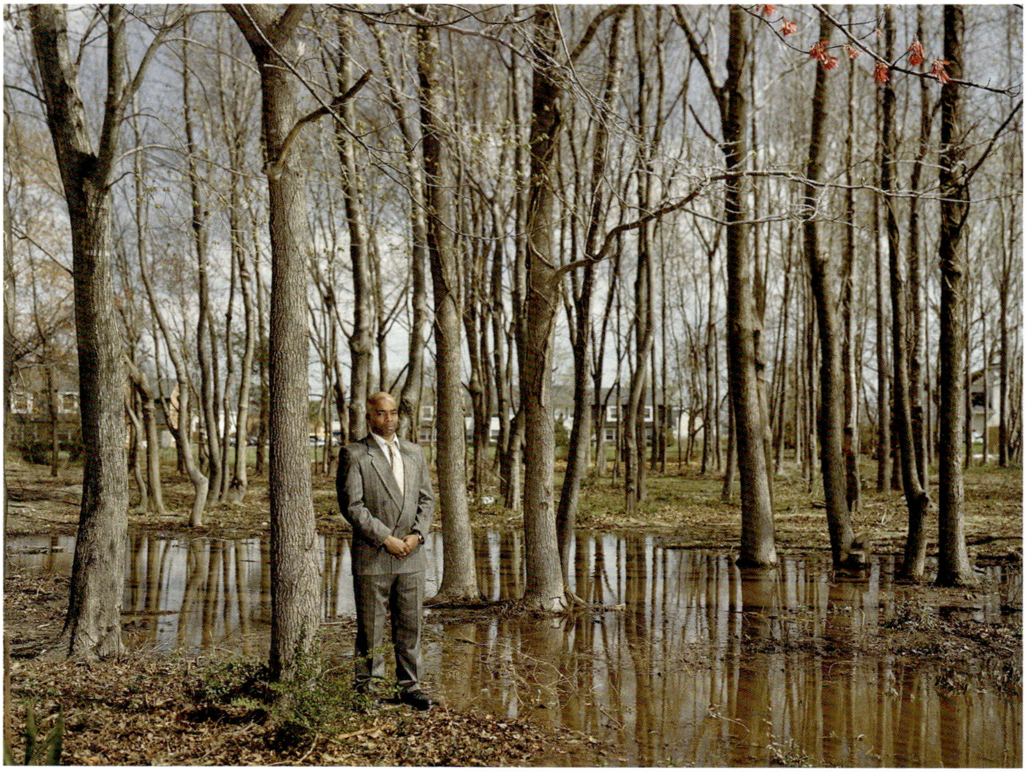

Troy Webb
Scene of the crime, The Pines, Virginia Beach, Virginia
Served 7 years of a 47-year sentence for kidnapping, rape and robbery, 2002

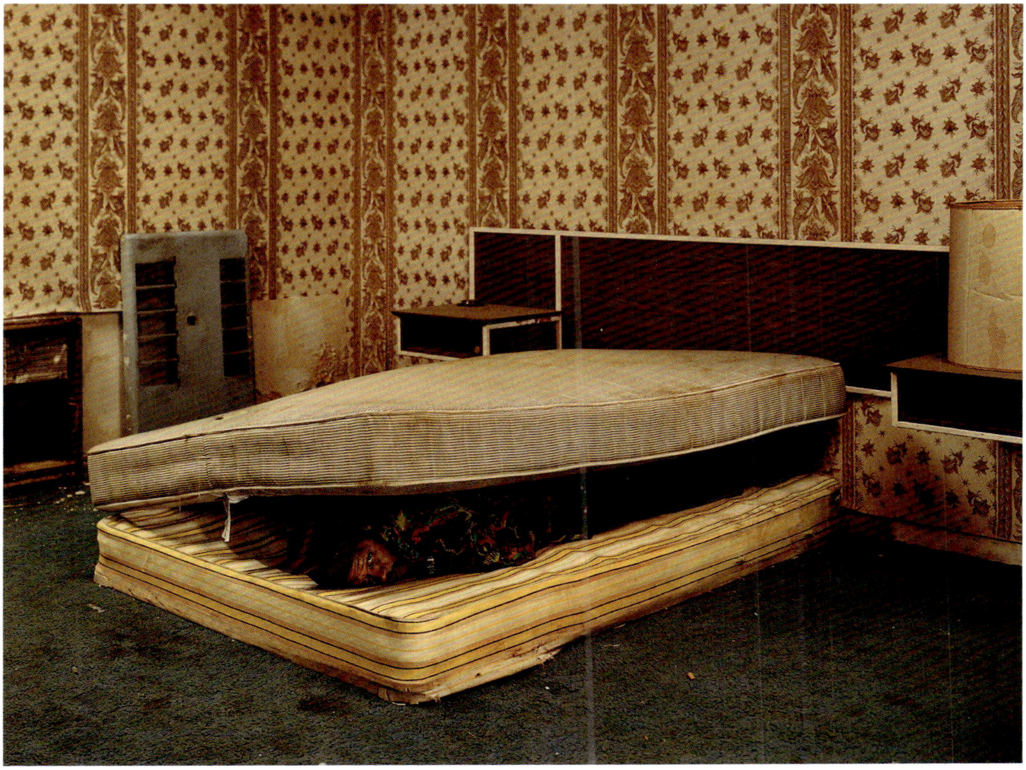

Larry Mayes
Scene of arrest, The Royal Inn, Gary, Indiana
Police found Mayes hiding beneath a mattress in this room
Served 18.5 years of an 80-year sentence for rape, robbery and unlawful deviate conduct, 2002

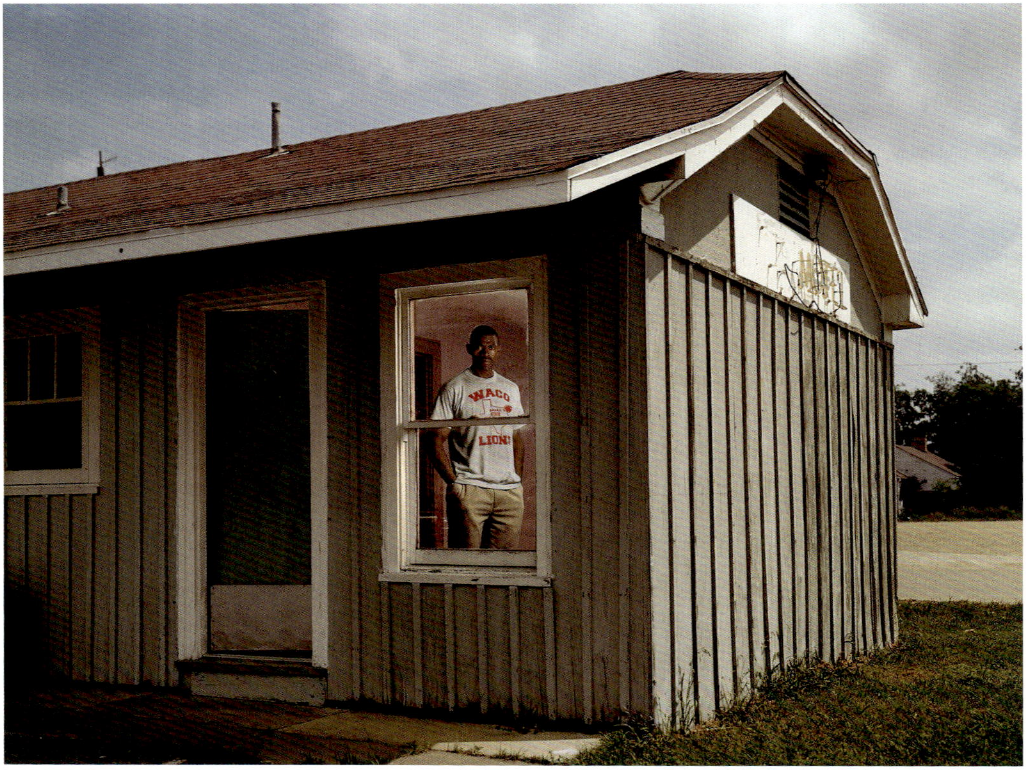

Calvin Washington
C&E Motel, Room No. 24, Waco, Texas
Where an informant claimed to have overheard Washington confess
Served 13 years of a life sentence for capital murder, 2002

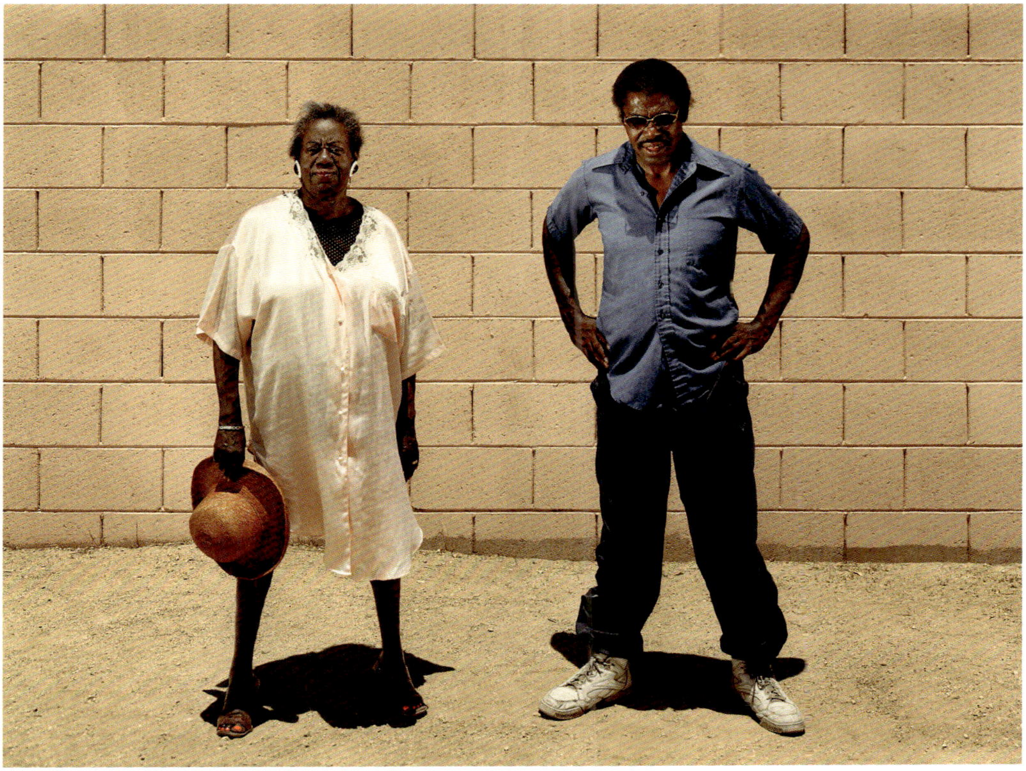

Larry Youngblood
Alibi location, Tucson Arizona
With Alice Laitner, Youngblood's girlfriend and alibi witness at trial
Served 8 years of a 10.5 year sentence for sexual assault, kidnapping and child molestation, 2002

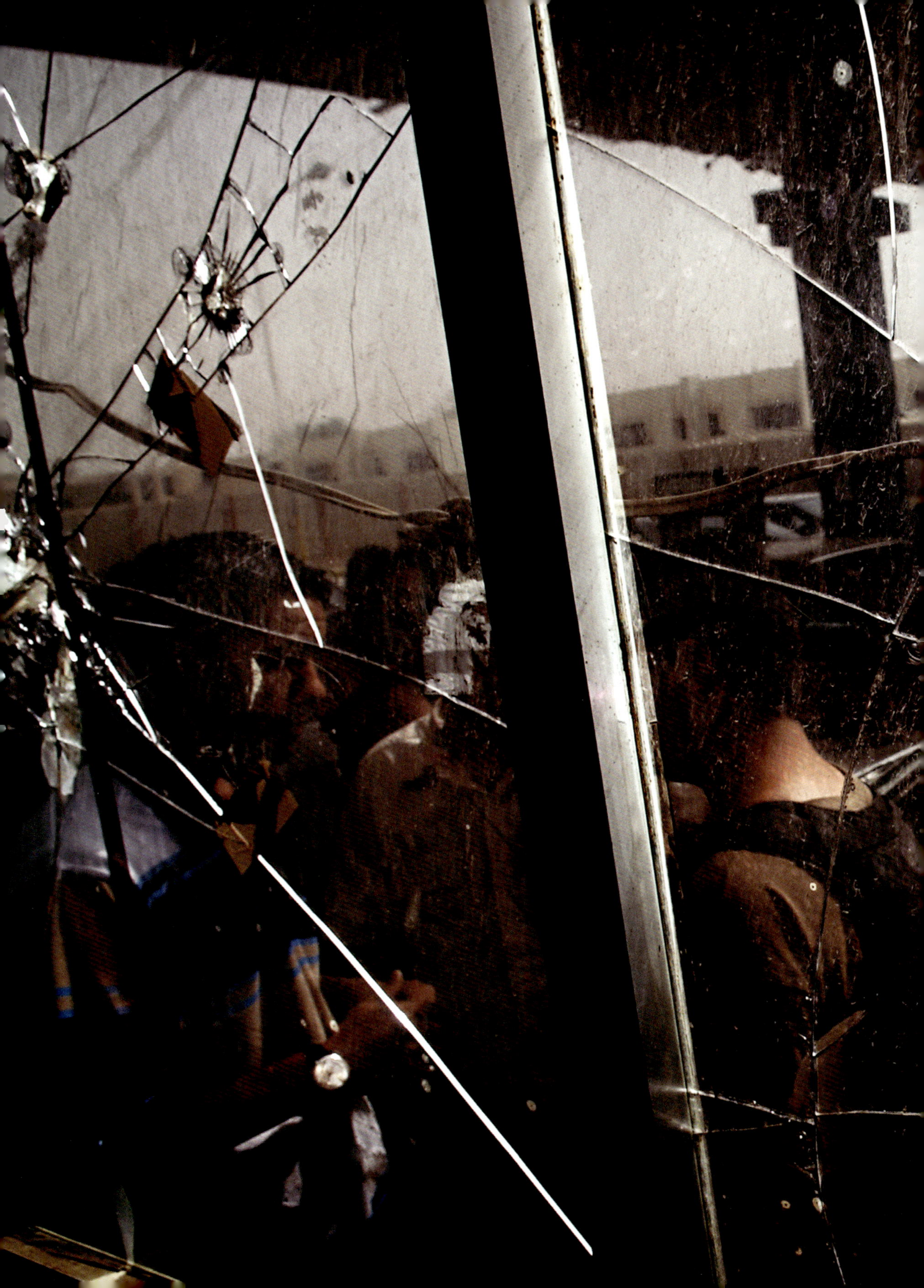

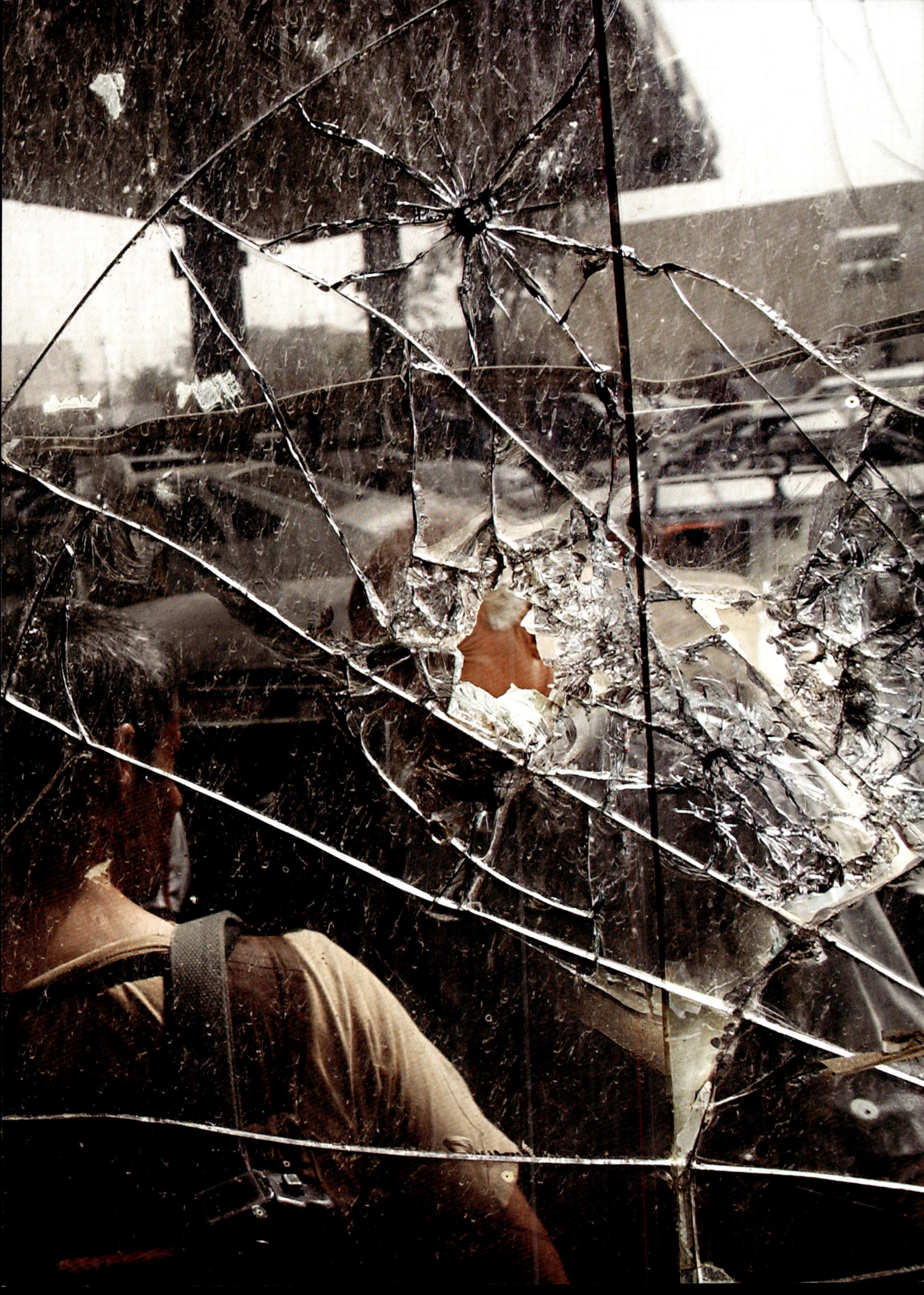

‘A gas station in Hayy al Amel was terrorized for months by a sniper, who would take potshots at locals queuing for hours to get petrol and cooking gas. Baghdad, 2007’

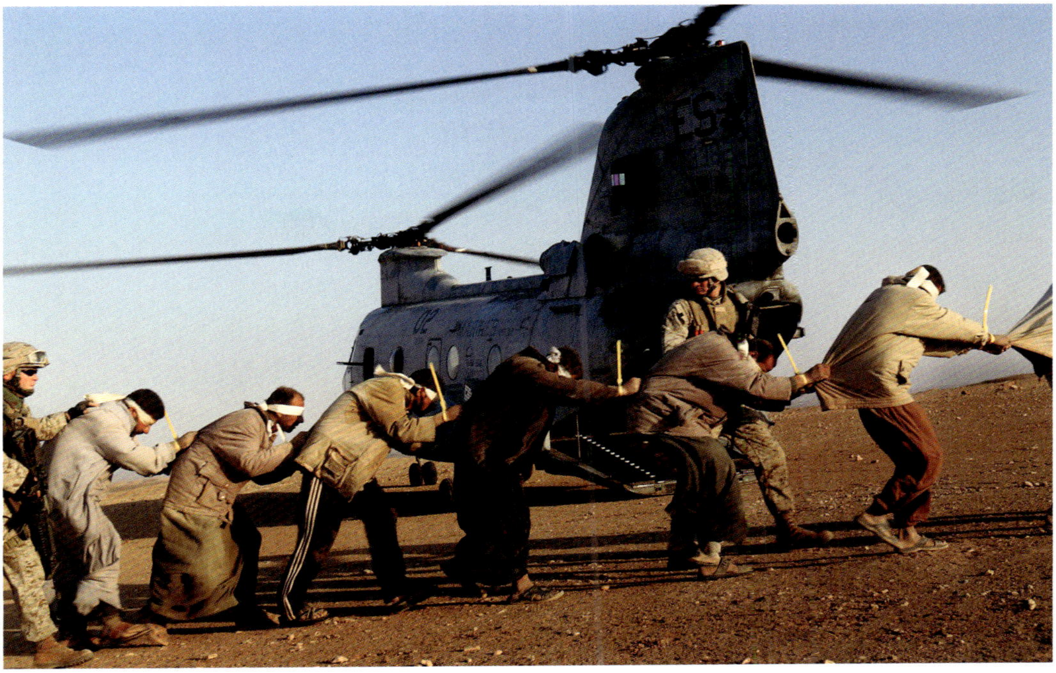

'Detainees swept up in an operation near the Syrian border are taken onto a helicopter by US Marines. Ramanah, Iraq 2005'

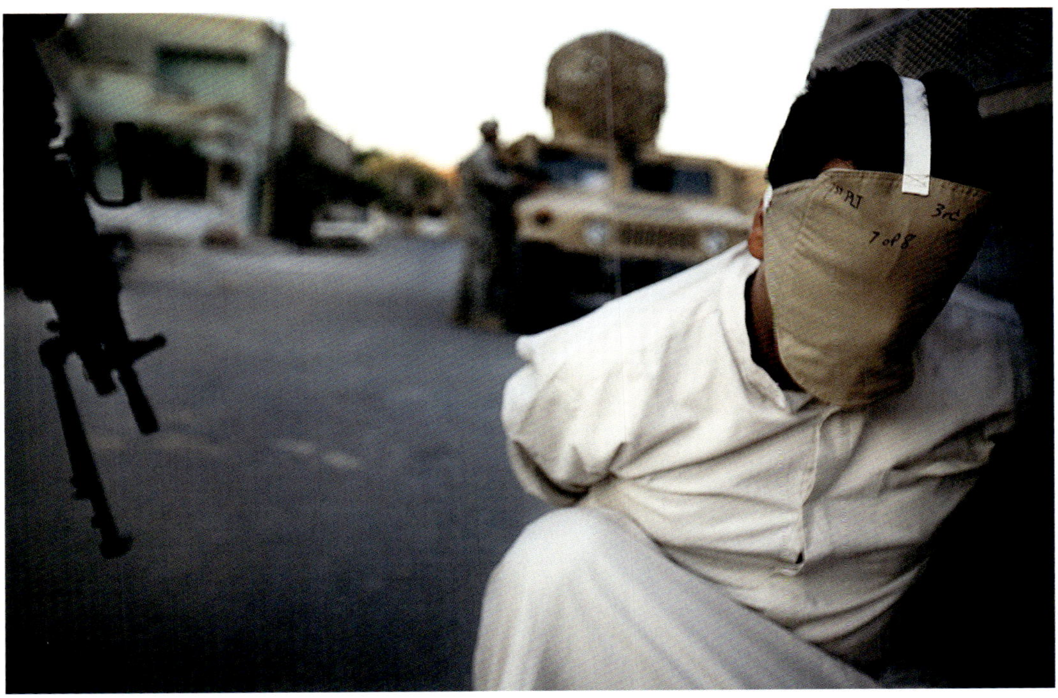

'A suspected Mahdi Army militiaman is blindfolded in the street before being taken away by American forces. Baghdad, Iraq, 2005'

Johan Spanner, aus / from *Iraq Series*, 2003-2009

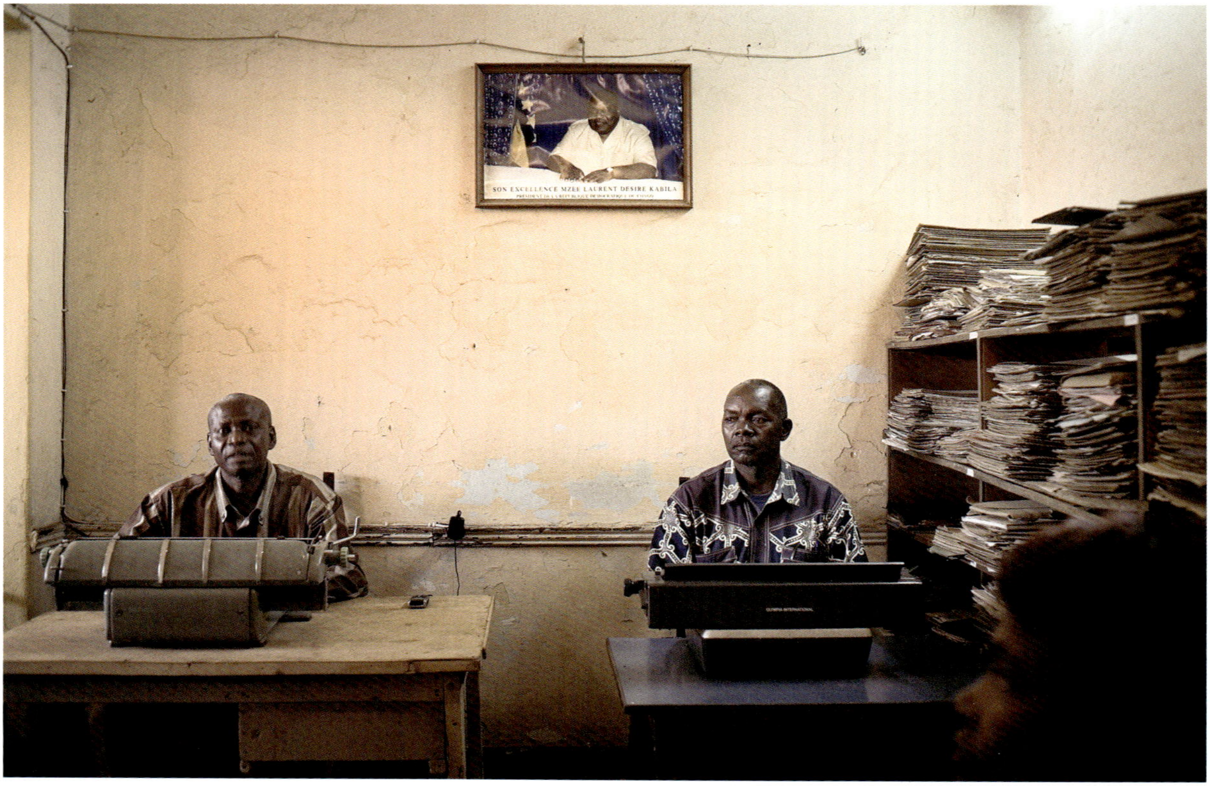

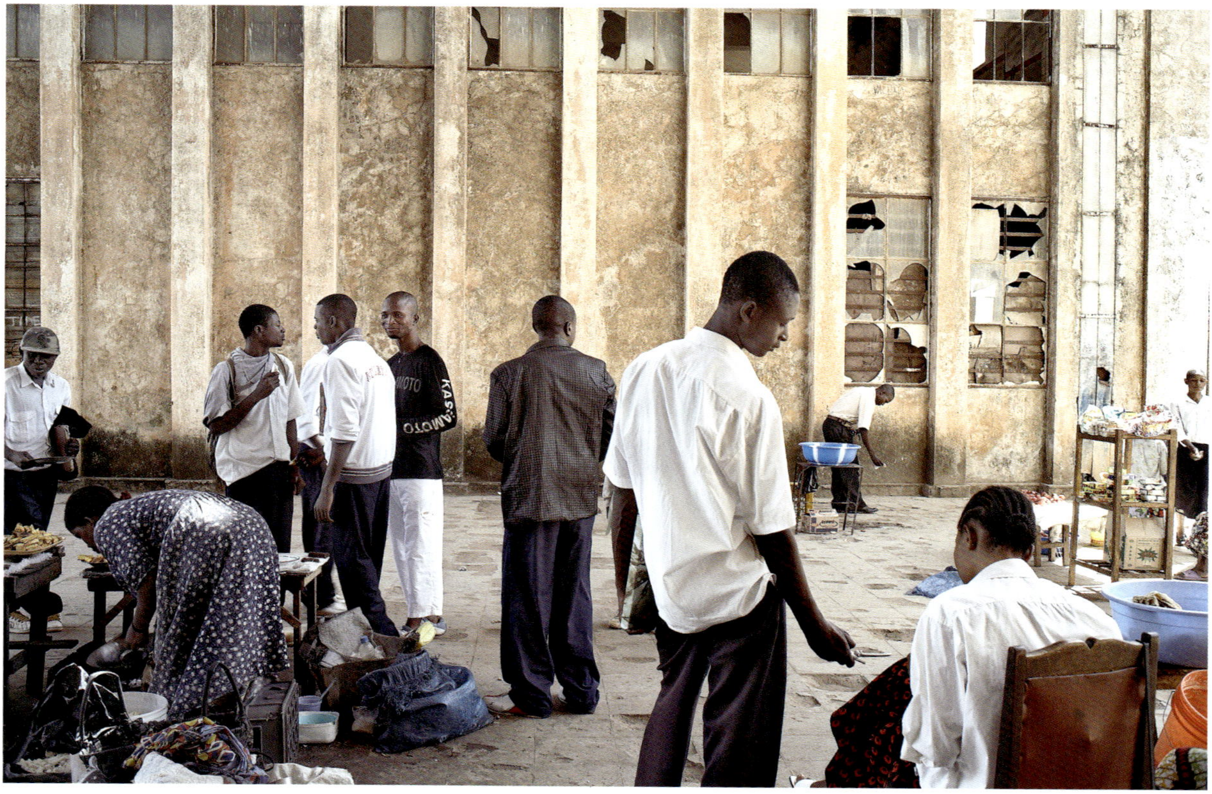

Guy Tillim, *Typing pool, Town Hall, Likasi, DR Congo* und / and *Athénée Royal High School, Lubumbashi, DR Congo*, 2007

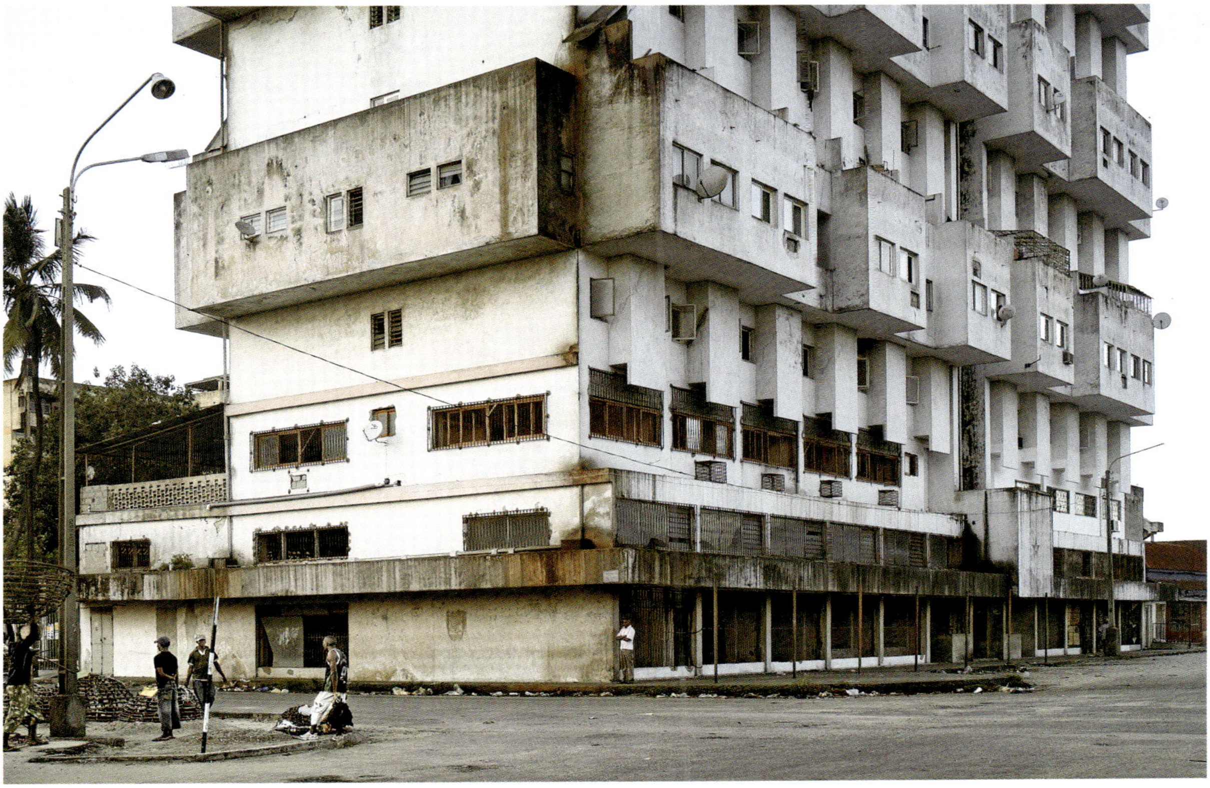

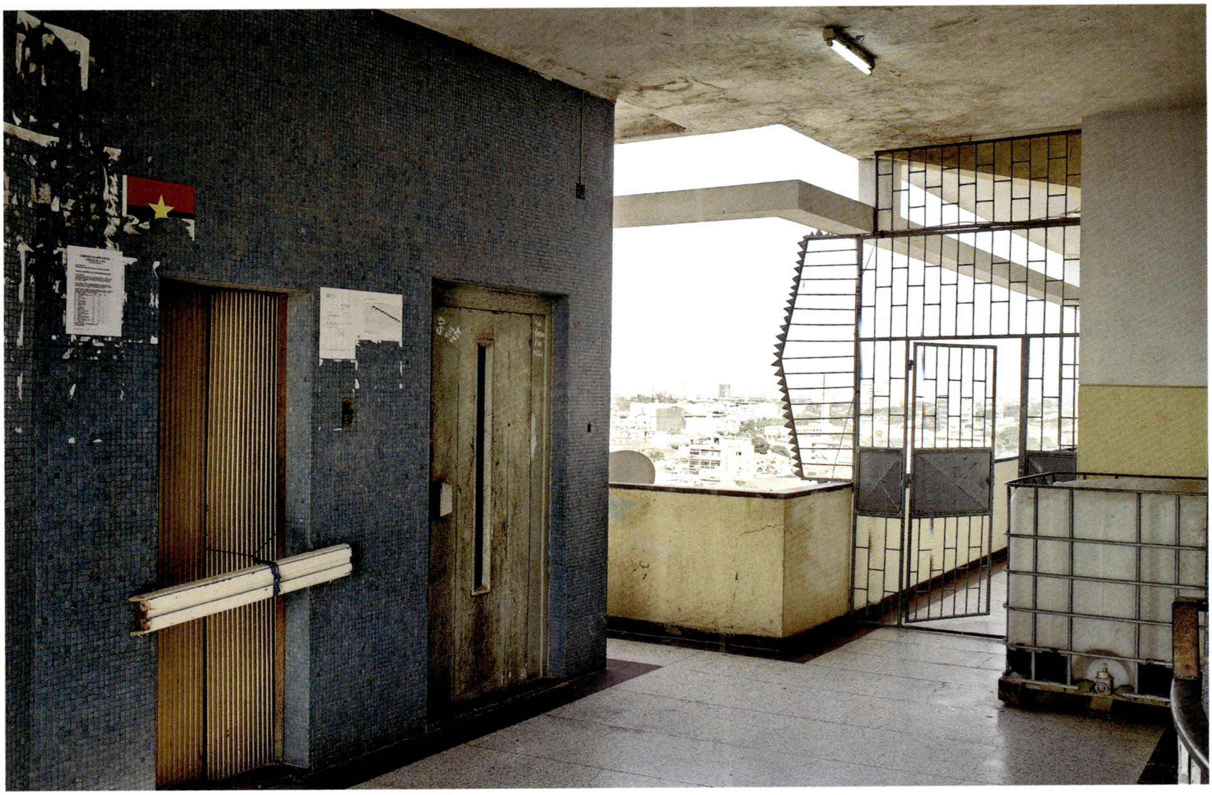

Guy Tillim, *Apartment building, Beira, Mozambique*, 2008 und / and *Apartment building, Luanda, Angola*, 2007

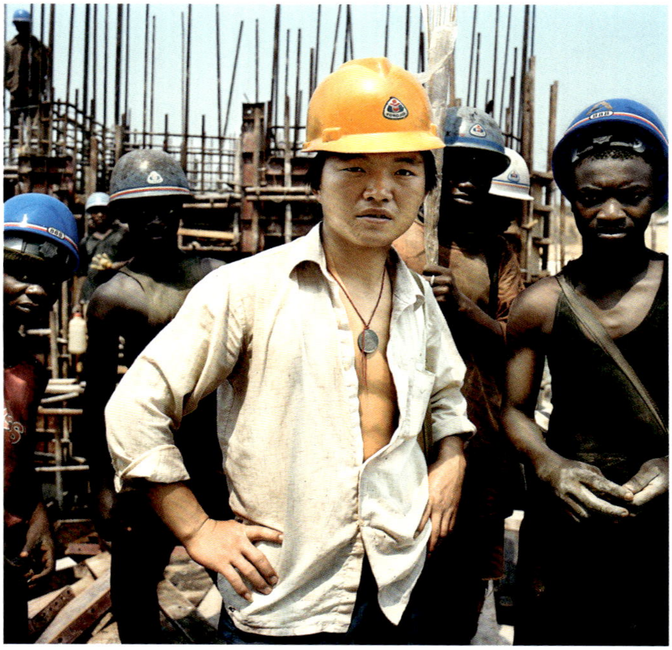

'On the building site of the Imboulou dam, Republic of the Congo, 200km north of the capital Brazzaville. In the foreground a Chinese worker of the China National Mechanical & Equipment Corporation (CMEC) company.'

Paolo Woods, *Congo, Imboulou dam*, aus der Serie / from the series *Chinafrica*, 2007

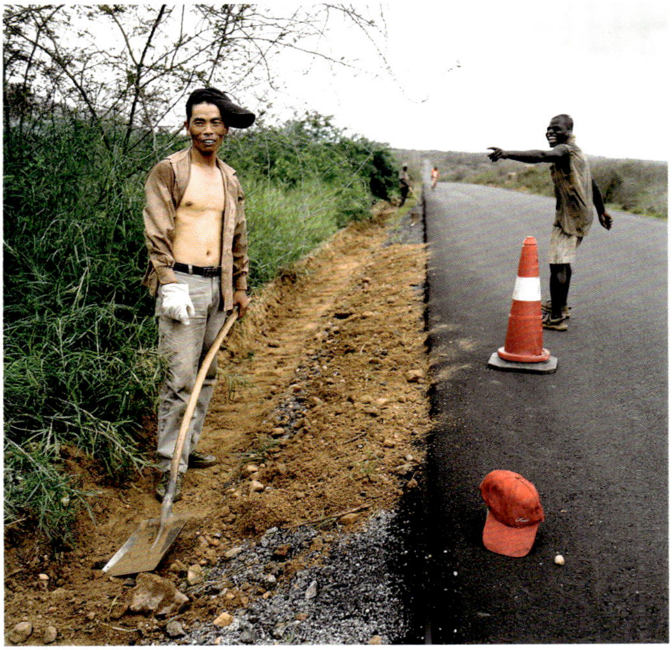

'A Chinese laborer and an Angolan colleague working on the coastal highway. China International Fund (CIF), the Chinese holding based in Hong Kong that oversees many contracts in Angola, has rebuilt this road, which unites the capital Luanda with Lobito, in record time.'

Paolo Woods, *Angola, Between Luanda and Lobito*, aus der Serie / from the series *Chinafrica*, 2007

Ecological Circuits

Ökologische Kreisläufe

Wilhelm-Hack-Museum, Ludwigshafen

Dieser Bereich des Fotofestivals soll das Verhältnis des Menschen zu seiner natürlichen Umgebung erkunden – ein Verhältnis, das sich im Laufe der Zeit ständig verändert hat. Zur Zeit der Romantik beispielsweise wurde die Natur als etwas Geheimnisvolles, Heroisches und sogar Transzendentes empfunden. Mit dem Aufkommen der Industriellen Revolution sah man sie dann als etwas an, das gezähmt, beherrscht und geradezu in Besitz genommen werden musste. Resultate einer solchen Einstellung sind die ungezügelte Ausbeutung natürlicher Ressourcen, der Missbrauch der Umwelt und die Gefährdung oder Zerstörung fragiler Ökosysteme. Heute stellen sich uns neue Aufgaben und wir sind gezwungen, unser Verhältnis zur natürlichen Umgebung zu überdenken. Angesichts unserer bisherigen Handlungen müssen wir die Konsequenzen ziehen und Verantwortung übernehmen.

Aktuell werden Symptome einer beunruhigenden Erkrankung der Umwelt sichtbar: Das schmelzende Eis der Polkappen verändert die arktische Landschaft unwiderruflich; Öl, Kohle und Gas werden rasend schnell gefördert und konsumiert, während wir die Auswirkungen auf die Umwelt noch immer leugnen; überall auf unserem Planeten wachsen die Städte explosionsartig an und dehnen sich aus wie schnellwüchsige Wälder. Die Landschaftsaufnahmen in der Ausstellung „Ökologische Kreisläufe" schaffen ein visuelles Bewusstsein für die Auswirkungen der unkontrollierten menschlichen Eingriffe in die Natur und ihre Ressourcen, den Teufelskreis von Produktion und Konsum und signalisieren zugleich die Tendenz zu einem neuen ökologischen Bewusstsein und einer neuen ökologischen Verantwortlichkeit.

Die Fotografien der Ausstellung dokumentieren wie kein anderes Medium das gewaltige Ausmaß der Veränderungen der natürlichen Umgebung als Resultat menschlicher Eingriffe im 20. und 21. Jahrhundert. In ihnen werden die ökologischen Ungleichgewichte und Missverhältnisse sichtbar, zugleich wird aber auch die andauernde Erhabenheit der Natur gepriesen und im Bewusstsein wachgerufen.

Heute sind wir mit den dramatischen Auswirkungen unserer modernen Hybris gegenüber den natürlichen Kreisläufen und Systemen, die das ökologische Gleichgewicht schaffen, konfrontiert. Diese ökologischen Kreisläufe werden unter anderem durch unseren Energieverbrauch, durch die Land- und die Forstwirtschaft und durch den städtischen Lebensstil überall auf der Welt beeinflusst. Als Ausgangspunkt dienen den ausstellenden Künstlern die kultivierten und dem heutigen Leben angepassten „zivilisierten" Landschaften, die der moderne Mensch ohne Rücksicht auf die Folgen geschaffen hat – die aber zwangsläufig im Wandel begriffen sind. Welche Rolle spielt der Mensch gegenüber der Natur in Zukunft? Wie kann unsere Beziehung zur Natur neu definiert werden, sodass dem Ticken der von uns selbst gelegten Zeitbombe Einhalt geboten werden kann? Wie können wir in uns tief verwurzelte, aber längst nicht mehr nachhaltige Haltungen und Praktiken verändern? Dies sind einige der wesentlichen Fragen, denen die Menschheit heute gegenübersteht.

Katerina Gregos &
Solvej Helweg Ovesen

Ecological Circuits

Wilhelm-Hack-Museum, Ludwigshafen

This chapter of the Fotofestival explores the changing attitude of man to the natural environment, a relationship that has been constantly shifting. During the Romantic period, for example, nature was seen as something mysterious, heroic and transcendental. With the advent of the industrial revolution, nature came to be seen as something to be tamed, mastered and possessed. The result of this attitude has been the boundless exploitation of natural resources, the abuse of the environment and the endangering or destruction of fragile ecosystems. Today we are faced with new responsibilities and forced to reconsider our relationship to the natural environment. We must now face the consequences of our prior actions.

Currently, symptoms of a worrying ecological pathology abound: the Arctic landscape is being redefined by melting ice; oil, coal and gas is being extracted and consumed at breakneck speed while we remain in denial of the effects of these on the environment; explosive urbanisation is occurring all over the planet, with cities growing at an unprecedented scale. The artworks presented in 'Ecological Circuits' generate a visual consciousness of the effects of unchecked human intervention in nature, our use of natural resources and the vicious cycle of production and consumption, and indicate a drive to a new ecological consciousness and responsibility.

The photographs presented in this exhibition document, as no other medium can, the vast scale of changes in the natural environment resulting from manmade interventions in the twentieth and twenty-first centuries. Ecological imbalances and dystopias become visible – yet the persisting sublime dimension of nature is also evoked and celebrated.

Today we face the dramatic consequences of our modern attitude towards the natural systems that maintain ecological balance. These ecological circuits are influenced by, among other things, our energy consumption, farming, forestry and urban lifestyles, on a worldwide basis. The exhibiting artists take as their point of departure the cultivated, modernised and 'civilised' landscapes that modern man has created without taking into account the consequences. This is something that is, by necessity, changing. What will be the role of man towards nature in the future? How can our relationship to nature be redefined in a way that reverses the ticking ecological timebomb that we have created? How can we change ingrained attitudes and practices that are no longer sustainable? These are some of the key questions facing mankind today.

Katerina Gregos &
Solvej Helweg Ovesen

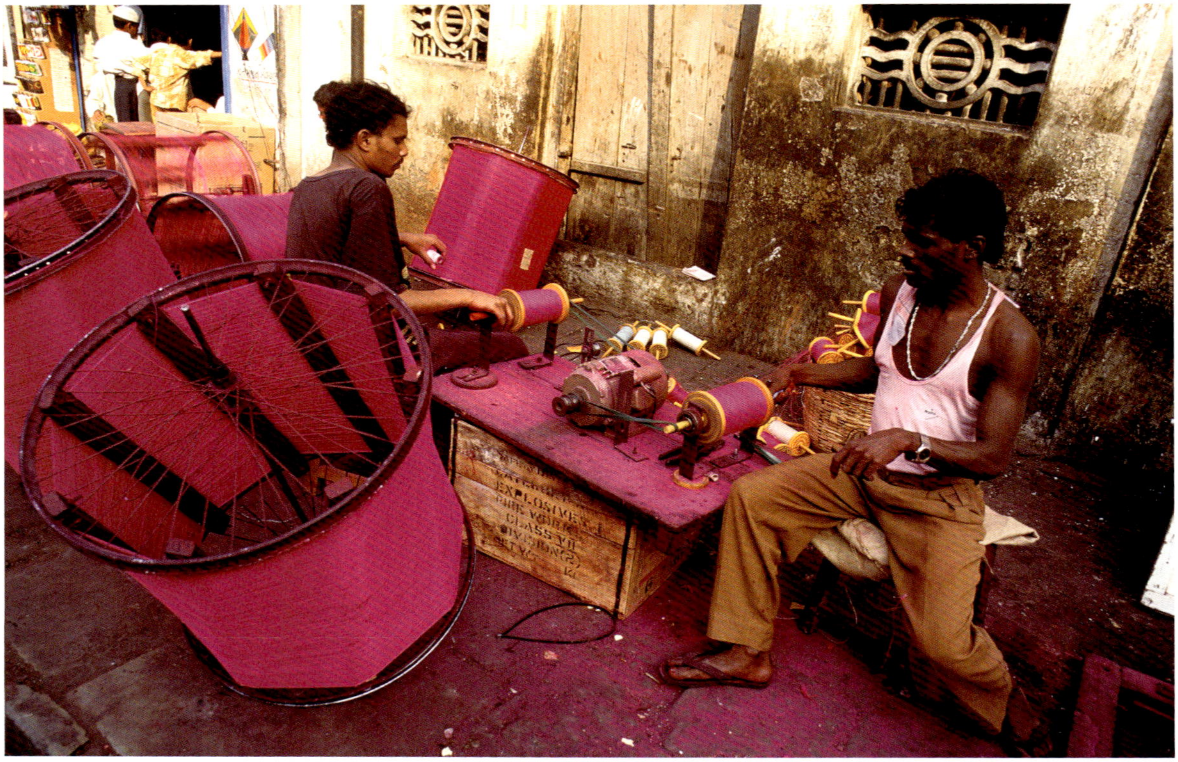

Ravi Agarwal, *Kite string making, Surat, India*, aus der Serie / from the series *Down and Out*, 1997–2000

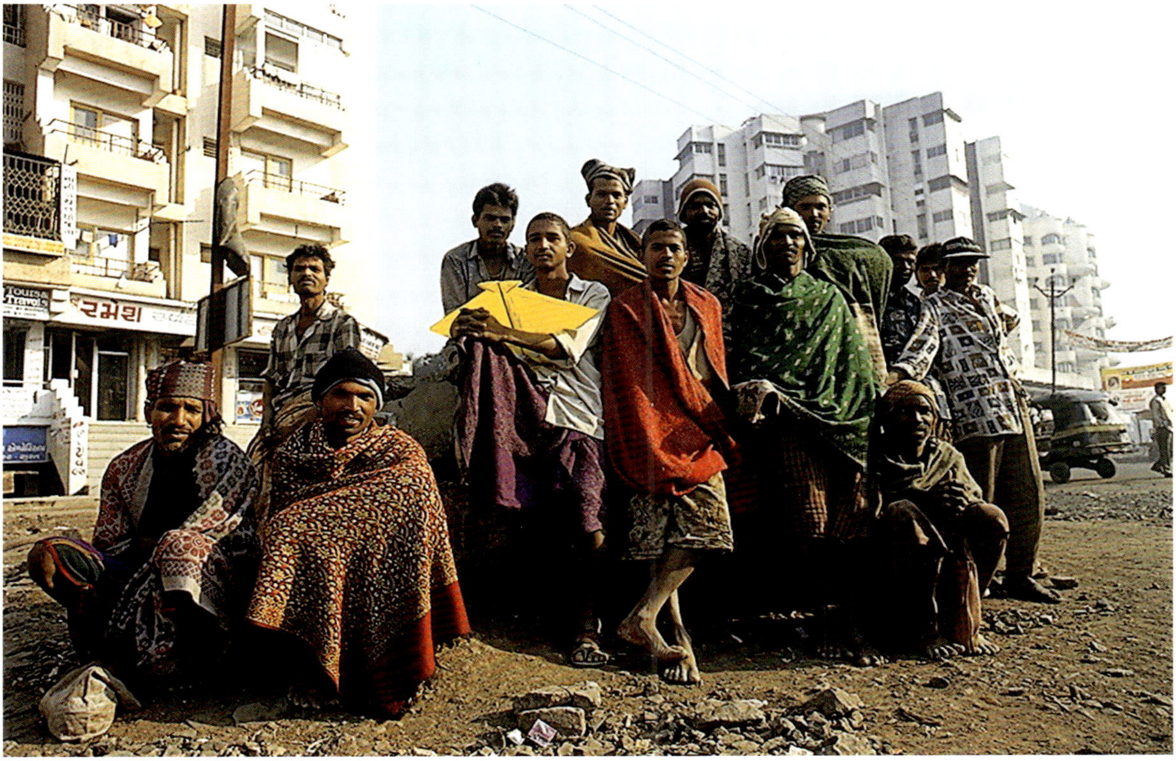

Ravi Agarwal, *Waiting for work, Surat, India*, aus der Serie / from the series *Down and Out*, 1997–2000

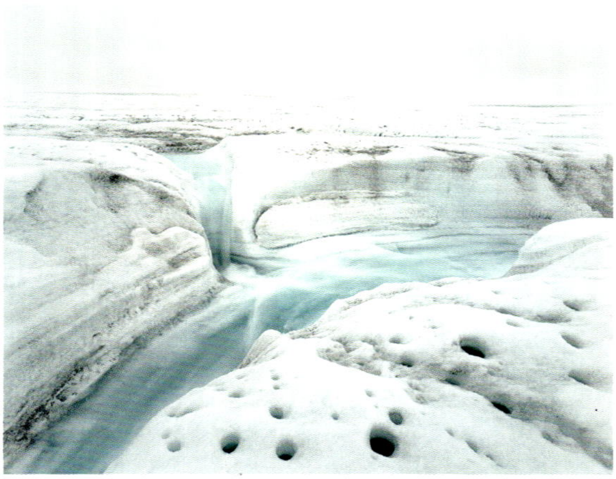

Olaf Otto Becker, *River 2, Position 1*, 2008

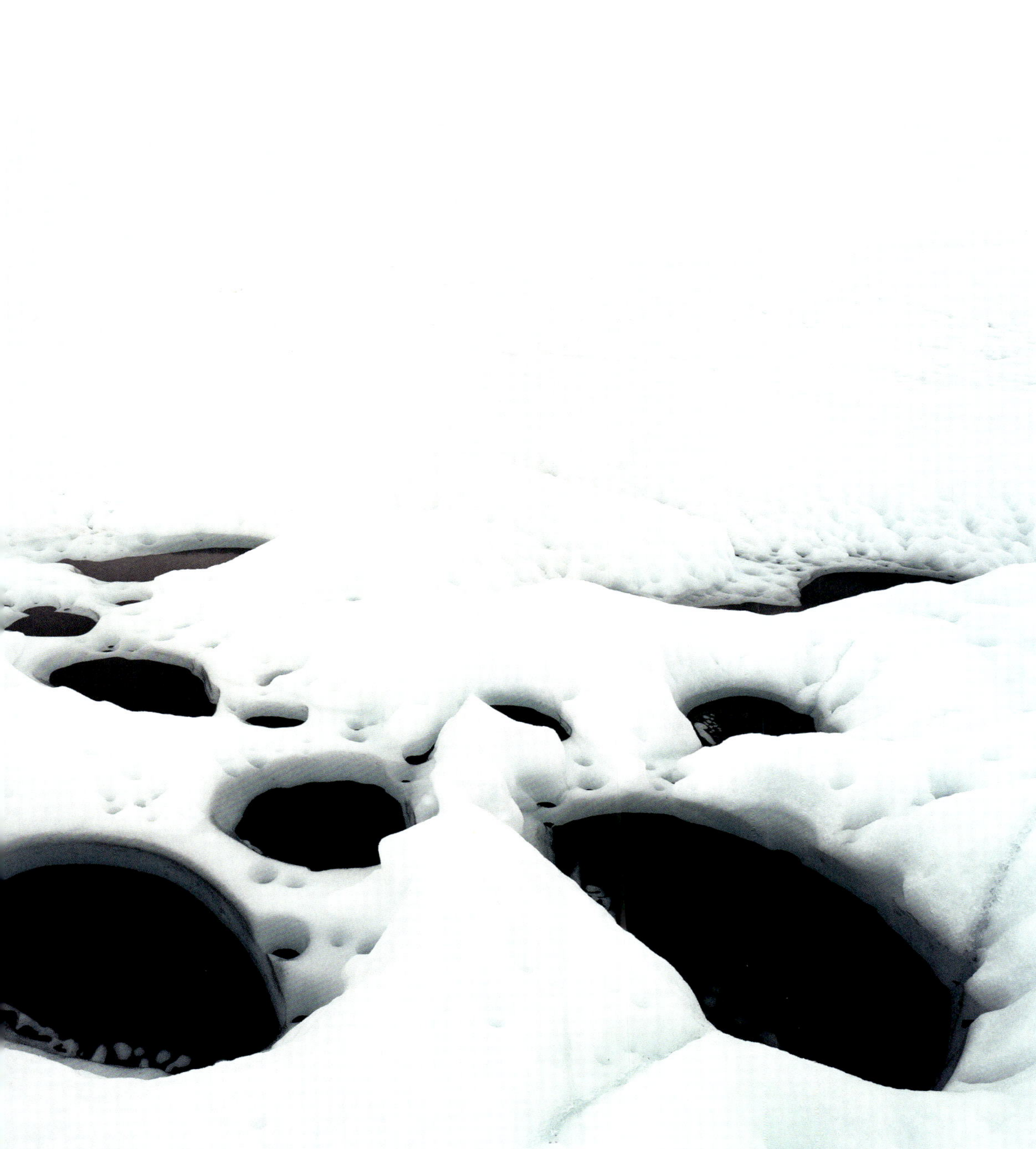

Olaf Otto Becker, *River 1, Position 1*, 2007

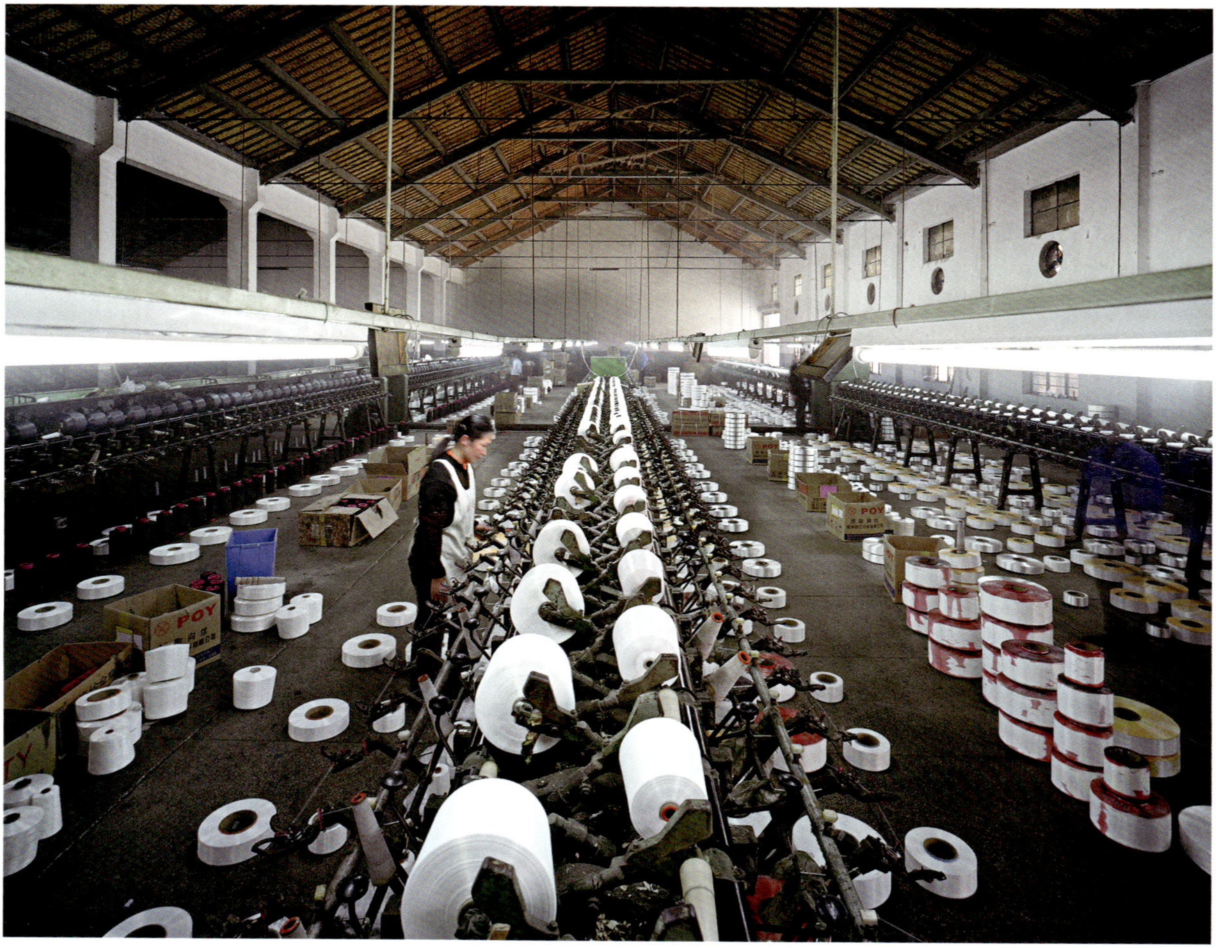

Edward Burtynsky, *Manufacturing #8, Textile Mill, Xiaoxing, Zhejiang, China*, 2004

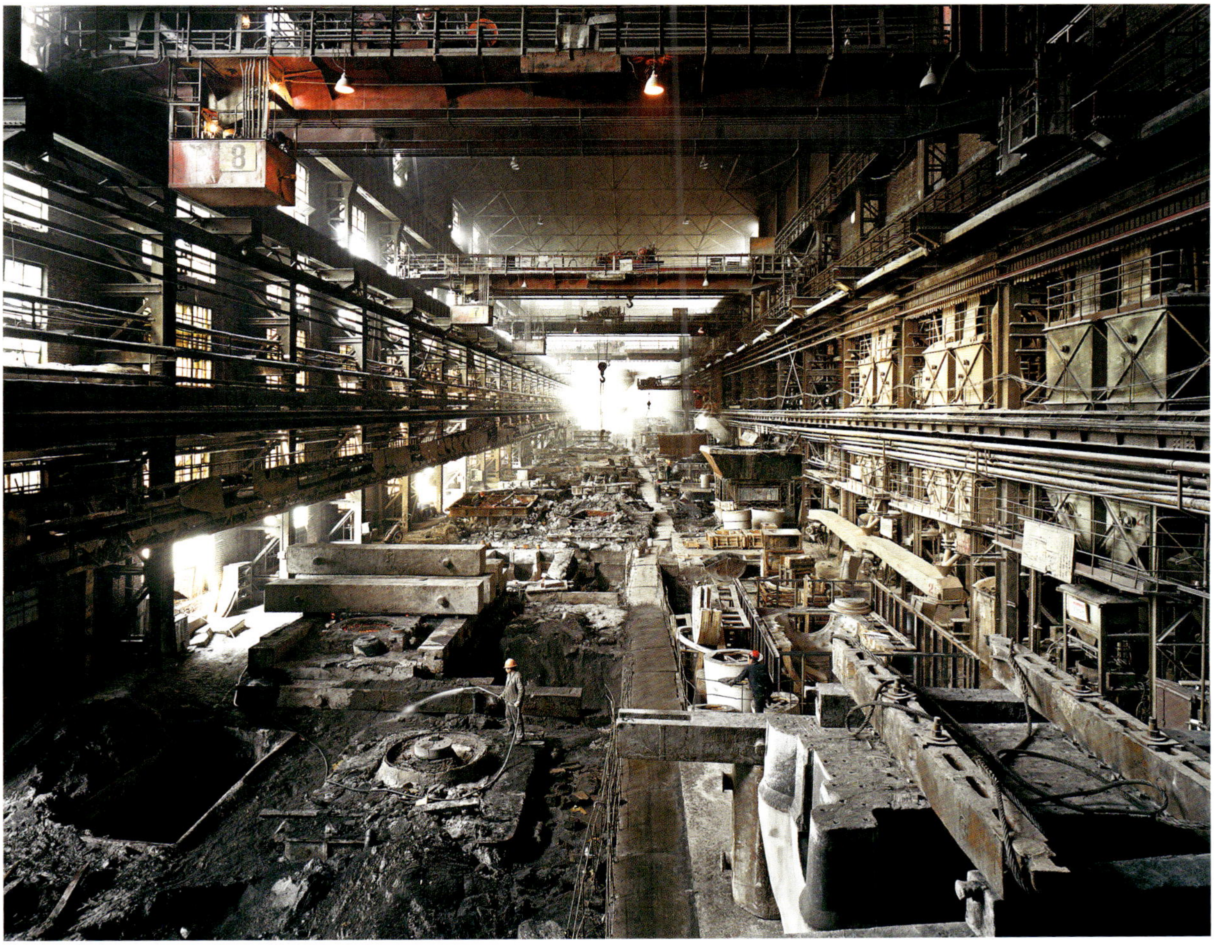

Edward Burtynsky, *Old Factories #4*, 2005

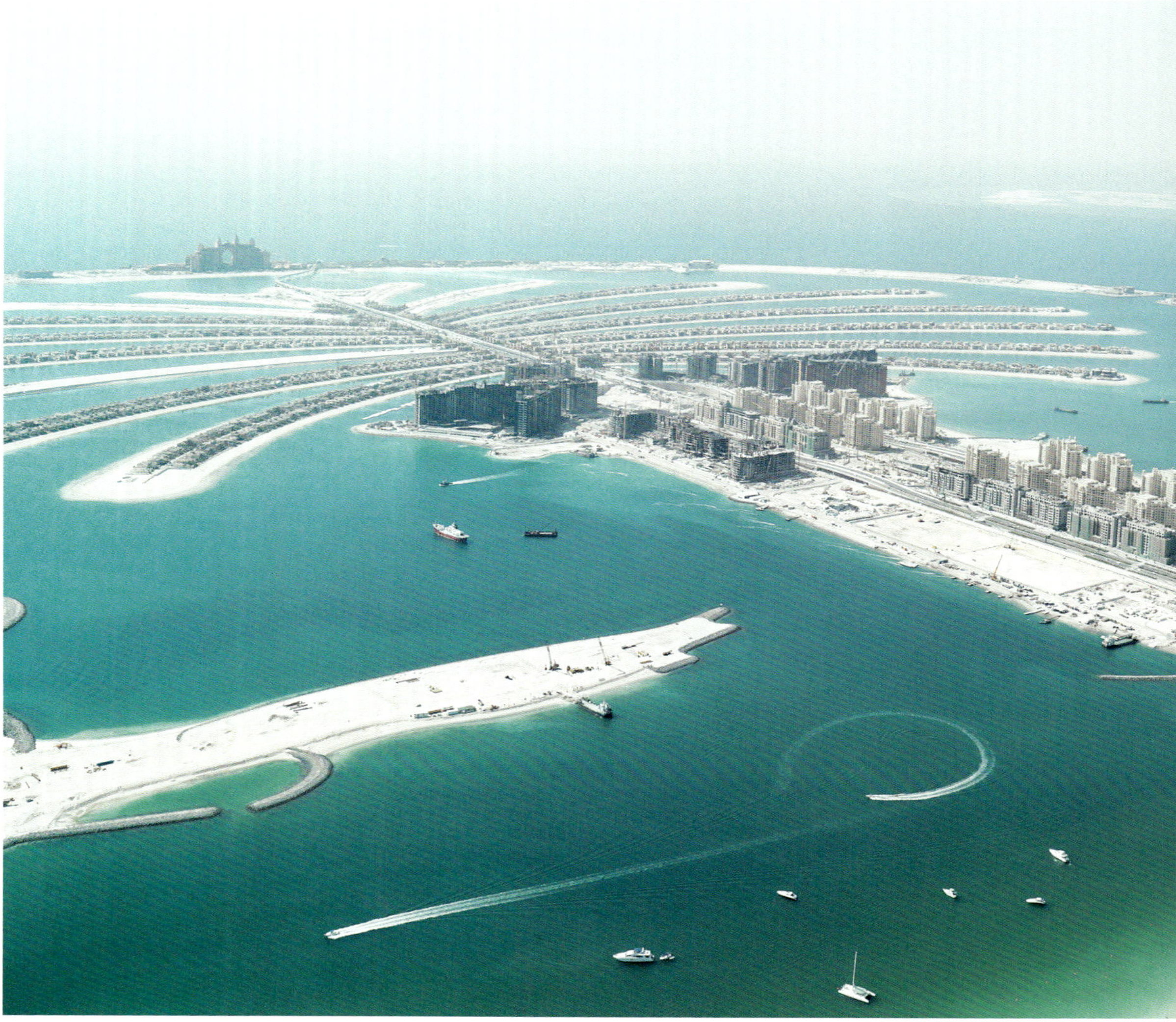

Philippe Chancel, *Palm island,* aus der Serie / from the series *Desert Spirit,* 2007–2010

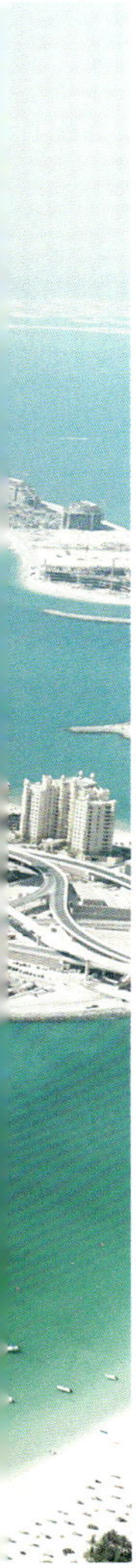

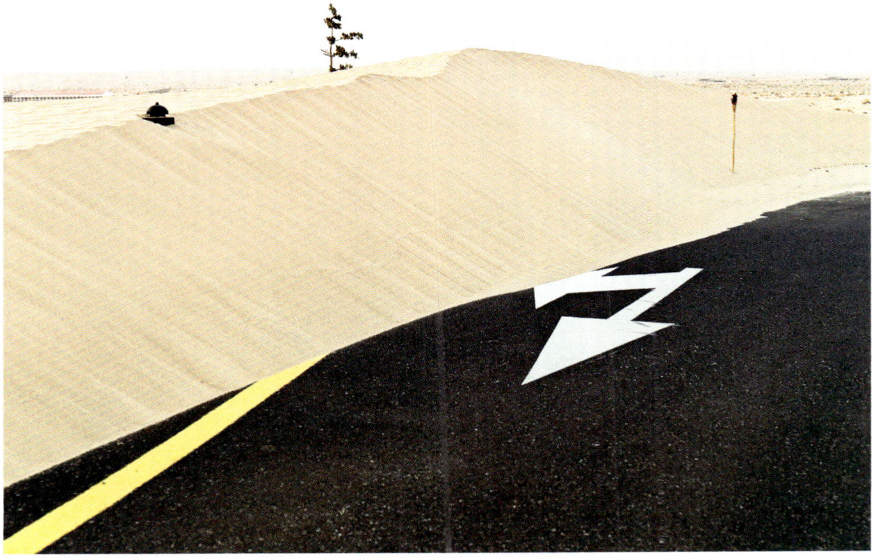

Philippe Chancel, *Yellow line,* aus der Serie / from the series *Desert Spirit,* 2007–2010

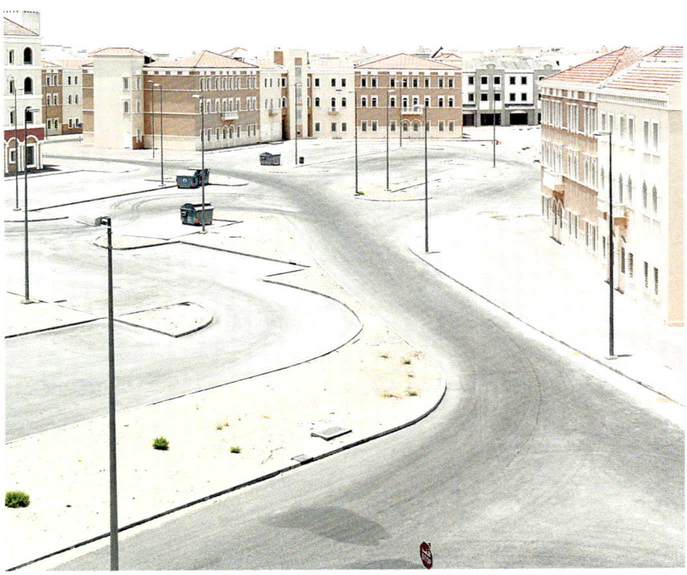

Philippe Chancel, *Ghost city,* aus der Serie / from the series *Desert Spirit,* 2007–2010

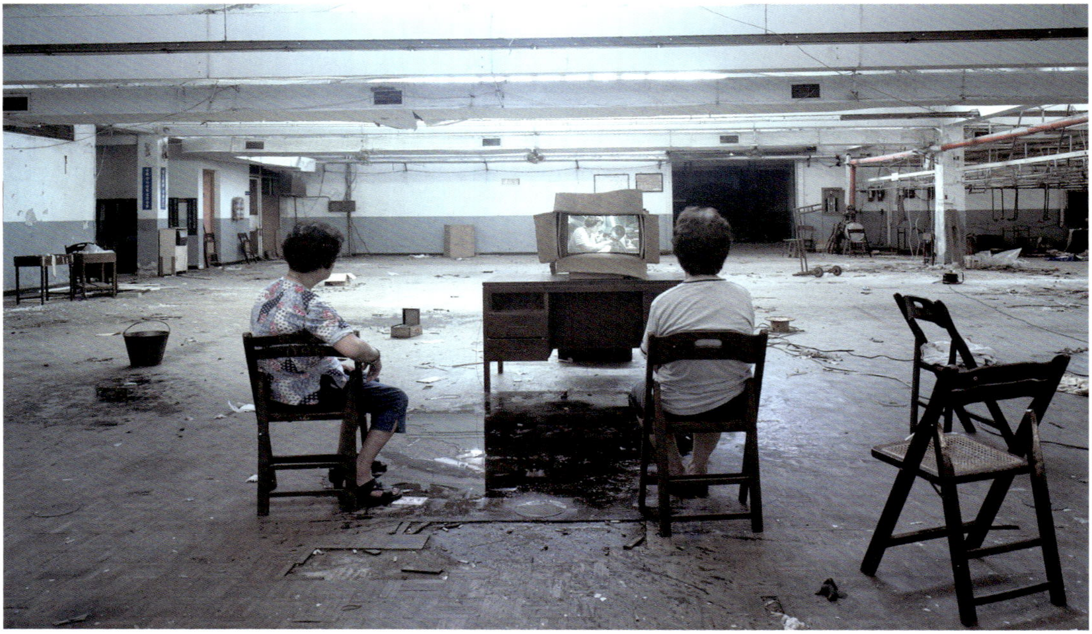

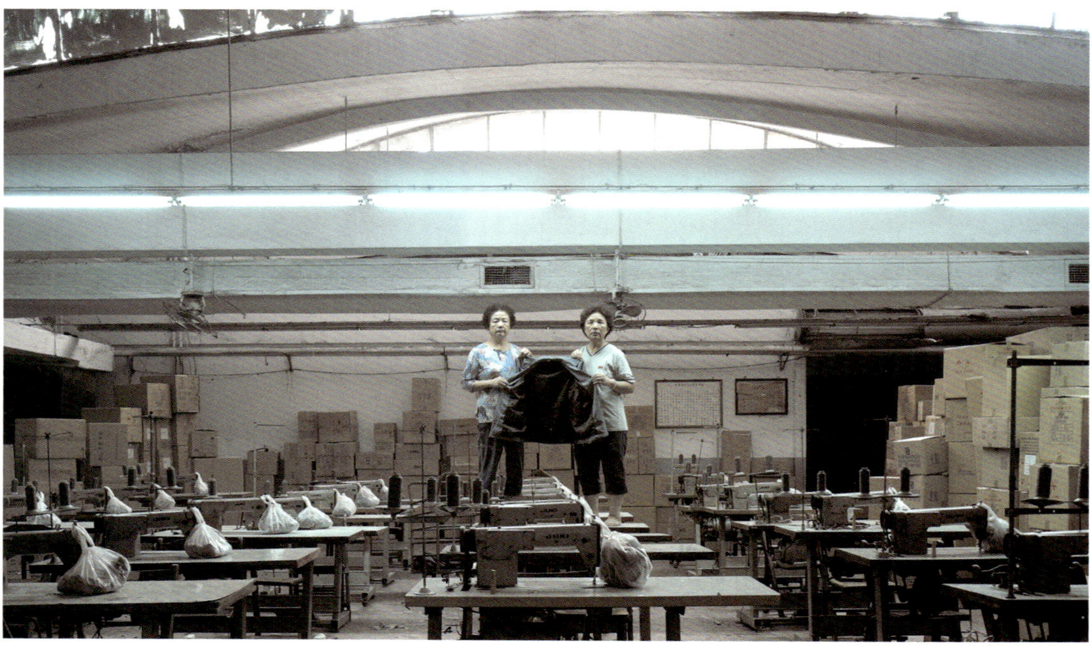

Chen Chieh-Jen, Standbilder aus / film stills from *Factory*, 2003

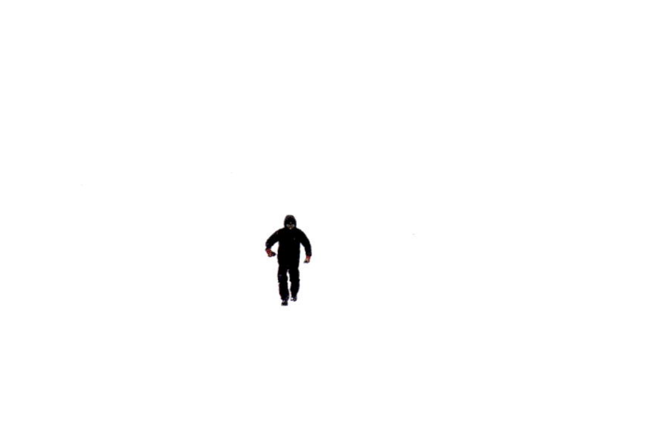
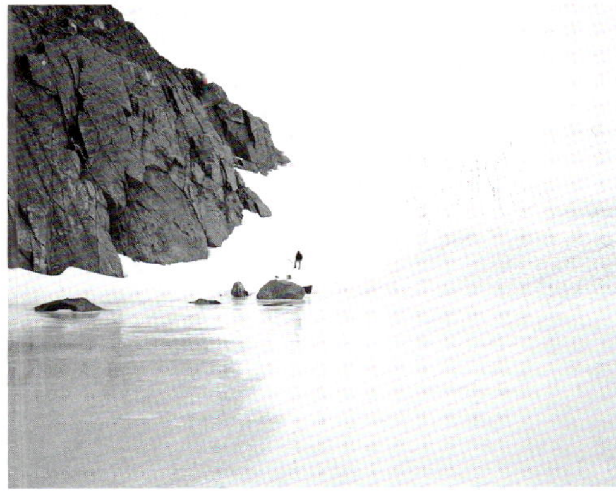

Geert Goiris, *#6/38* und / and *#9/38* aus / from *Whiteout*, 2009–2011

Geert Goiris, *#8/38* aus / from *Whiteout*, 2009–2011

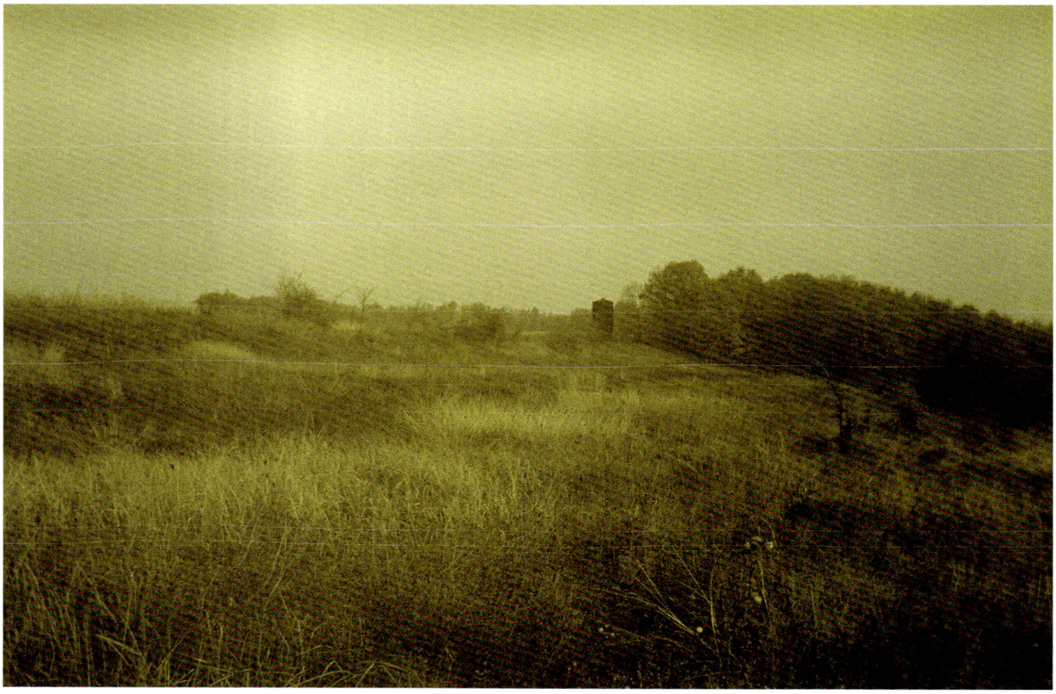

Nicu Ilfoveanu, *SPA_lipatti,* aus der Serie / from the series *Steampunk Autochrome,* 2004–2008

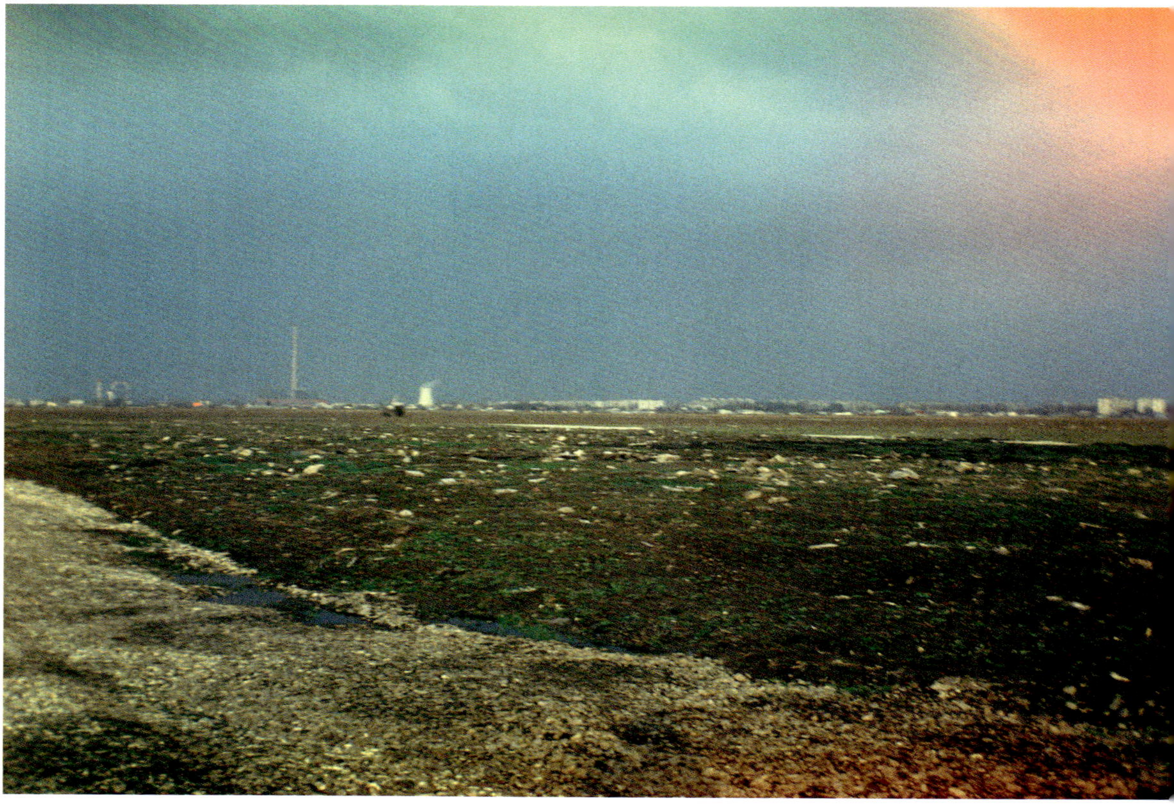

Nicu Ilfoveanu, *SPA_măgurele,* aus der Serie / from the series *Steampunk Autochrome,* 2004–2008

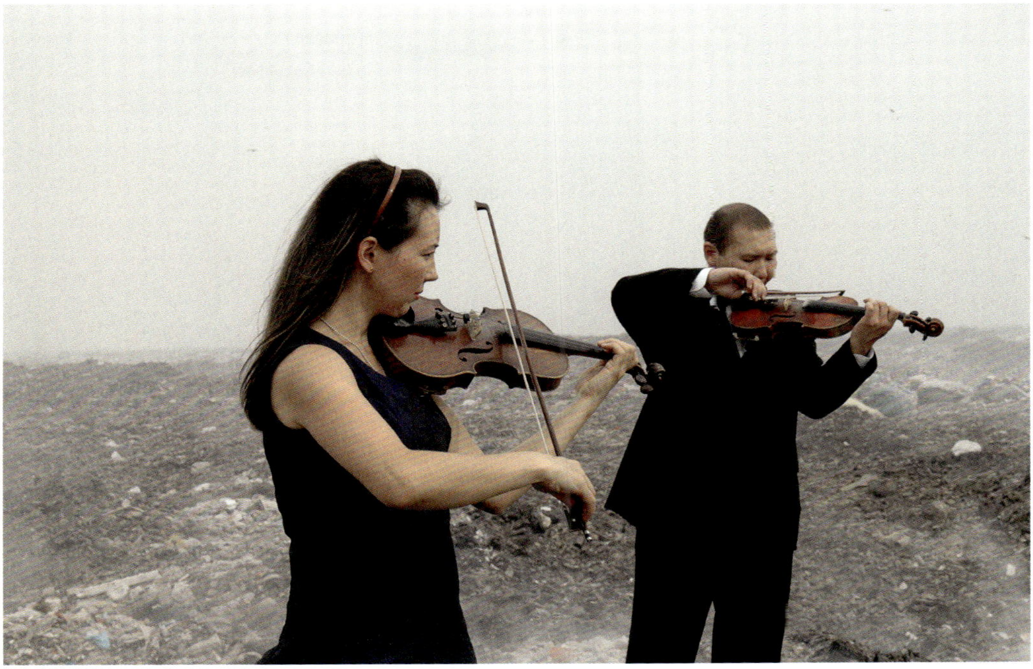

Gulnara Kasmalieva & Muratbek Djumaliev, Standbild aus / production still from *Spring*, 2009
Nächste Seite / next page: Panos Kokkinias, *Circle*, 2010

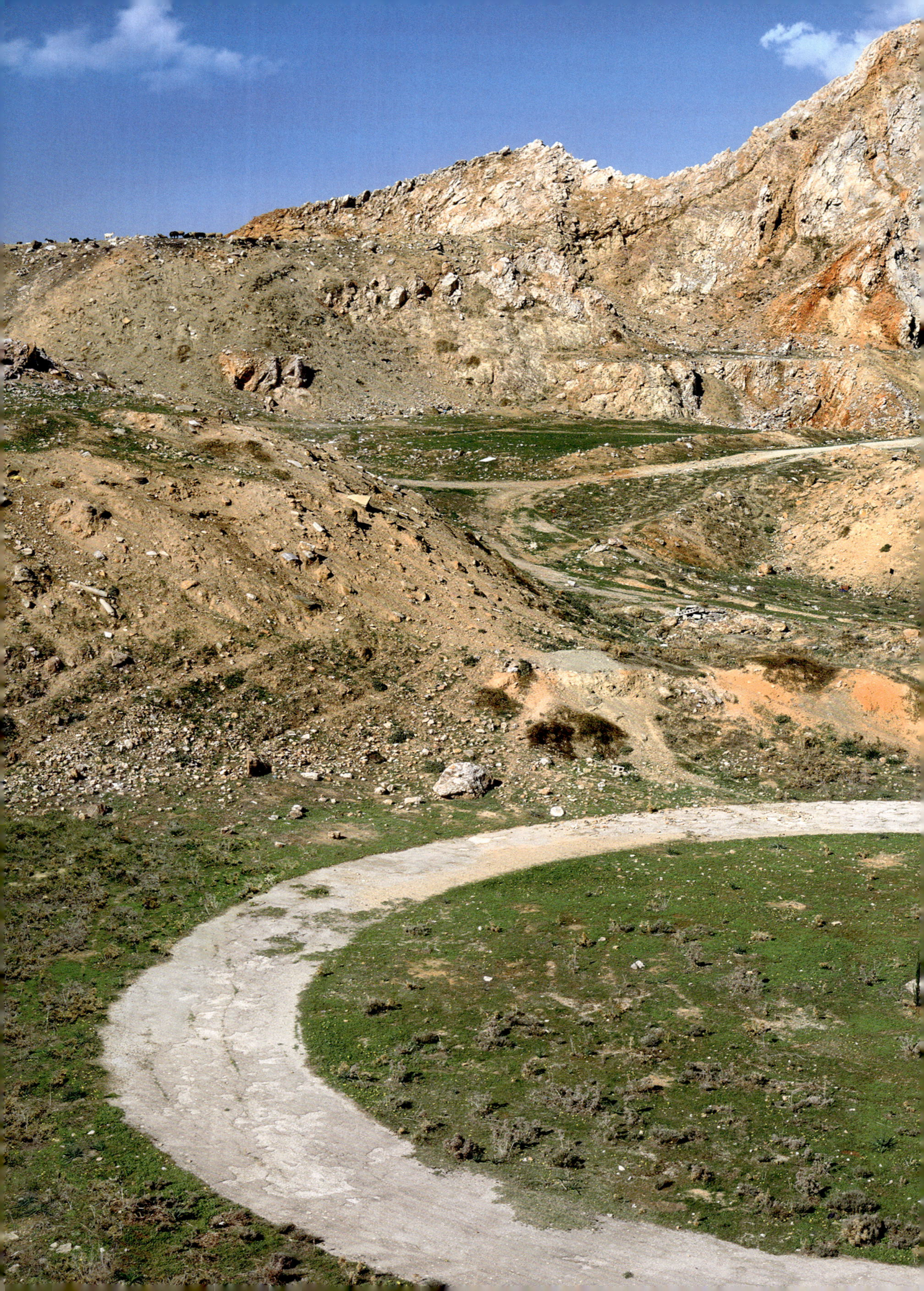

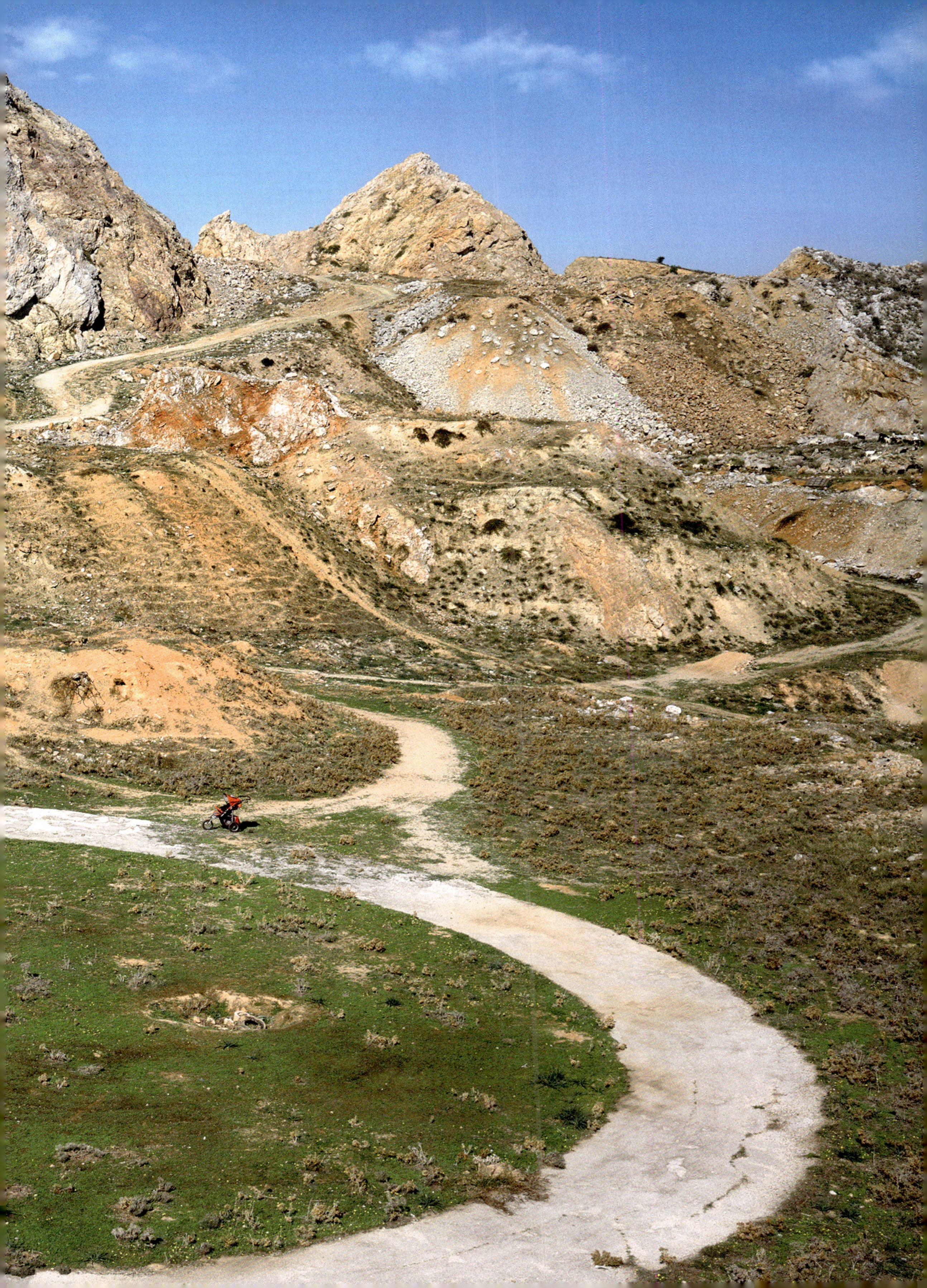

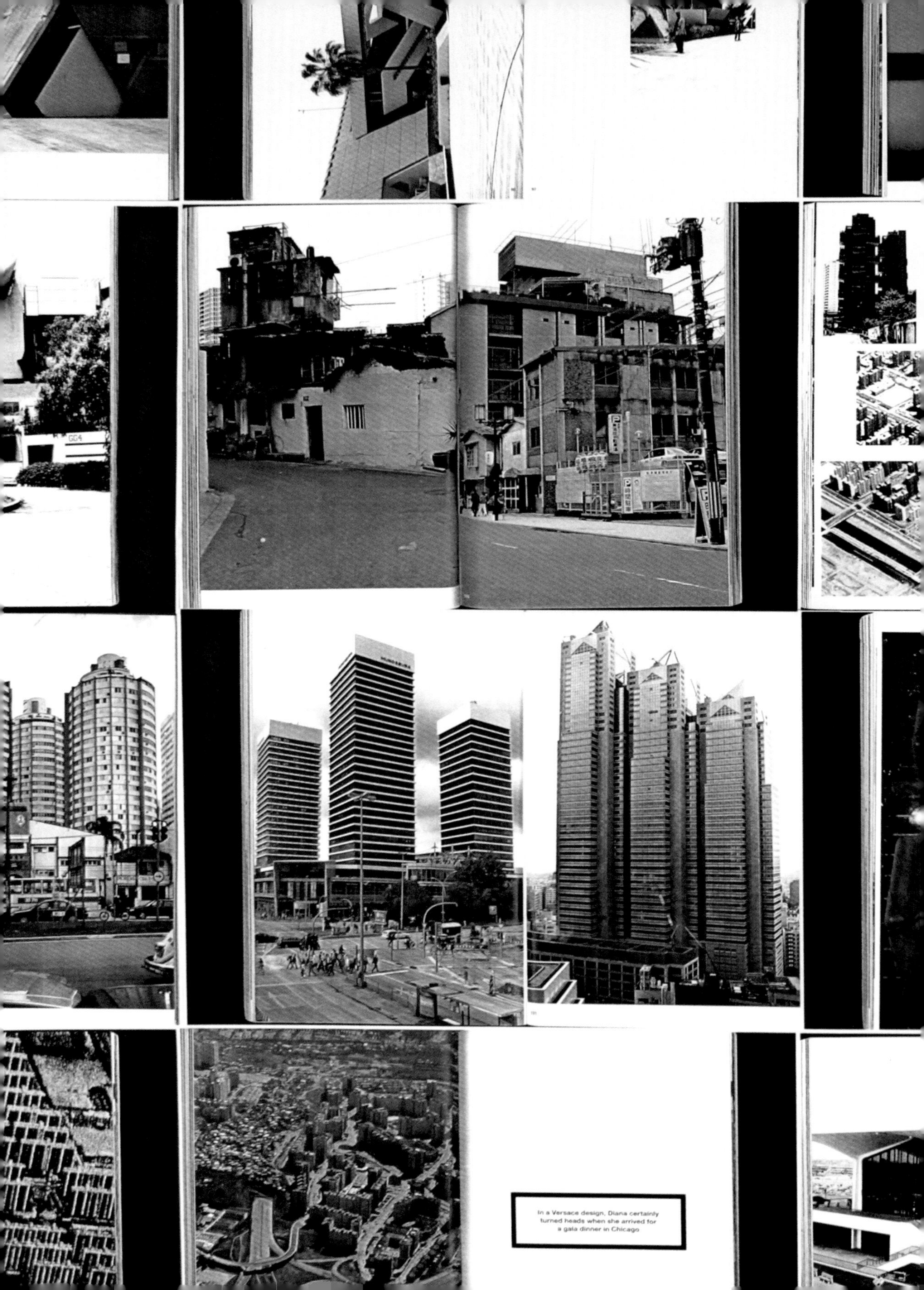
In a Versace design, Diana certainly
turned heads when she arrived for
a gala dinner in Chicago

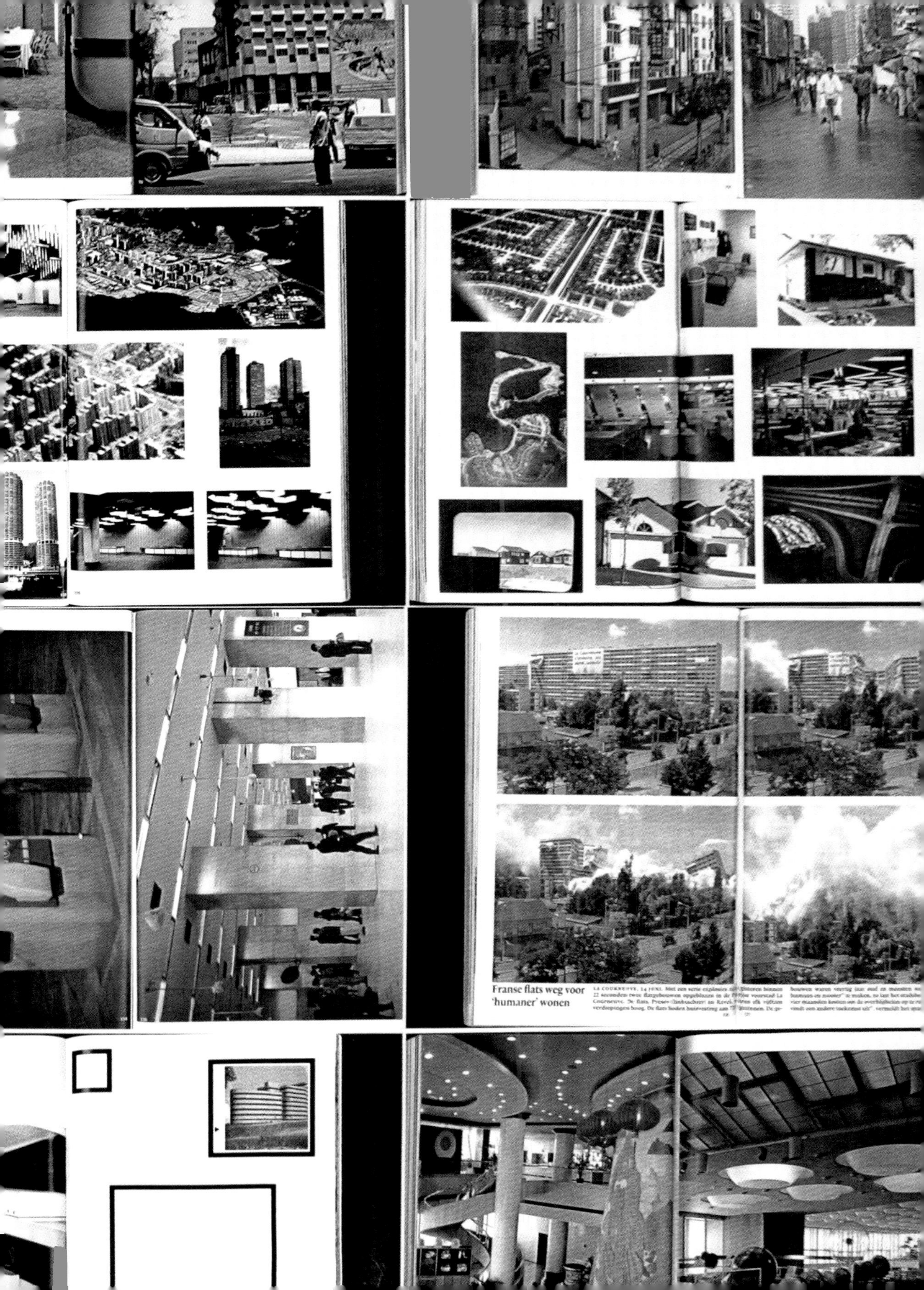
Franse flats weg voor 'humaner' wonen

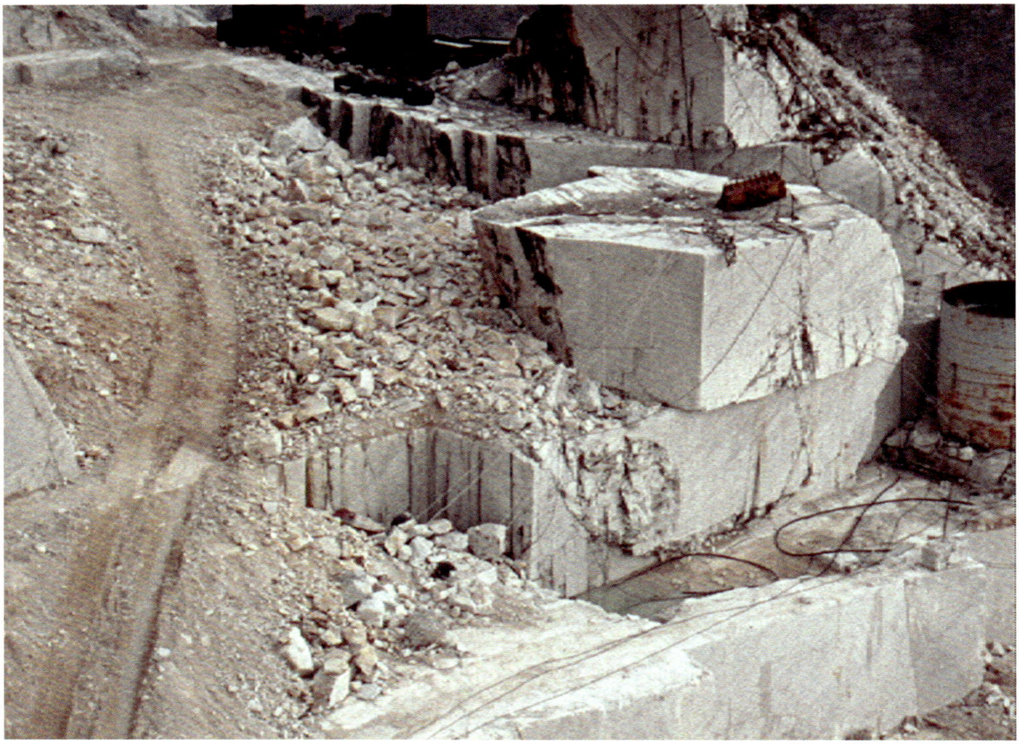

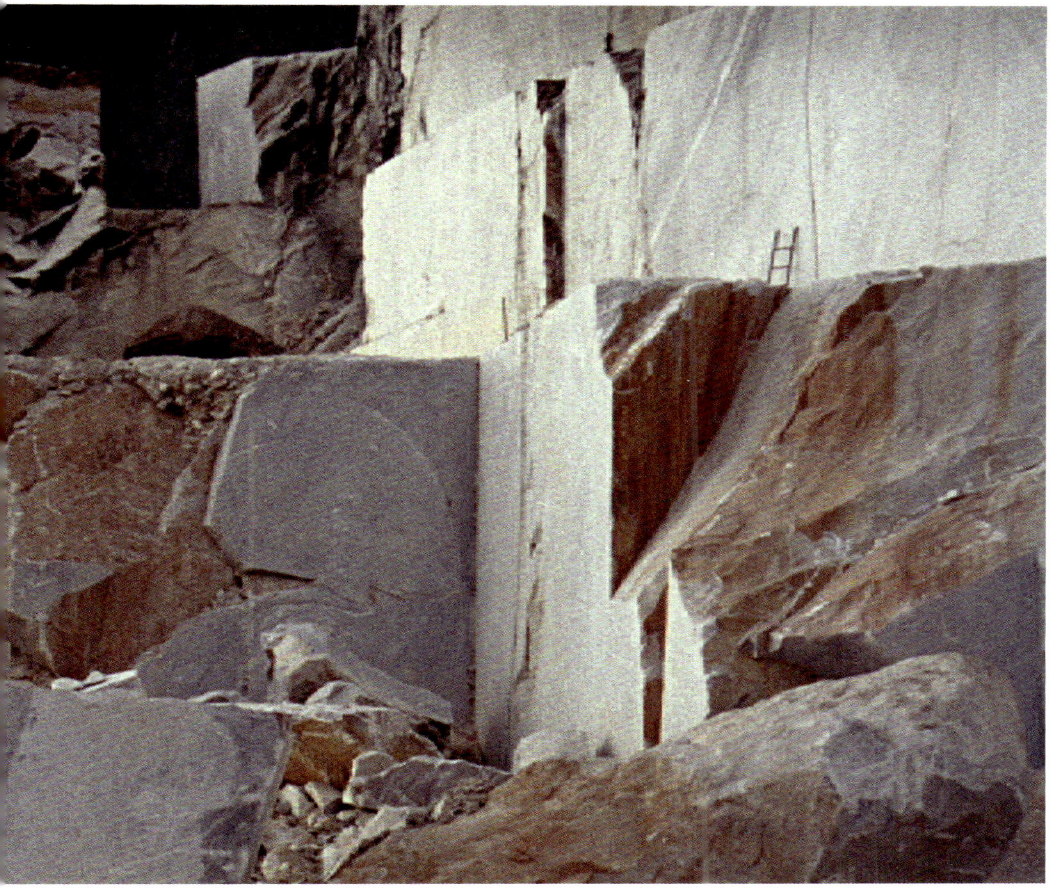

Vorige Seite / previous page: Aglaia Konrad, *Iconocopycity*, 2011
Aglaia Konrad, Standbilder aus / stills from *Concrete & Samples III – Carrara*, 2010

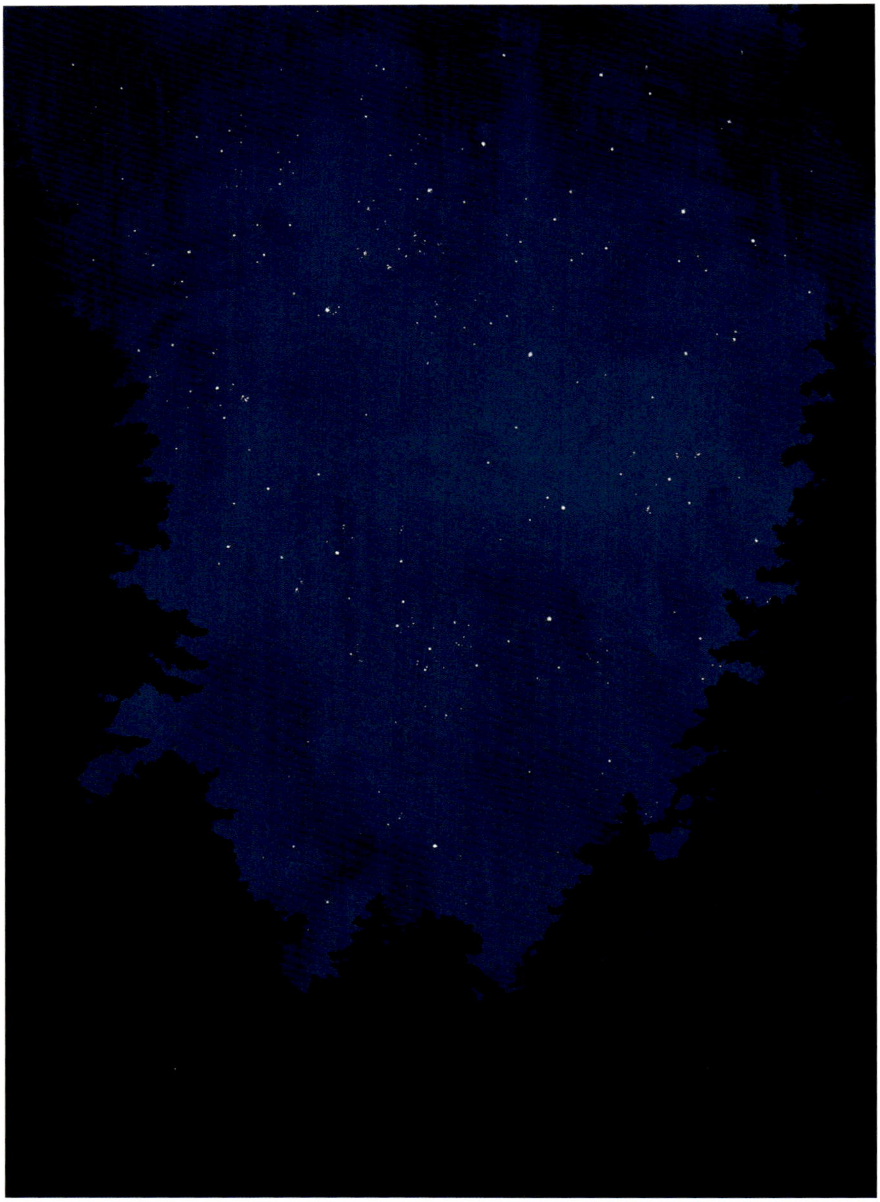

Links und rechts / left and right: Florian Maier-Aichen, *Untitled*, 2011
Nächste Seiten / next pages: Yang Yongliang, *Artificial Wonderland No. 1*, 2010

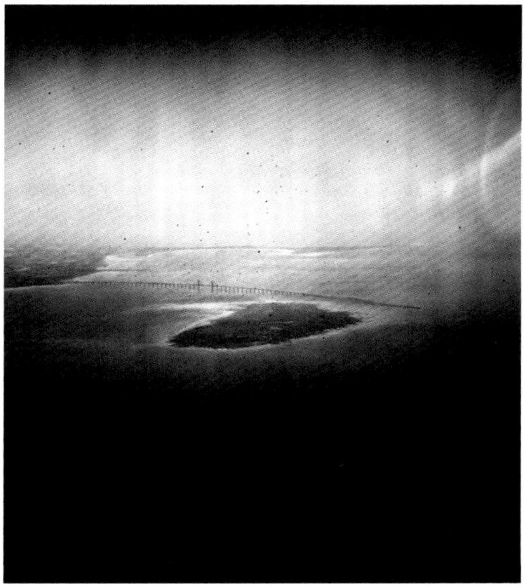

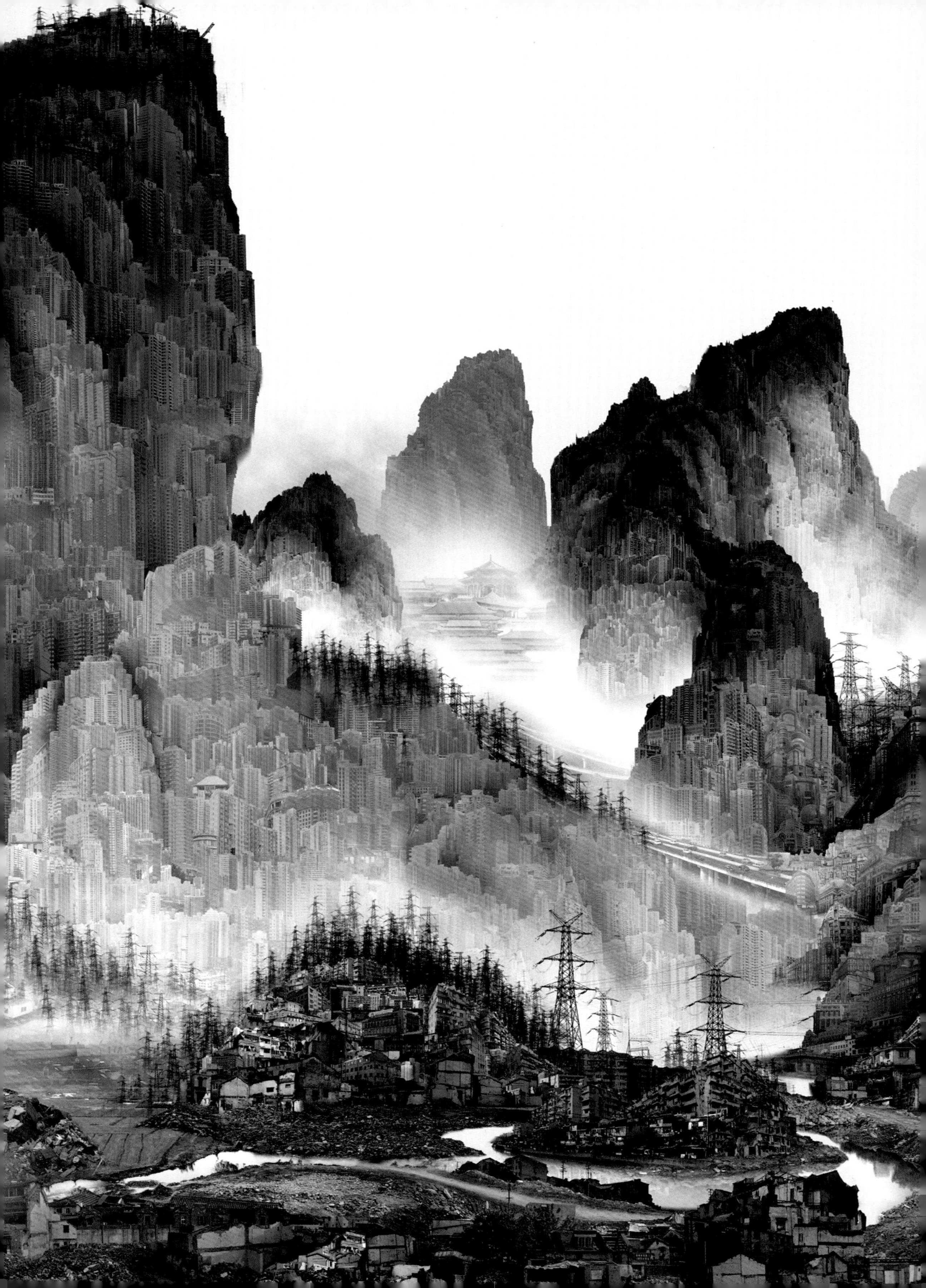

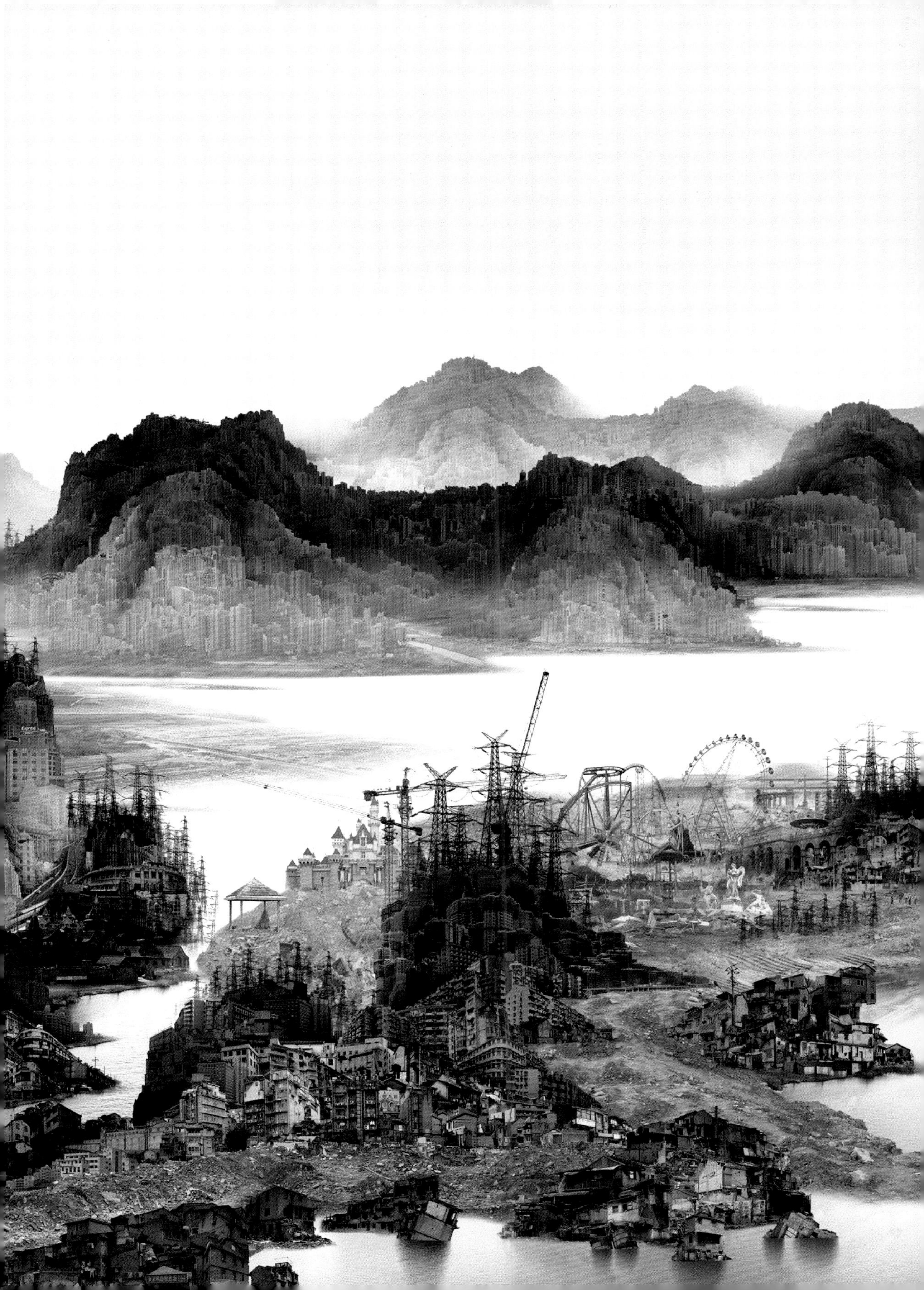

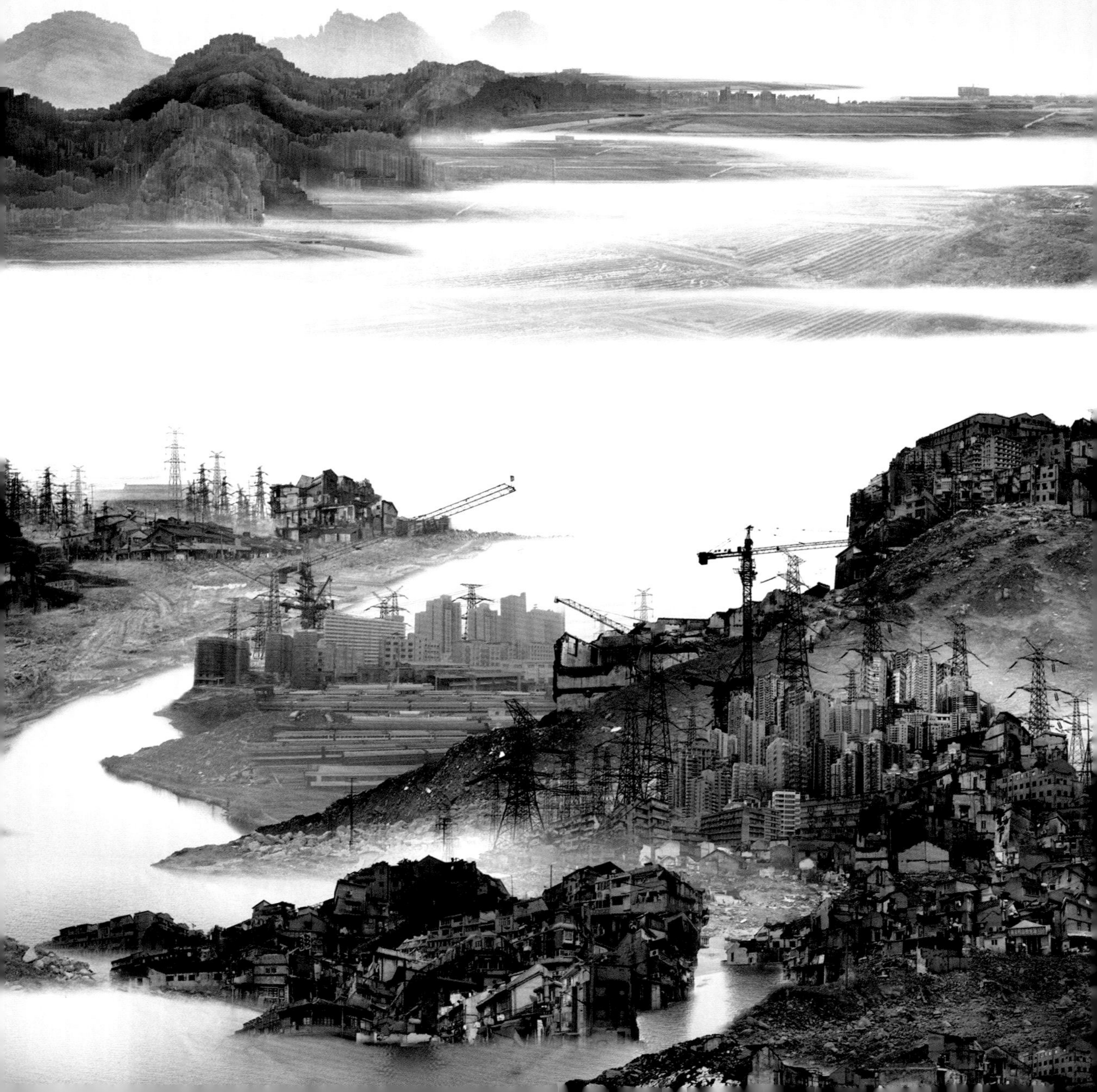

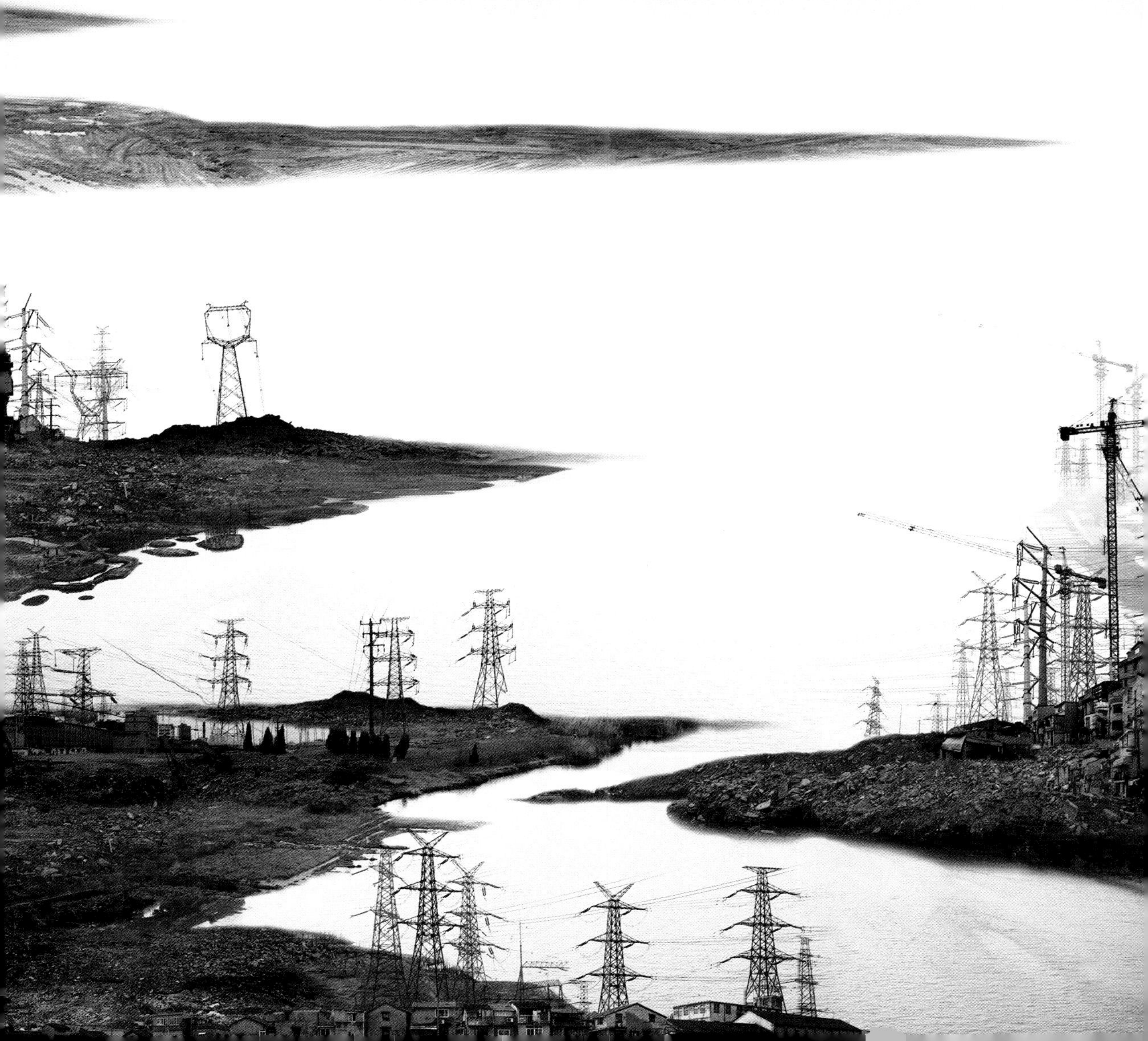

Role and Ritual

Rolle und Ritual

Kunsthalle Mannheim

Das Thema „Rolle und Ritual" wird durch künstlerische und anthropozentrische Fallstudien von Ritualkulturen und Rollenspielen präsentiert, die lokalspezifisch sind, zugleich aber einem postkolonialen, globalen Kontext angehören.

Rituale sind wesentliche Aktionsarten, welche die menschliche Kultur, Spiritualität und Sozialität schaffen und aufrechterhalten. Bei ihnen handelt es sich sowohl um geschichtlich überlieferte als auch um neu erfundene kollektive Handlungen, die einer allgemein bekannten Dramaturgie gemäß ablaufen und häufig von einer leitenden Person „dirigiert" werden. Rituale ermöglichen Menschen das Erleben, die Teilnahme an und das Deuten von gemeinschaftlichen Ereignissen – sind sie nun feierlich oder schockierend –, sie bekräftigen das Gefühl einer kollektiven Erfahrung und erzeugen in einigen Fällen sogar ein kollektives Bewusstsein.

Da Rituale häufig in gemeinschaftlichen Glaubenssystemen gründen, welche, wie Moderne und Postmoderne gezeigt haben, im Westen auf sich selbst bezogen sind, kommen in dieser Ausstellung dem spirituellen, aber auch dem theatralischen und dem visuellen Aspekt besondere Bedeutung zu. „Rolle und Ritual" zeigt Dokumentationen von Ritualen und stellt dabei sowohl ihre äußere Erscheinung in den Mittelpunkt wie auch die sozialen Rollen und Codes, die in ihnen offenbar werden. Hierbei spiegelt sich auch die Rolle des Künstlers als Forscher – als „einsamer Jäger" auf der Suche nach bestimmten Situationen und Bildern –, der die Kulturen und Völker beobachtet. Dies stimmt mit den Vorstellungen des französischen Filmemachers und Anthropologen Jean Rouch überein, der sich selbst als „Künstler" bezeichnete und dem diese subjektive Rolle viel mehr zusagte als die des „klassischen" Anthropologen, wobei es Rouch darum ging, die Definition seiner eigenen Position im Hinblick auf die von ihm beobachteten kulturell konditionierten Situationen zu erleichtern.

Rituale bringen Menschen zusammen, können sie aber auch voneinander trennen. Durch seine Teilnahme an einem Ritual ordnet sich das Individuum einer gesellschaftlich anerkannten Rolle und Vorgehensweise unter und erlangt eine Rolle in der Gemeinschaft. Auch allein kann das Individuum sich rituell und somit symbolisch aufgeladenes Verhalten aneignen, das einer bestimmten rituellen Rolle zuzuordnen ist, und die so entstehende Persönlichkeit in Situationen des wirklichen Lebens einbringen. „Rolle und Ritual" zeigt eine Reihe von Ritualen und ihre offensichtlichen theatralischen Momente durch fotografische oder filmische Erzählungen von Ritualen in den Kulturen der Gegenwart.

Katerina Gregos & Solvej Helweg Ovesen

Role and Ritual

Kunsthalle Mannheim

'Role and Ritual' features diverse artistic and anthropocentric case studies of local ritualistic culture and role-playing cited in a postcolonial, global context.

Rituals are essential forms of action that create and sustain human culture, spirituality and sociality. Rituals are both historically inherited and contemporarily collective actions ordered in a commonly known dramaturgy, often 'directed' by a leading person. Through rituals, humans, partake of and interpret communal events, whether celebratory or cathartic. These events confirm and generate a sense of collective experience and consciousness.

As rituals are often founded in shared belief systems, the spiritual, but also the theatrical and the visual aspect take up a special place in this exhibition as manifestations of these belief systems. 'Role and Ritual' presents documentations of rituals focusing on their appearance and the social roles and codes manifested therein. Here, the role of the artist as researcher – as the 'lonely hunter' of specific situations and images – is reflected upon taking into account the cultures and peoples observed. This is in line with the ideas of French filmmaker and anthropologist Jean Rouch, who called himself an 'artist' and much preferred this subjective role to the one of the 'classical' anthropologist.

Rituals bring people together, but they can also separate them. By taking part in a ritual, the individual succumbs to a socially agreed role and procedure and gains a role in the community. When alone, individuals may also appropriate the symbolically loaded behaviour ascribed to a certain ritual role. 'Role and Ritual' presents specific photographic or filmic fables of rituals in contemporary cultures, both on an individual but also on a collective level.

Katerina Gregos & Solvej Helweg Ovesen

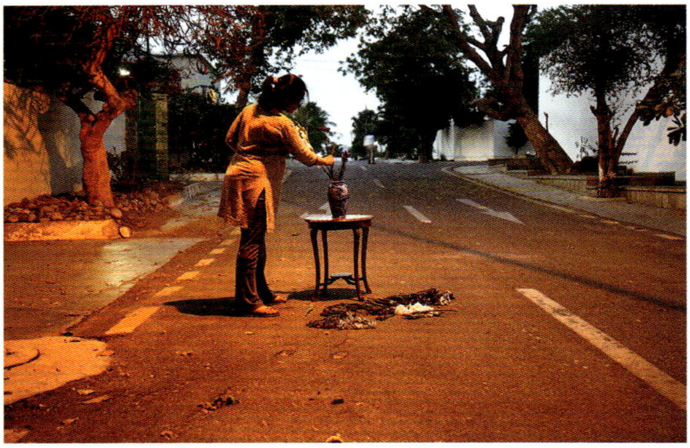

Jacky Mirza, 7:45 pm, 26 August 2008, Ramadan, Karachi

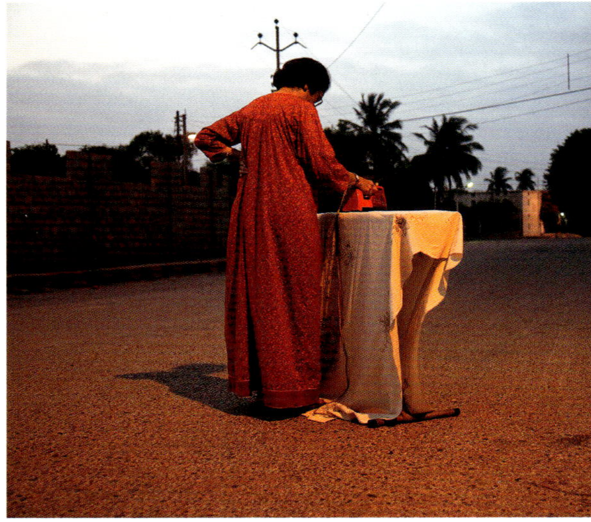

Pari Wania, 7:42 pm, 22 August 2008, Ramadan, Karachi

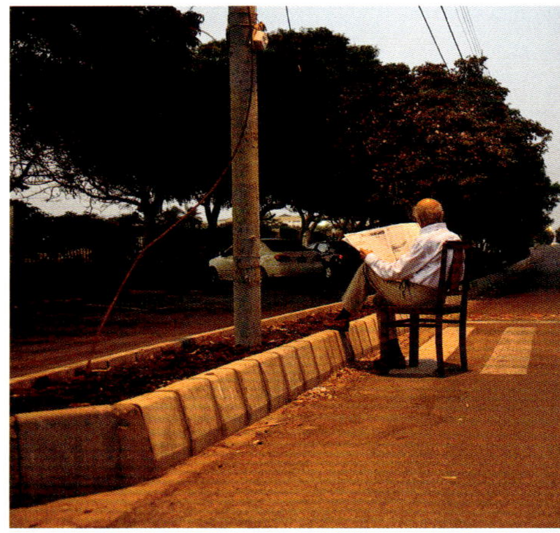

Jerry Fernandez, 7:45 pm, 21 August 20(Ramadan, Karachi

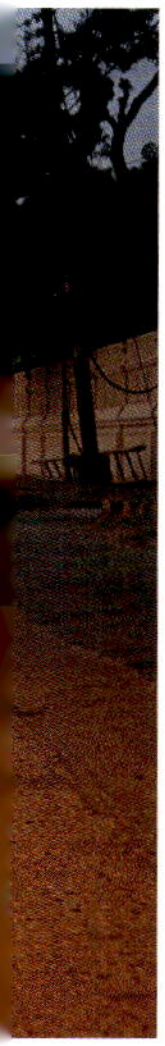

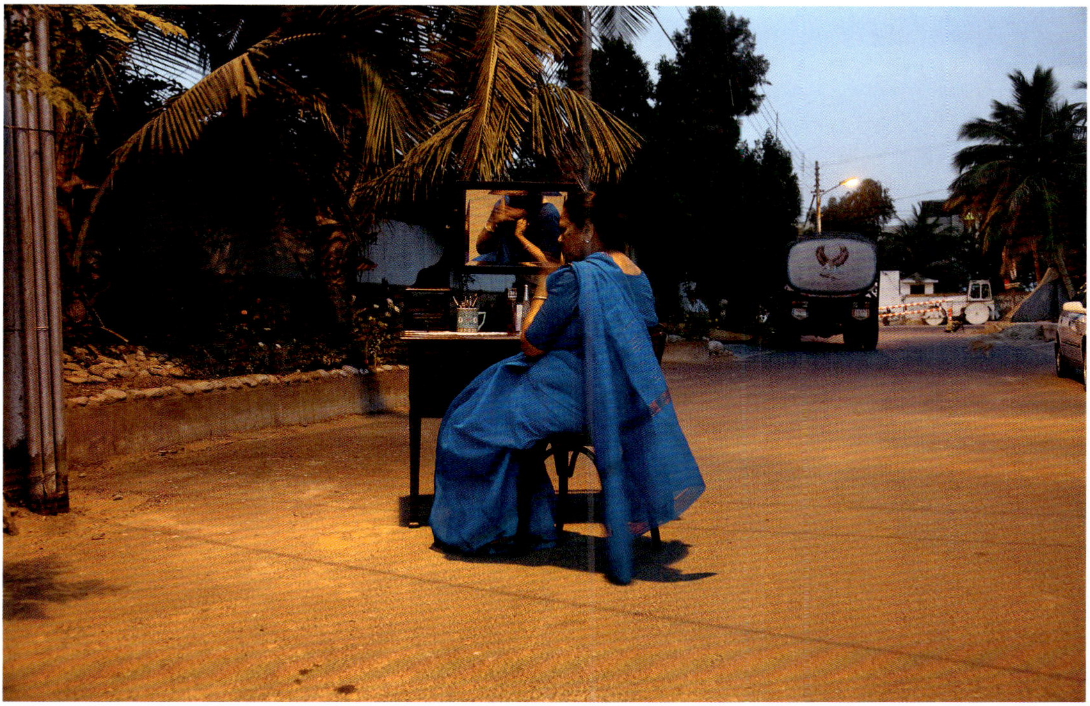

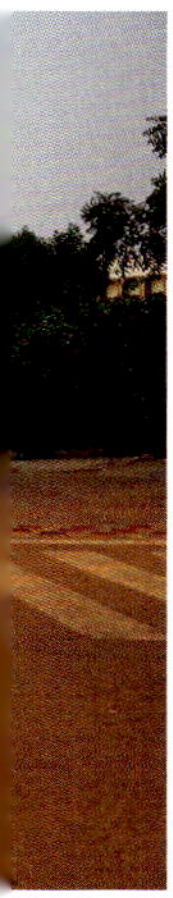

Chandra Acharya, 7:50 pm, 30 August 2008, Ramadan, Karachi

Bani Abidi, aus / from *Karachi Series 1*, 2009

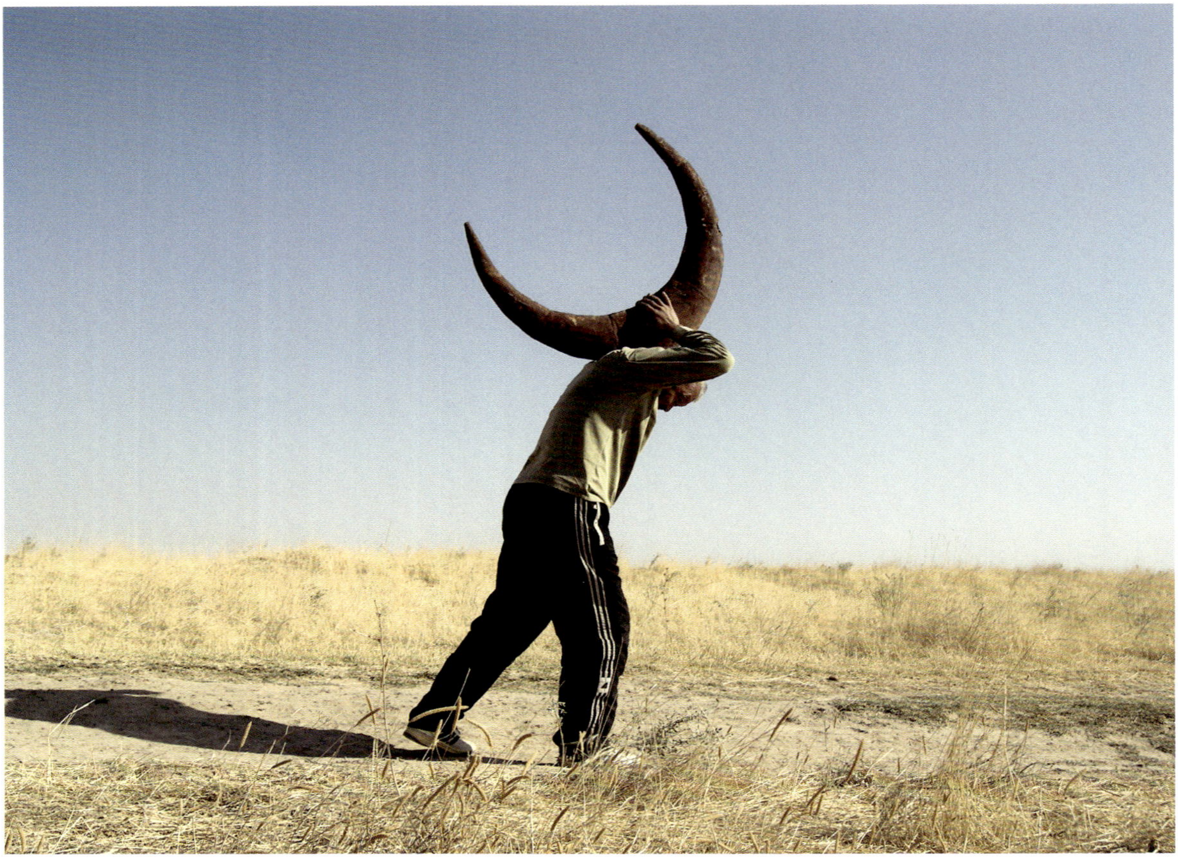

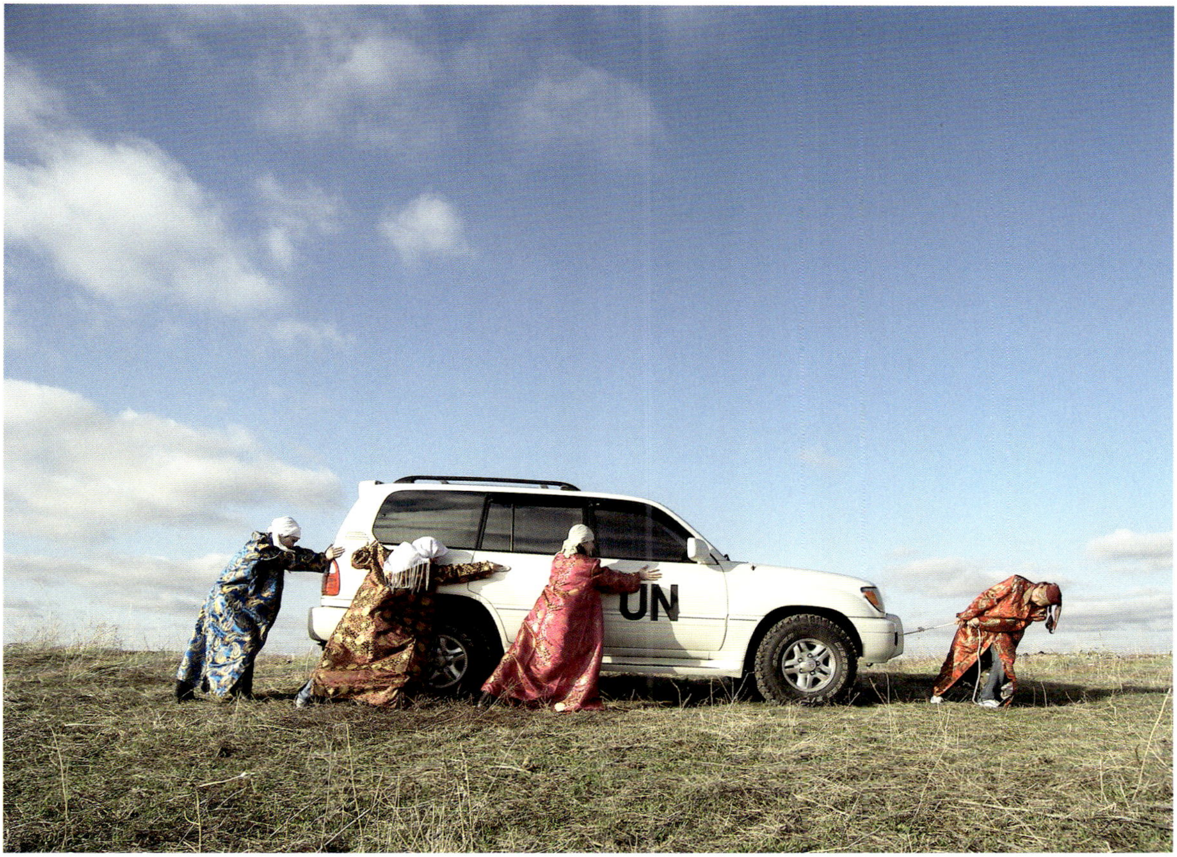

Said Atabekov, aus der Serie / from the series *Way to Rome,* 2007

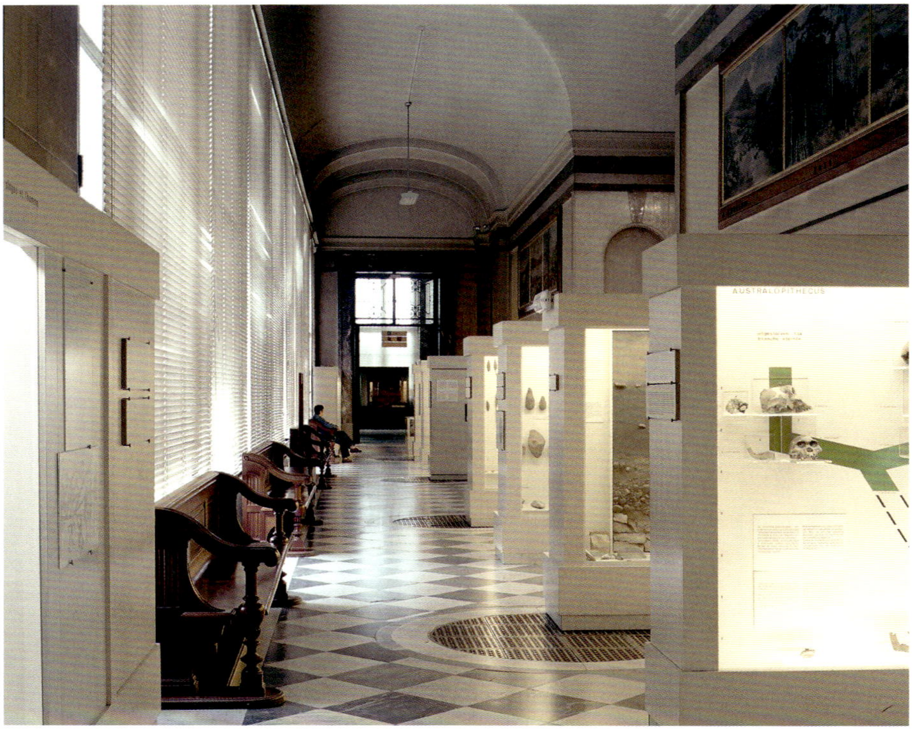
AUSTRALOPITHECUS

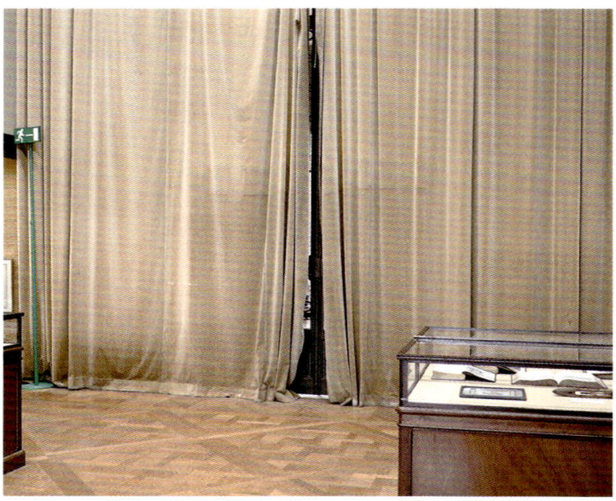

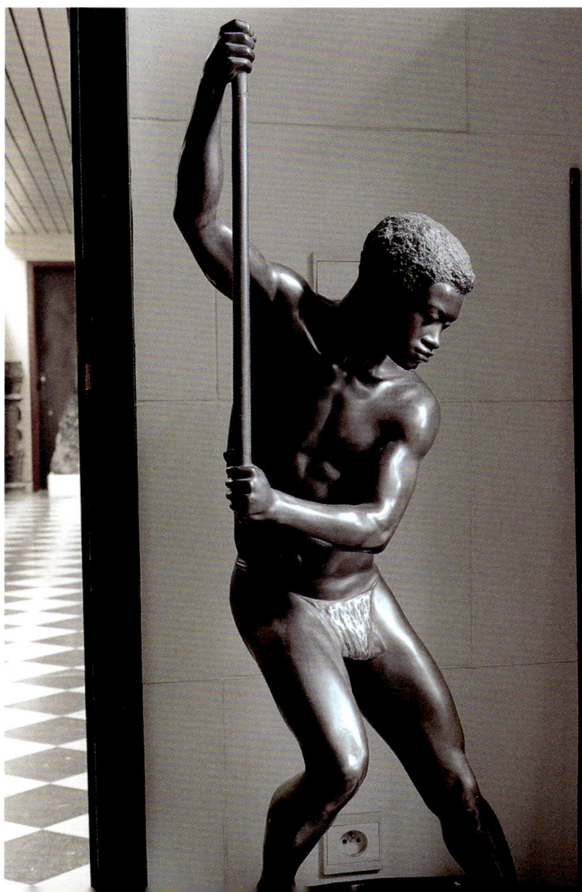

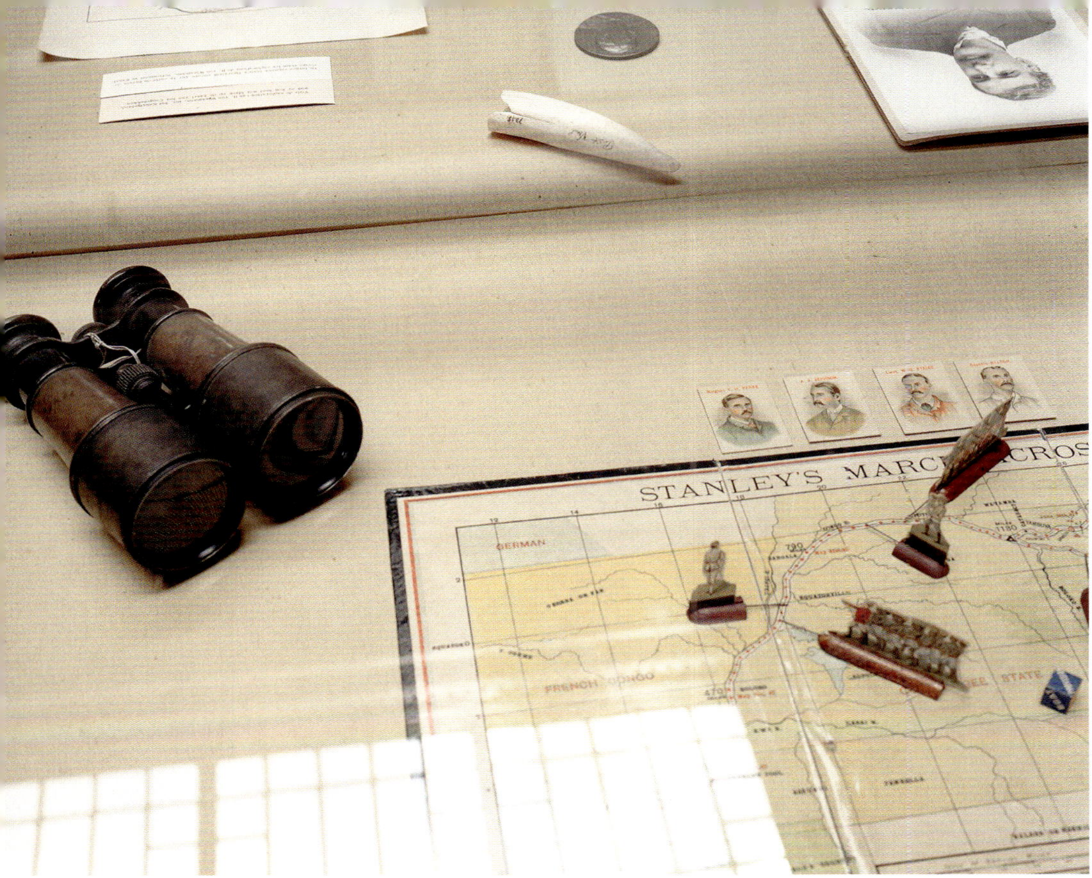

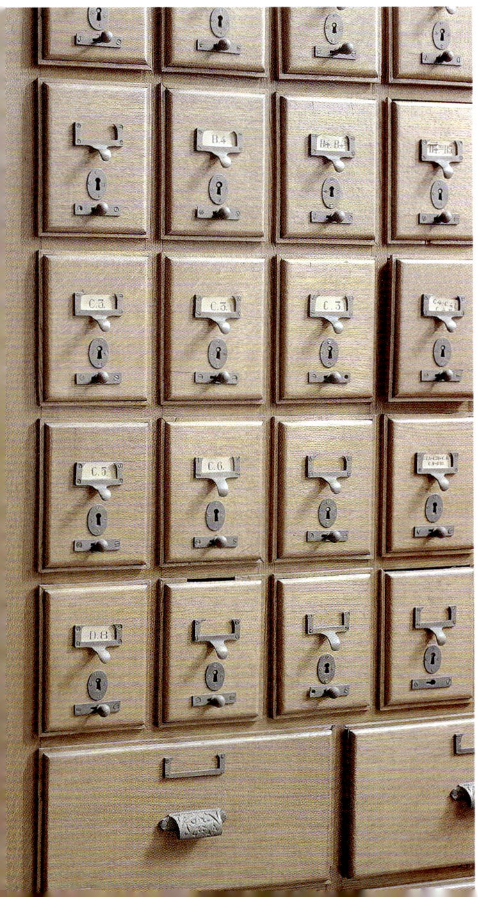

Peggy Buth, *Desire in Representation (Travelling through the Musée Royale)*, 2004–2009

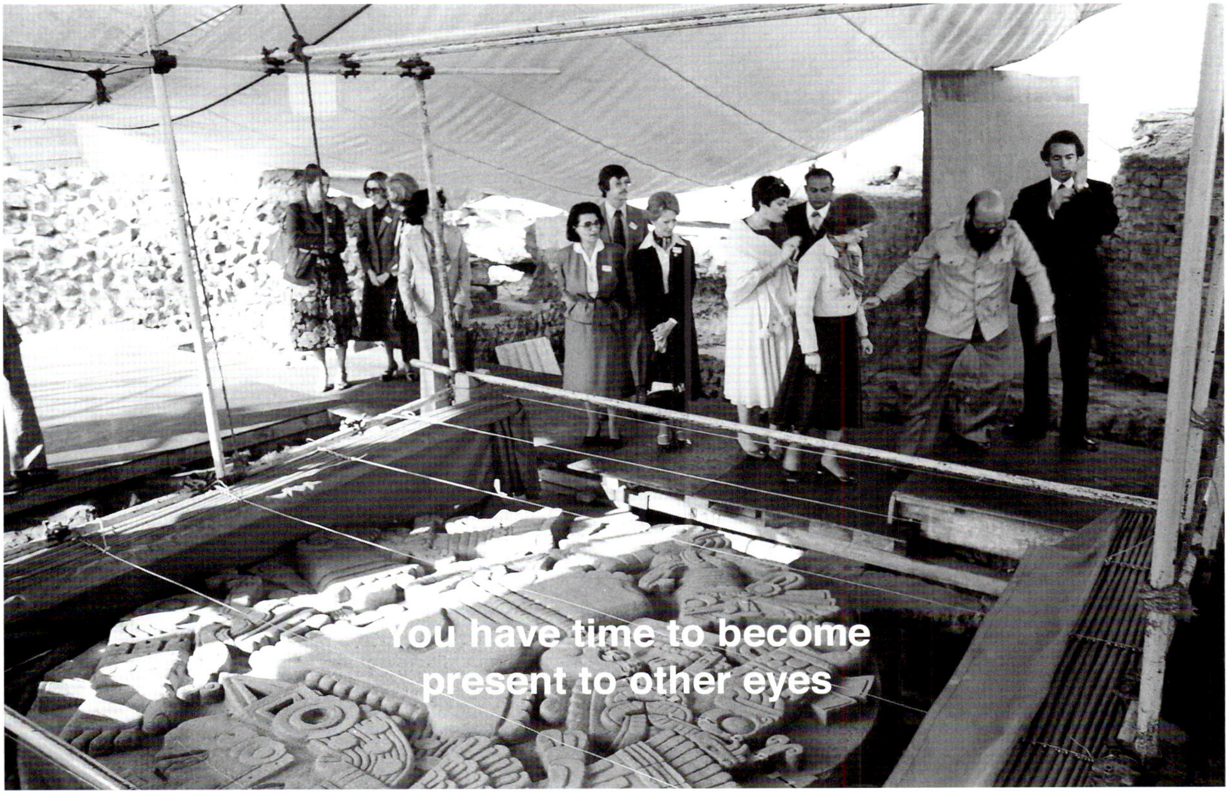

Mariana Castillo Deball, Standbild aus / video still from *There Is a Space Later in Time Where You Are Just a Memory,* 2010
Nächste Seite / next page: Philippe Chancel, *#1*; *#2; #3; #4* aus der Serie / from the series *Arirang,* 2005

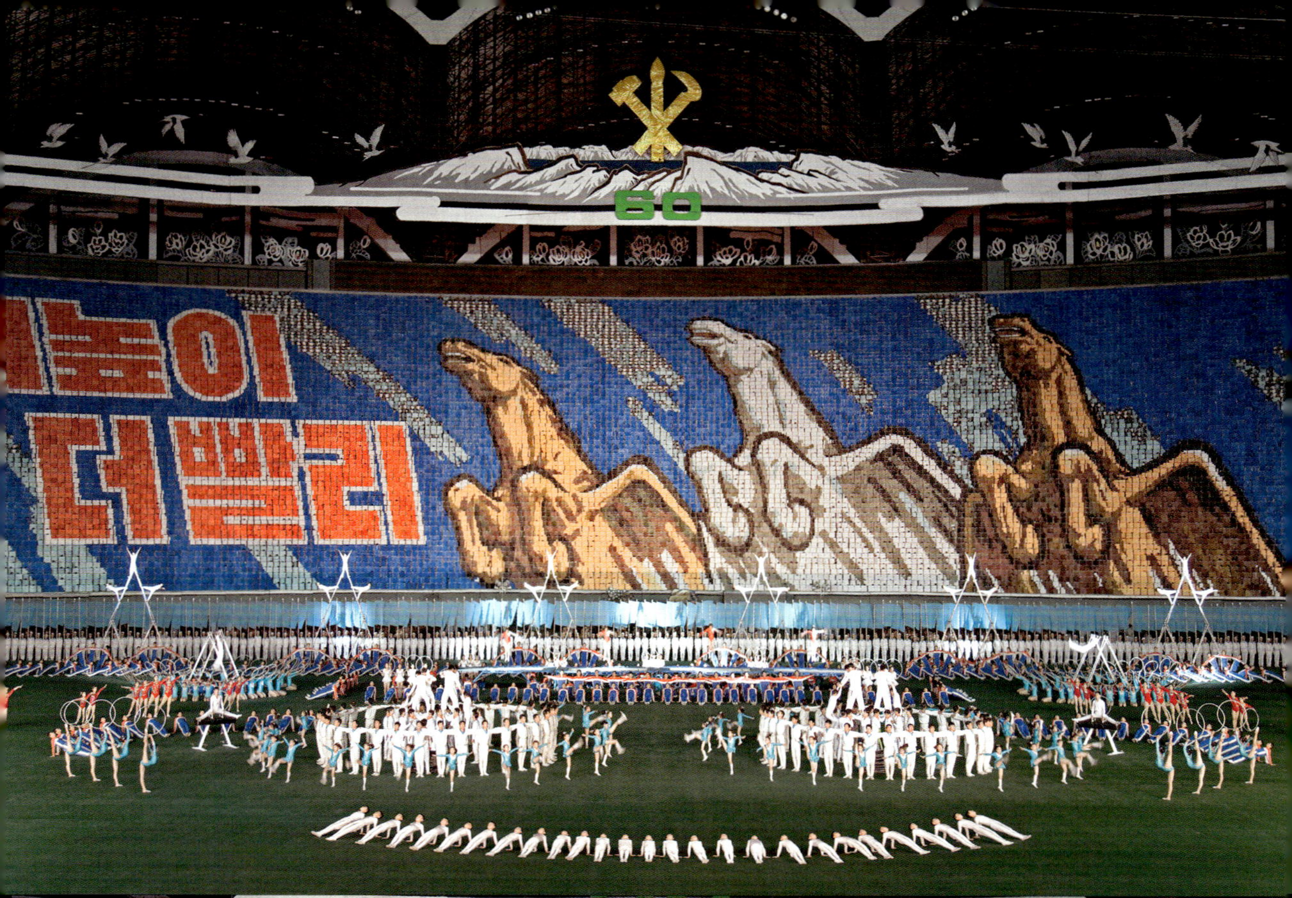
60
높이
더빨리

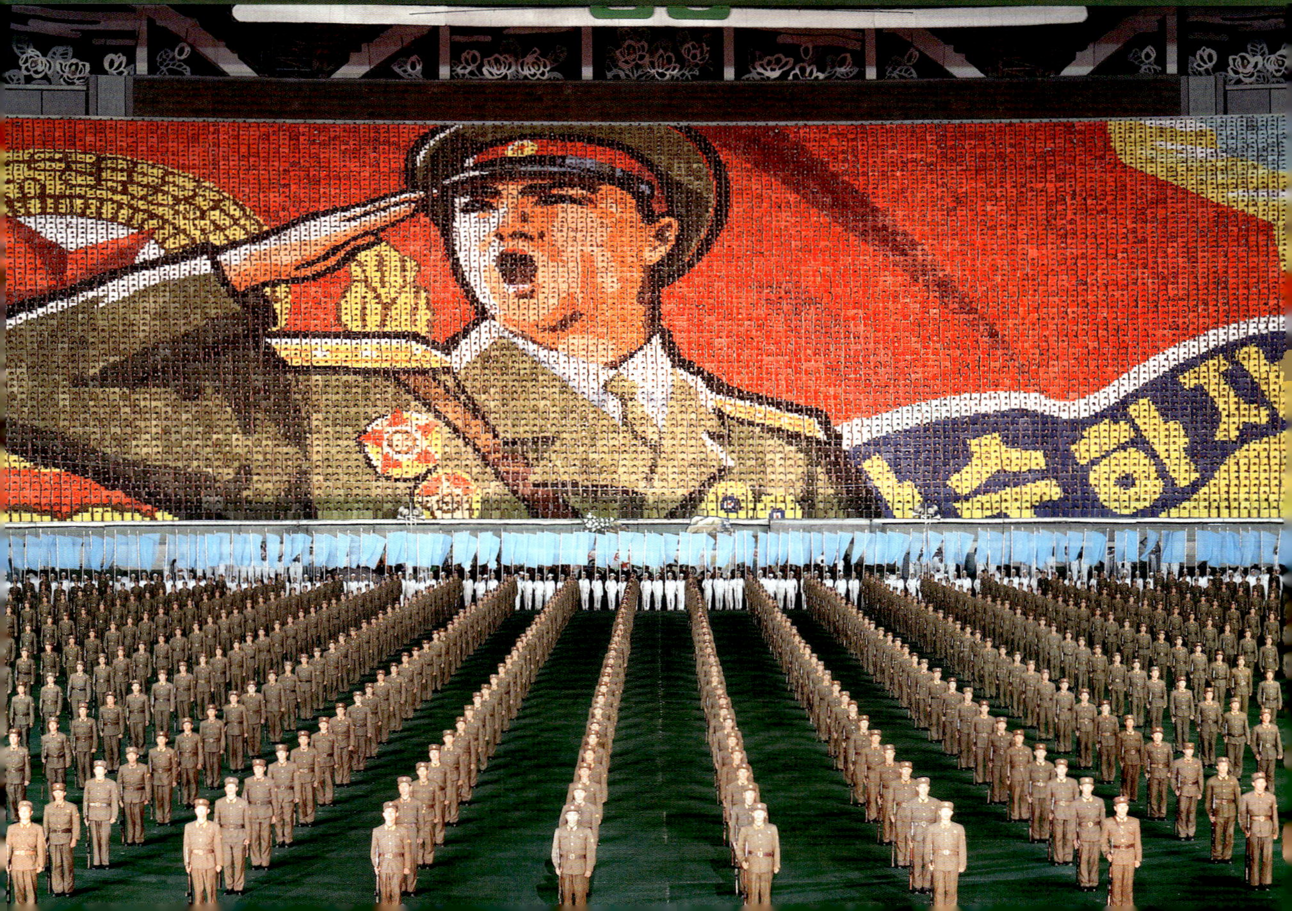

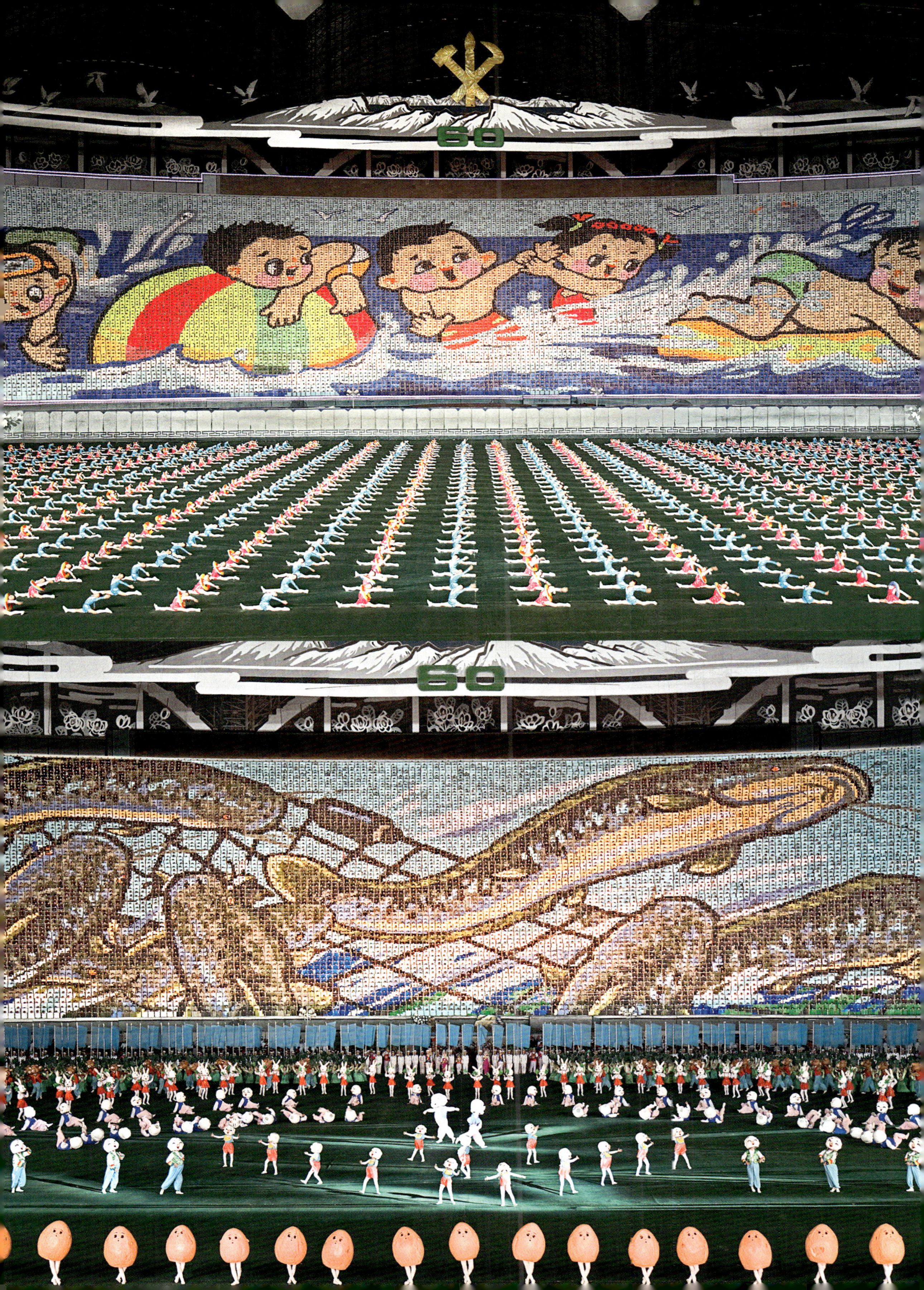
60
60

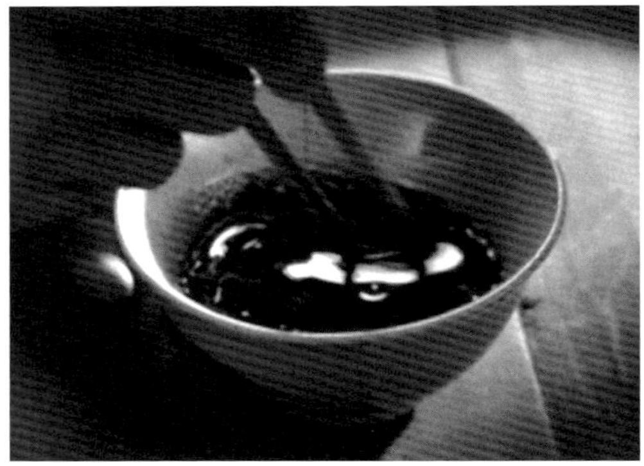

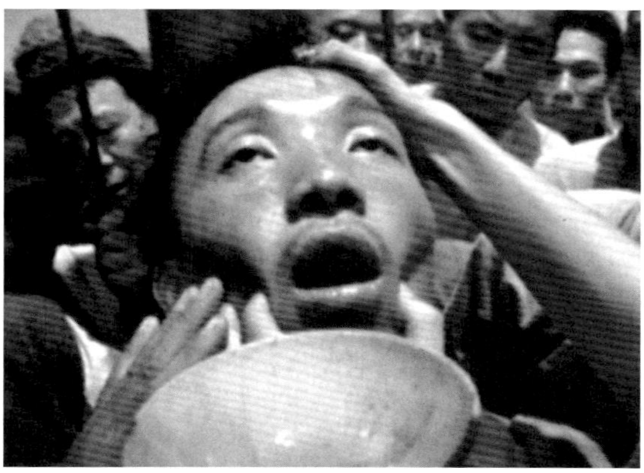

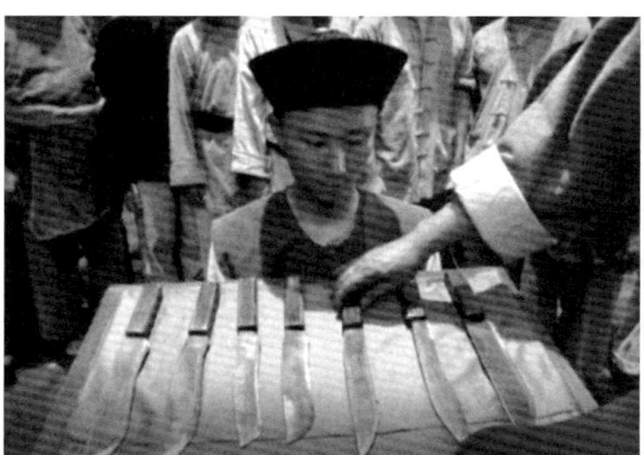

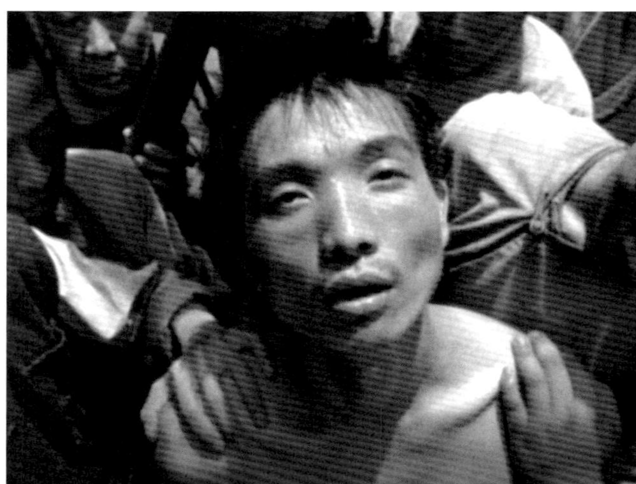

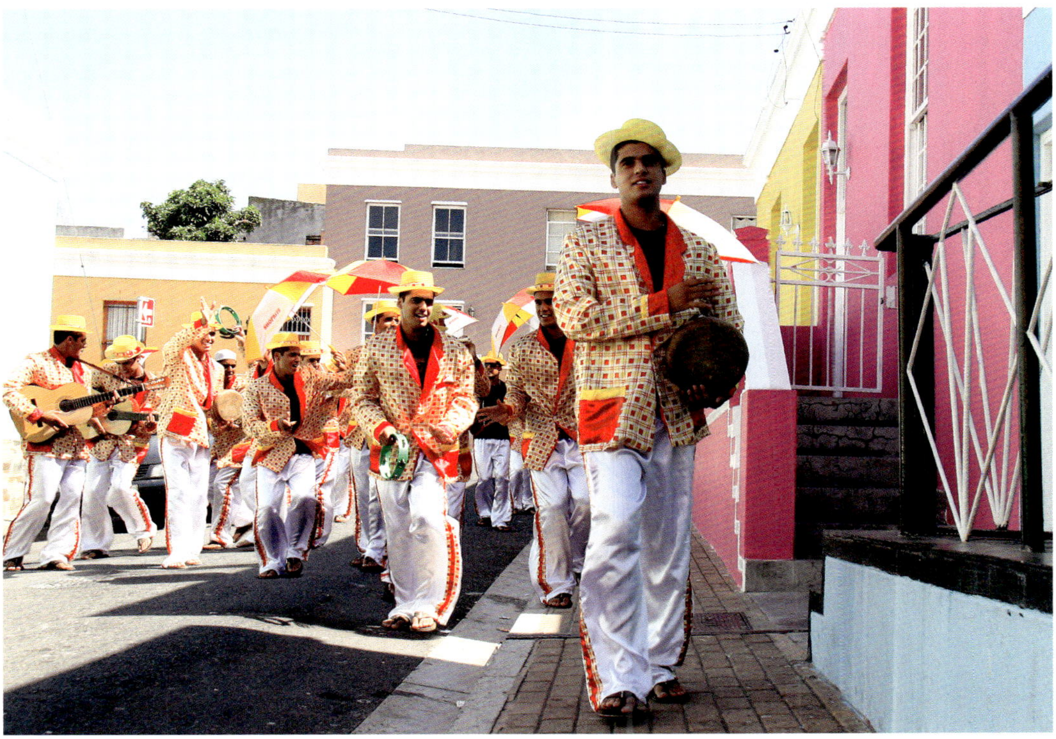

Hasan & Husain Essop, *Pennsylvanians*, 2008
Links / left: Chen Chieh-Jen, Standbilder aus / film stills from from *Lingchi – Echoes of a Historical Photograph*, 2002

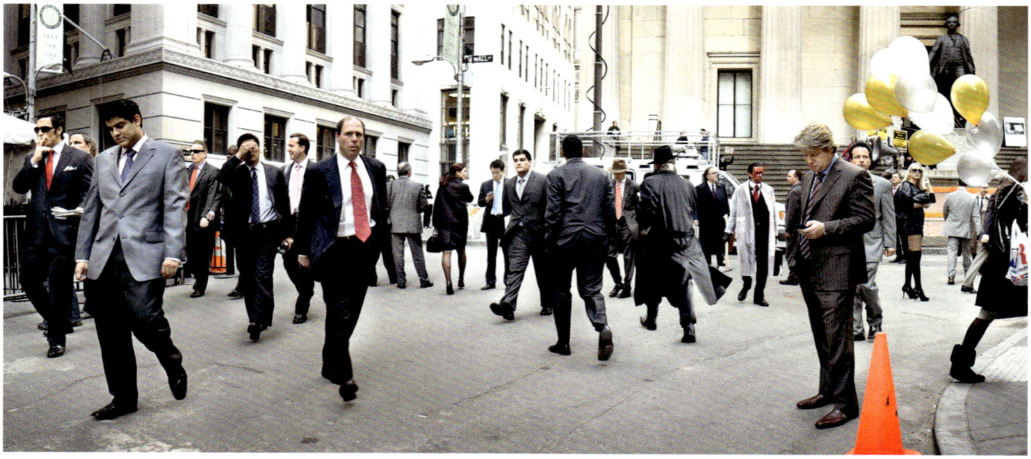

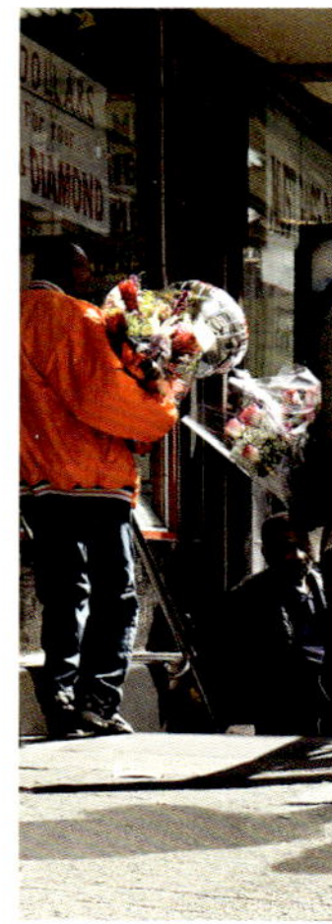
DIAMOND

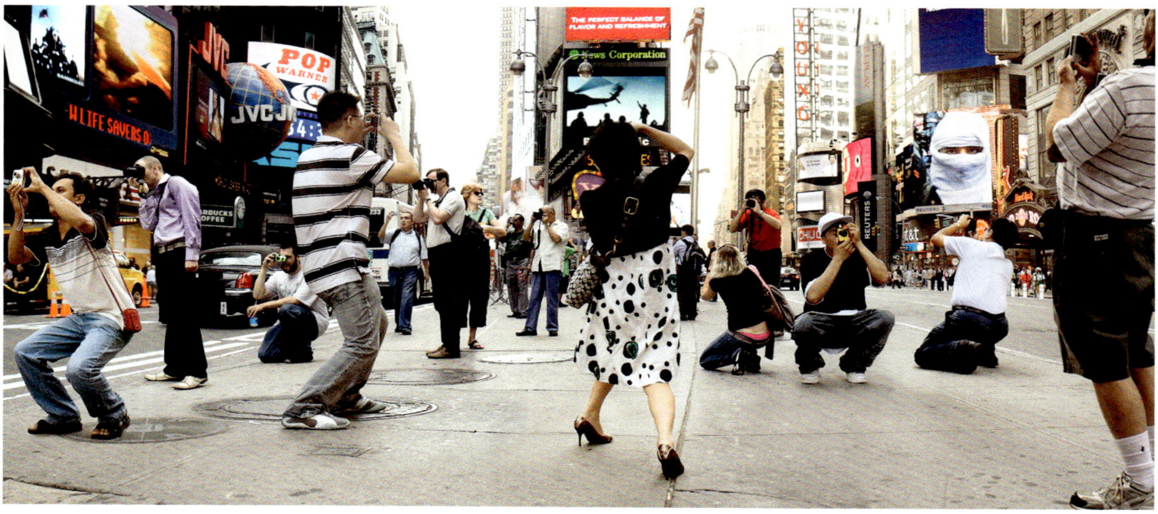
POP
WARNER
JVC
THE PERFECT BALANCE OF
FLAVOR AND REFRESHMENT
News Corporation
REUTERS

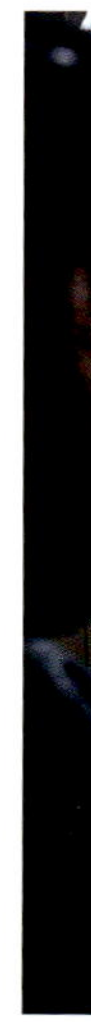

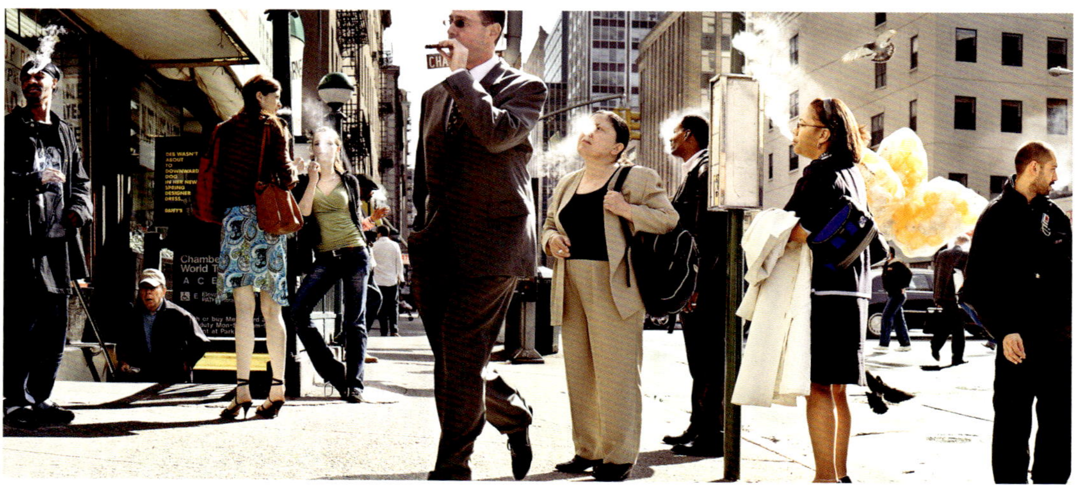

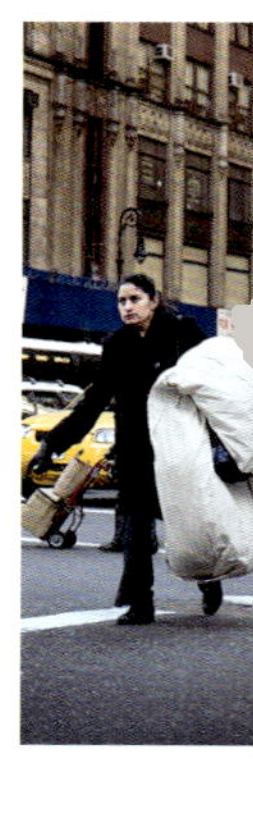

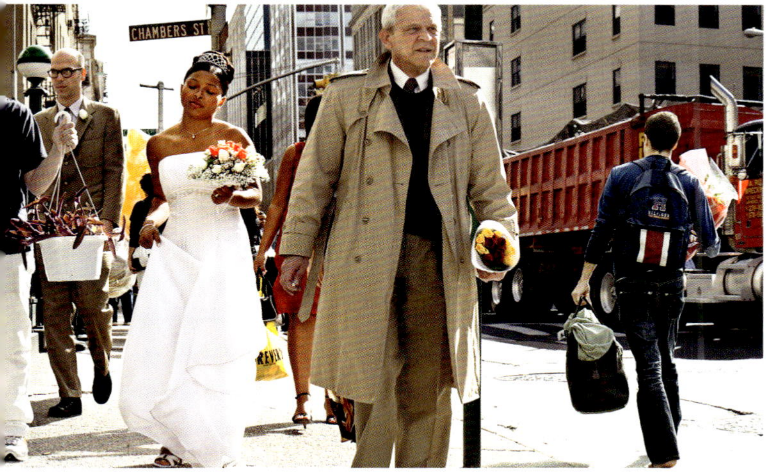

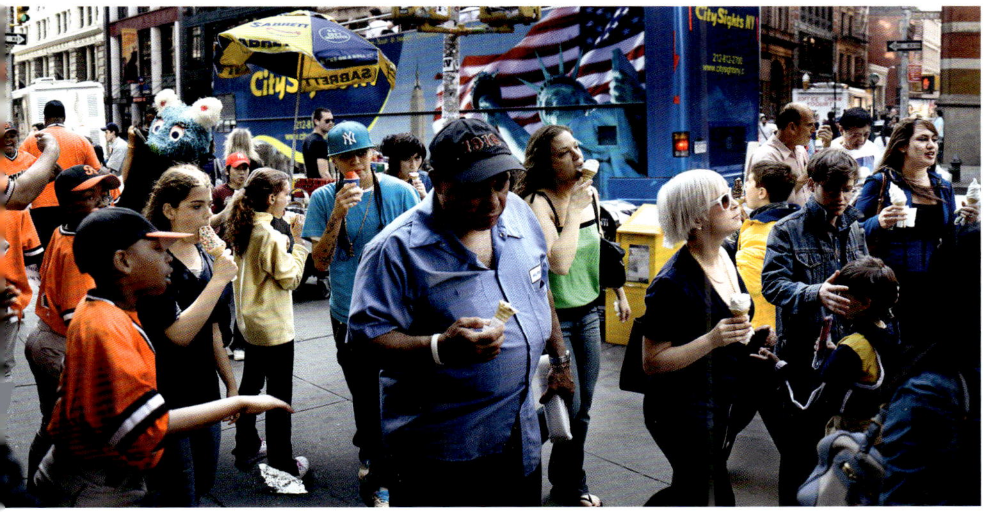

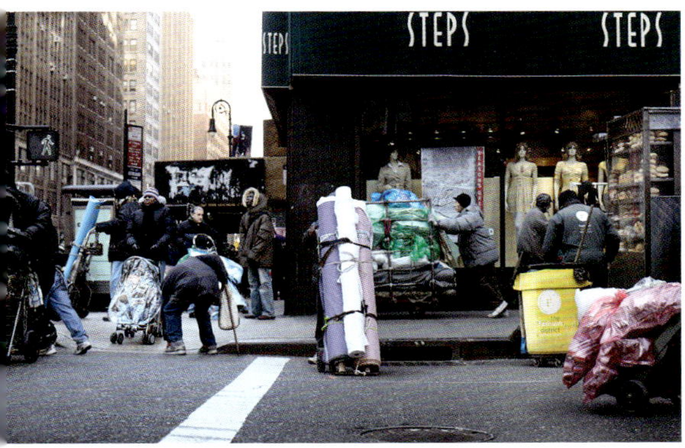

Von links nach rechts / from left to right: Peter Funch, *Hommage a Ellis*, 2010; *Loving Lovers*, 2007; *Memory Lane*, 2008; *Pantone Pantomime*, 2010; *Smoking Smokers*, 2006; *Mass Transit*, 2007 aus der Serie / from the series *Babel Tales*, 2006–2010

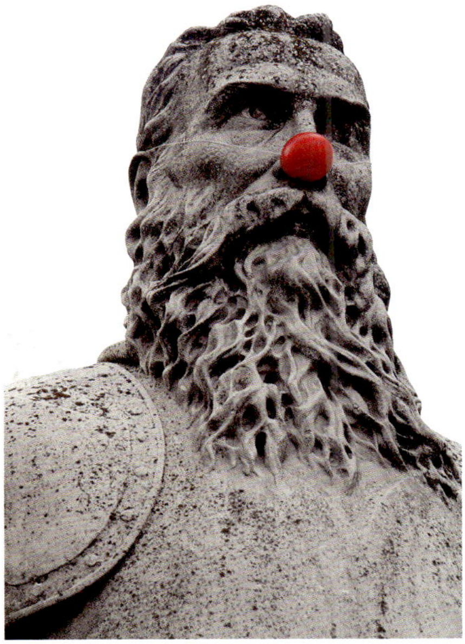

Igor Grubić, *366 Liberation Rituals,* 2008–2009

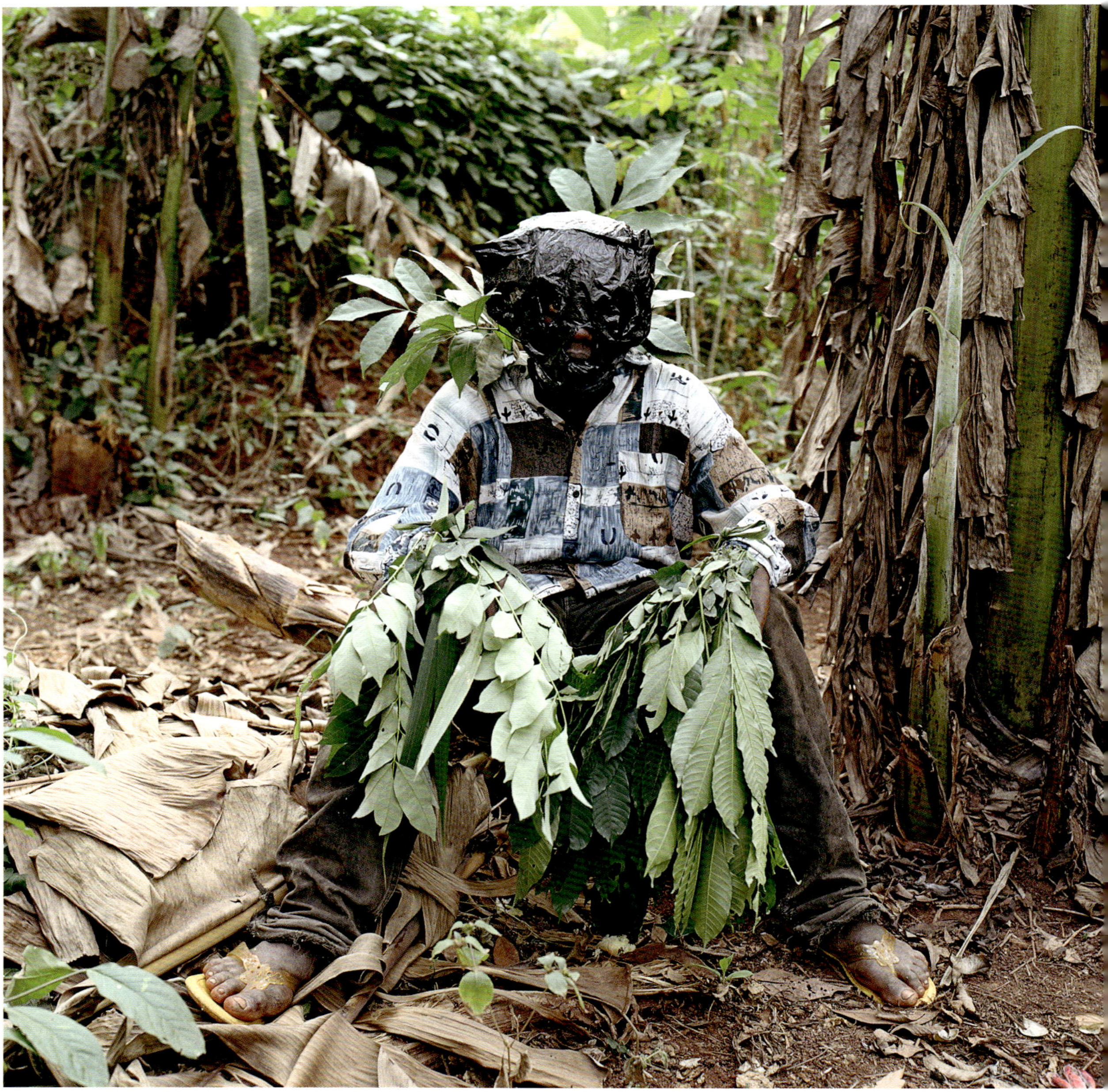

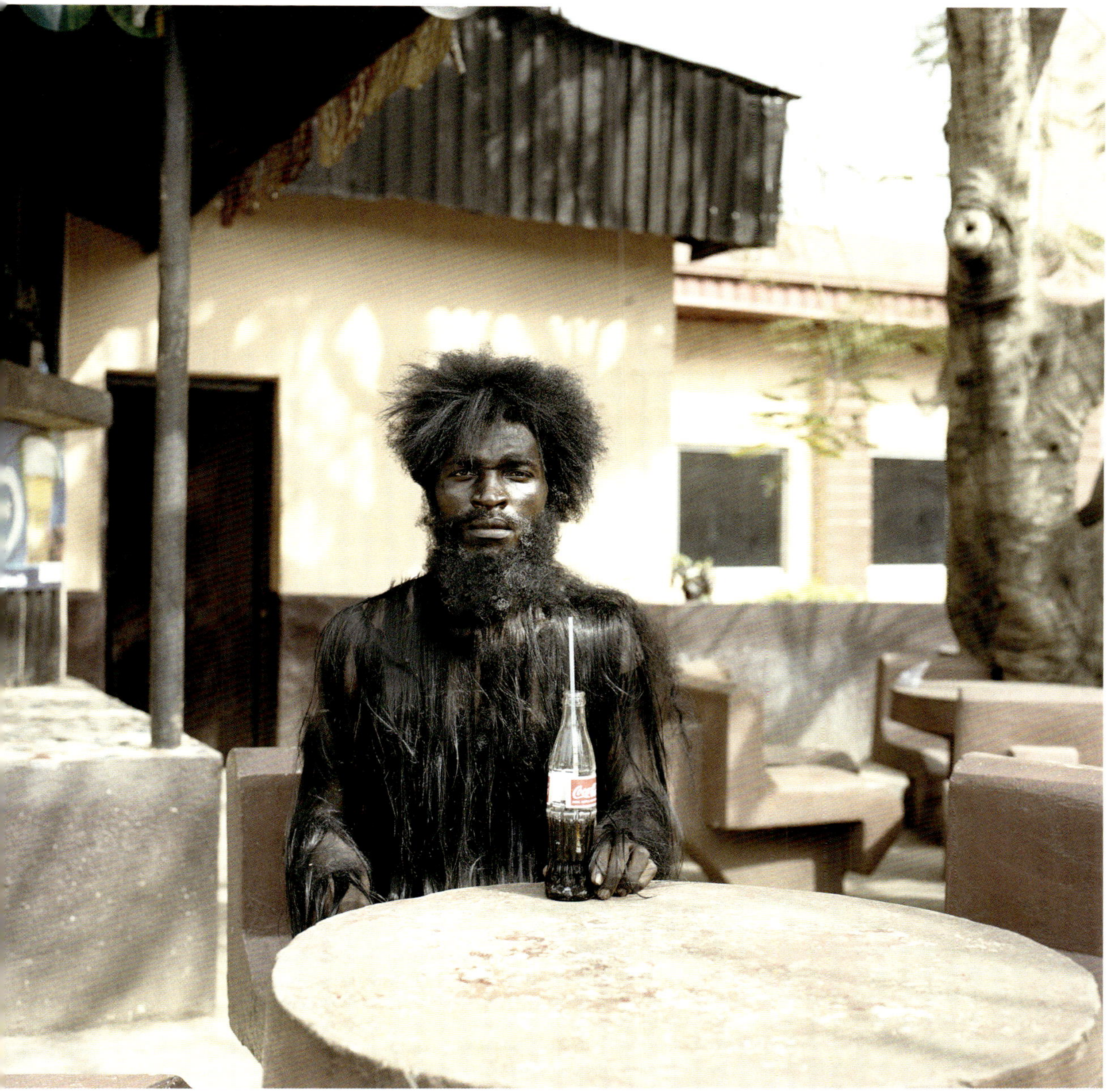

Pieter Hugo, *Emeka Uzzi. Enugu, Nigeria,* 2009
Links / left: Pieter Hugo, *Steven Amoako, Wild Honey Collector, Techiman District, Ghana,* 2005

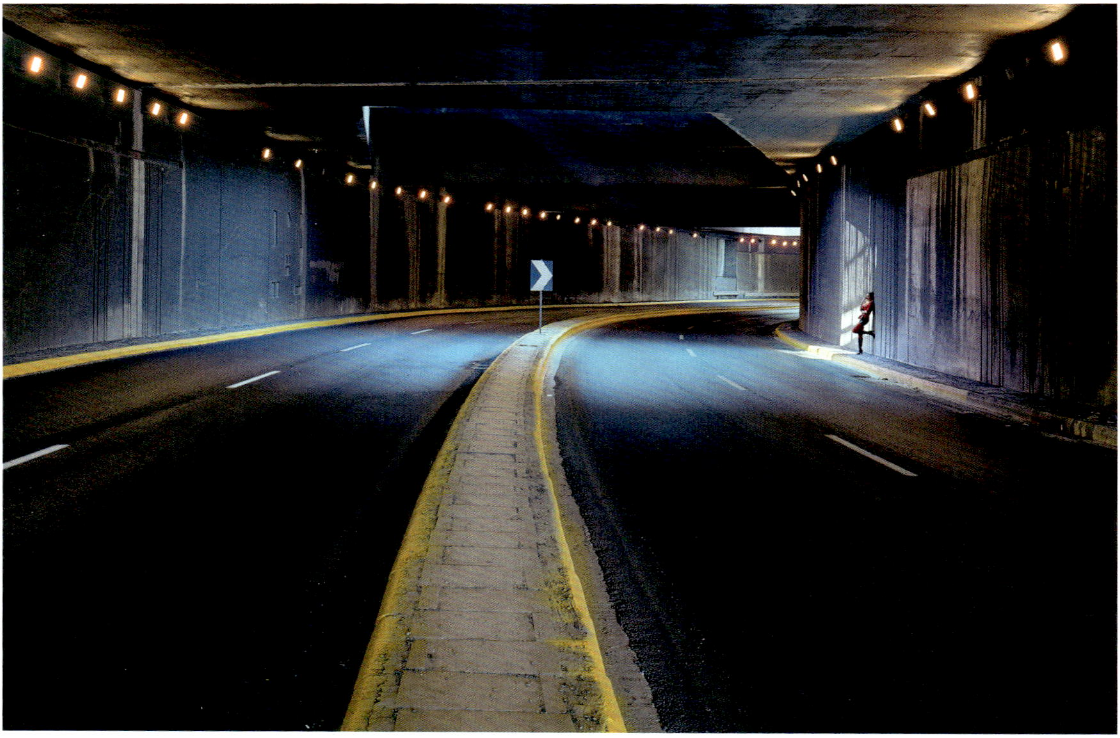

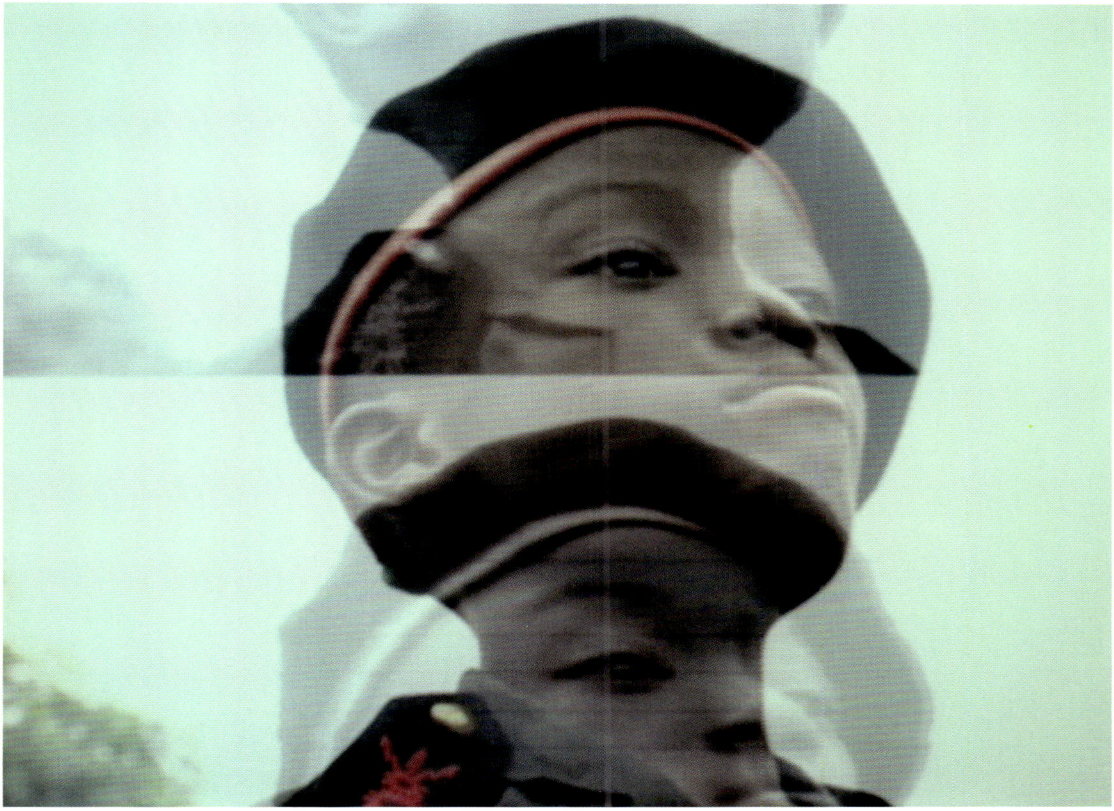

Vincent Meessen, Standbild aus / video still from *Vita Nova,* 2009
Links / left: Panos Kokkinias, *Aliki,* 2007
Nächste Seite / next page: Kirstine Roepstorff, *The Six Realms,* 2007

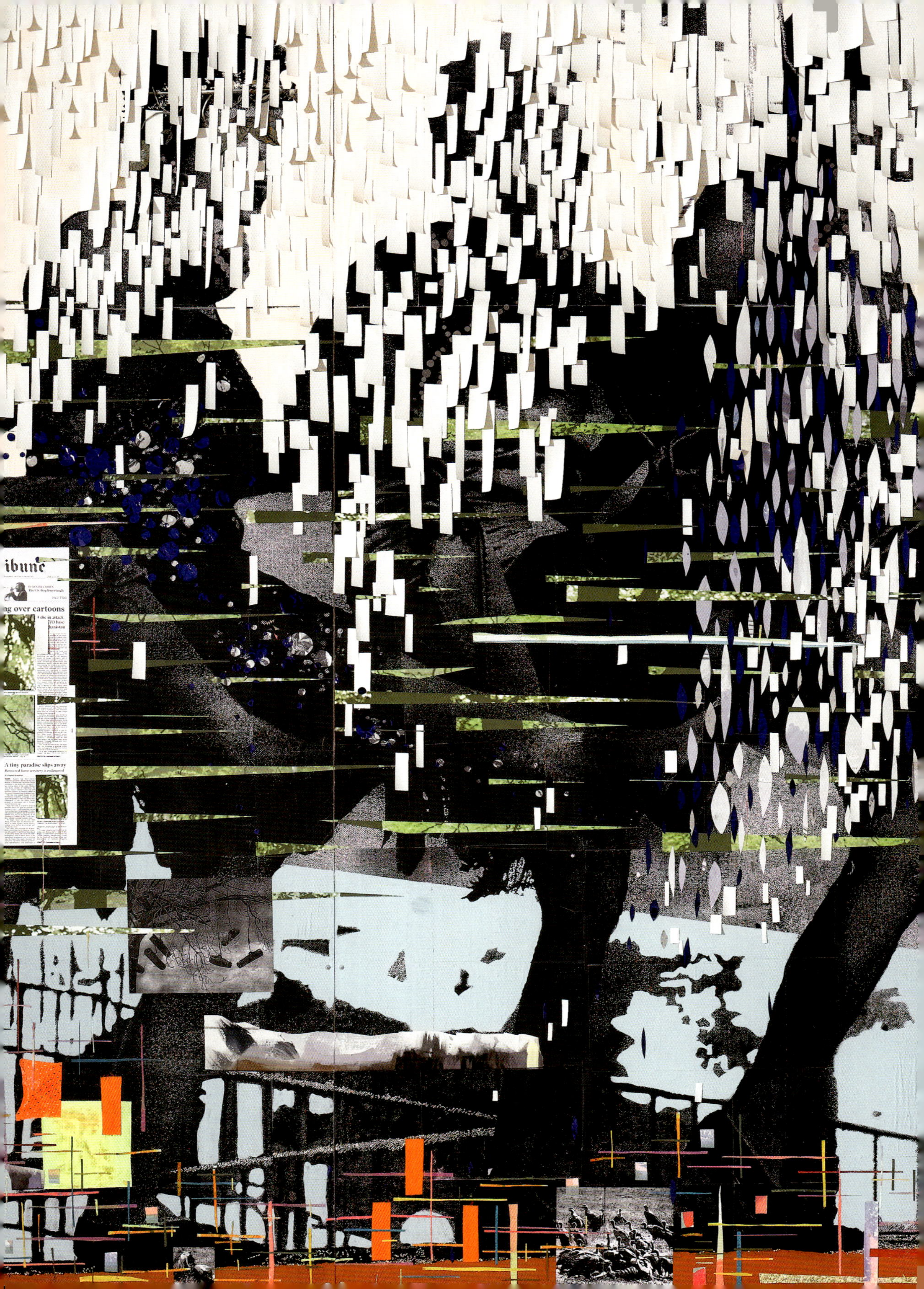
ibune
ng over cartoons
A tiny paradise slips away

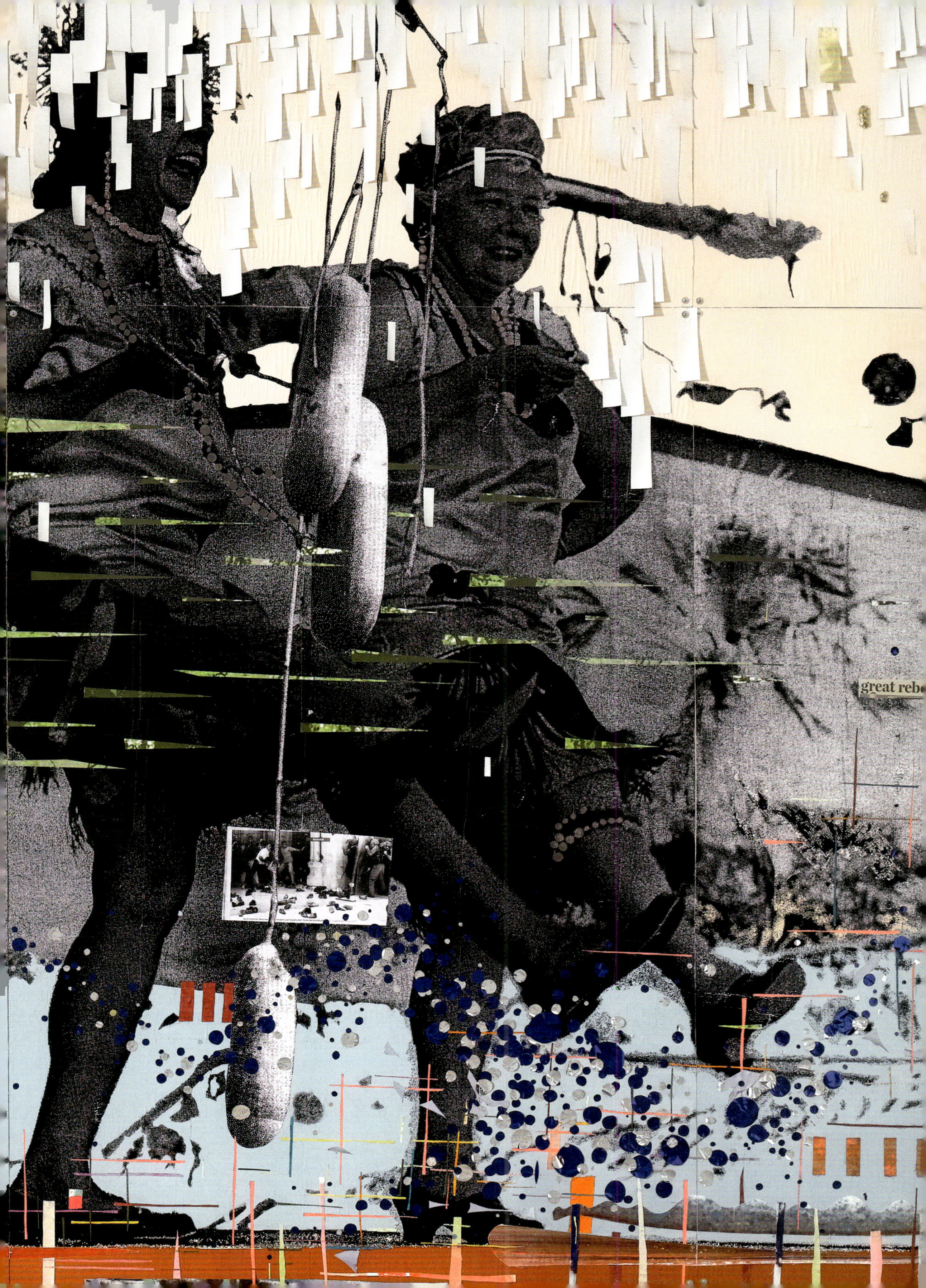
great reb

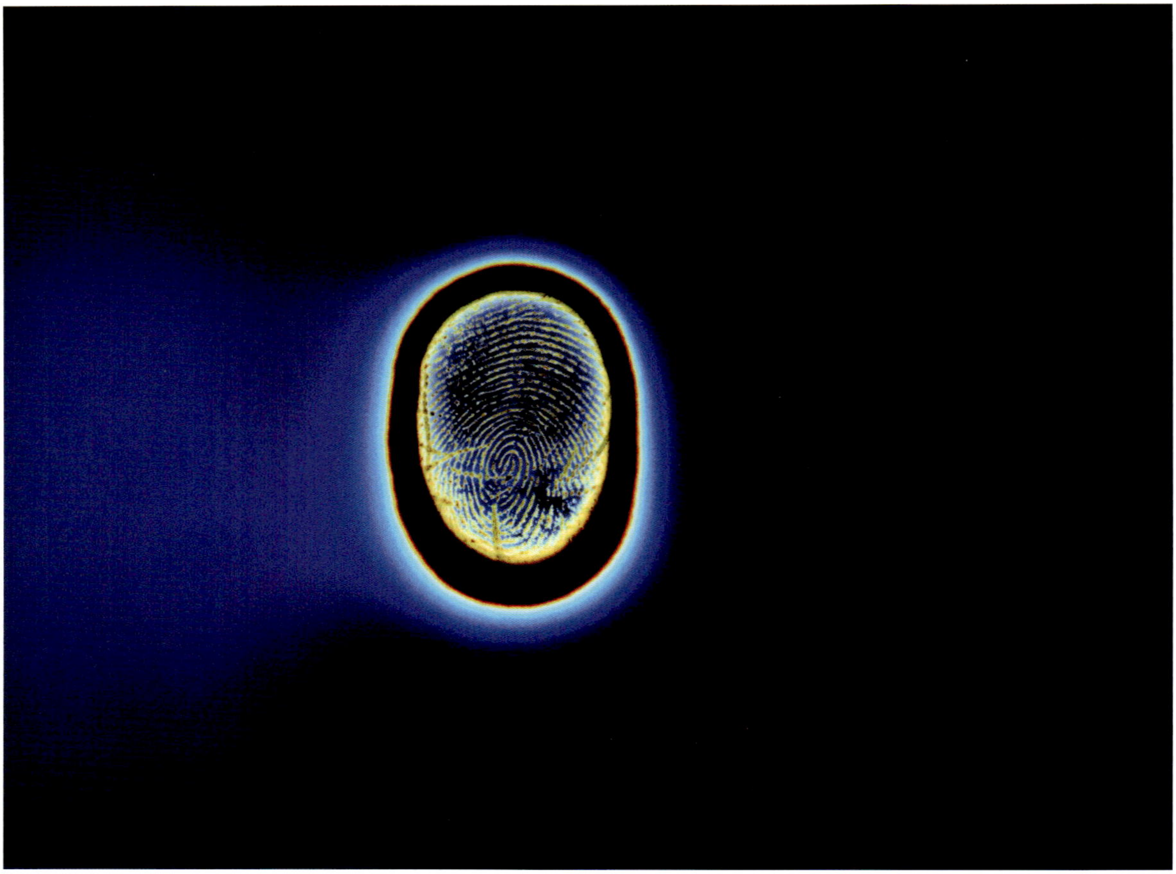

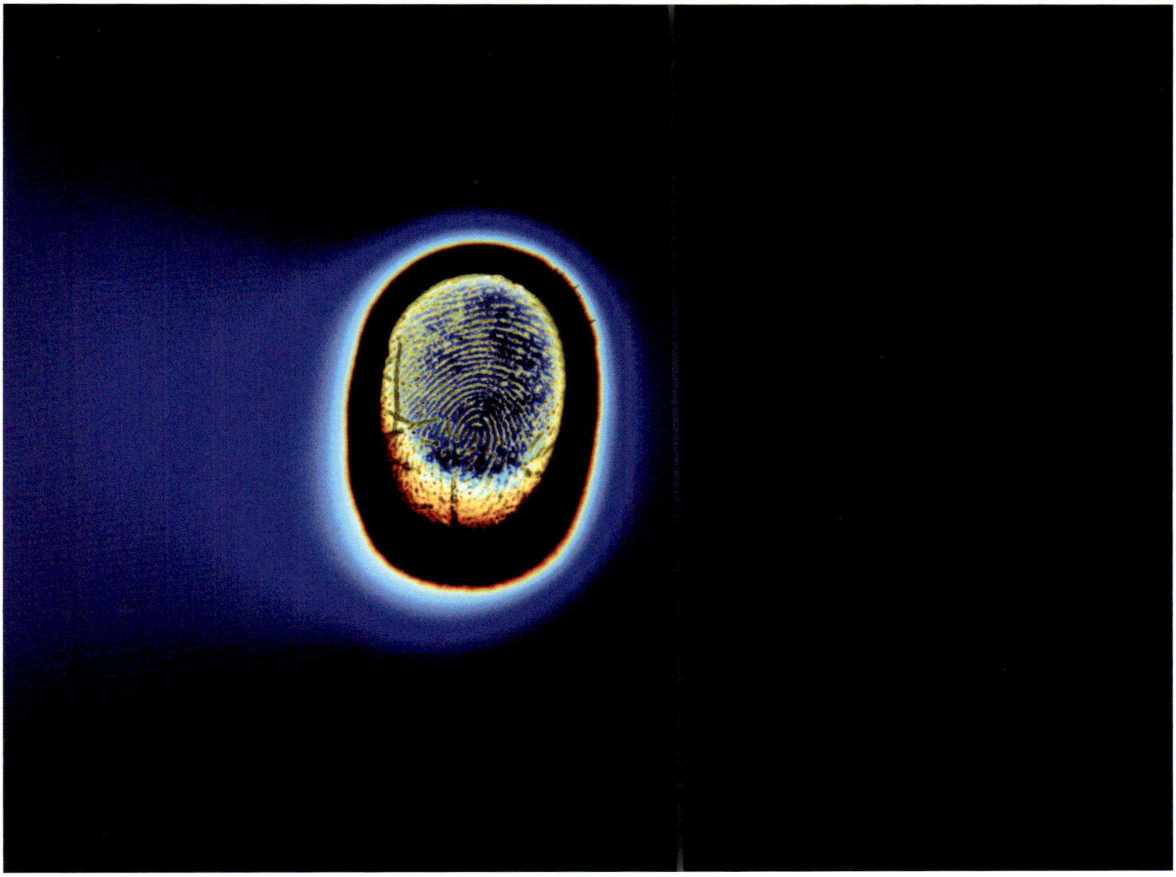

Jeremy Shaw, *Transcendental Capacities (Electronic Dance Music Grid – 1978 – 2001), detail: Coco Steel and Love Bomb – Feel It; Transcendental Capacities (Electronic Dance Music Grid – 1978 – 2001), detail: Joey Beltram – Energy Flash, 1990*, 2011

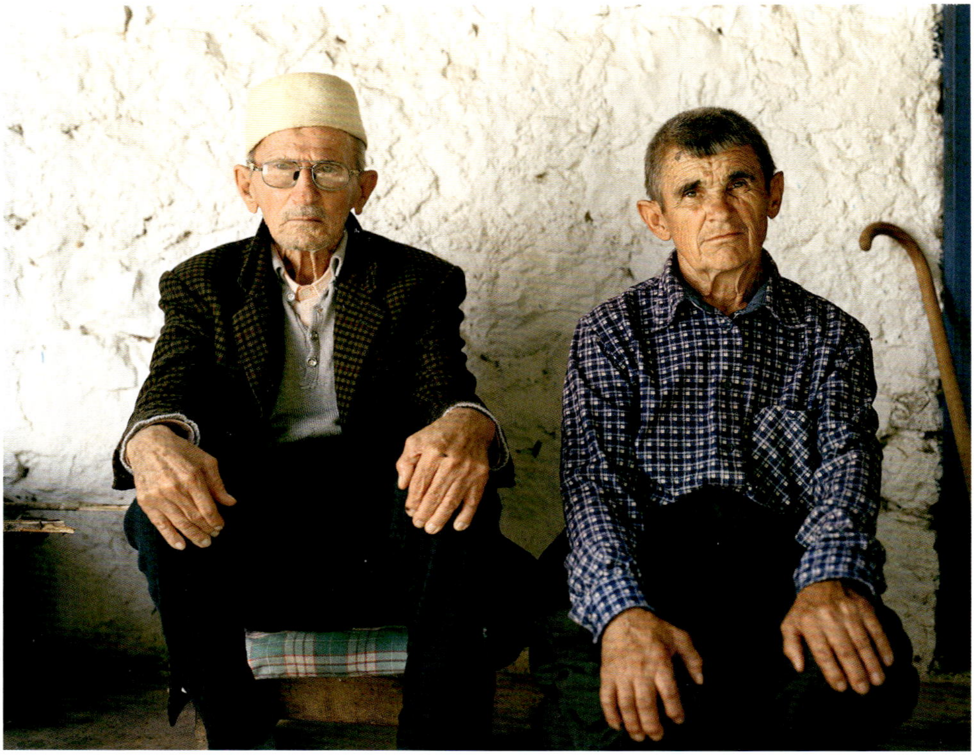

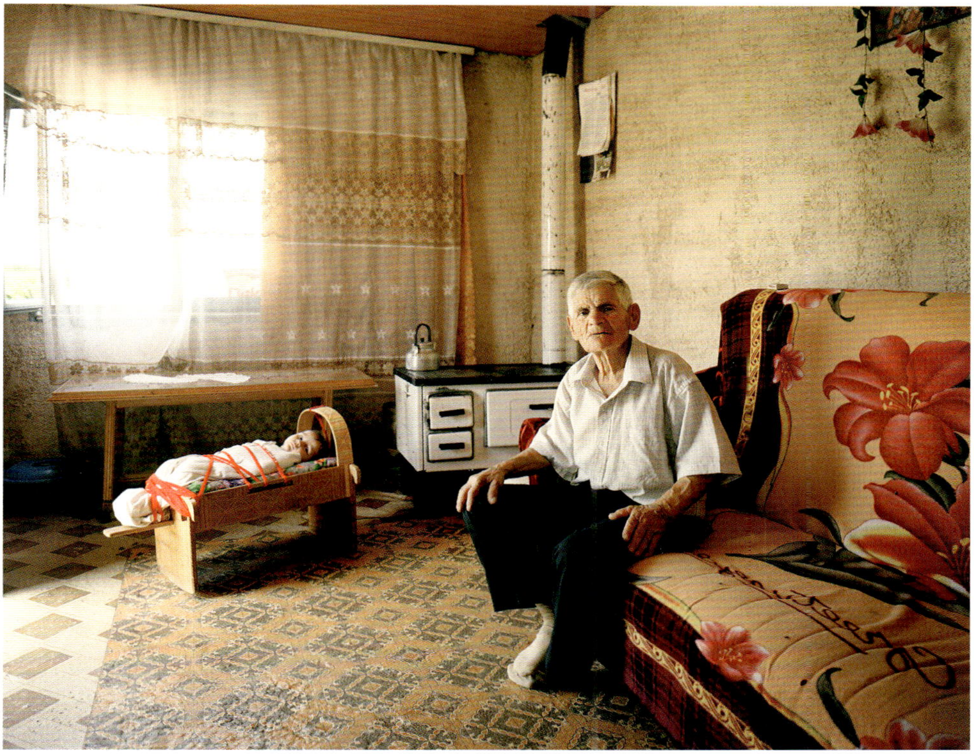

'Marte became a sworn virgin at age 20, but had dressed like a man since age 6, when her parents died. She was born in 1930 in Xhuxhë.'

Links / left: 'Have, who was born in '43, lives on a mountain with a long-standing tradition for sworn virgins. Until the recent death of her hundred-year old father, she was living and working alongside him. She became a man at age 6.'

Johan Spanner, aus der Serie / from the series *Sworn Virgins,* 2009

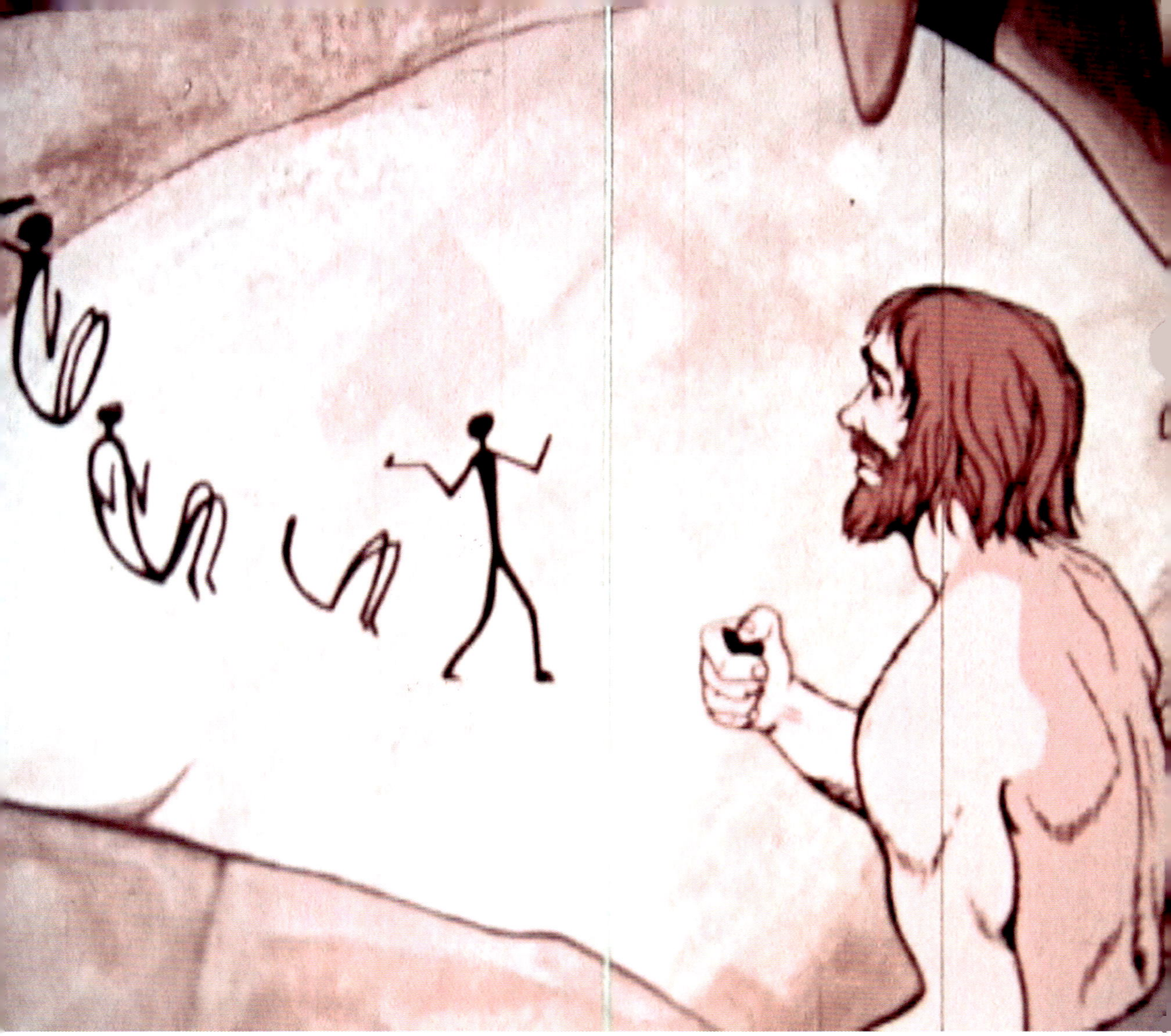

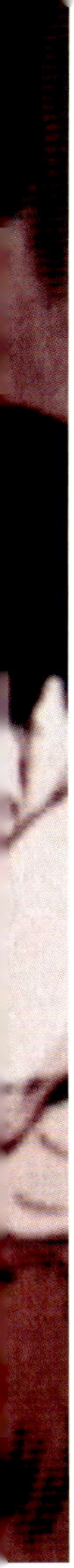

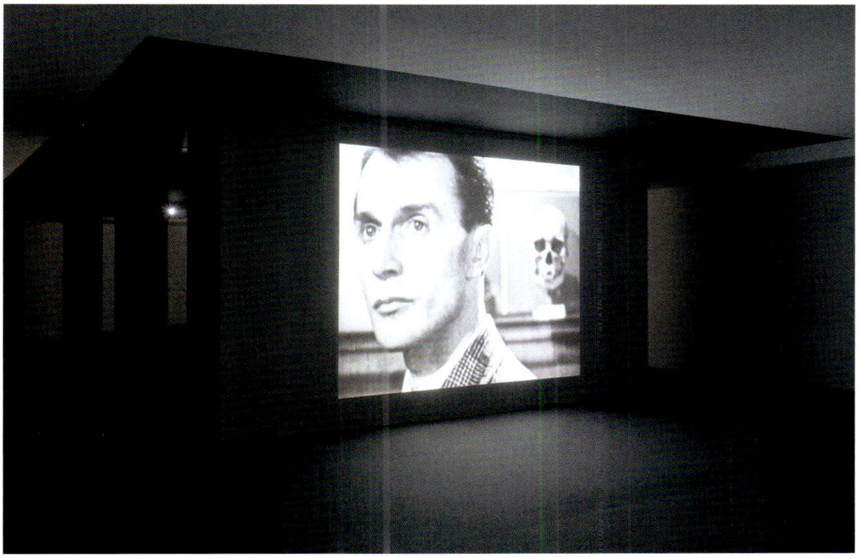

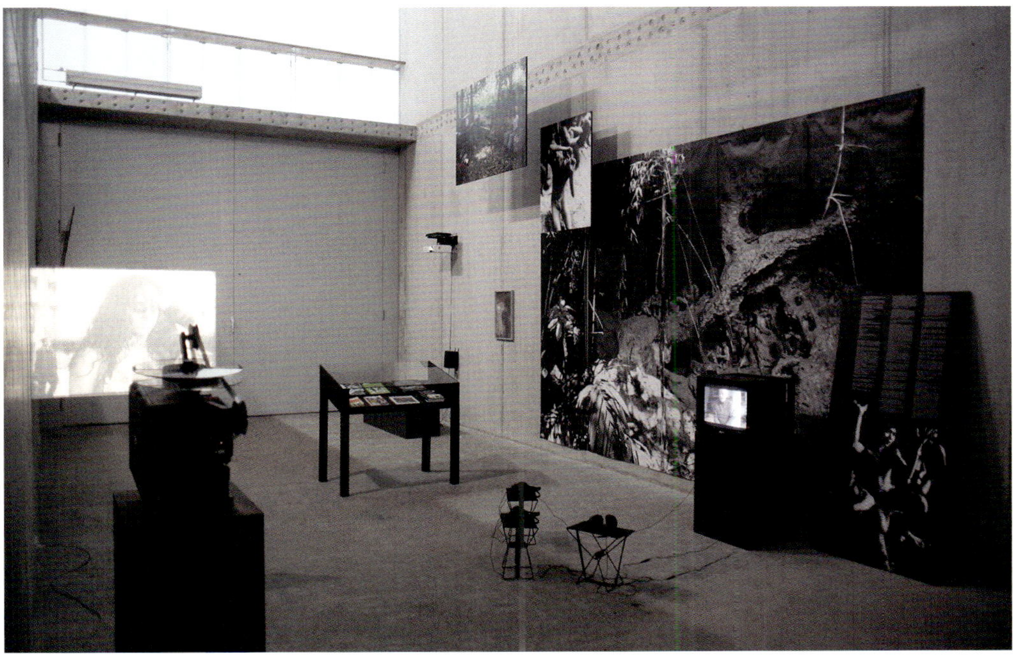

Von links nach rechts / from left to right: Clemens von Wedemeyer, Standbild aus / video still from *Found Footage,* als Teil von / part from *The Fourth Wall,* 2009; Standbild aus / video still from *Found Footage,* 2009, Ausstellungsansicht / exhibition view, Galleria Civica, Trento; *The Fourth Wall,* 2009, Ausstellungsansicht / exhibition view, KOW, Berlin

Life

Cycles

Lebenskreisläufe Heidelberger Kunstverein

Das Unterthema „Lebenskreisläufe“ im Heidelberger Kunstverein präsentiert sich in Form von fotografischen Zeugnissen, die Einblicke in alle das Leben neu bestimmenden Schritte vermitteln: von der Geburt über das Erwachsenwerden, das Erwachsensein, das Altern und schließlich den Tod. Auch wenn sie Teil eines gemeinsam wahrnehmbaren Gefühls der Menschlichkeit sind, befreiende Momente der Liebe, des Lachens, der Freude und des Teilens, genauso wie Themen des Kampfes, des Leids und des Verlusts, erfahren Menschen in unterschiedlichen Kulturen diese auf eine jeweils andere Weise.

Ein Lebenskreislauf bezeichnet eine Daseinskurve, zu der auch Geburt und Tod gehören, und die Lebensbahn eines einzelnen Wesens zwischen diesen beiden Polen. Doch auch wenn das Leben als ein Kreislauf wahrgenommen werden kann, obgleich ein linearer, endlicher, sind das Werden, der Zerfall und das Vergessen Teil dieses unaufhaltsamen Prozesses. Die Fotografien der Ausstellung „Lebenskreisläufe“ erfassen und durchdringen die existenziellen, biografisch wesentlichen Momente, die unsere persönliche Erfahrung von der Welt beeinflussen und schließlich bestimmen, das große Glück und das schmerzliche Leid in unserem Leben.
Sie beziehen sich auf die ephemere Natur ebenso wie auf die materiellen und physischen Auswirkungen der vergehenden Zeit. Aus diesem Grund präsentiert diese Ausstellung die klassischen, symbolhaften Manifestationen des Übergangs von einem Lebensstadium zum anderen – die sogenannten Übergangsriten, die heute gepflegt werden. Hierbei handelt es sich zum Beispiel um Hochzeitszeremonien oder Begräbnispraktiken, doch vermittelt die Zusammenstellung der Kunstwerke auch Einsichten in die eher abstrakten und von Kultur zu Kultur unterschiedlichen Bedingungen, denen Menschen in verschiedenen Lebensphasen unterworfen sind und untersucht, wie diese als fotografisches Zeugnis erscheinen: vom laienhaften Familienalbum bis zum sorgfältig in Szene gesetzten Porträt.

Man kann heutzutage starke Veränderungen bezüglich der Haltung zum Altern wahrnehmen. Zum einen geschieht dies aufgrund eines neoliberalen Gebots der Bio-Macht, das die Jugend als einen elementaren gesellschaftlichen Wert bevorzugt. Man könnte dies „das Zeitalter der anti-aging Altersdiskriminierung“ nennen, eine Zeit, in der wir unseren fortschreitenden Zerfall und unsere unvermeidliche Entropie verweigern. Auch wenn der Begriff des Alterns ein natürlicher Teil des Lebenskreislaufs ist, wird er oft als negativ und unerwünscht wahrgenommen. Dies ist vor allem in Ländern der Fall, in denen der Konsumgeist eine der Hauptantriebskräfte dafür ist, den Mythos von ewiger Schönheit und Jugend zu verbreiten. Zum anderen ist die Jugend, und sind vor allem Teenager (ein vor gerade einmal 50 Jahren erfundener Begriff), zu einer Handelsware geworden, die von den globalen Medien aus konsumförderlichen Gründen unaufhörlich ausgebeutet und im Umlauf gehalten wird. Generell ist der Begriff „Lifestyling“ der Schlüssel zum Verständnis davon, wie in vielen kapitalistischen Ländern bestimmte Lebensphasen und Konsumverhalten propagiert, inszeniert und auf allen Ebenen des privaten und öffentlichen Lebens verkauft werden.

„Lebenskreisläufe“ kann als „Punktum“ der Ausstellungsreihe angesehen werden: der Augenblick, an dem das Leben durch das Medium der Fotografie in einem Moment fixiert wird.

Katerina Gregos & Solvej Helweg Ovesen

Life Cycles Heidelberger Kunstverein unfolds as a photographic testimony of insights into all the stages of life from birth to coming of age, adulthood, old age and death. Although part of a commonly experienced sense of humanity, liberating moments of love, laughter, pleasure and sharing, as well as questions of struggle, mourning and loss are experienced with great difference in diverse cultures.

A lifecycle represents the existential curve from birth to death and the trajectory of an individual existence between the two. Yet, if life can be perceived as a cycle albeit a linear and finite one, then becoming, decay, and oblivion are part and parcel of this inexorable process. The photographs in 'Life Cycles' capture and cut through the existential moments of biographical importance that impact upon and eventually constitute our subjective experience of the world and the deeper bliss or painful hardships of life. They allude to the ephemeral nature as well as the material and physical consequences of the passage of time. This exhibition venue therefore showcases the classical symbolic manifestations of the movement of life from one state to another: rites of passage such as wedding ceremonies or burial practices, for example. It also provides insight into the different conditions that human beings are subjected to in various stages of life and explores how these appear as a photographic testimonies: from the amateur family album to the carefully staged portrait.

We are today experiencing great shifts in attitudes towards aging. This is in part due to a neoliberal biopolitical order that privileges the concept of youth as a primary societal value. One could call this 'the ageist age of anti-aging', a time in which we seem to be in denial of our progressive decay and inevitable entropy. Although aging is a natural part of the cycle of life it is now, more often than not, perceived in a negative light, particularly in countries where consumerism is a driving force in propagating the myth of eternal beauty and youth. Youth, and in particular teenagers (a concept invented only fifty years ago) have become marketable commodities and are incessantly being exploited by the global media corporations. The notion of 'lifestyle' is a key concept in understanding how consumption is propagated, staged and sold micro-politically in many capitalist countries.

'Life Cycles', which can be considered to be the exhibition's epilogue, serves as the final and indeed contemporary 'punctum' which cuts through the visual consciousness of the cycle of life.

Katerina Gregos & Solvej Helweg Ovesen

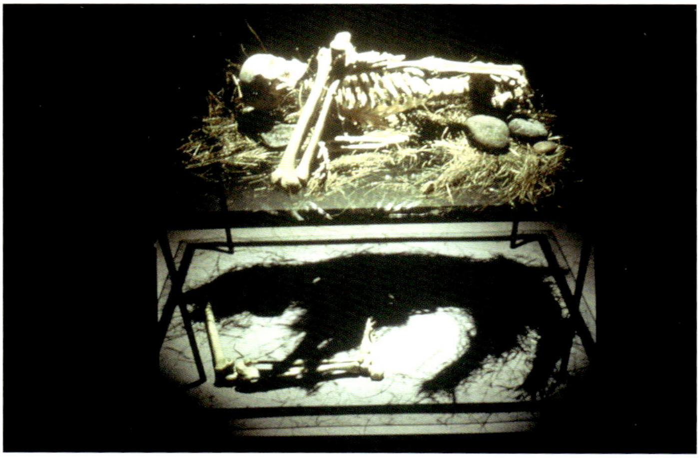

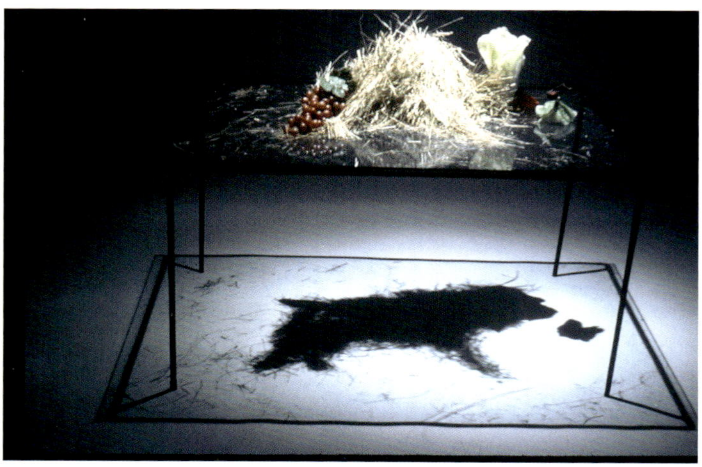

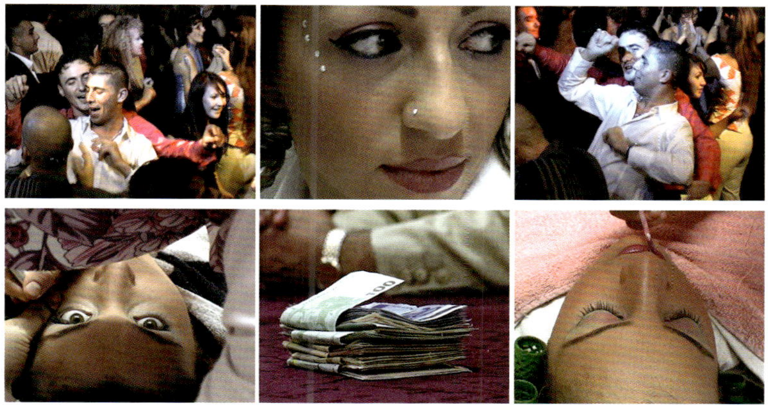

Köken Ergun, Standbilder aus / video stills from *Wedding*, 2007–2008

Links / left: Mac Adams, *Bones*; *Dog Chasing Butterfly* aus der Serie / from the series *Parallel Lives*, 1999

Nächste Seite / next page: Simon Fujiwara, *Before the Fall*, 2011

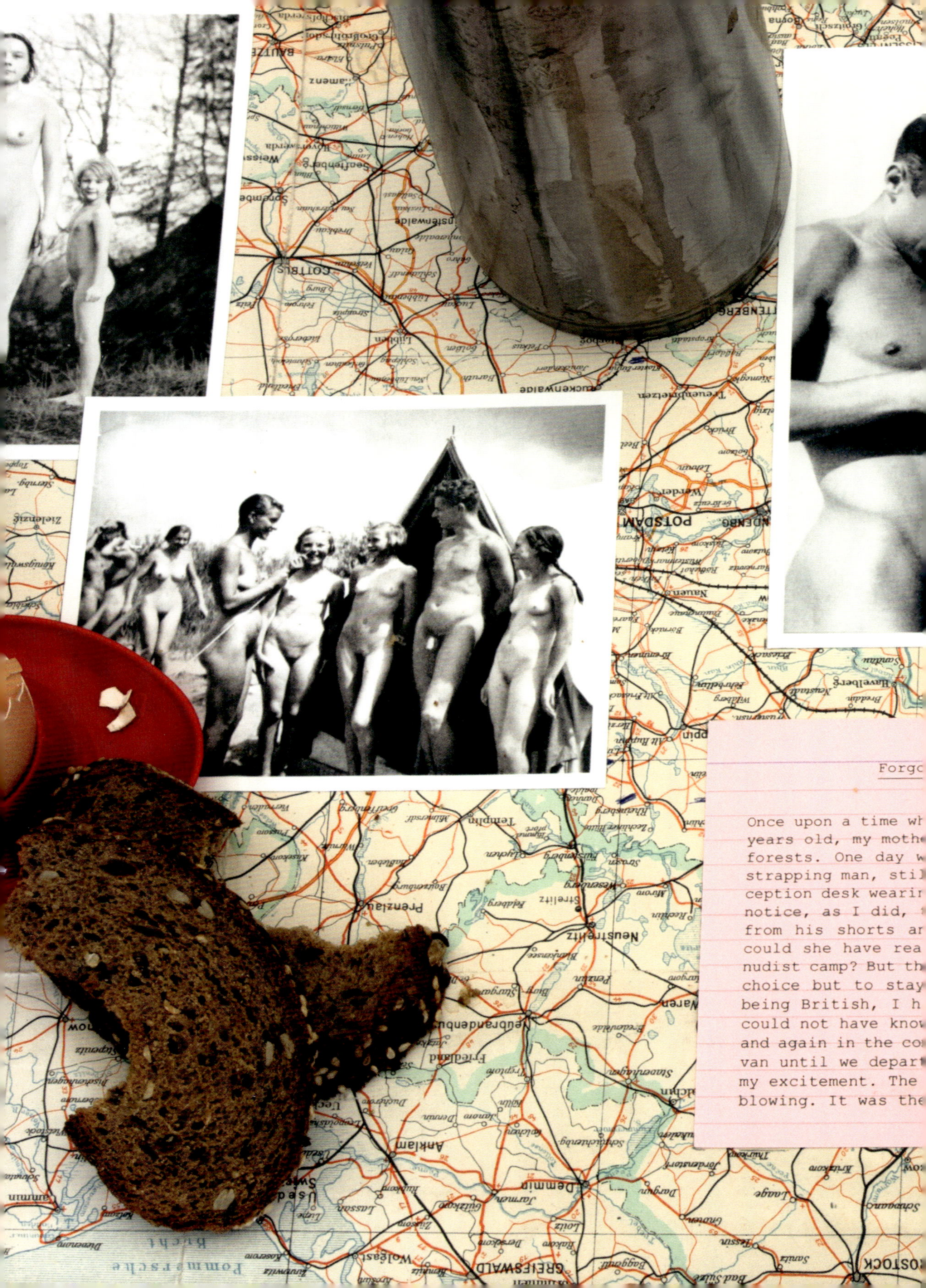
Forgc
Once upon a time wh
years old, my moth
forests. One day w
strapping man, sti
ception desk wearir
notice, as I did,
from his shorts ar
could she have rea
nudist camp? But th
choice but to stay
being British, I h
could not have know
and again in the co
van until we depart
my excitement. The
blowing. It was the

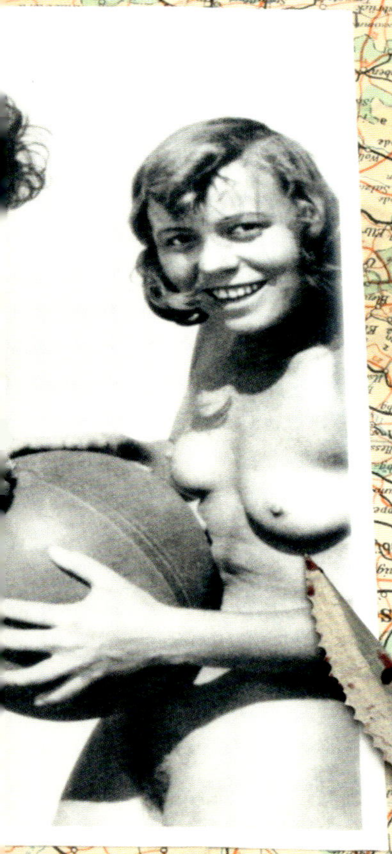

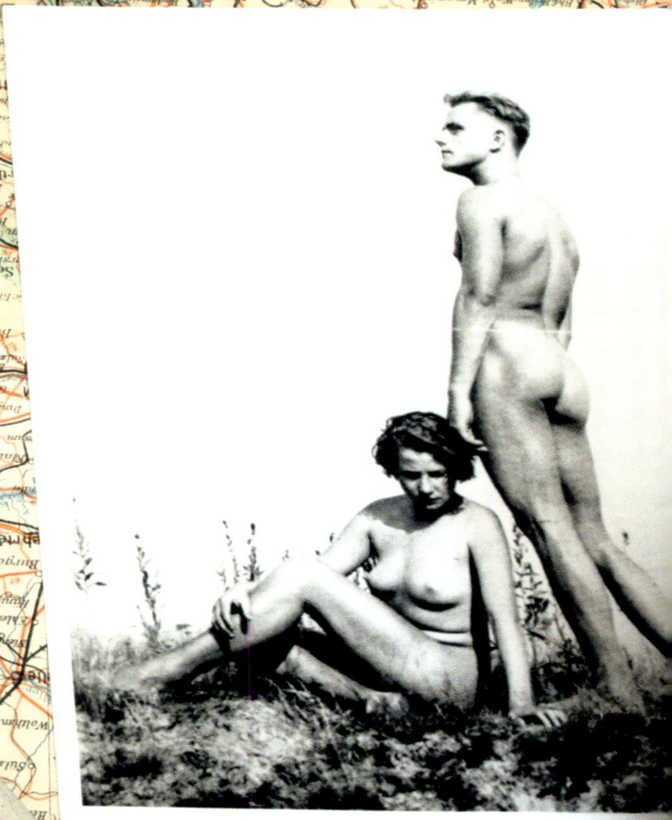

Fall, 1989.
Southern Germany.

young, innocent boy of only ten
on a camping trip to the German
at a lakeside campsite where a
swimming, greeted us at the re-
y shorts. Since my mother didn't
ong meaty schlong was poking out
down the side of his leg, how
we had booked ourselves into a
lready setting and we had little
was famous for its nudism, but
een a naked man before and so I
was a sight I would crave again
. I didn't dare leave the camper-
t day, for fear I couldn't hide
turning and a cooler breeze was
e summer.

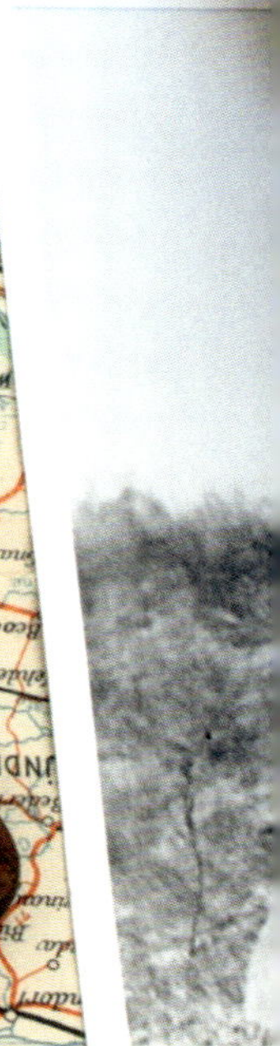

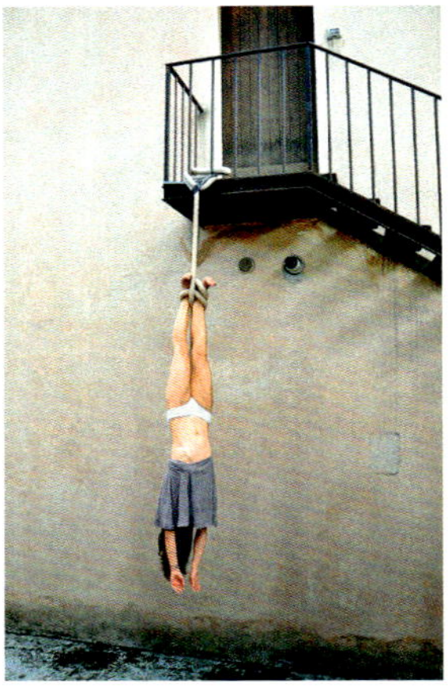

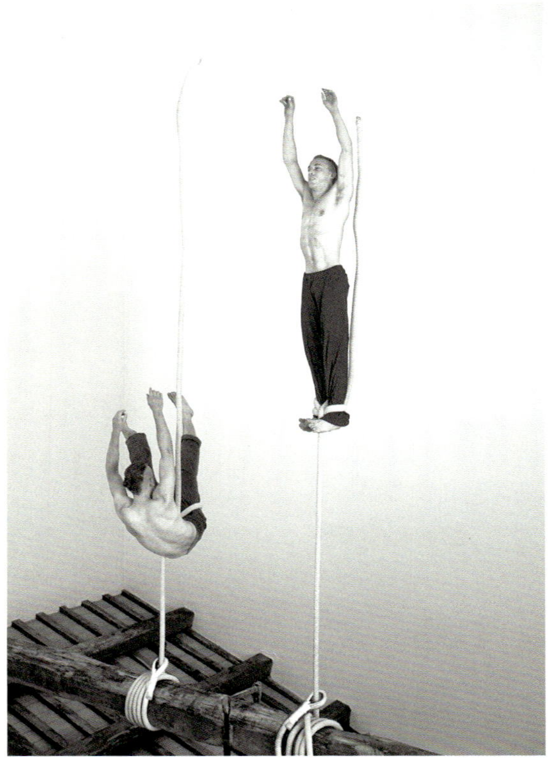

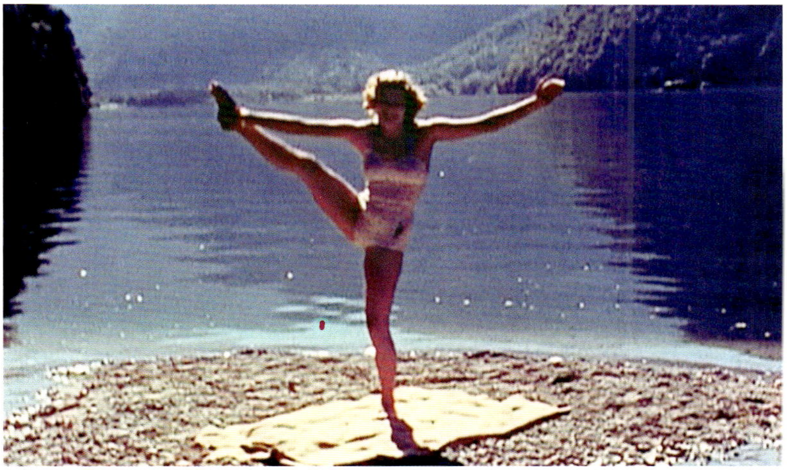

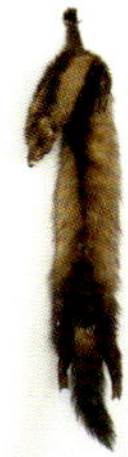

Von links nach rechts / from left to right: Agnès Geoffray, *Flétrissure; Infama; Eva Braun; Vanité* aus der Serie / from the series *Les suspendus*, 2010–2011

Nächste Seite / next page: Jacob Holdt, aus / from *American Pictures*, 1970–1975 'Paternal love on the 12th floor in the slum. Chicago, IL'; 'Red-haired redneck with her black girlfriend Union Springs, AL'; 'Prison guard with his step-grandchild. Tunica, LA'; '1977 – New York: Danish-American love'

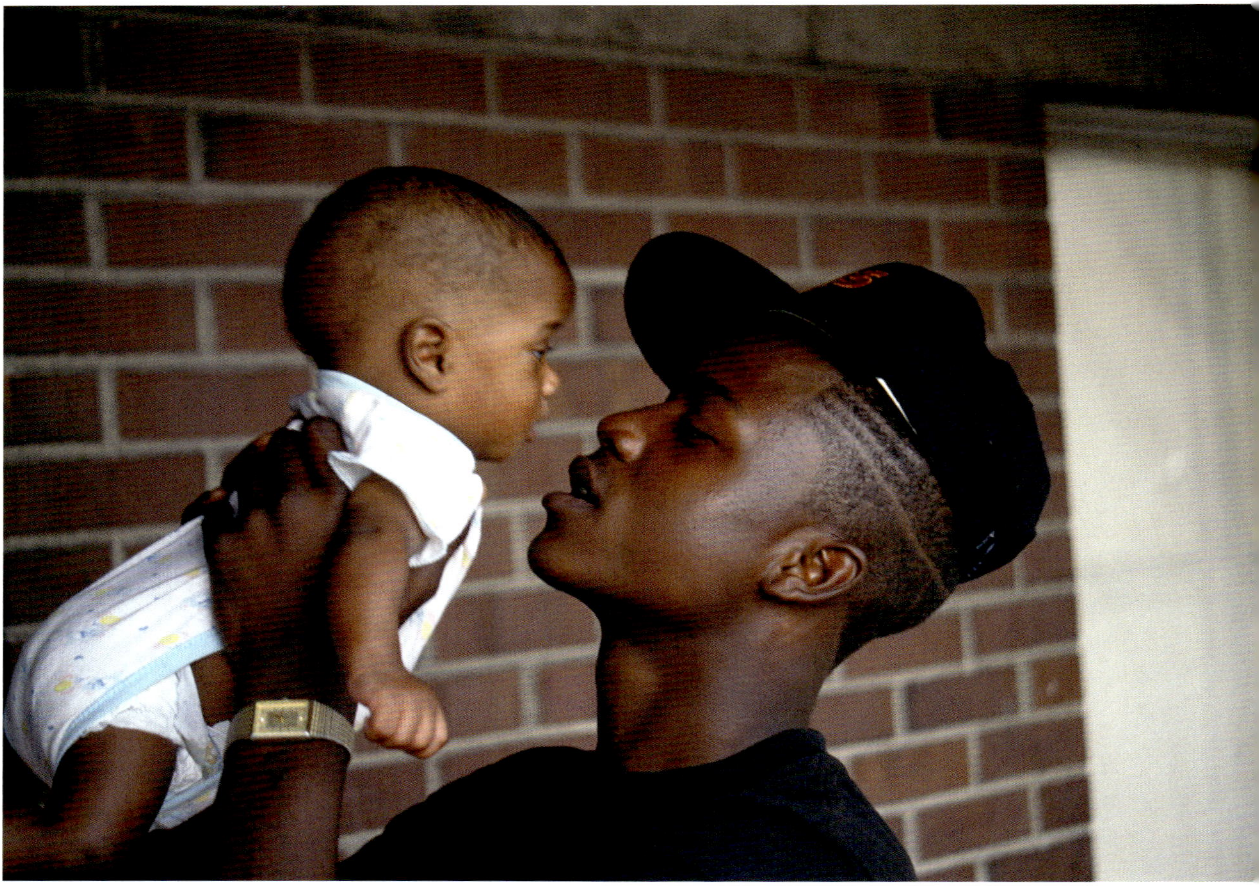

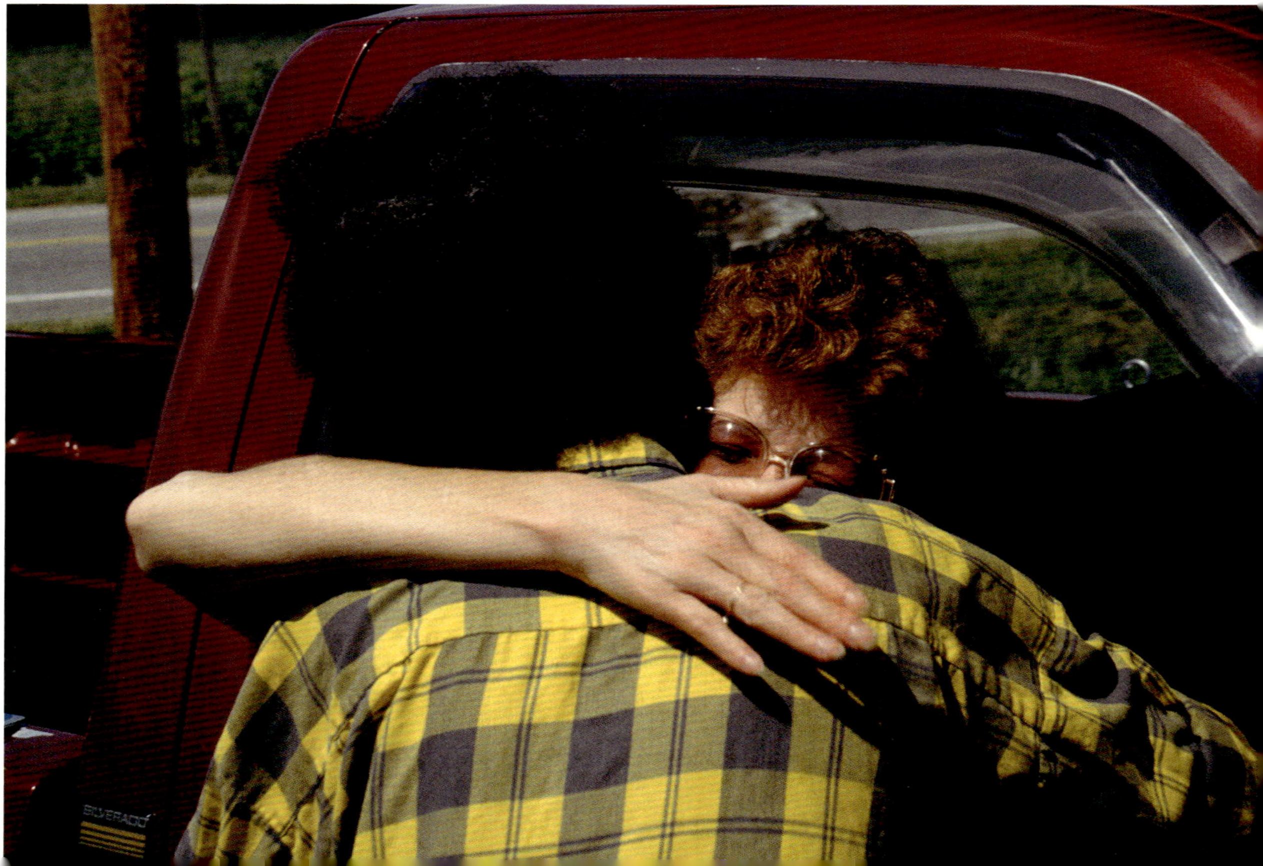

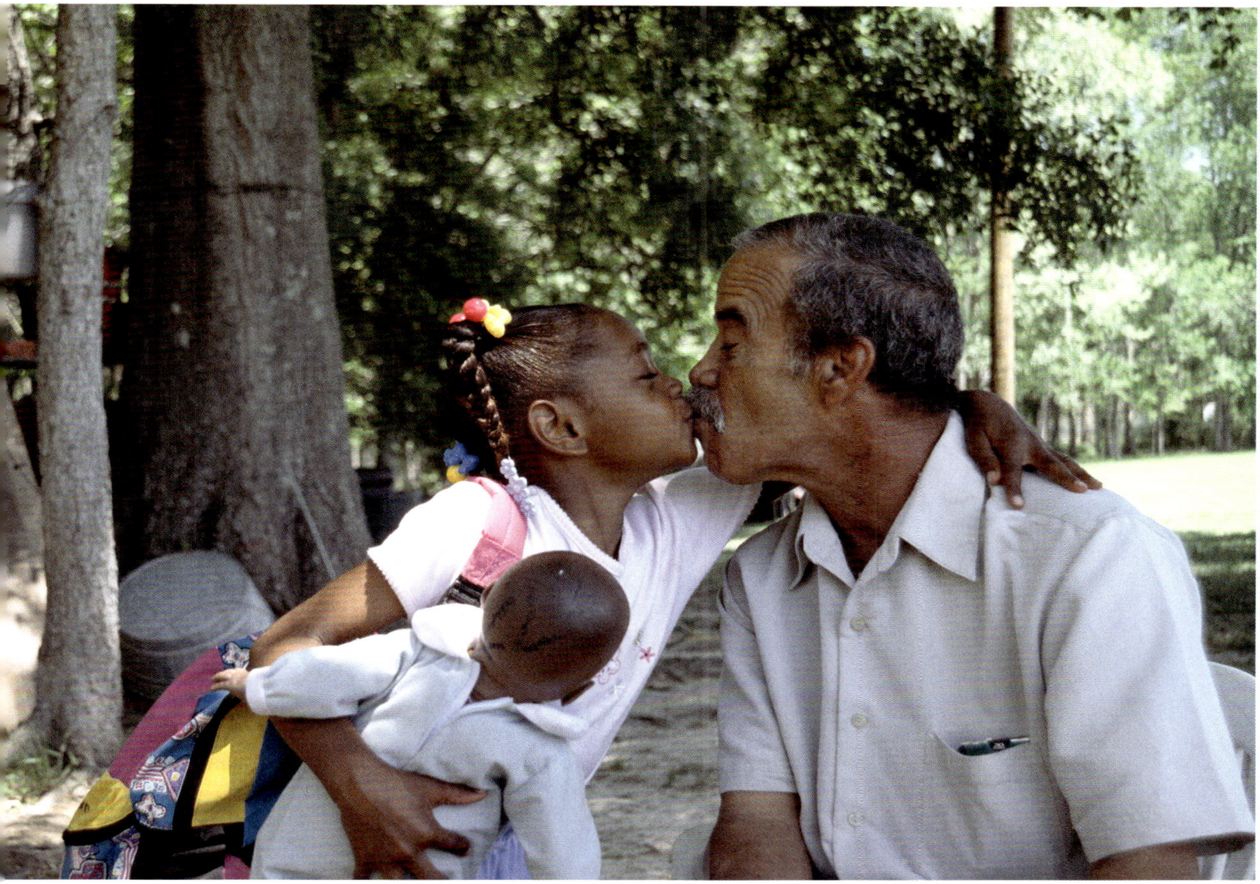

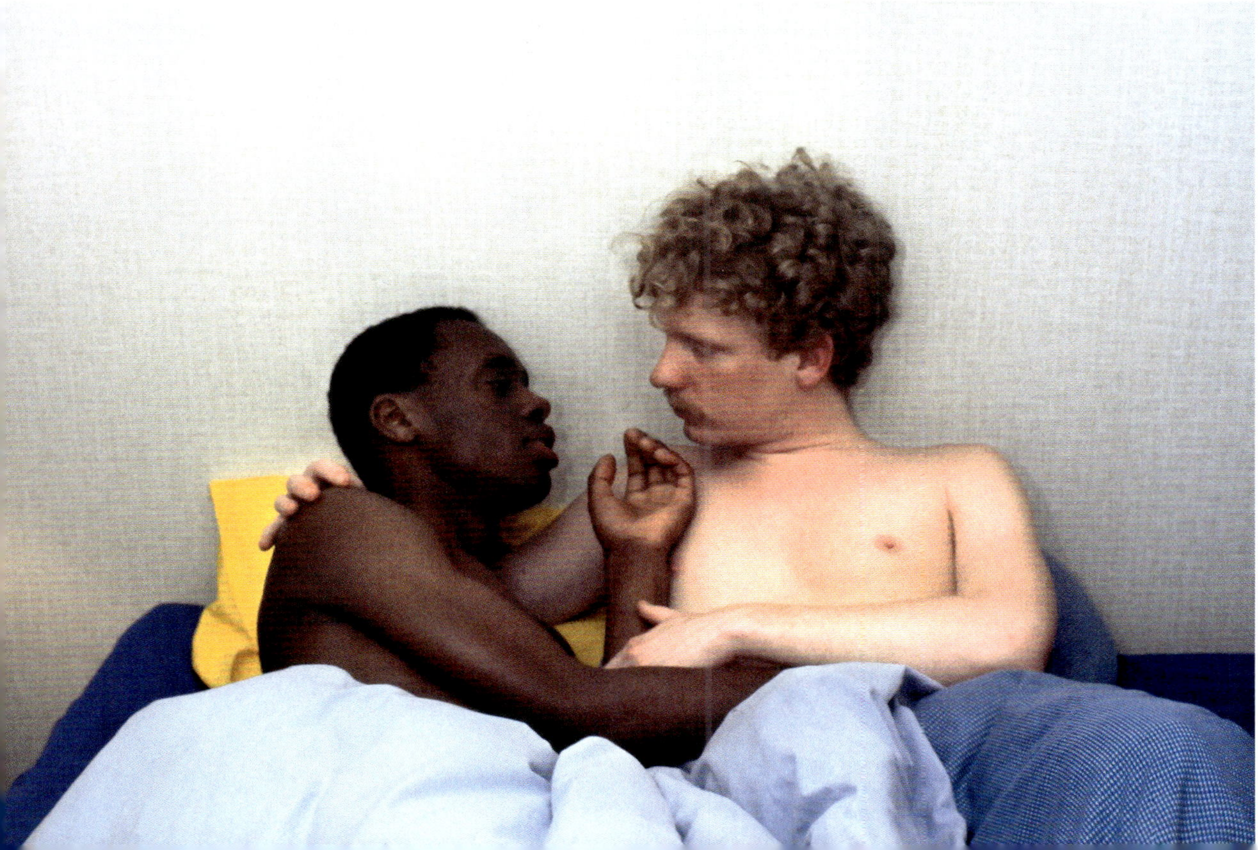

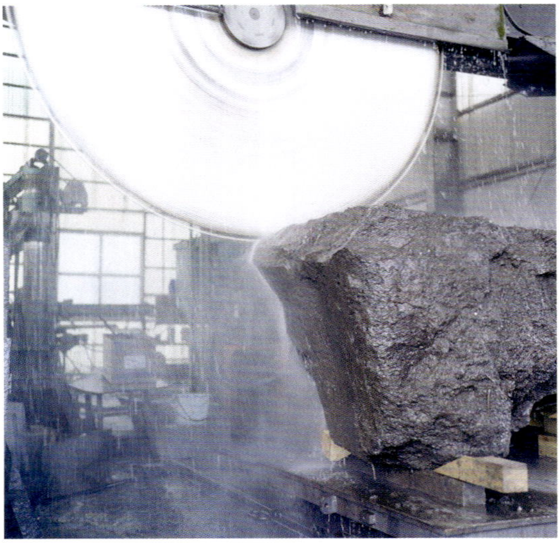
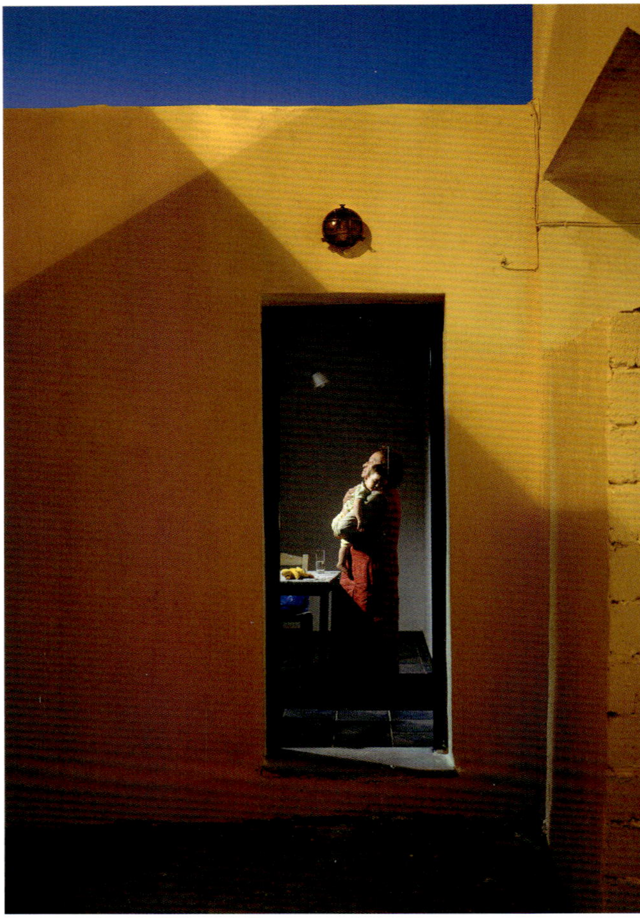
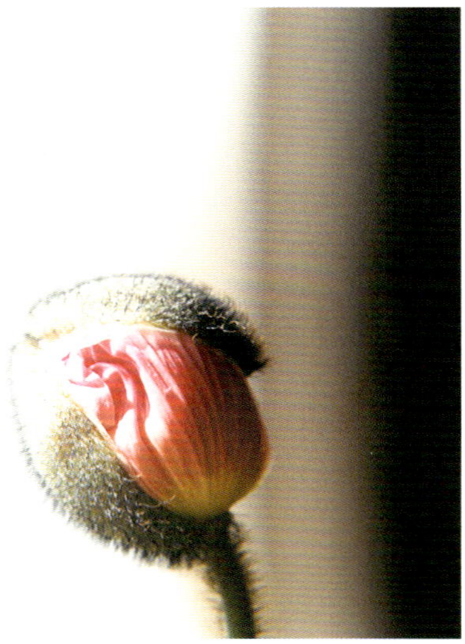

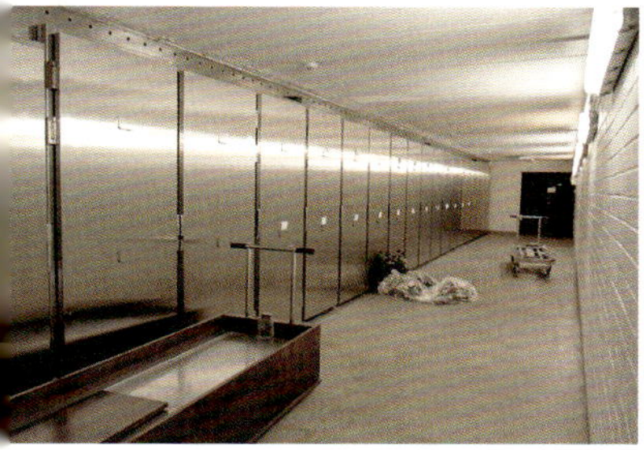

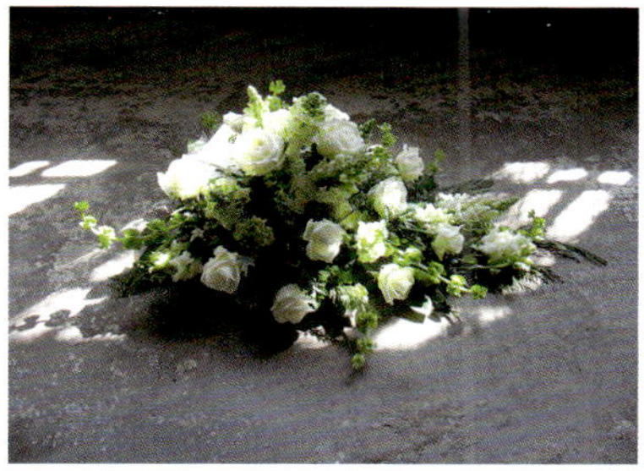

Von links nach rechts / from left to right: Rinko Kawauchi, *Untitled,* aus der Serie / from the series *Aila*, 2004

Panos Kokkinias, *Theoni*, 2006

Heta Kuchka, Standbilder aus / video stills from *Tuomo & Paavo*, 2009

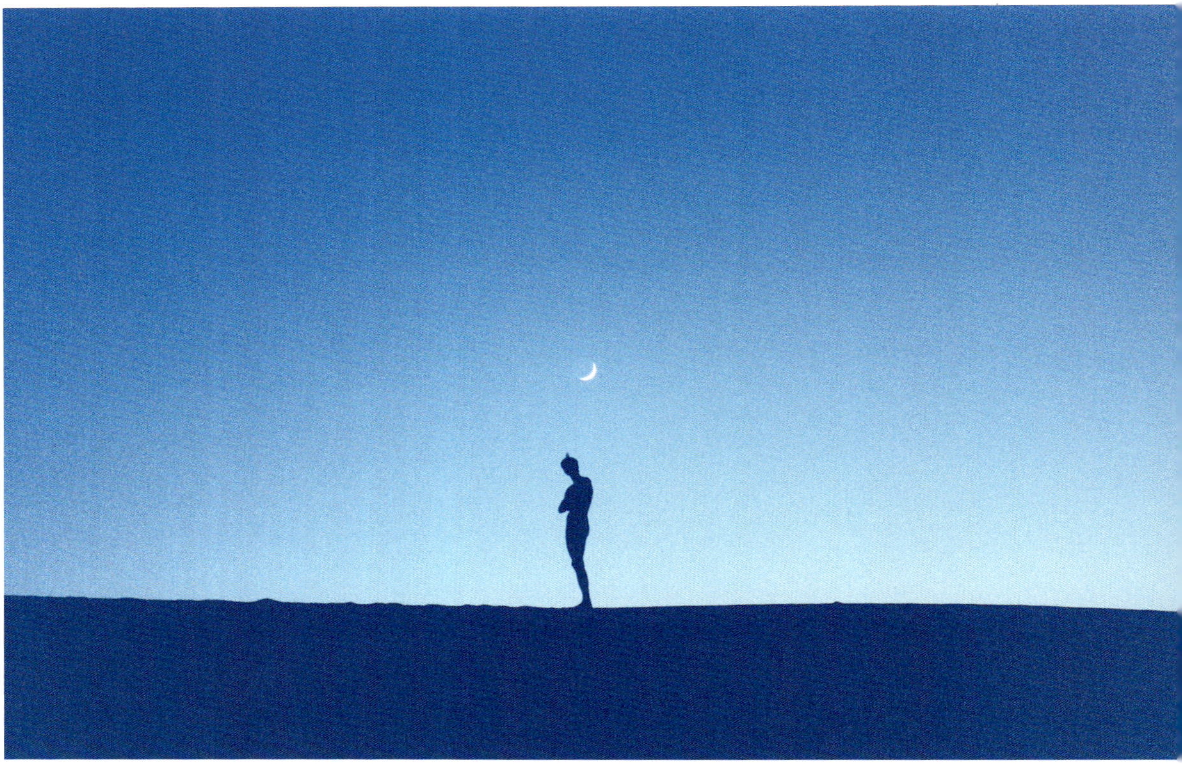

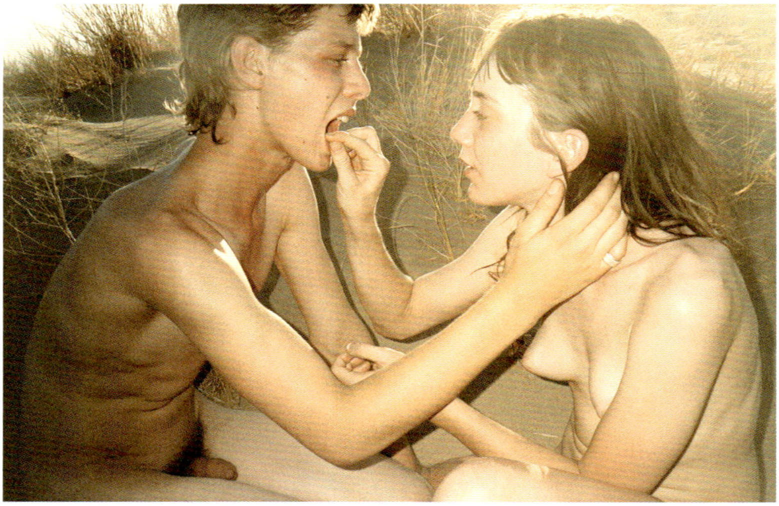

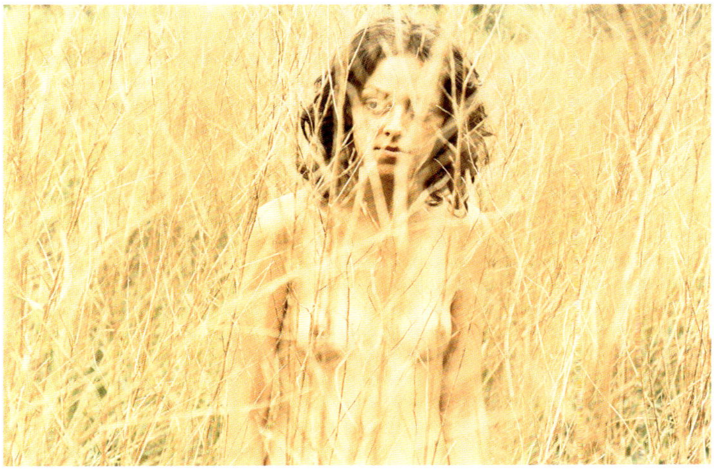

Von links nach rechts / from left to right: Ryan McGinley, *Blue Moon*; *Marlon and Rebecca*; *Hanna (Blonde Meadow)*; *Jake Falling Cut Chest*; *Fall Away (Leaves)* aus der Serie / from the series *Road Trips*, 2009

Nächste Seite / next page: Barbara Metselaar Berthold, aus / from *The Tall Tale of Freewill*, 1978–2011

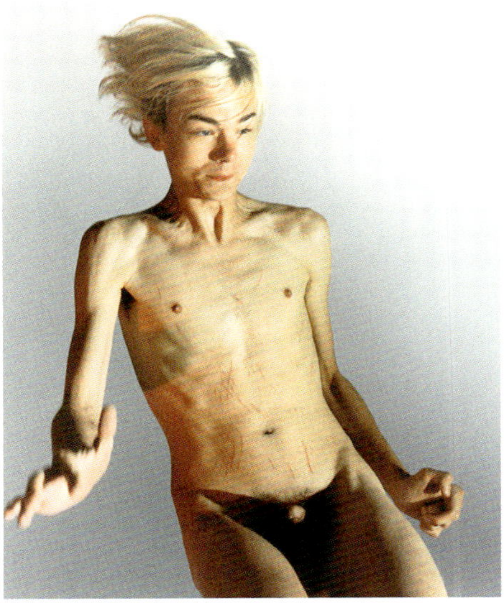

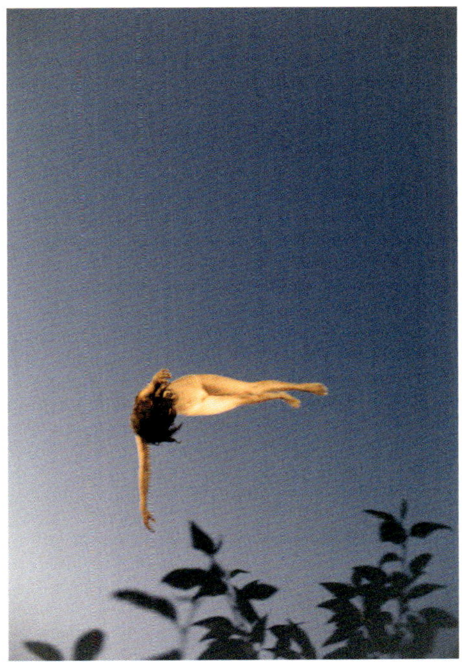

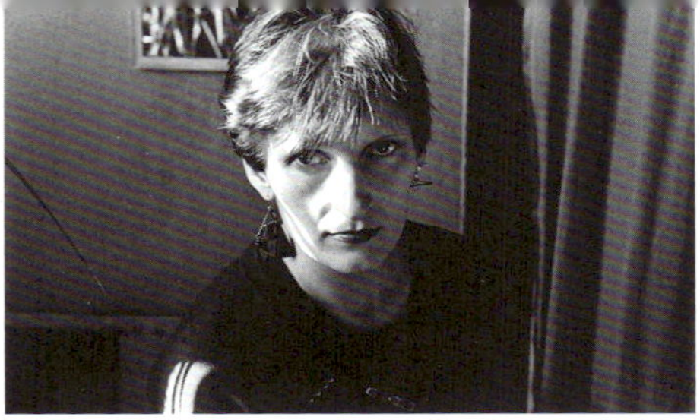
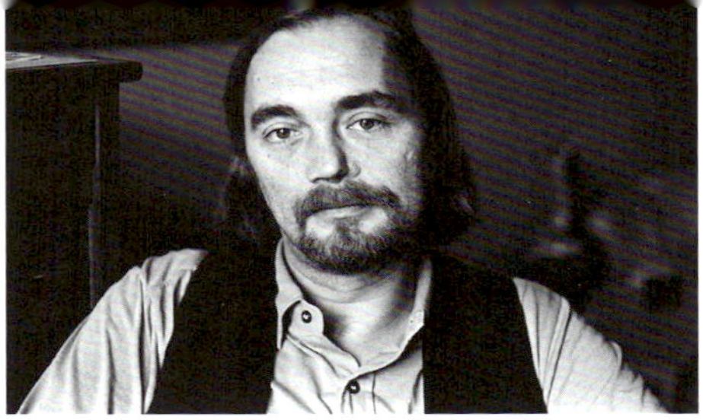
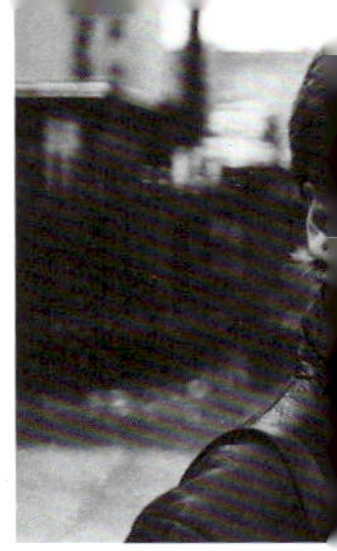
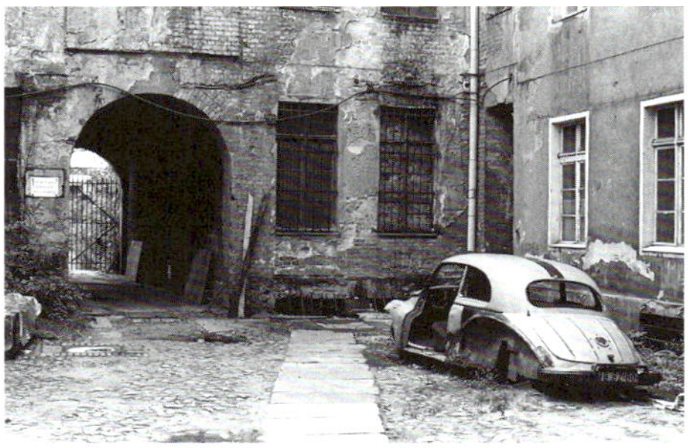
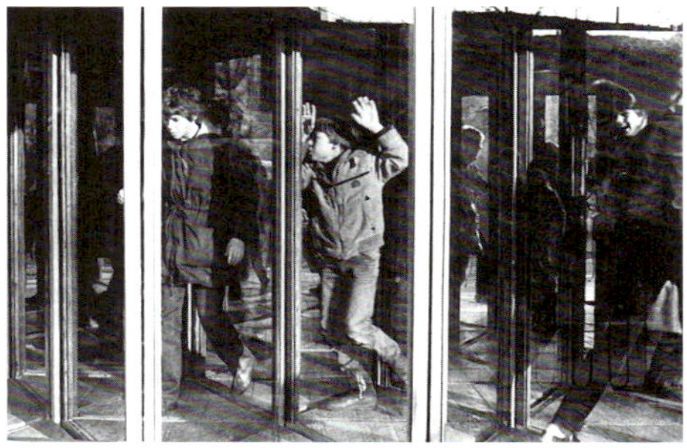
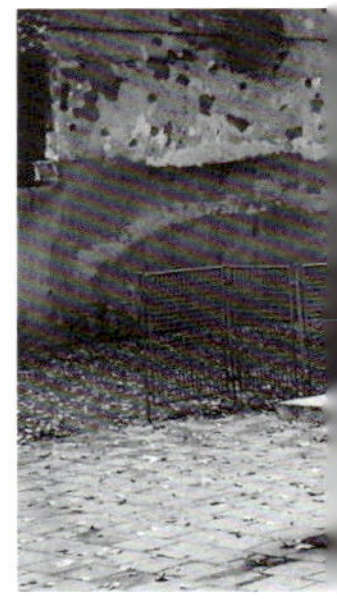
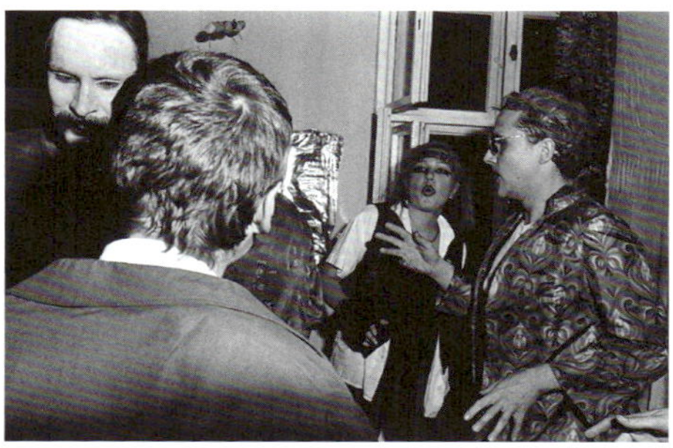
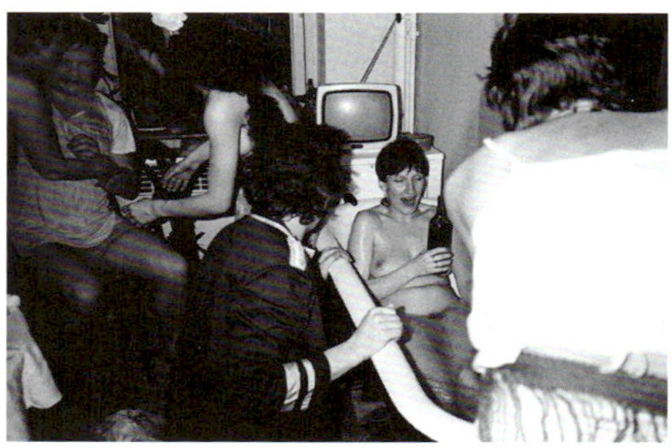
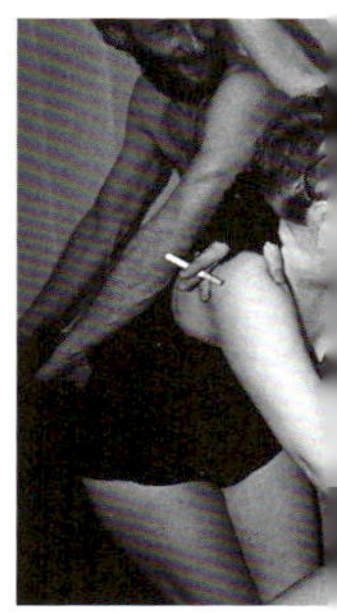
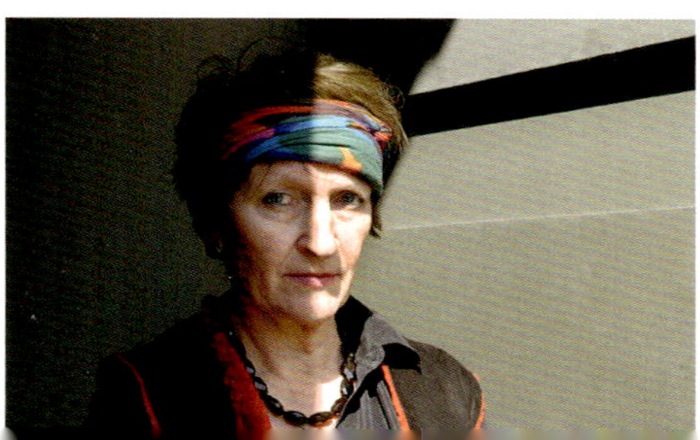
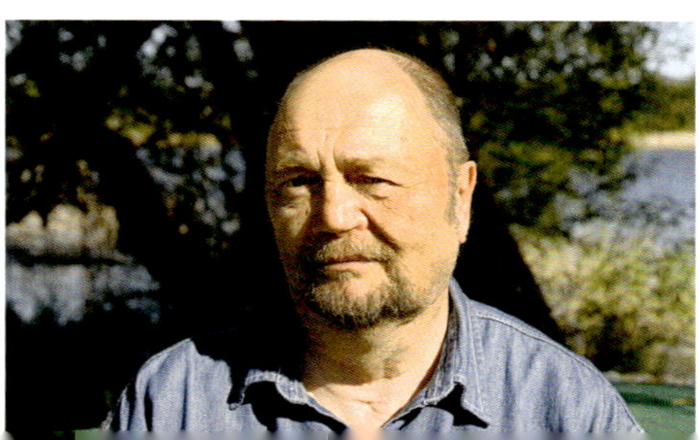
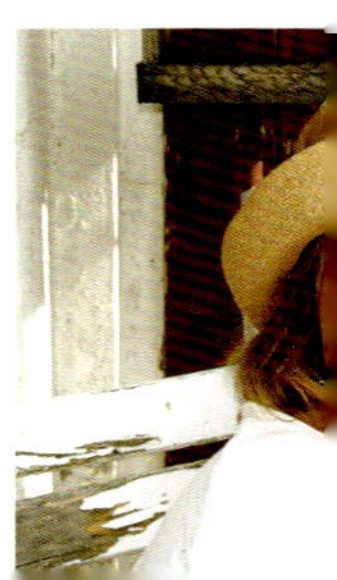

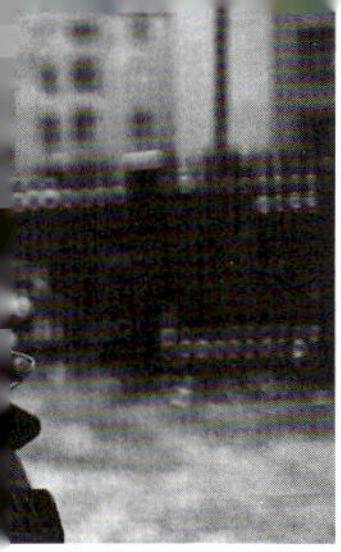

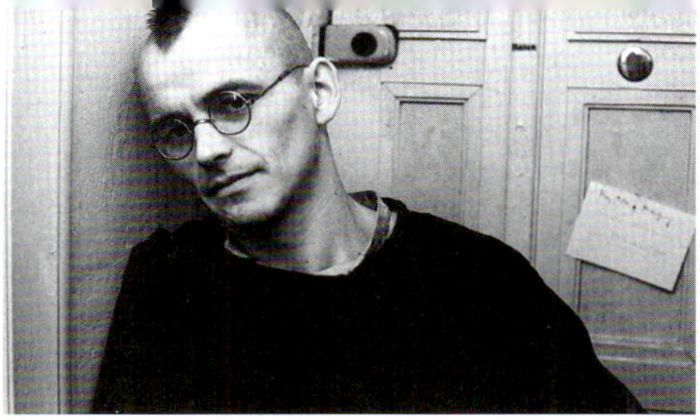

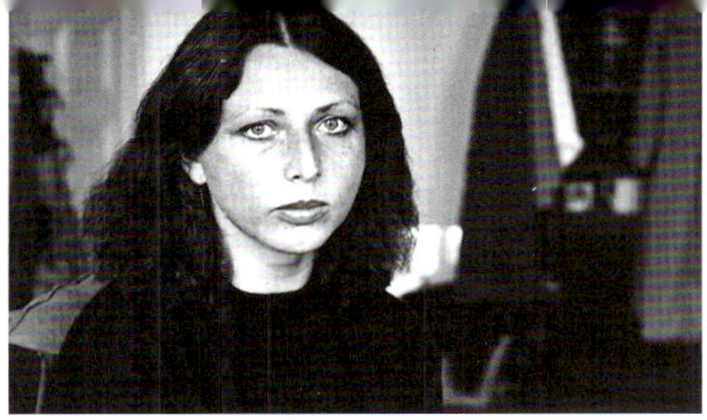

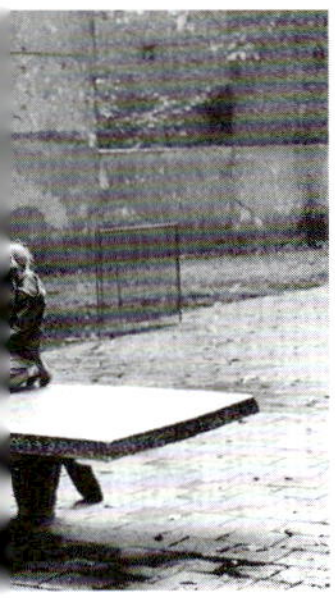

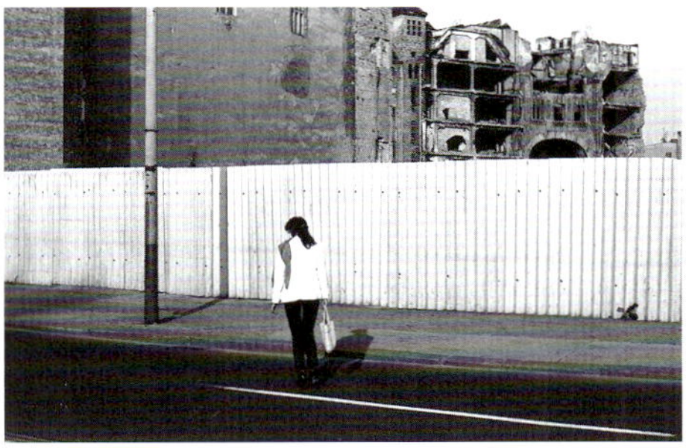

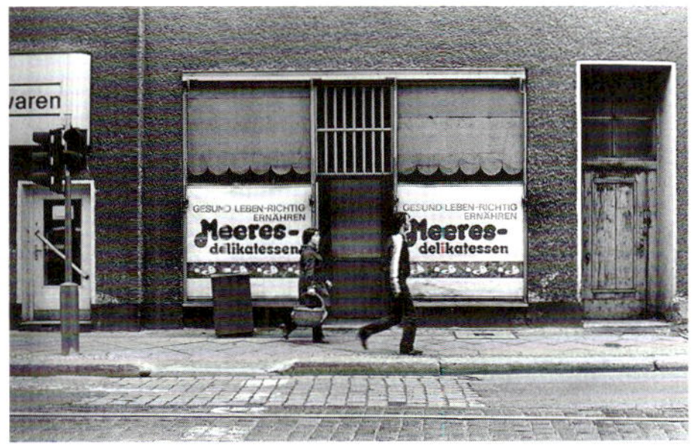
waren
GESUND LEBEN-RICHTIG ERNÄHREN
Meeres-
delikatessen
GESUND LEBEN-RICHTIG ERNÄHREN
Meeres-
delikatessen

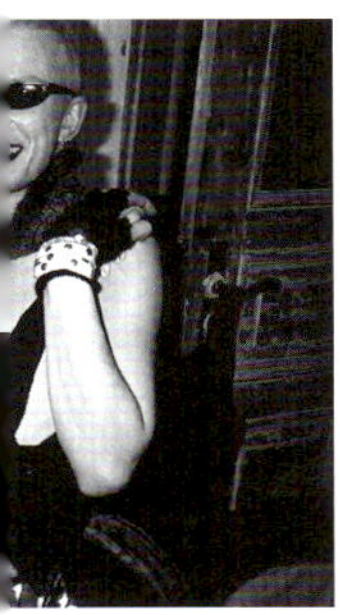

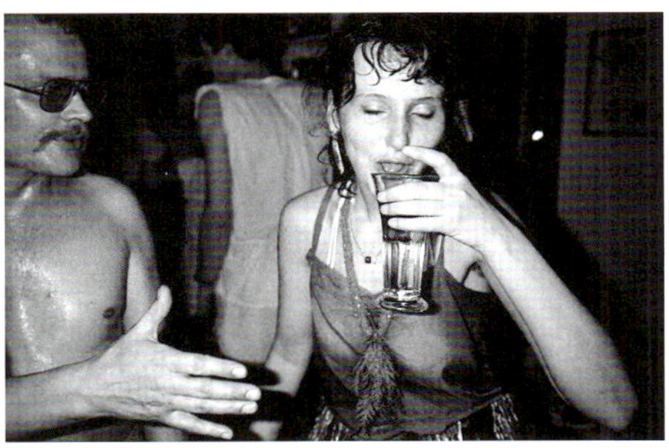

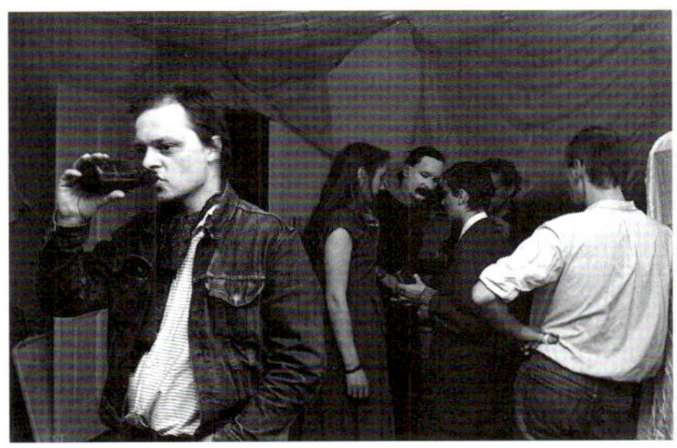

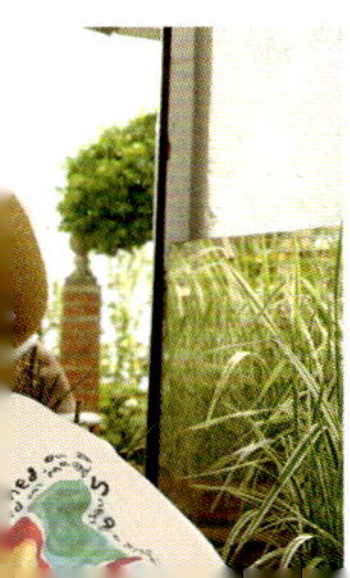

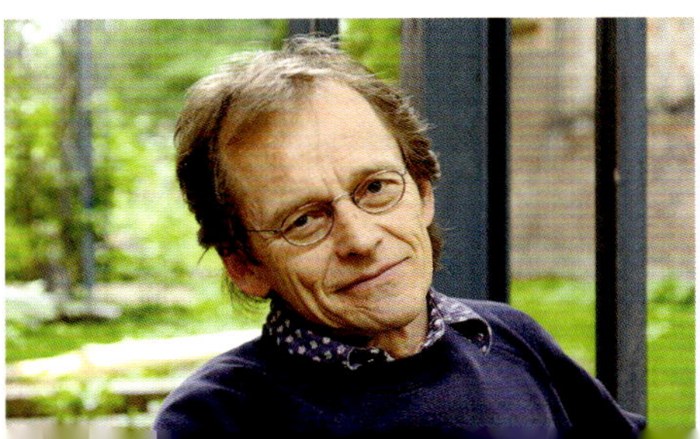

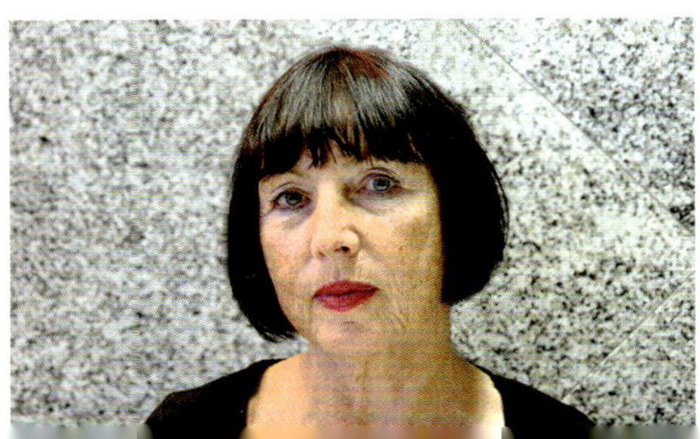

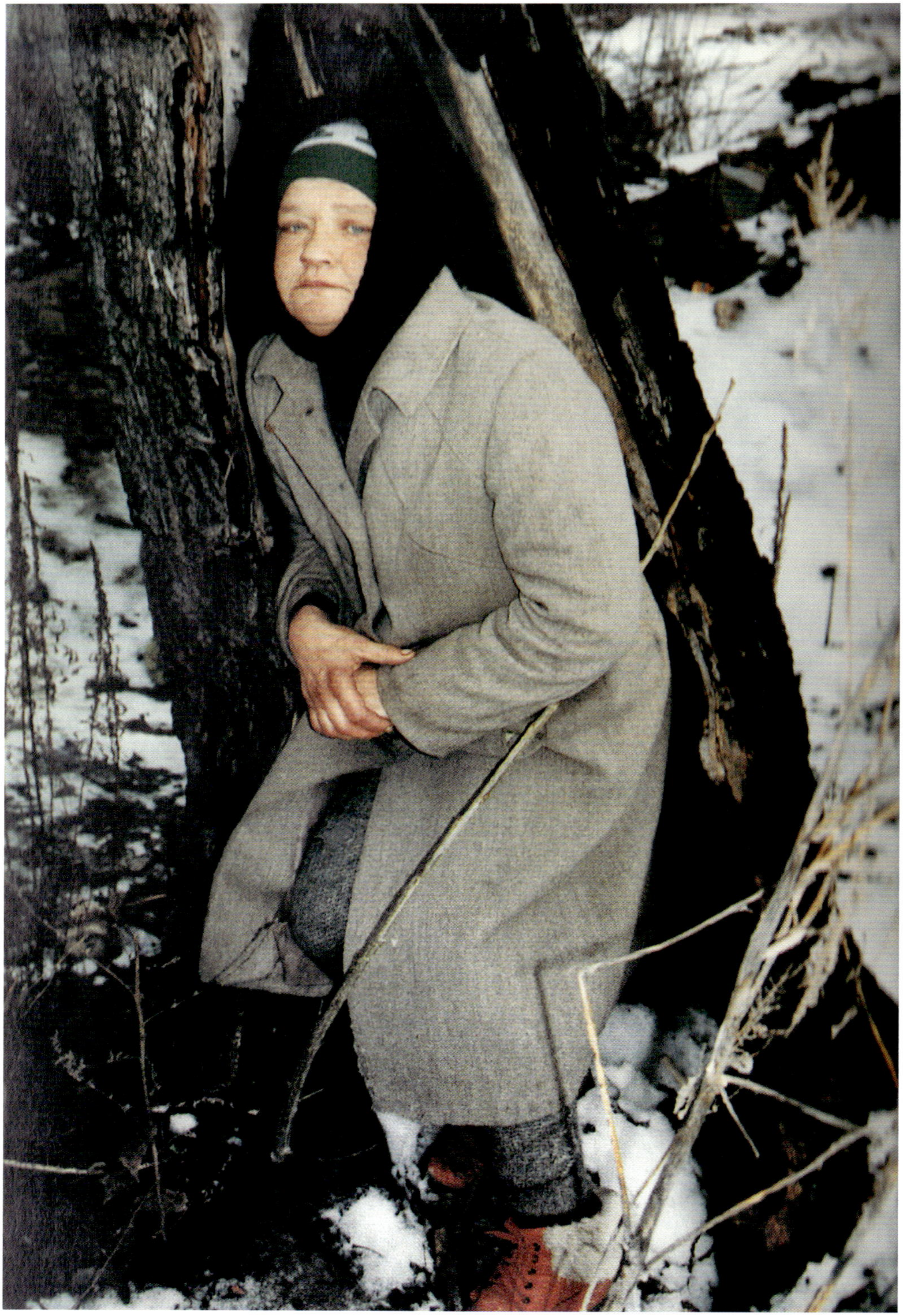

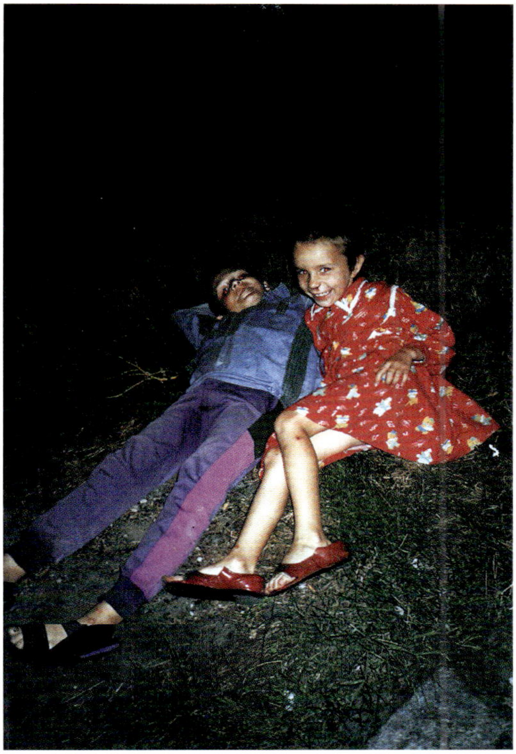

Links und rechts / left and right: Boris Mikhailov, *Case history*, 1997

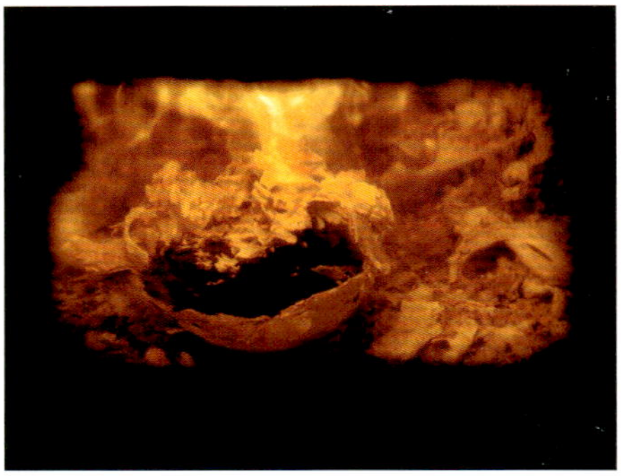

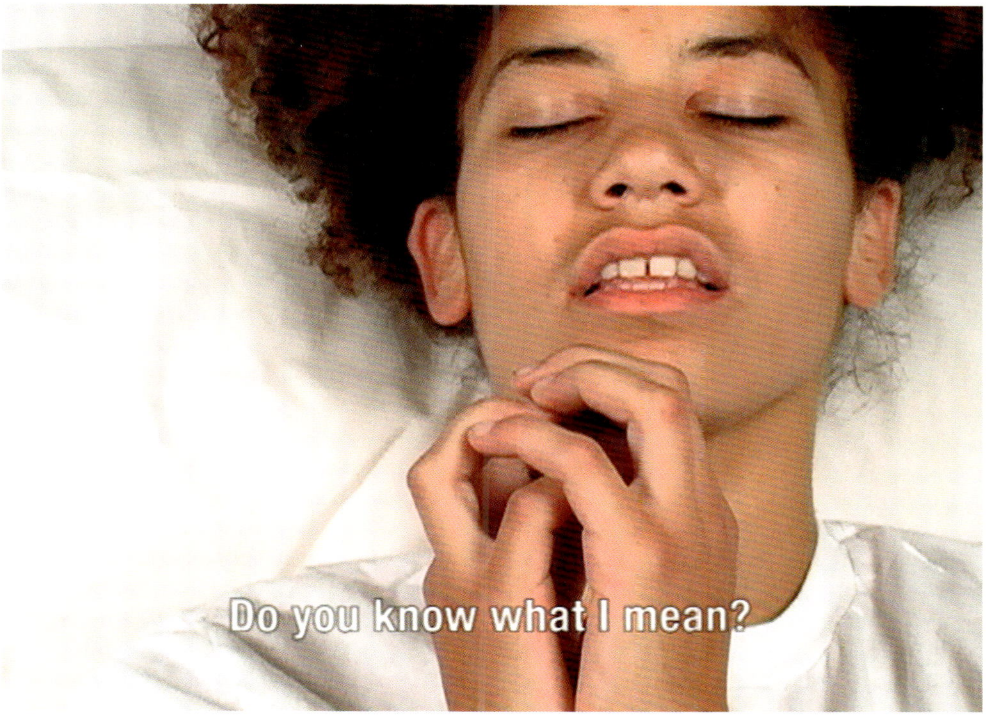

Jeremy Shaw, *Sara,*
Standbild aus /
video still from
DMT, 2004

Links / left: Torbjørn
Rødland, *Burning*
Skull no. 1,
2008–2010

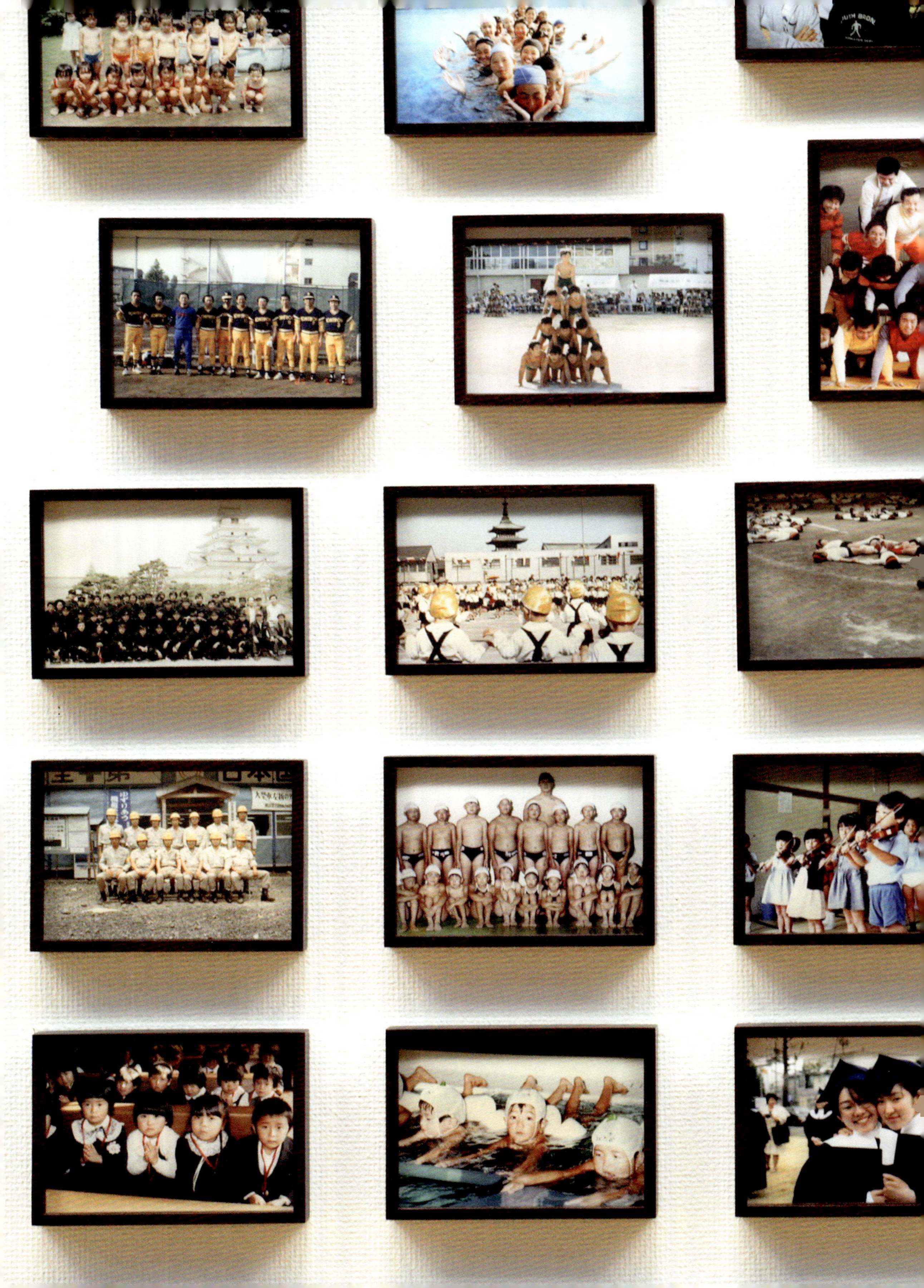

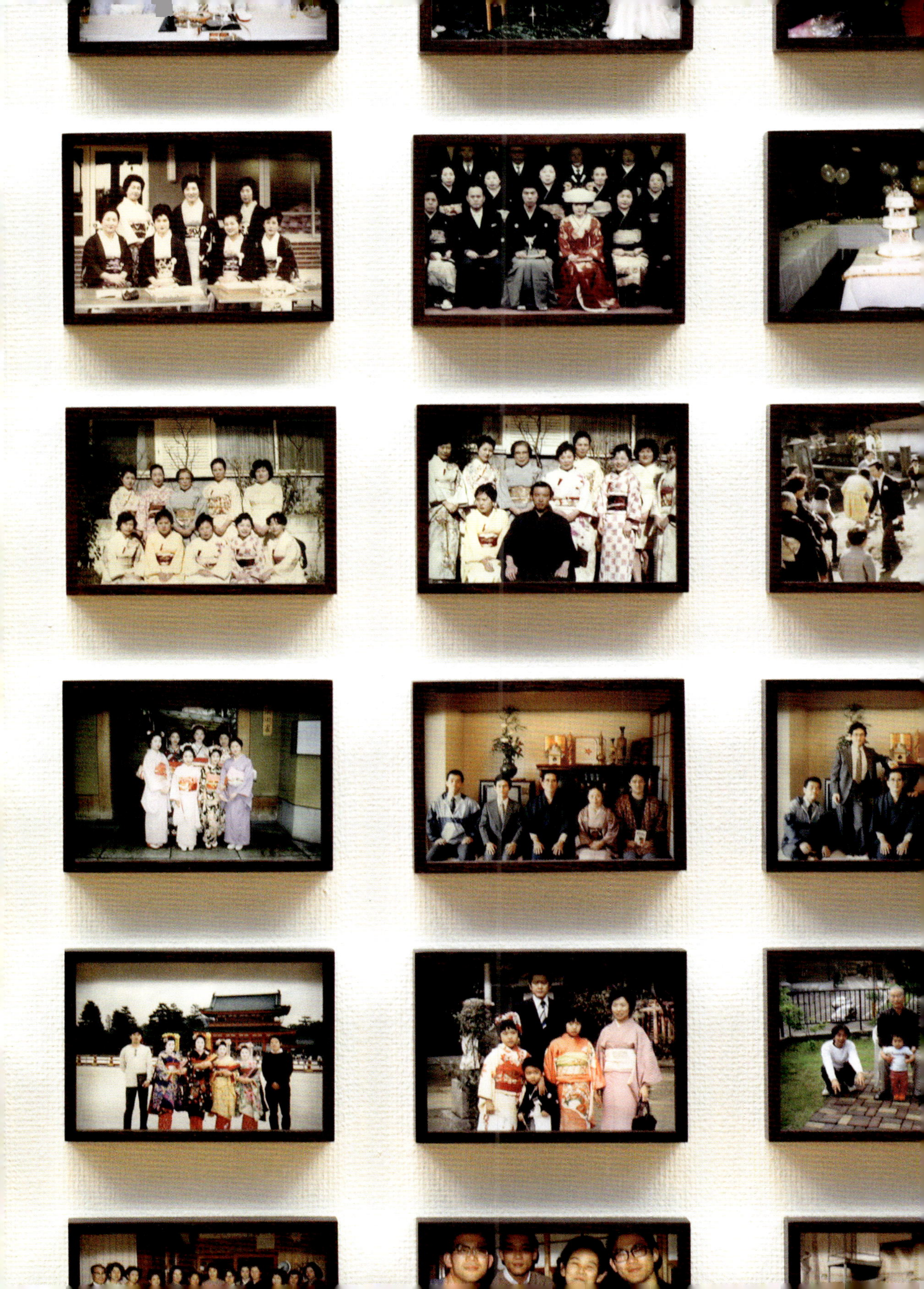

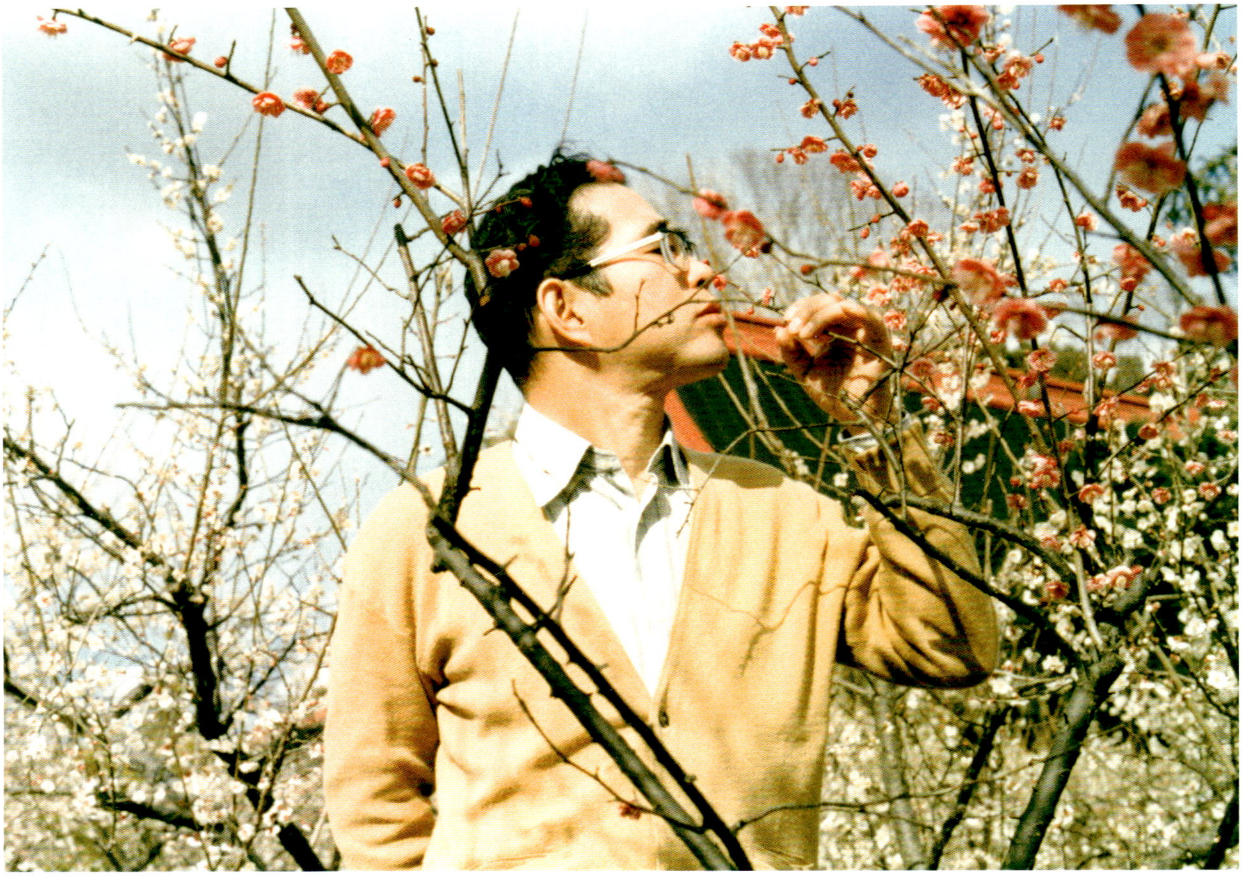

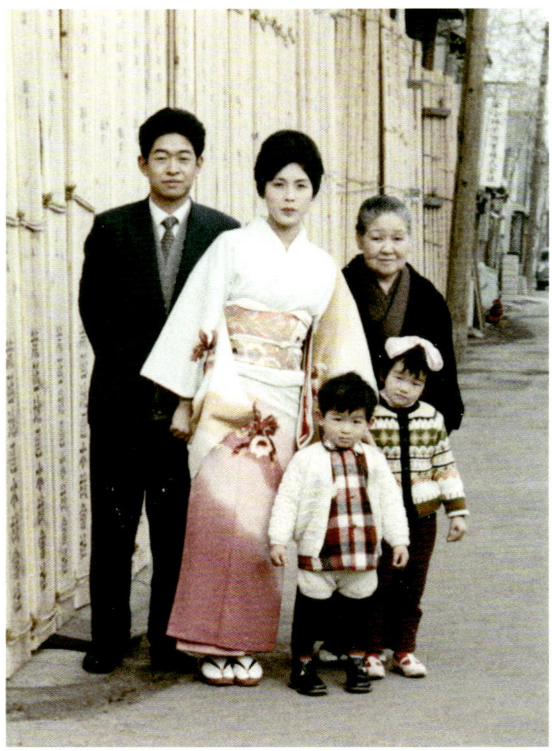

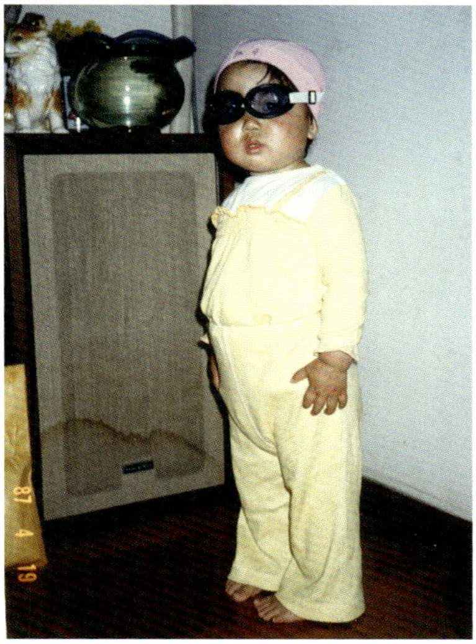

orige Seite und
nks und rechts /
revious page and
eft and right: Fiona
an, *Vox Populi*,
okyo, 2007

The Practice of Everyday Life

Das alltägliche Leben Kunstverein Ludwigshafen

Als Teil des 4. Fotofestivals Mannheim_ Ludwighafen_Heidelberg, *The Eye is a Lonely Hunter*, beinhaltet das Unterthema „Das alltägliche Leben" eine fotografische Untersuchung der Organisation, Durchführung und „Personalisierung" des täglichen Lebens – Aufgaben, denen sich alle Menschen gegenübergestellt sehen. Inspiriert wurde dieses Ausstellungssegment durch das Buch *L'invention du quotidien* (Deutsch: *Die Kunst des Handelns*) des Soziologen Michel de Certeau, der untersuchte, wie die Menschen ihre Kultur individualisieren und Dinge – von Gebrauchsgegenständen bis zu alltäglichen Handlungen – verändern oder modifizieren, um sie sich „anzueignen". Wie bewältigen wir das tägliche Leben? Wie durchleben wir die tagtäglichen Handlungen, Notwendigkeiten und Routinen? Wie ersinnen wir Strategien, mit denen wir den Alltag bezwingen? Wie bewegen wir uns im privaten wie auch im öffentlichen Raum und besetzen ihn – als Einzelpersonen und als Mitglieder einer Gruppe?

Die Ausstellung konzentriert sich auf einen wichtigen Aspekt des alltäglichen Lebens: die Möglichkeiten und Grenzen der individuellen Handlungsfähigkeit sowohl als Vermittlung eines mikrokosmischen Weltbilds wie auch als Beispiel für den Überlebenswillen. Sie erlaubt einen Einblick in die unterschiedlichen Rituale / Umsetzungen des täglichen Lebens überall auf der Welt, in ihrer Einfachheit, Eigenheit und ihrem Erfindungsreichtum. Sie fragt, ob es zwischen „Praxis" und „Routine" einen Unterschied gibt und, wenn ja, worin sich dieser manifestiert.

Tatsächlich gibt es „universale" Praktiken und Lebensweisen, wie das Essen, das Sich-Kleiden und der menschliche Kontakt, die uns allen gemein sind. Doch werden diese Praktiken in unterschiedlichen Kulturen auf unterschiedliche Weise offenbar: Während einige Gepflogenheiten eine gewisse Einheitlichkeit oder Normiertheit aufweisen mögen, sind andere eine Art von Widerstand gegenüber der Konvention und stellen die Verallgemeinerungen des menschlichen Alltagslebens infrage. Deshalb ist die Vorstellung von einer „Normalität" des Alltäglichen relativ: in der Auswahl der Fotografien kommen sowohl übliche und vertraute als auch recht ungewöhnliche tägliche Routinen und Praktiken zum Ausdruck. Das Hauptanliegen der Ausstellung *The Eye is a Lonely Hunter* und ihrer Teilbereiche ist es, einen Einblick in das Leben anderer zu vermitteln, der über den visuellen Mythos von Normalität und Universalität hinausgeht. „Das alltägliche Leben" bezeugt das Vermögen der Menschheit, angesichts der Herausforderungen des täglichen Lebens erfindungsreiche Überlebensstrategien zu entwickeln.

Katerina Gregos & Solvej Helweg Ovesen

The Practice of Everyday Life Kunstverein Ludwigshafen

'The Practice of Everyday Life' consists of a photographic investigation into the organisation, performance and 'personalising' of everyday life, a task all human beings face. This segment of the exhibition is inspired by the eponymous book by sociologist Michel de Certeau, in which he investigates how human beings individualise culture, and alter or modify things, from utilitarian objects to quotidian practices, in order to make them 'their own'. How do we 'practice' everyday life? How do we go through the processes of daily actions, necessities, and routines? How do we devise strategies that get us through the quotidian? How do we navigate and occupy private as well as public space, individually and collectively?

The exhibition focuses on an important aspect of the practice of everyday life, namely the possibilities and limits of individual agency both as a kind of communication of a microcosmic worldview and as an example of the will to survive. The exhibition offers insight into the diverse practices of everyday life around the world, in all its simplicity, idiosyncrasy, and inventiveness, and asks whether there is a difference between 'practice' and 'routine' and, if so, how this difference is manifested.

We nearly all share certain 'universal' practices and regimens such as eating, dressing, socialising – but these manifest themselves in different ways in different cultures. While some practices might be subject to a certain homogeneity or normalisation, others constitute a form of resistance to convention, thus challenging universalising representations of the quotidian life of humankind. The notion of 'normality' in relation to the everyday is one that is therefore relative, and this photographic selection displays both habitual and familiar as well as perhaps less familiar routines and practices of everyday life. The overall aim of *The Eye is a Lonely Hunter*, and its several components, is to provide insight into the lives of others beyond the visual mythologies of normality and universality. 'The Practice of Everyday Life' testifies to humankind's capacity for inventive survival strategies in the face of quotidian existence.

Katerina Gregos & Solvej Helweg Ovesen

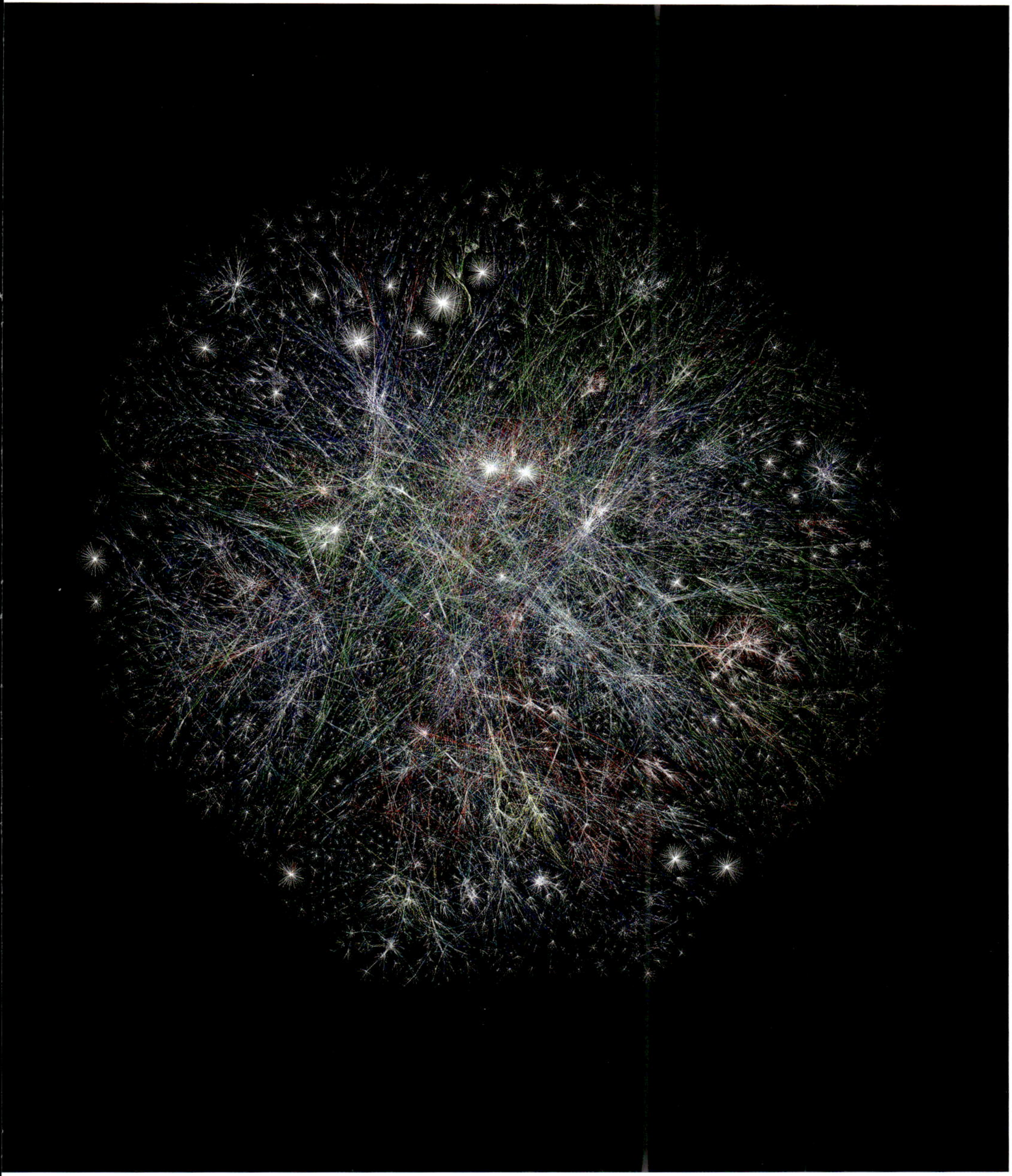

Sofia Burchardi & Plamen Bontchev, *Alone Together,* 2011

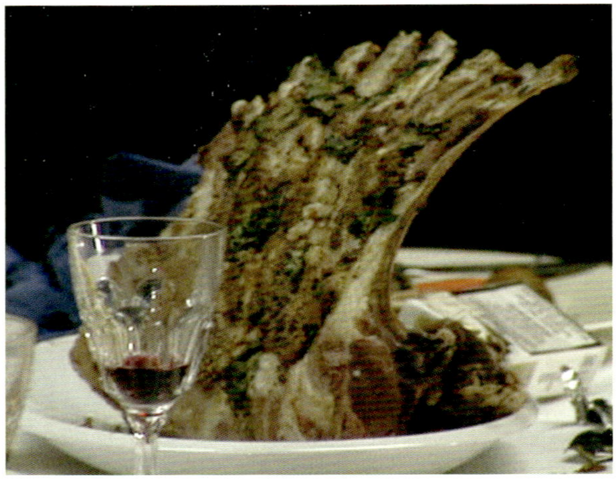

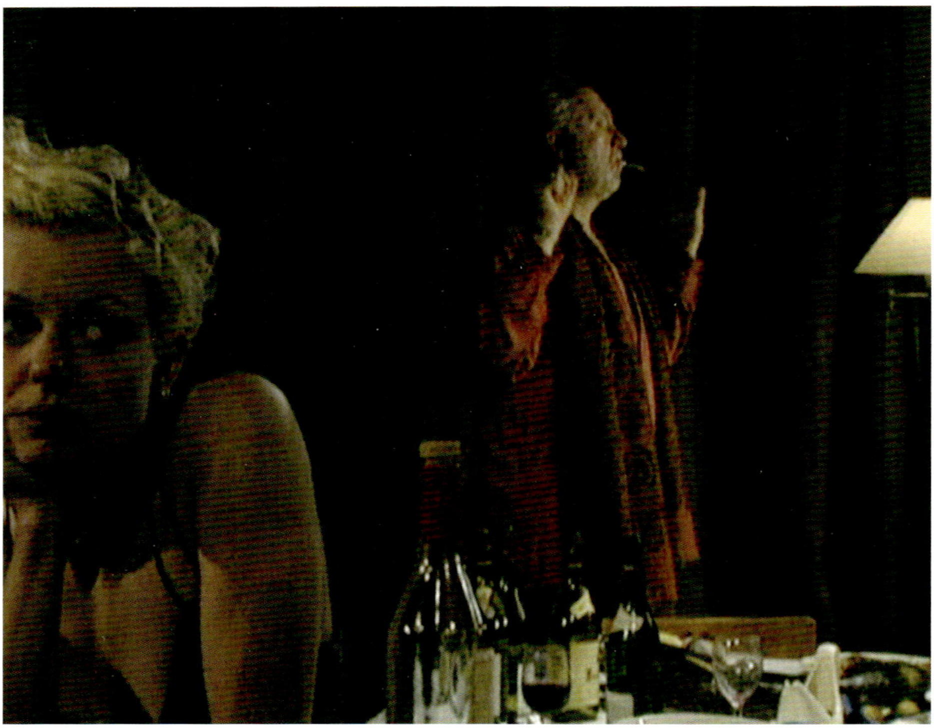

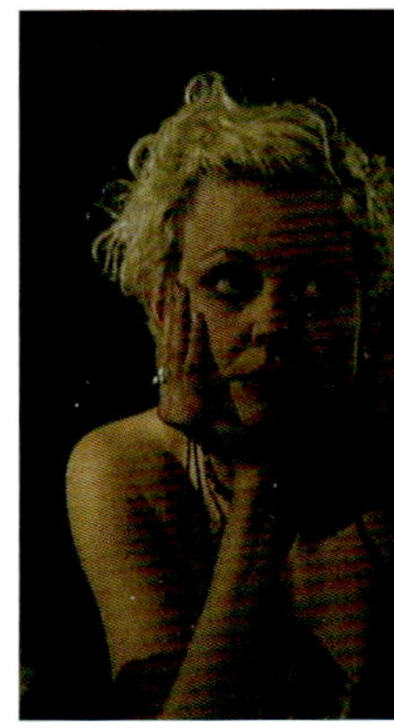

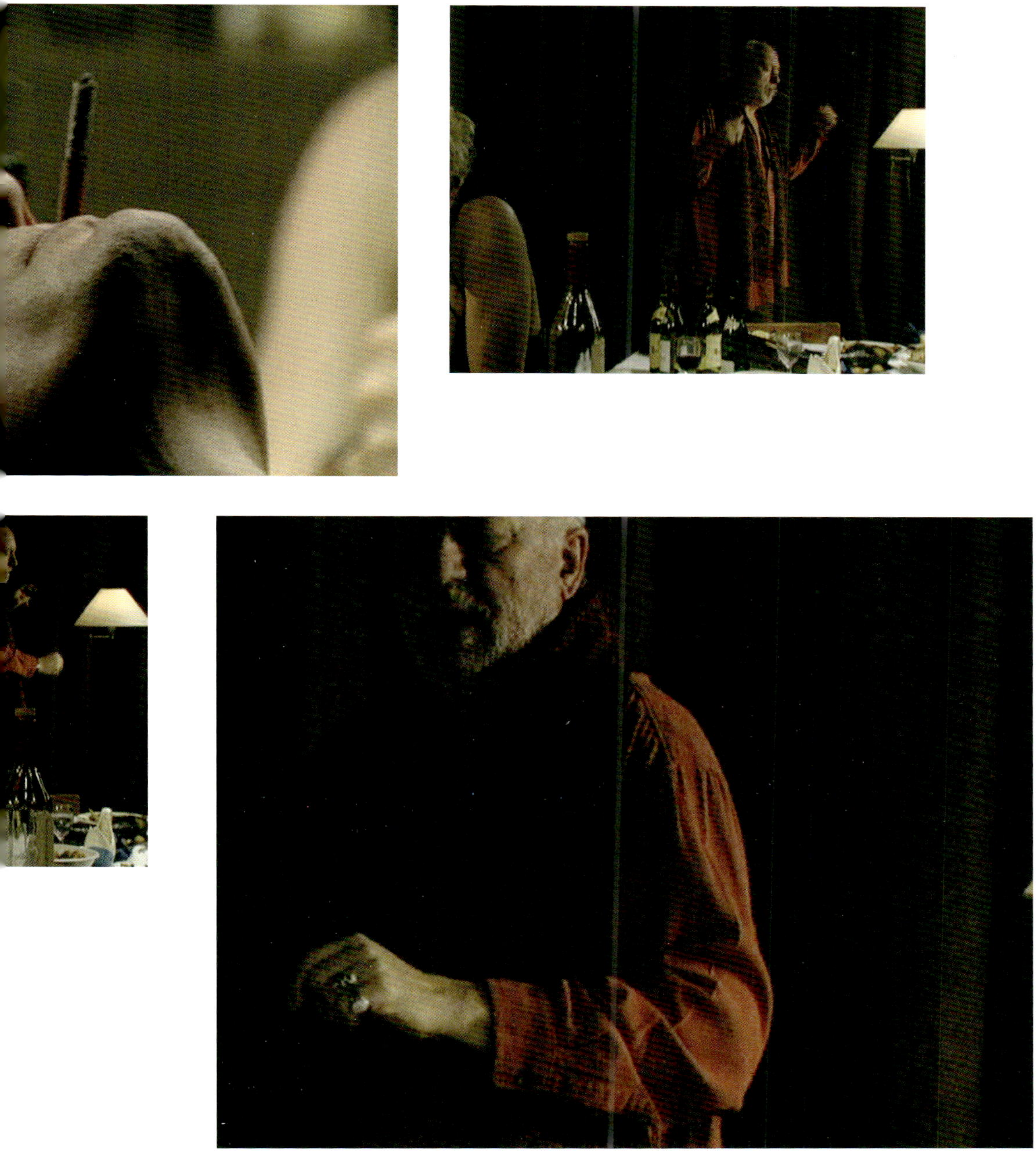

Marie José Burki, Standbilder aus / video stills from *De nos jours (dedans)*, 2004

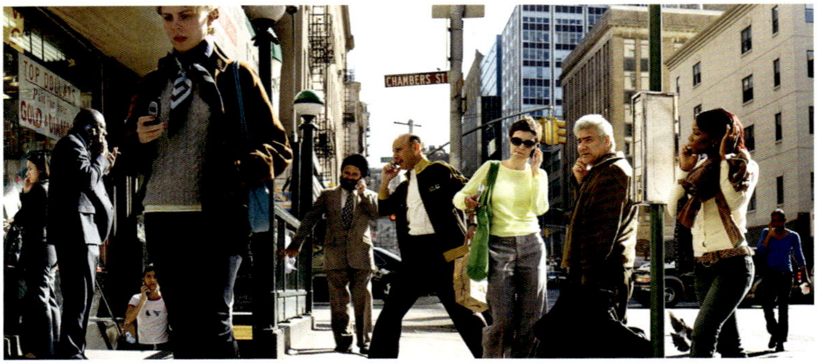
CHAMBERS ST

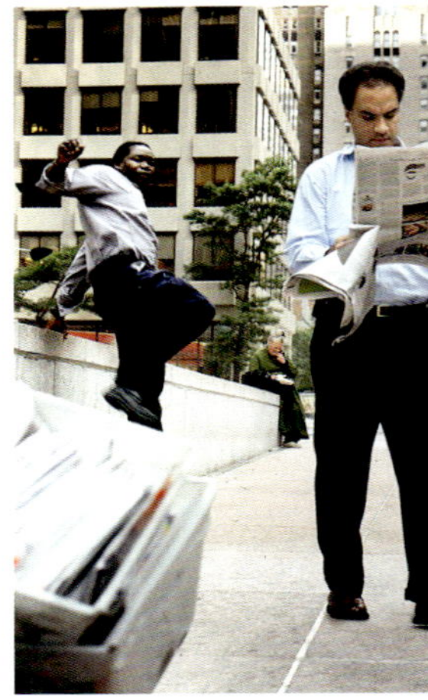

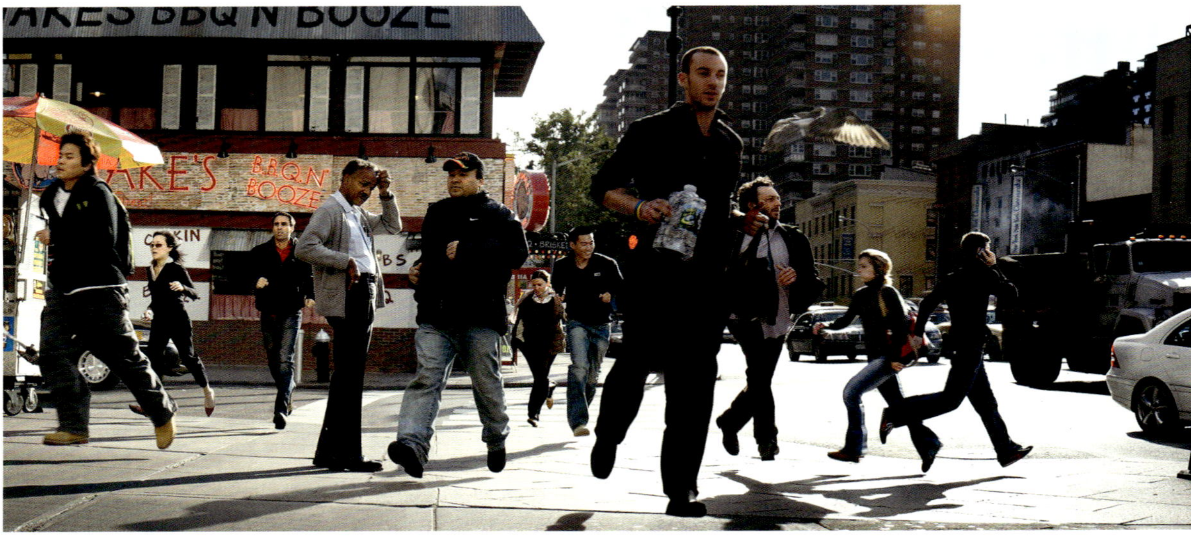
AKES BBQ N BOOZE

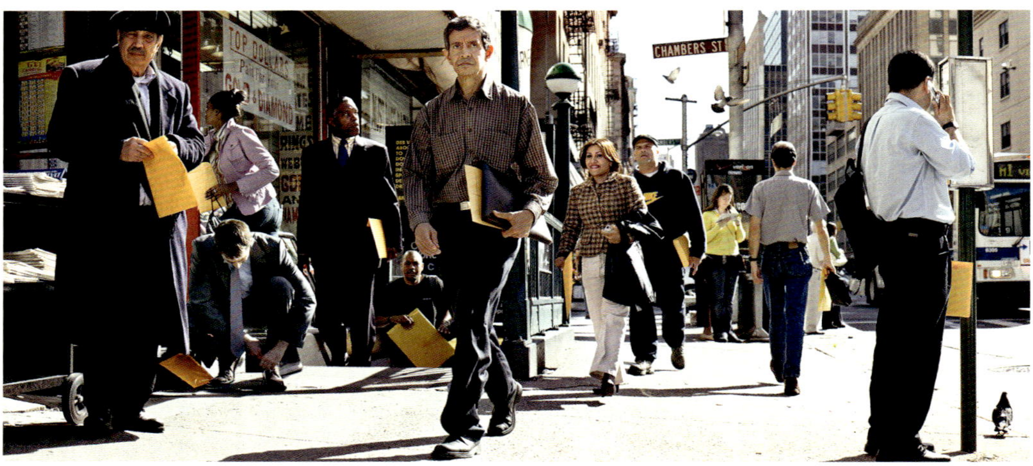
CHAMBERS ST

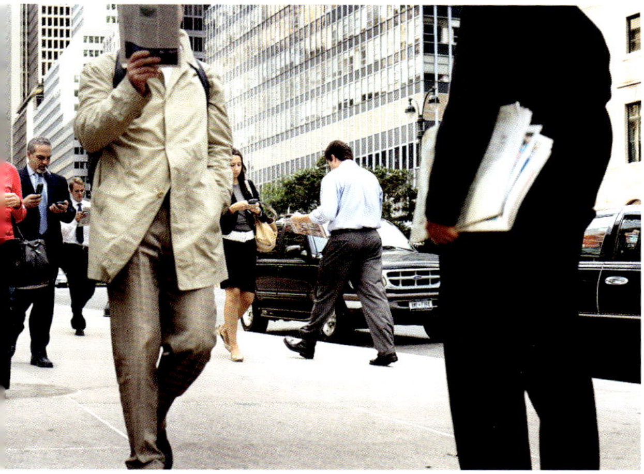

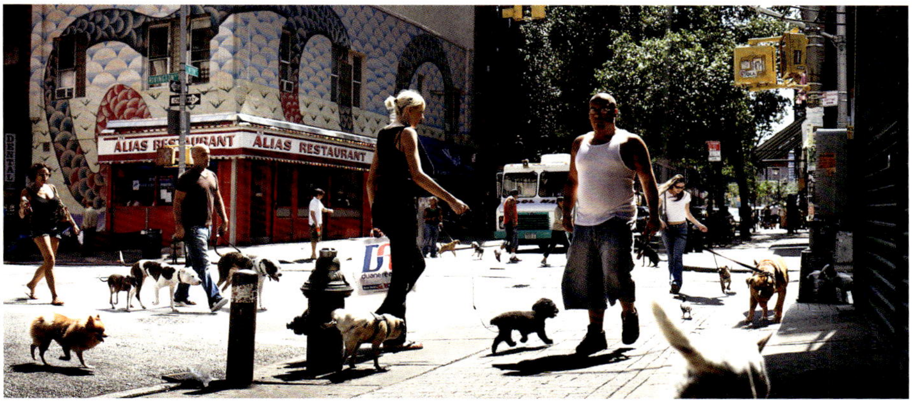

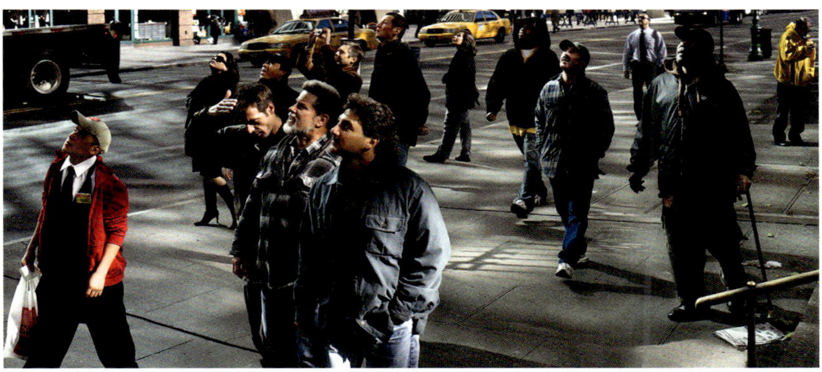

Von links nach rechts / From left to right: Peter Funch, *Communicating Community*, 2007; *Diverting Diversions*, 2007; *Exigent State*, 2007; *Following Followers*, 2007; *Informing Informers*, 2006; *Observing Observers*, 2007 aus der Serie / from the series *Babel Tales*, 2006–2010

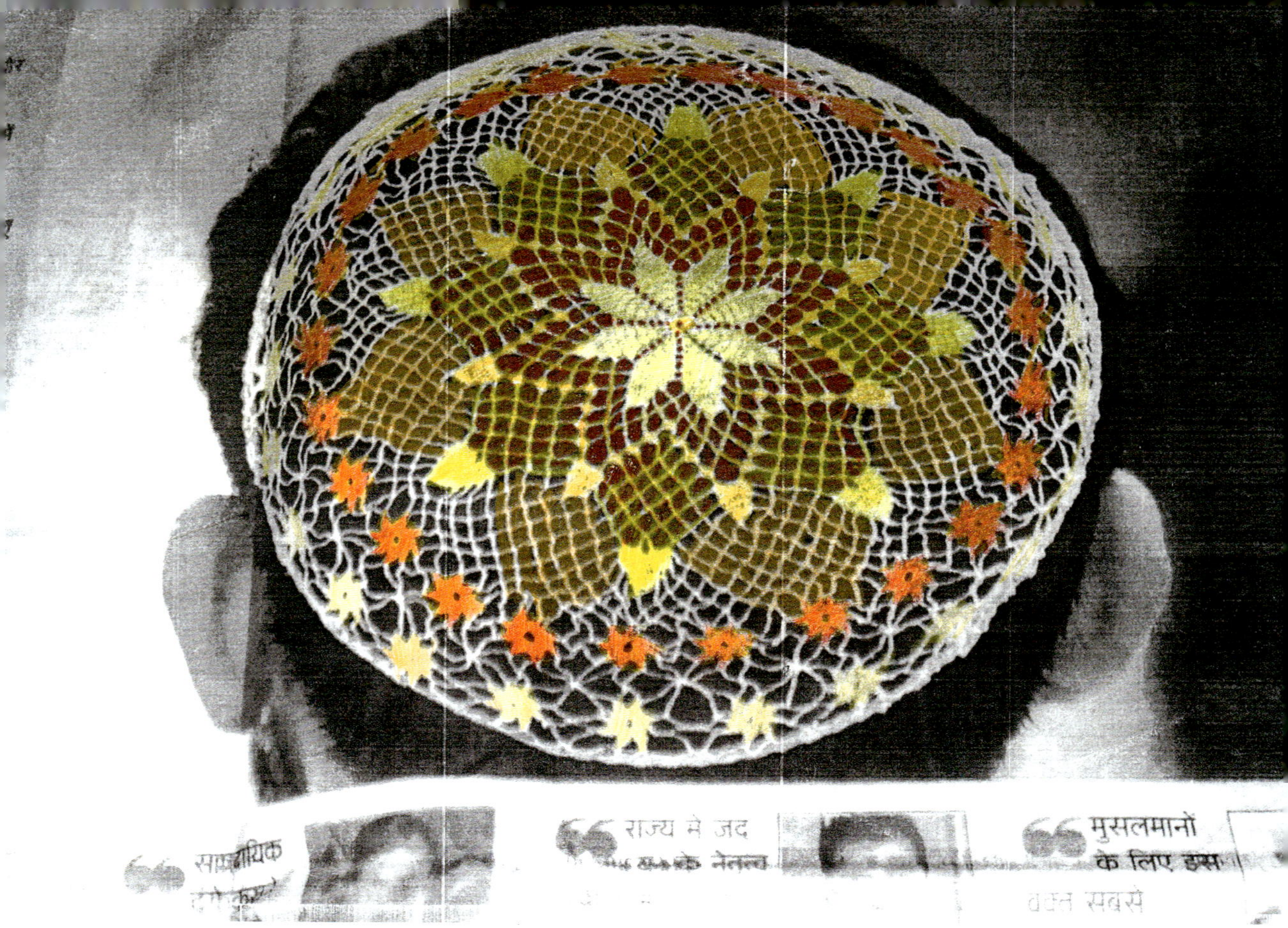

Alexandros Georgiou, *Everyday Islam*, 2009-2010, aus der Serie / from the series *Without My Own Vehicle, Varanasi*, 2009–2010

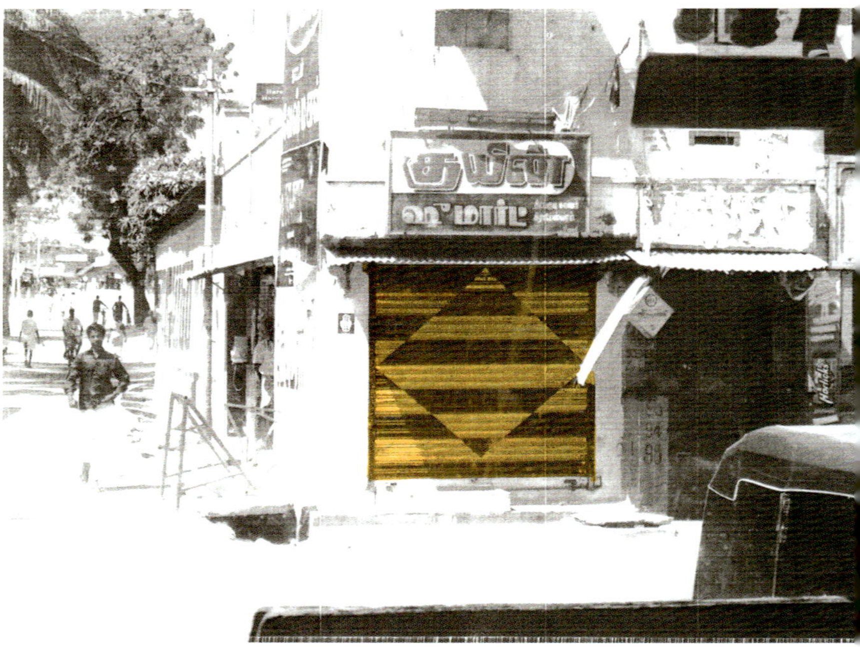

Alexandros Georgiou, *Mystical Mundane*, 2010, aus der Serie / from the series *Without My Own Vehicle, Varanasi*, 2009–2010

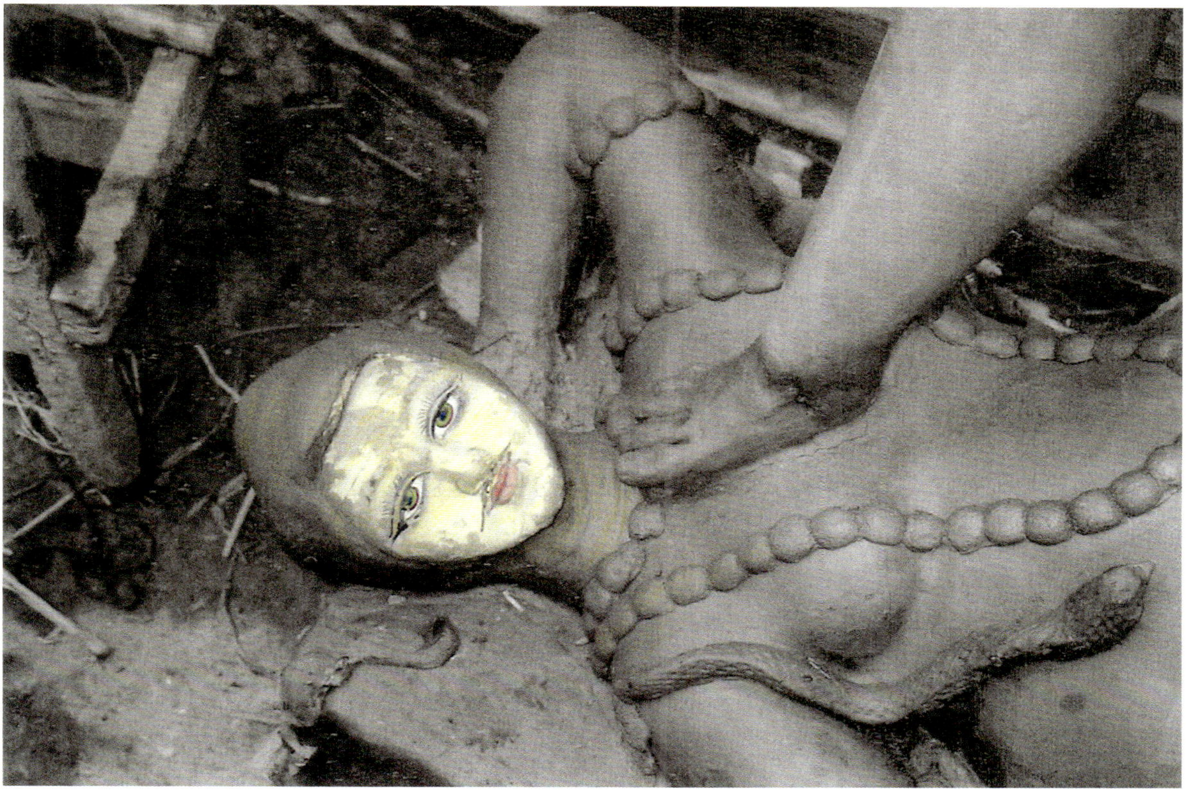

Alexandros Georgiou, *Shiva under Kali's foot*, 2010, aus der Serie / from the series *Without My Own Vehicle, Varanasi*, 2009–2010

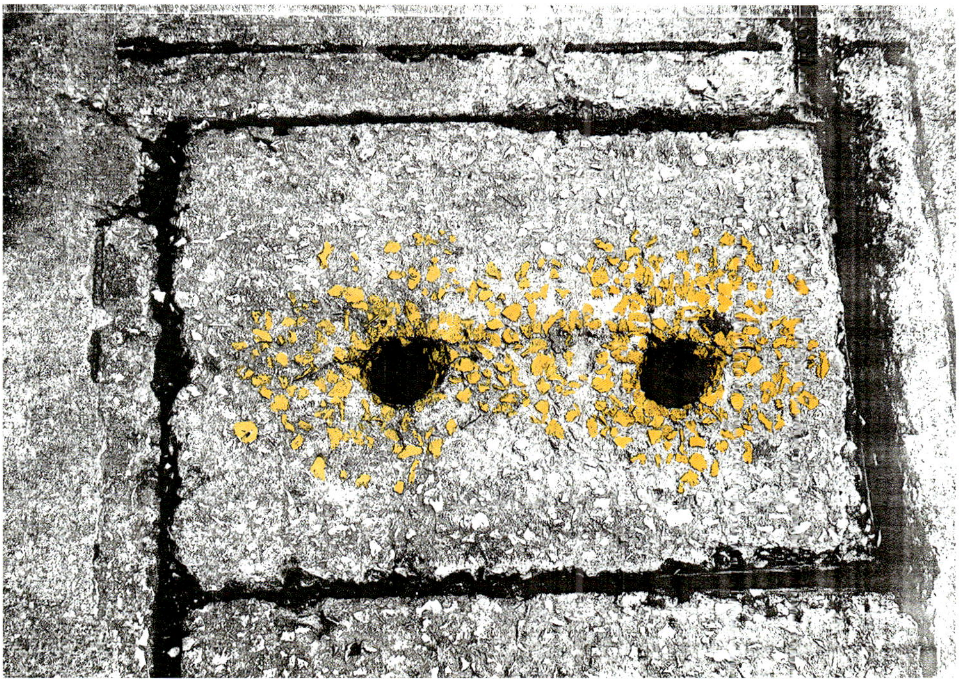

Alexandros Georgiou, *The Eyes Of The Gutter*, 2010, aus der Serie / from the series *Without My Own Vehicle, Varanasi*, 2009–2010

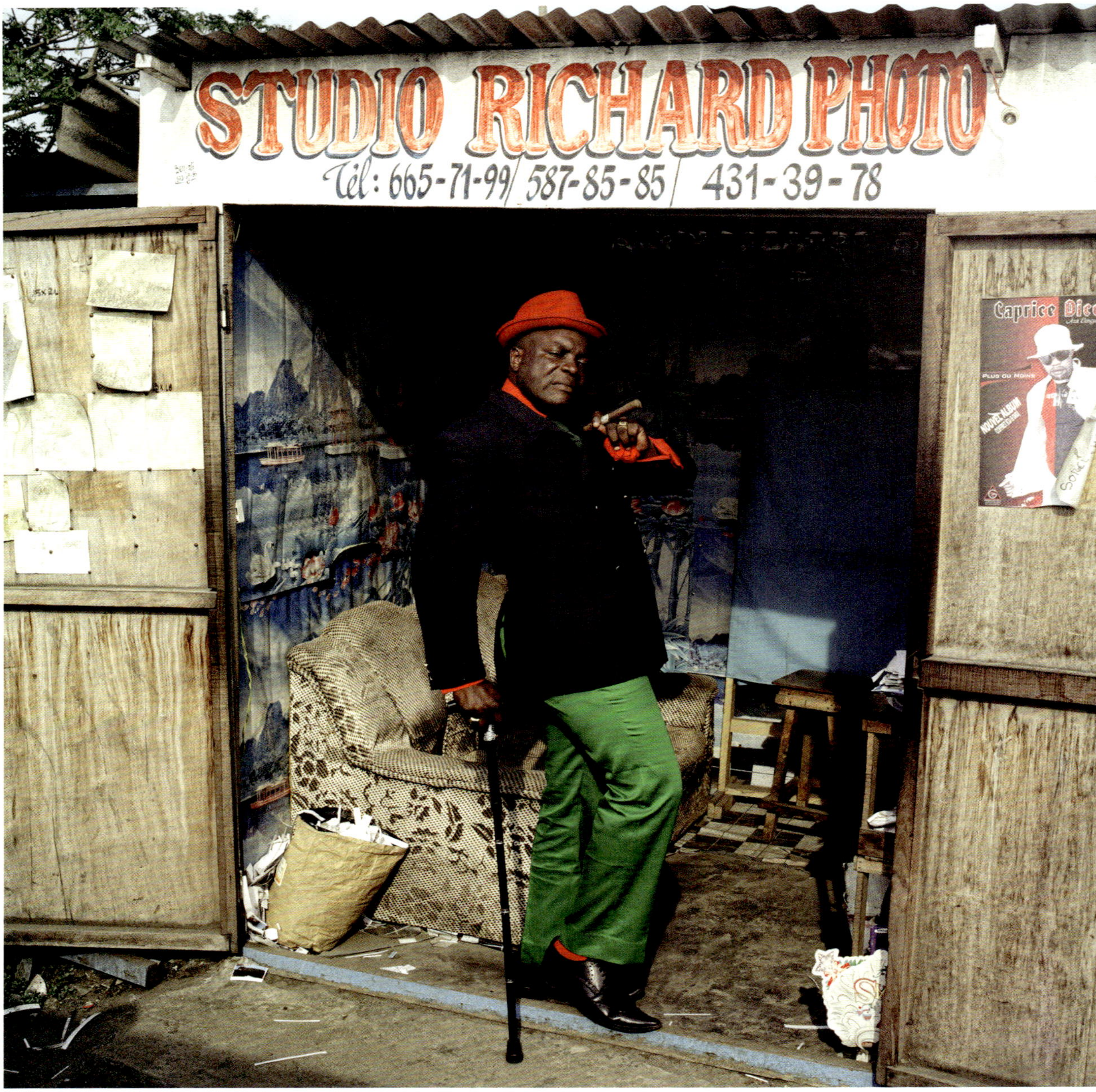

Francesco Giusti, *MABIOS DE M'PAKA' – Republic of the Congo – Pointe-Noire*, aus der Serie / from the series *Sapologie*, 2009

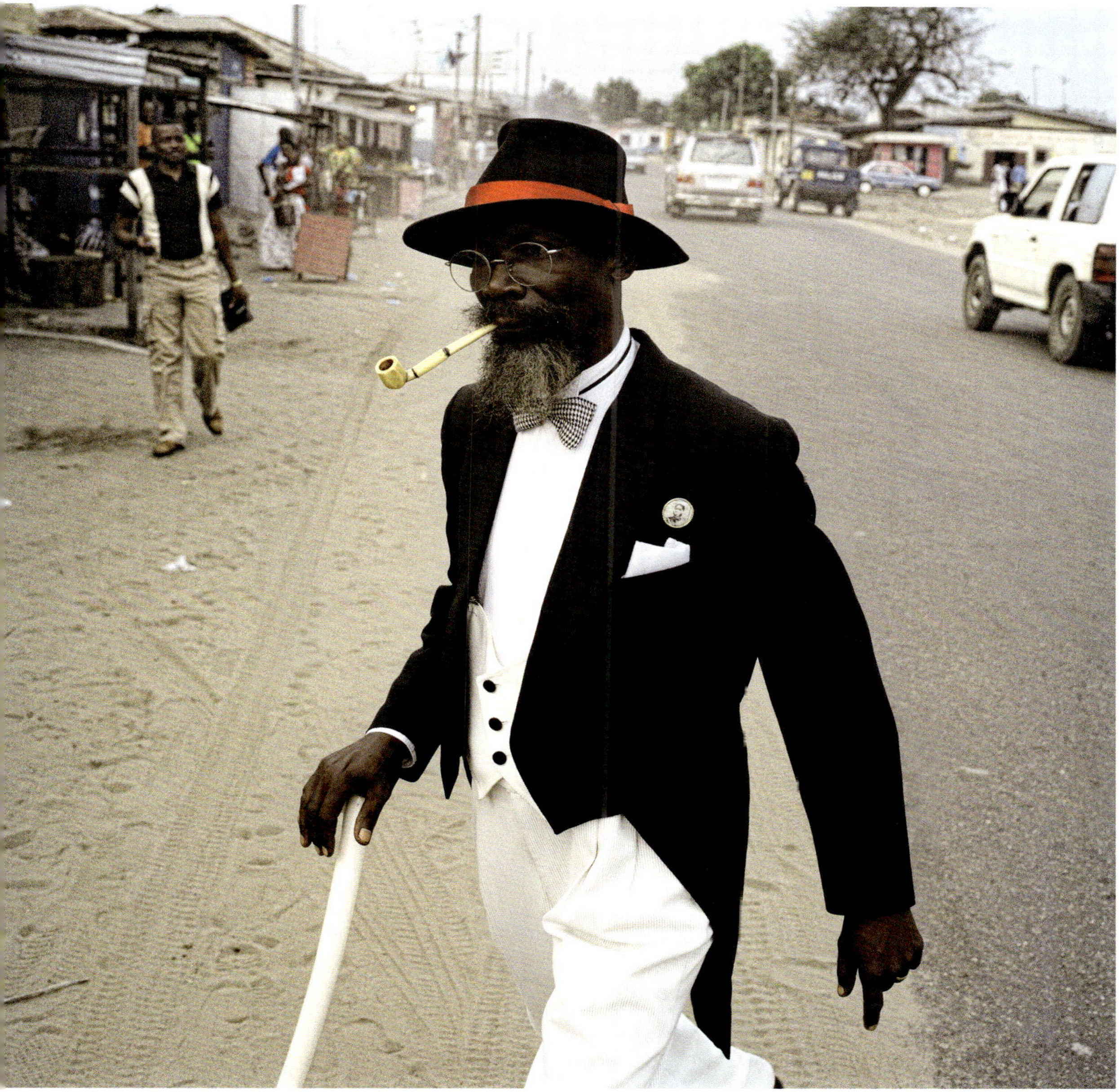

rancesco Giusti, *BONGA BONGA – Republic of the Congo – Pointe-Noire,* aus der Serie / from the series *Sapologie*, 2009

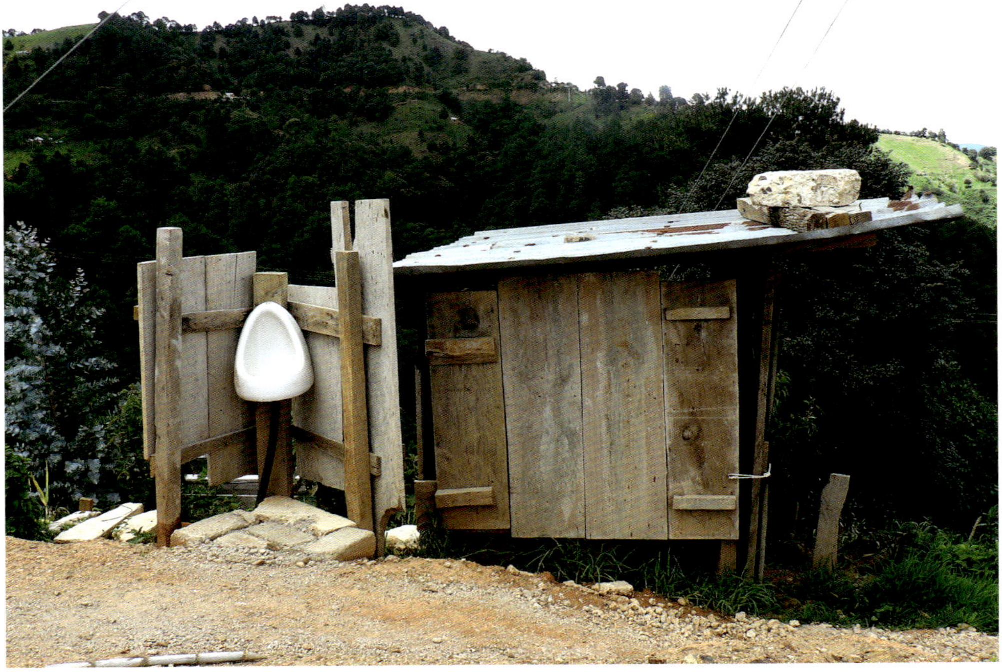

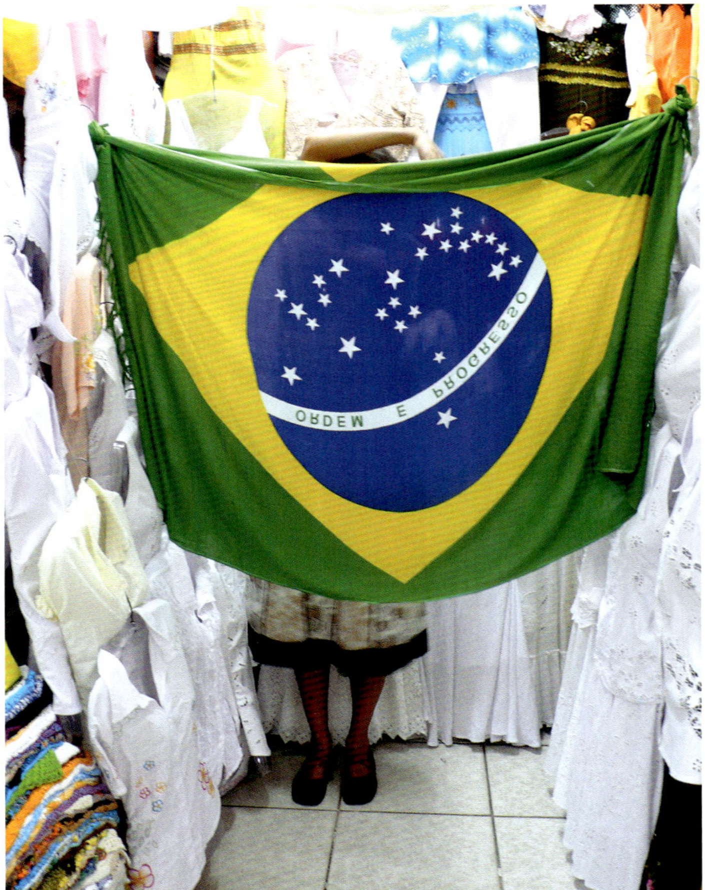

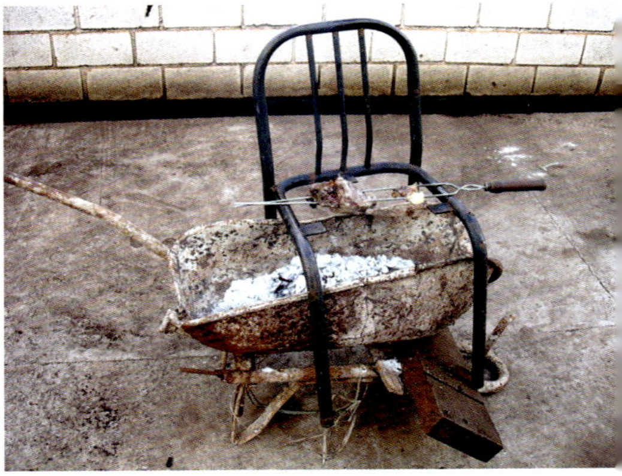

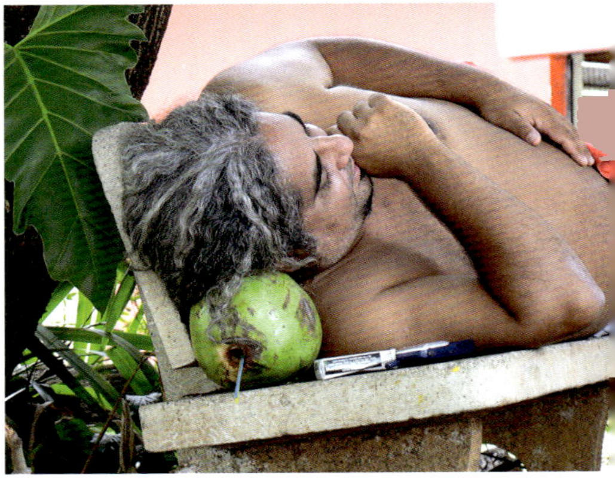

Links / left: Cao Guimarães, aus der Serie / from the series *Gambiarras*, 2000–2011

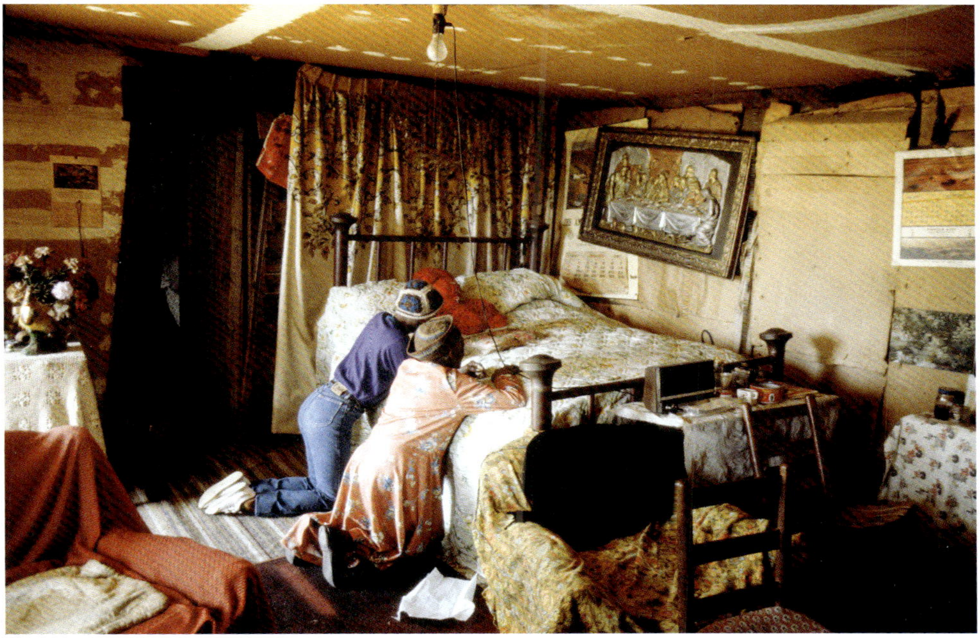

'Mary praying with her 92-year-old aunt. Perote, AL'
Jacob Holdt, aus / from *American Pictures*, 1970–1975

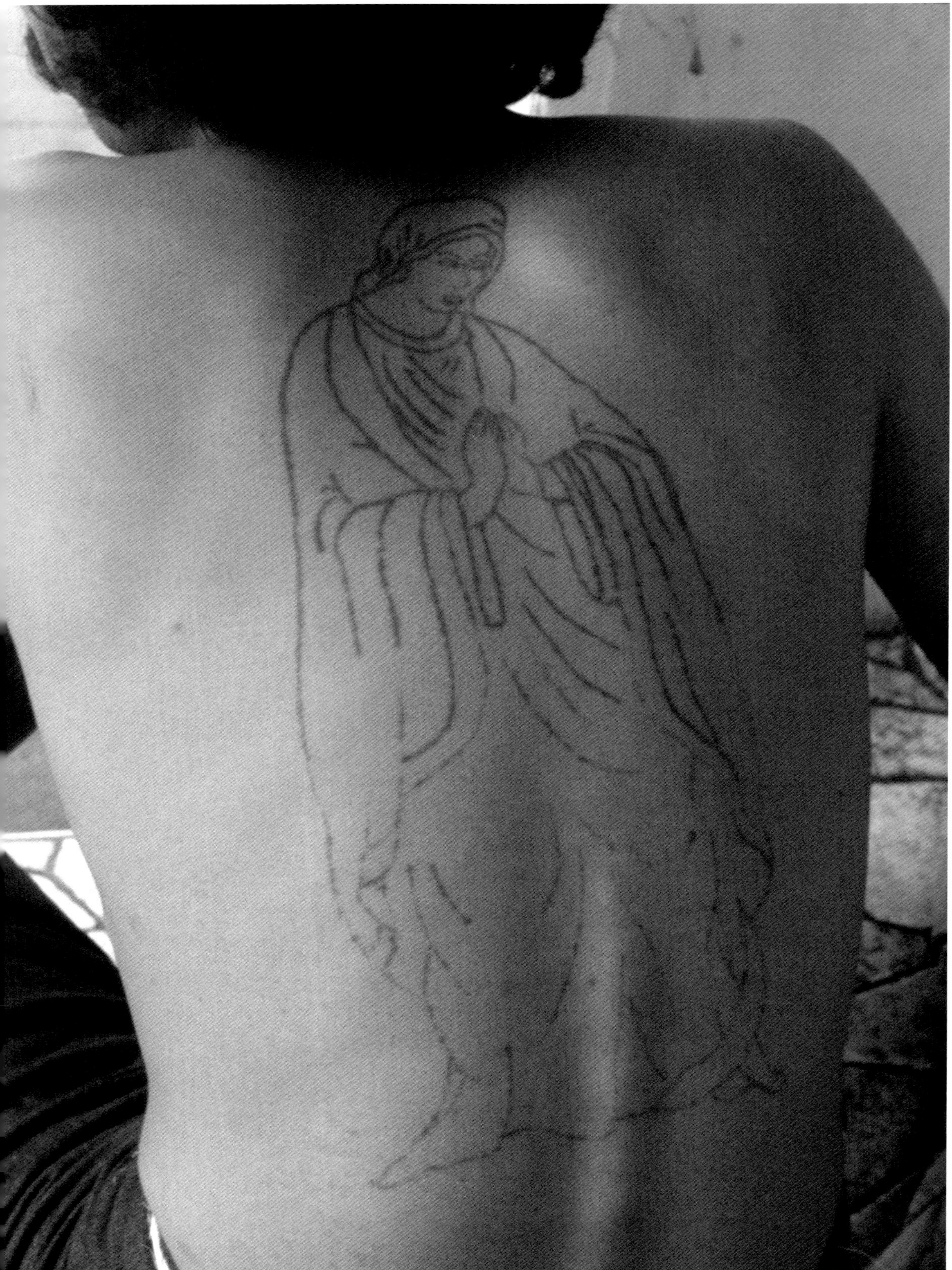

'Tatoo. New Orleans'
Jacob Holdt, aus / from *American Pictures*, 1970–1975

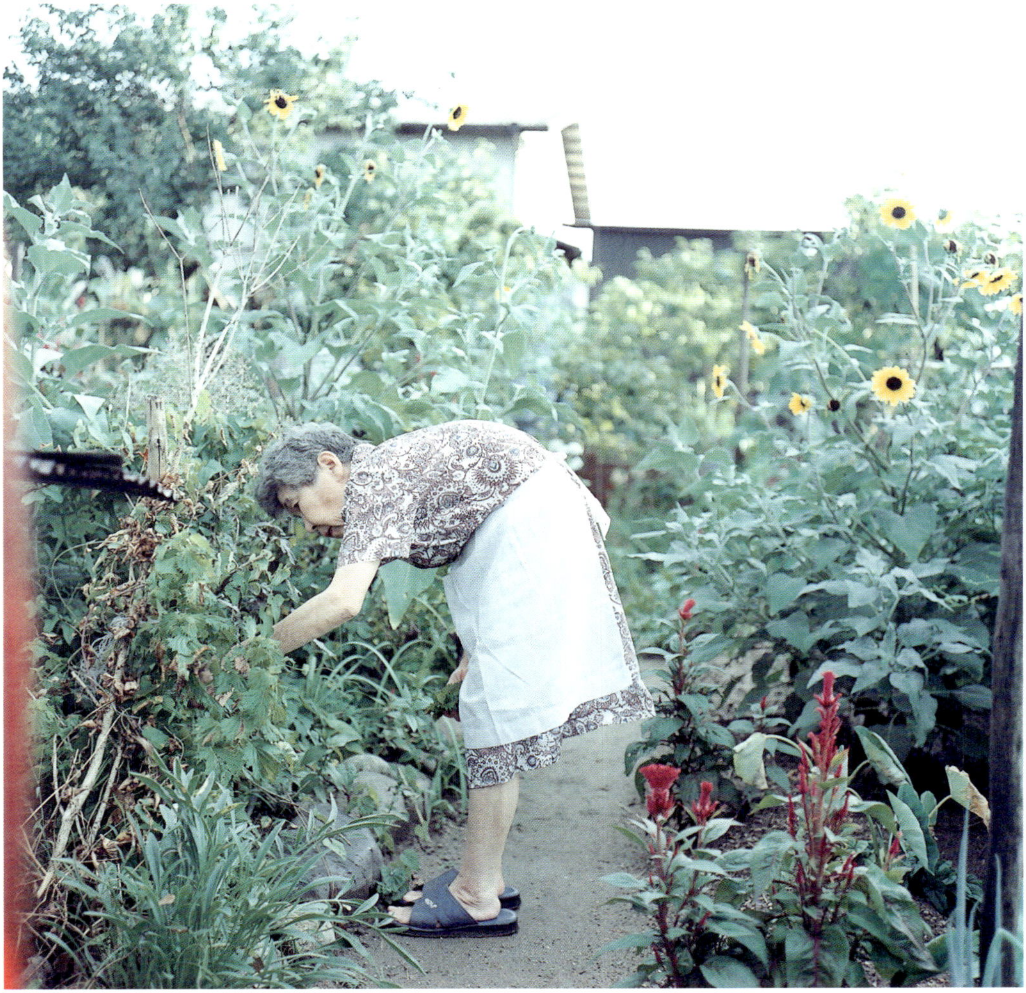

Rinko Kawauchi, *Untitled,* aus der Serie / from the series *Cui Cui*, 2005

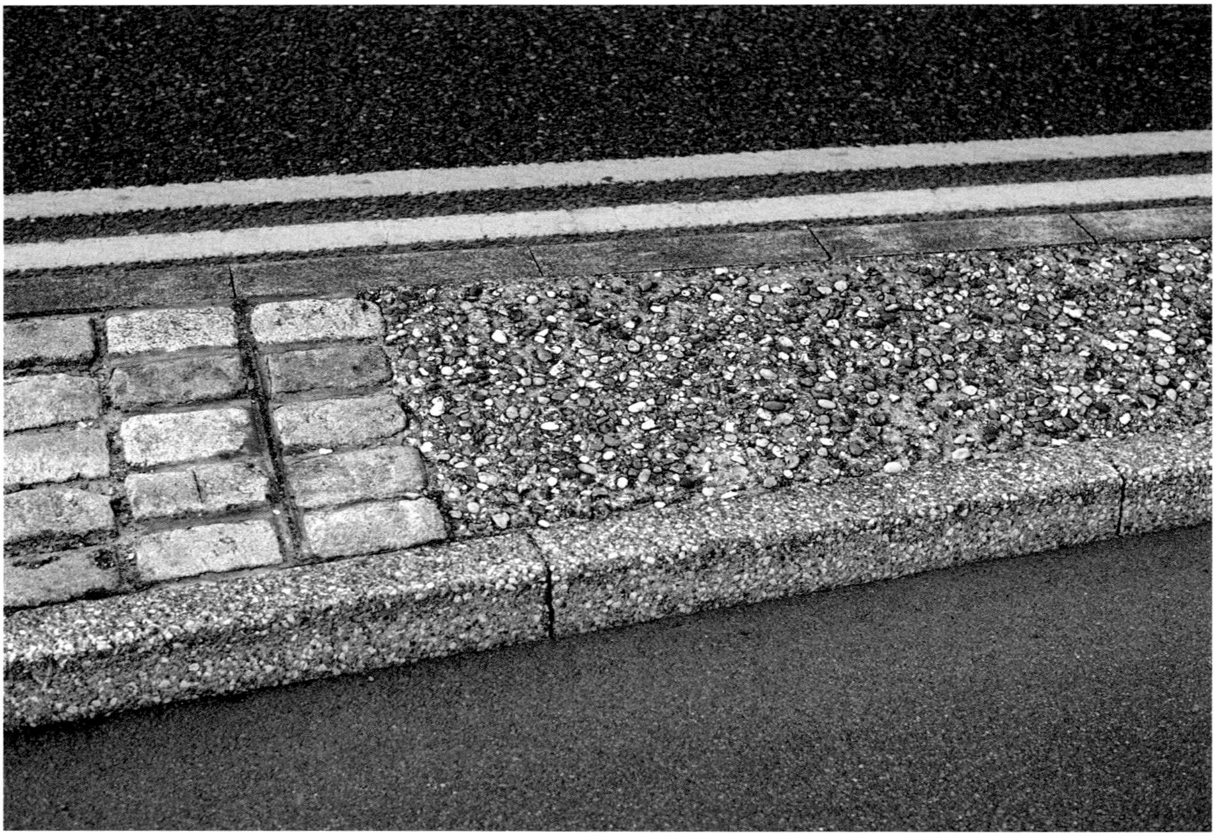

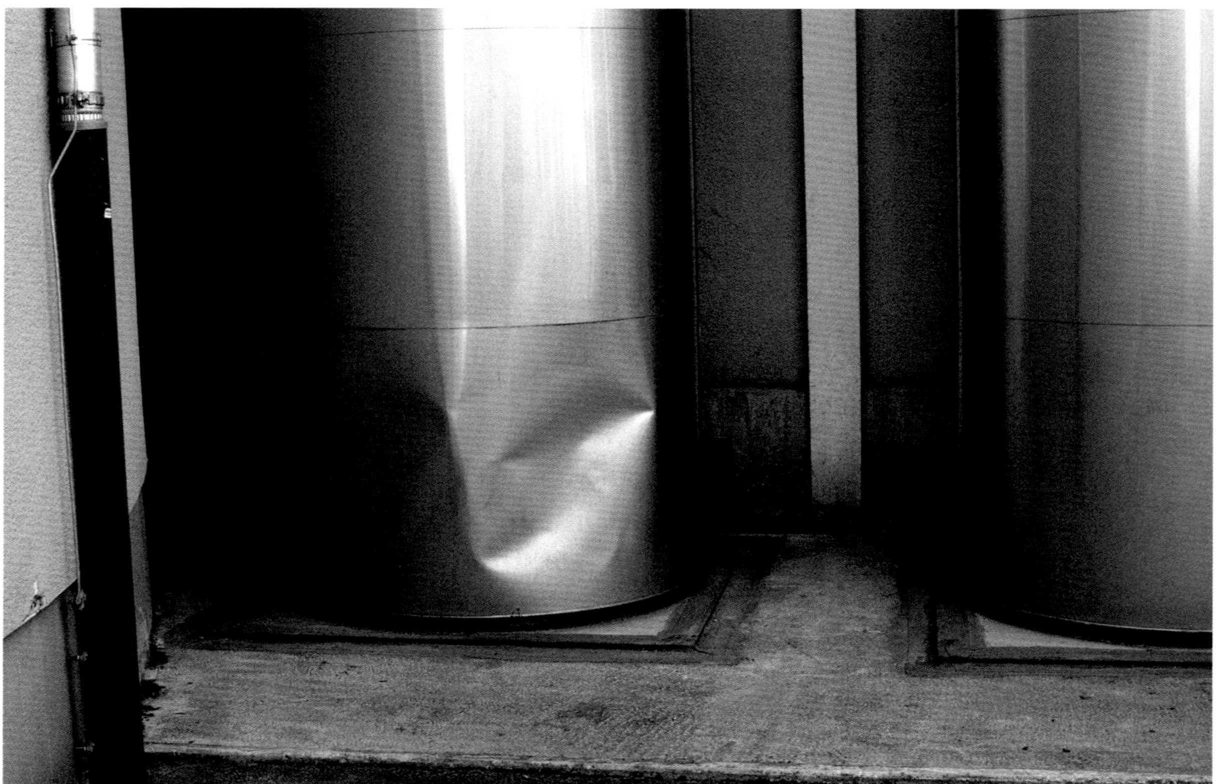

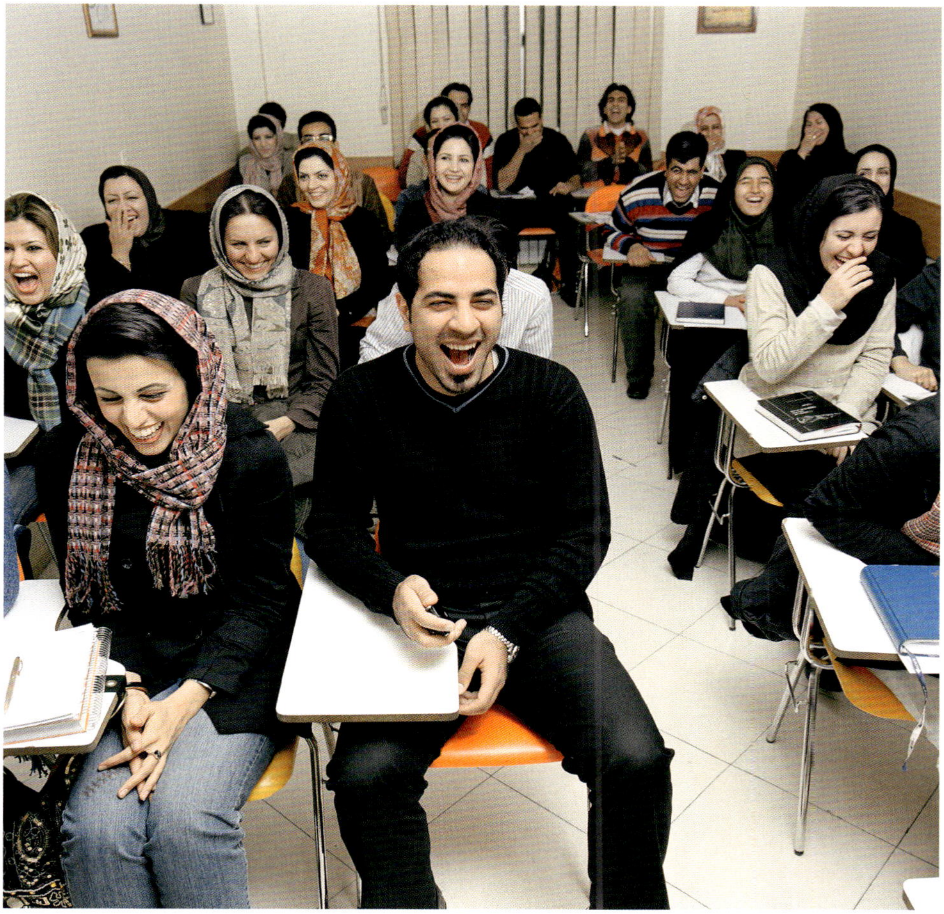

'The Tehran Laughing School during a practical exercise. Mr Mohtashemi, who directs the school, believes that the physical act of laughing has positive effects on people's well-being and self confidence. In these classes, Mohtashemi first guides his students through laughing exercises, followed by lectures modeled on American self-help master, Anthony Robbins. Students pay $200 a year to attend his courses.'

Paolo Woods, aus der Serie / from the series *Walk on my Eyes*, 2004–2009 (veröffentlicht / released 2010)

Links / left: Tris Vonna-Michell, Quellenmaterial aus / source material from *endless tapes*, 2011

Sc

Presen

lo

tations

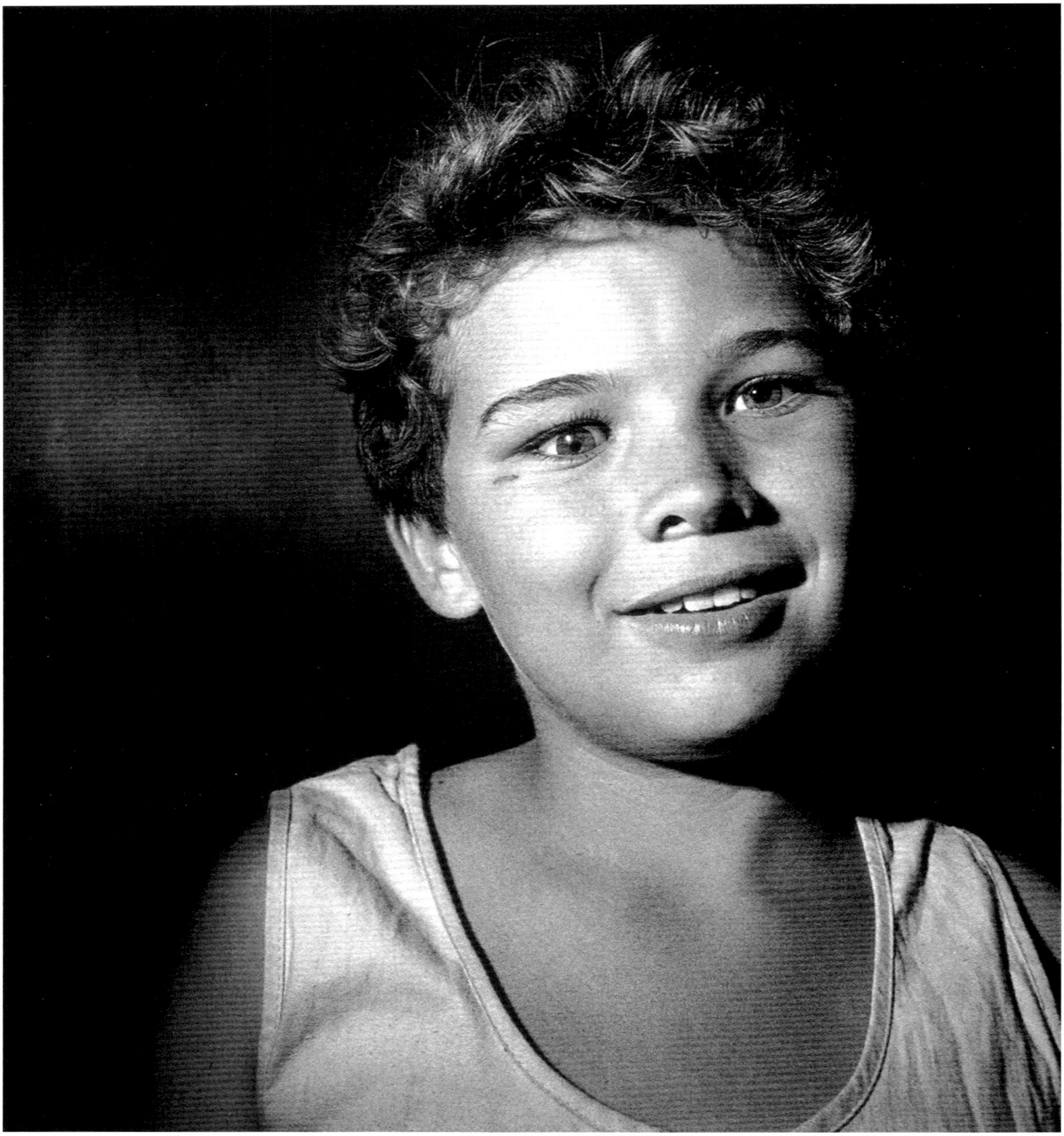

Roger Ballen, *Teenager with glass eye, Western Transvaal*, 1994, aus der Serie / from the series *Outland* (Sammlung Prinzhorn, Heidelberg)

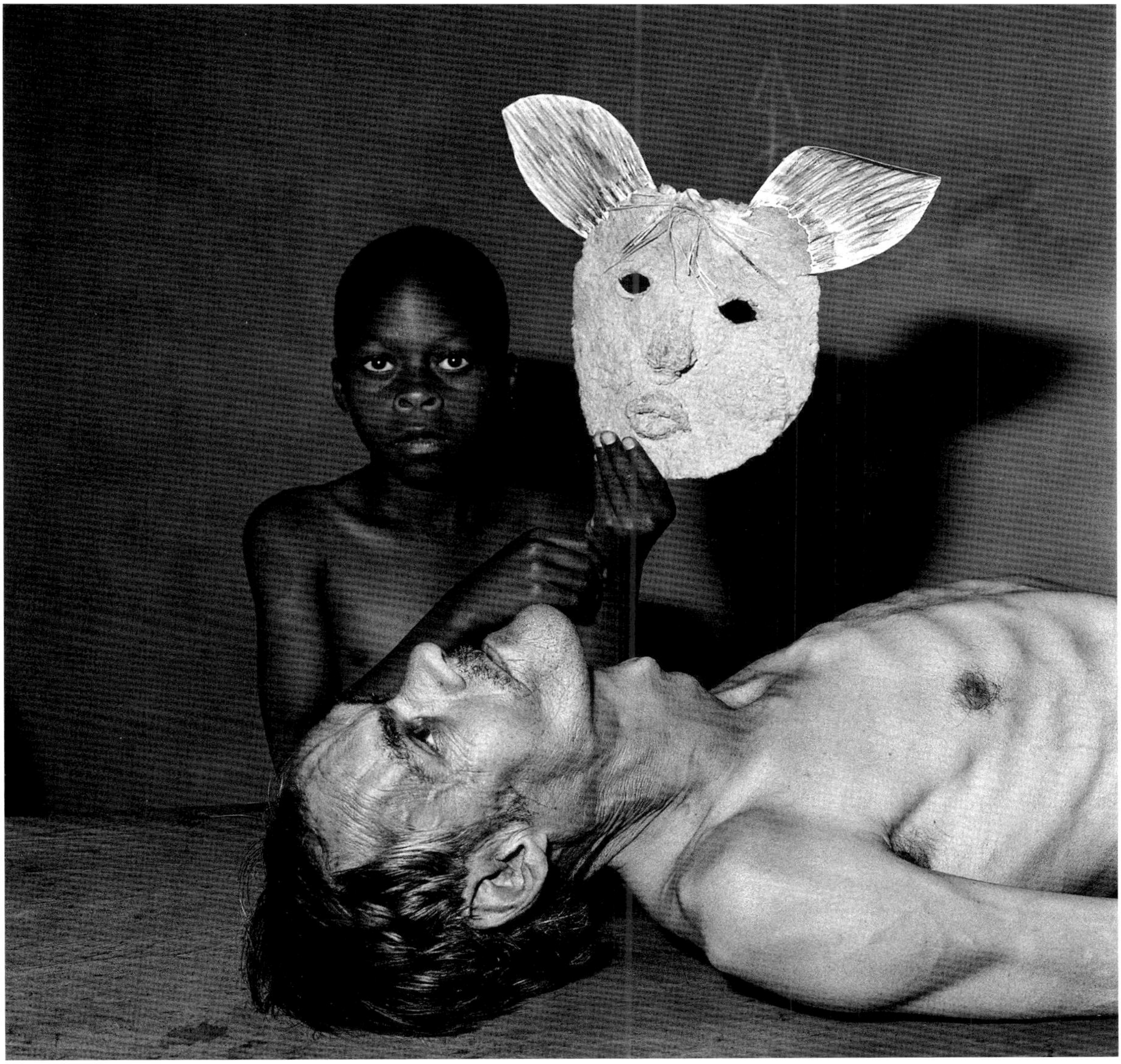

Roger Ballen, *Tommy Samson and a mask*, 2000, aus der Serie / from the series *Outland* (Sammlung Prinzhorn, Heidelberg)

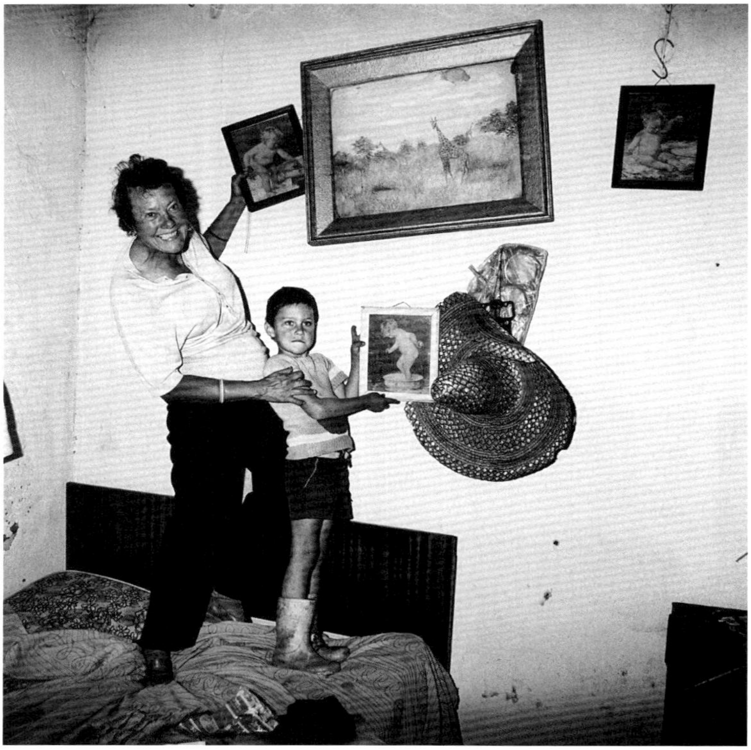

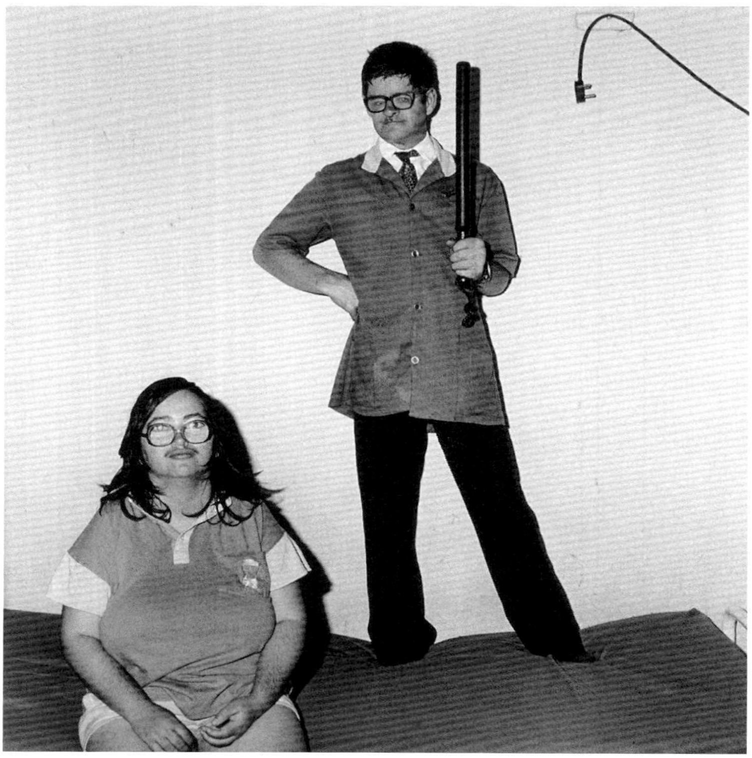

Roger Ballen, *Diamond digger and son standing on bed, Western Transvaal*, 1987 und / and Roger Ballen, *Security guard and girlfriend*, 1997, aus der Serie / from the series Outland (Sammlung Prinzhorn, Heidelberg)

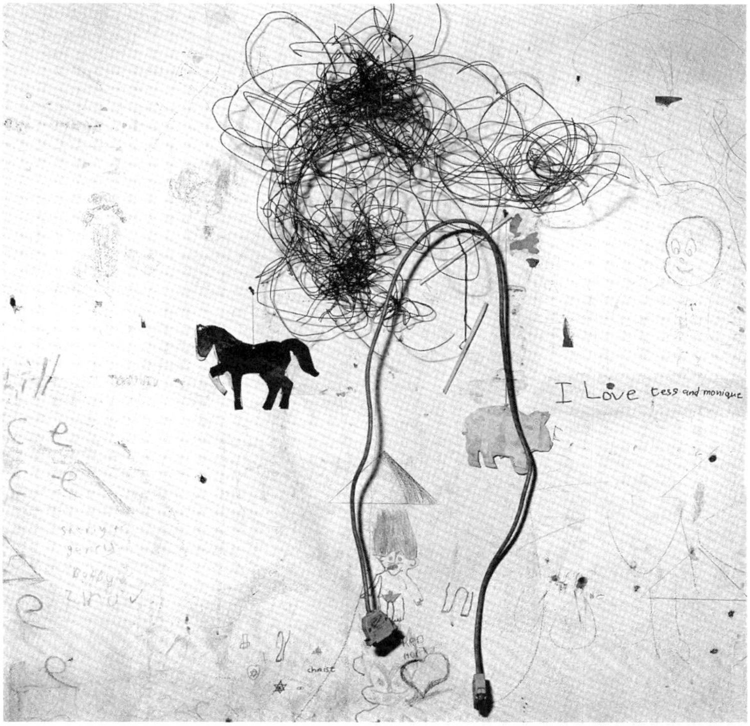

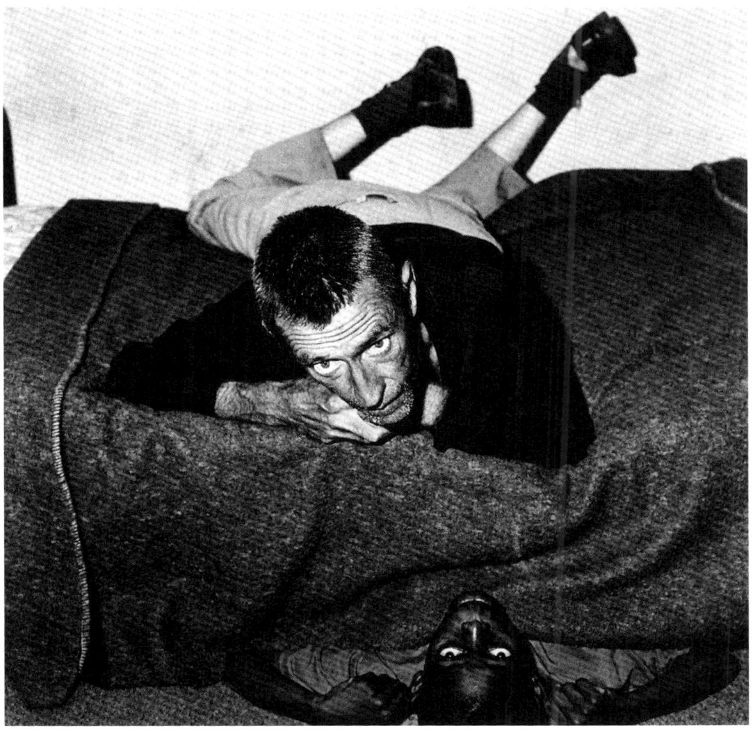

Roger Ballen, *Children's Bedroom Wall*, 2000 und / and Roger Ballen, *Elias coming from under John's Bed*, 1999, aus der Serie / from the series (Sammlung Prinzhorn, Heidelberg)

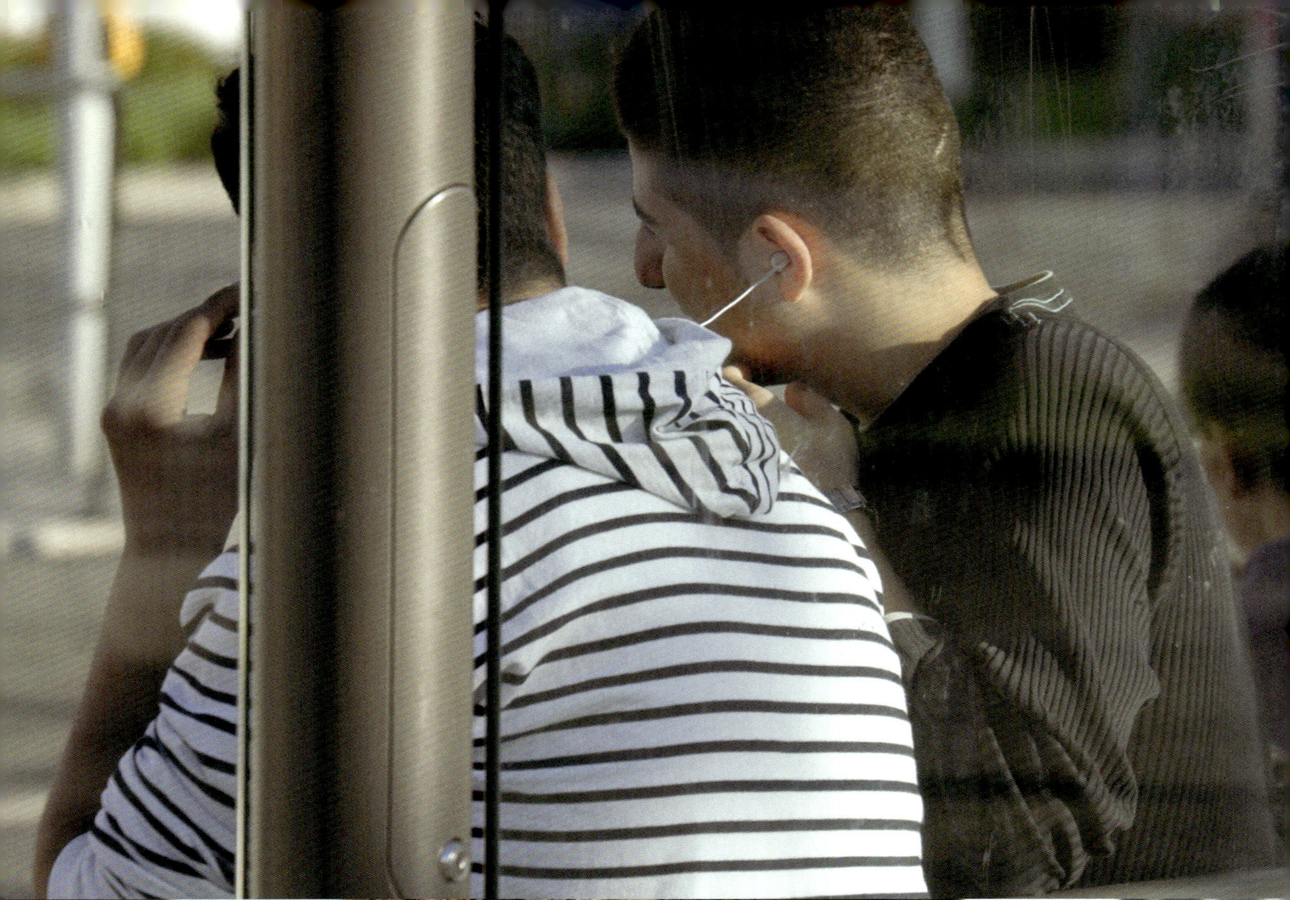

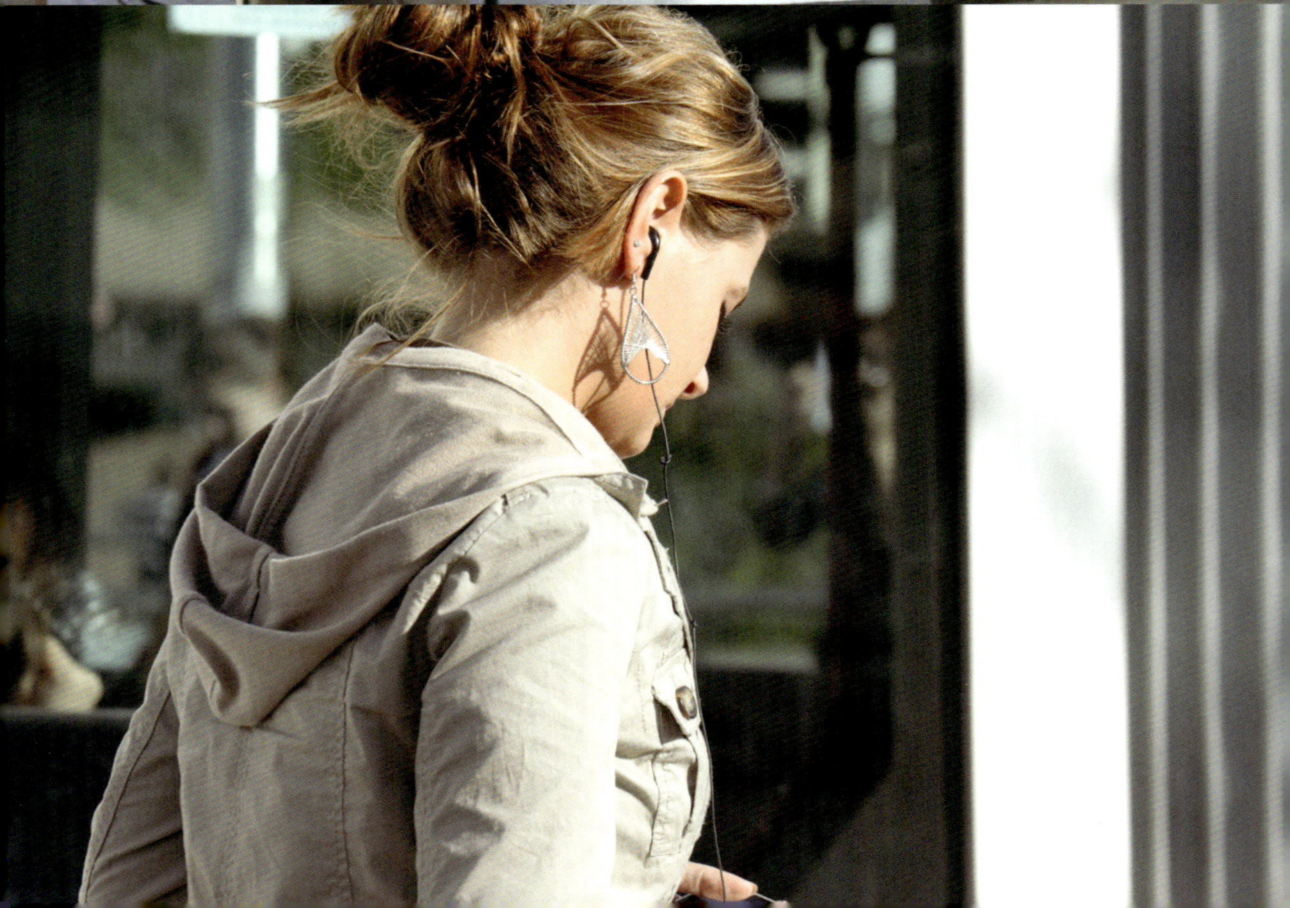

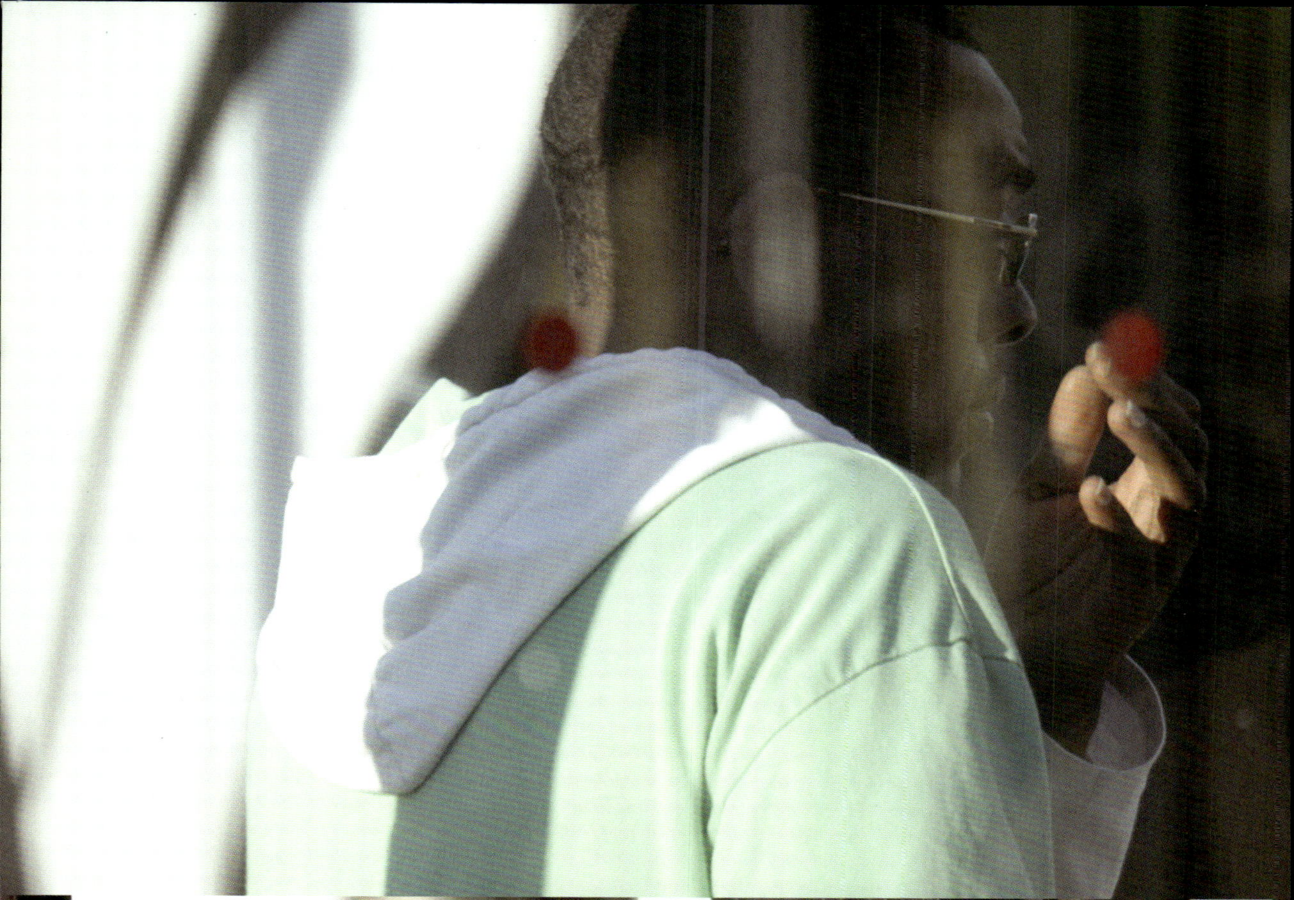

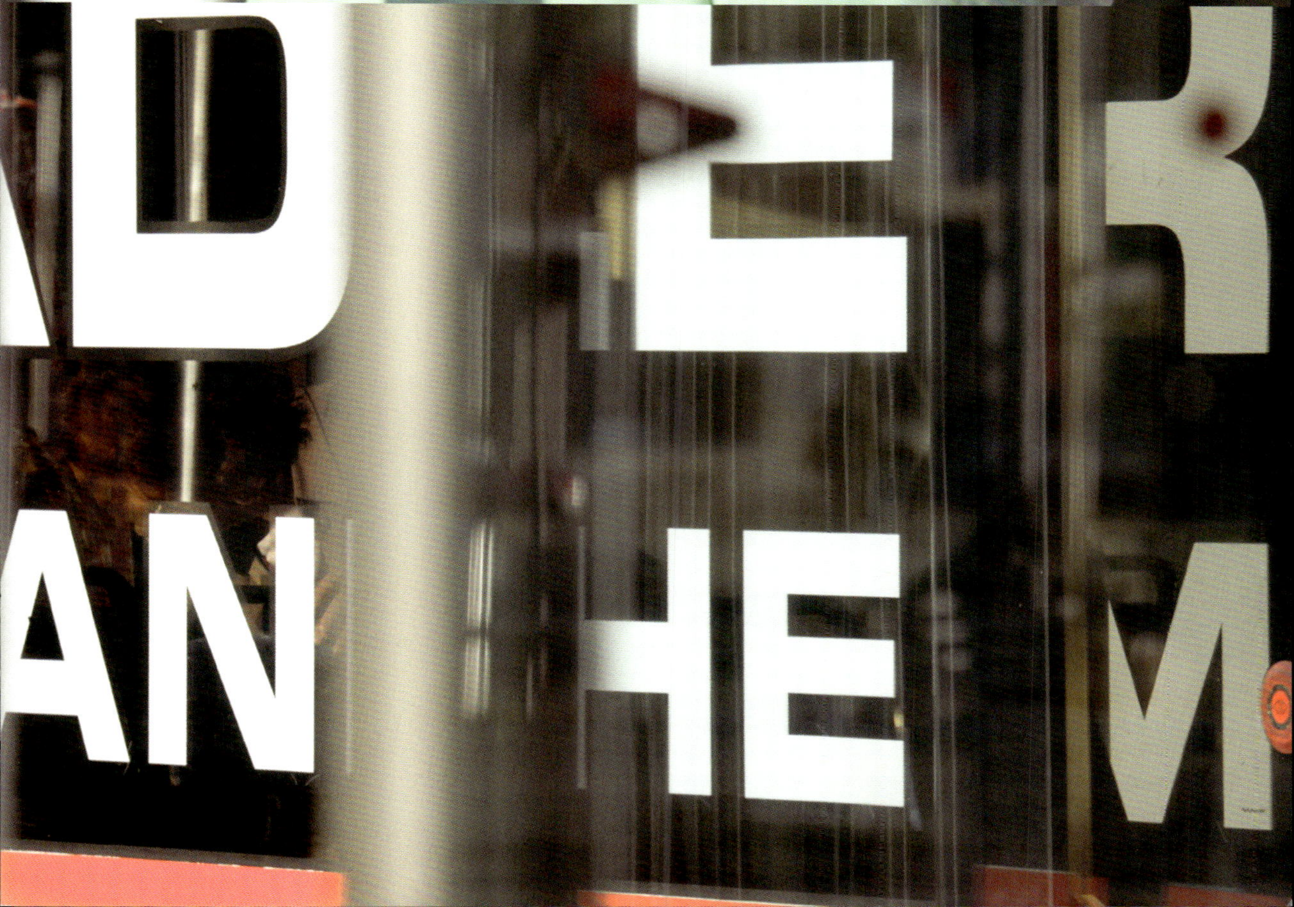

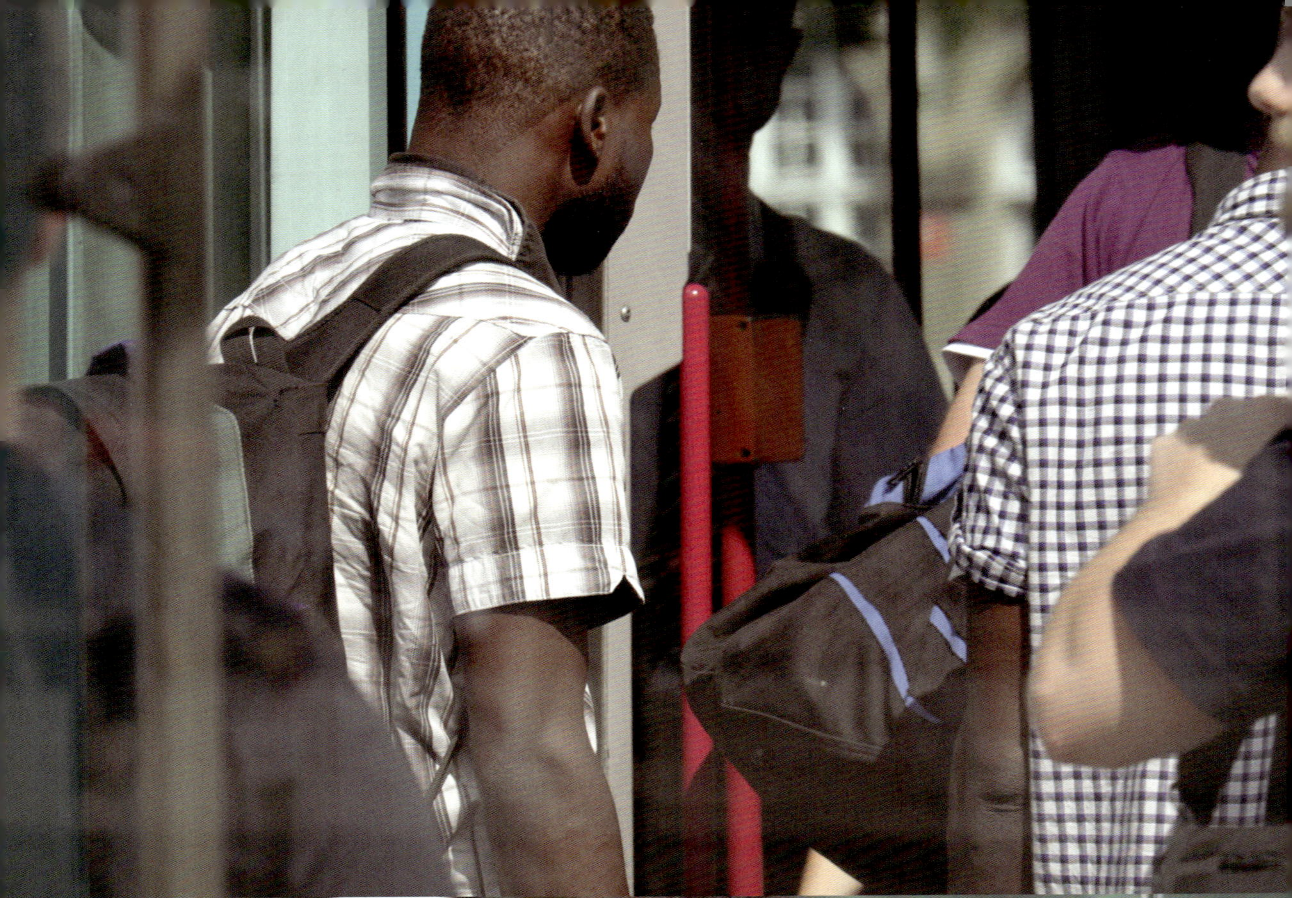

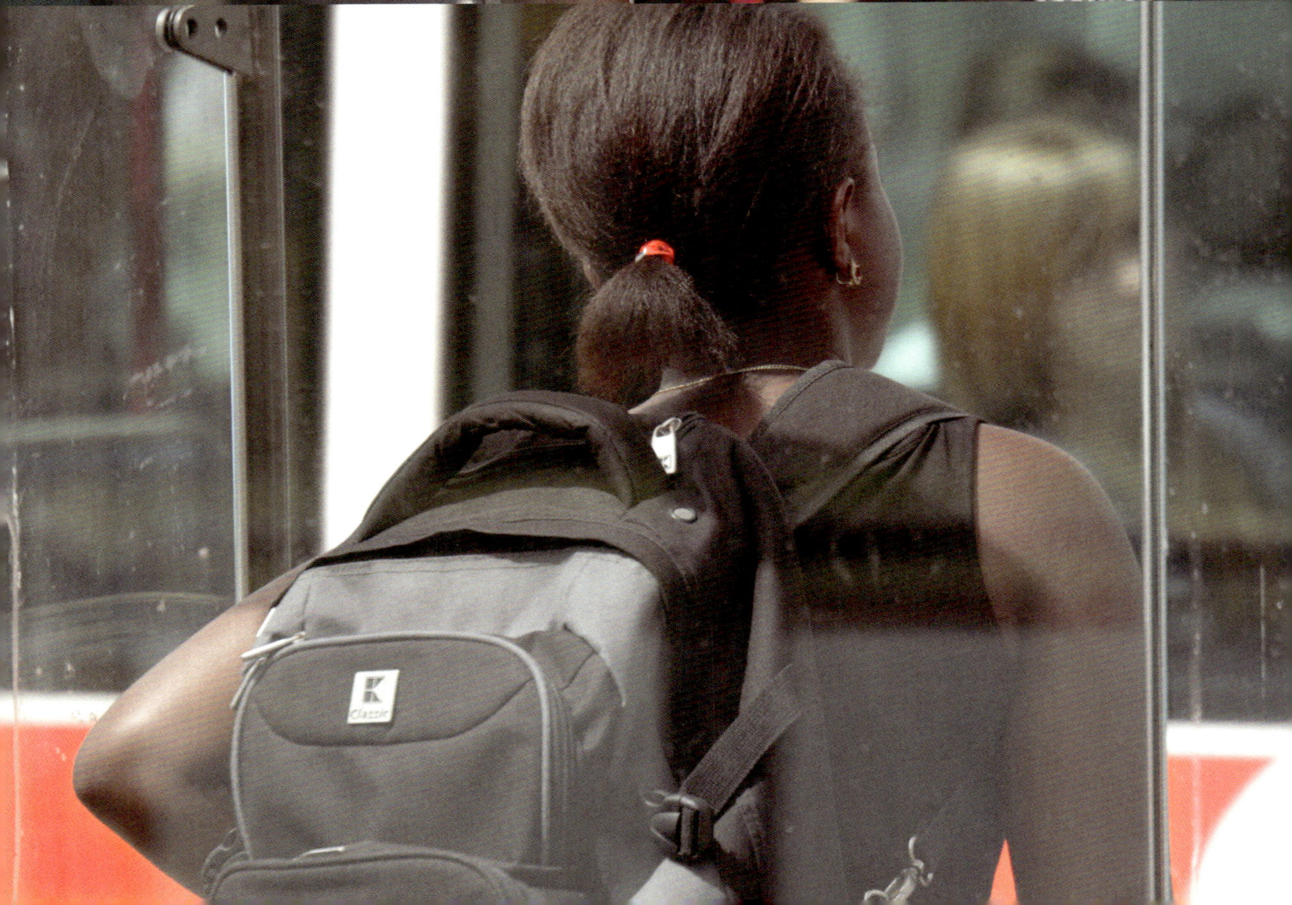
K
Classic

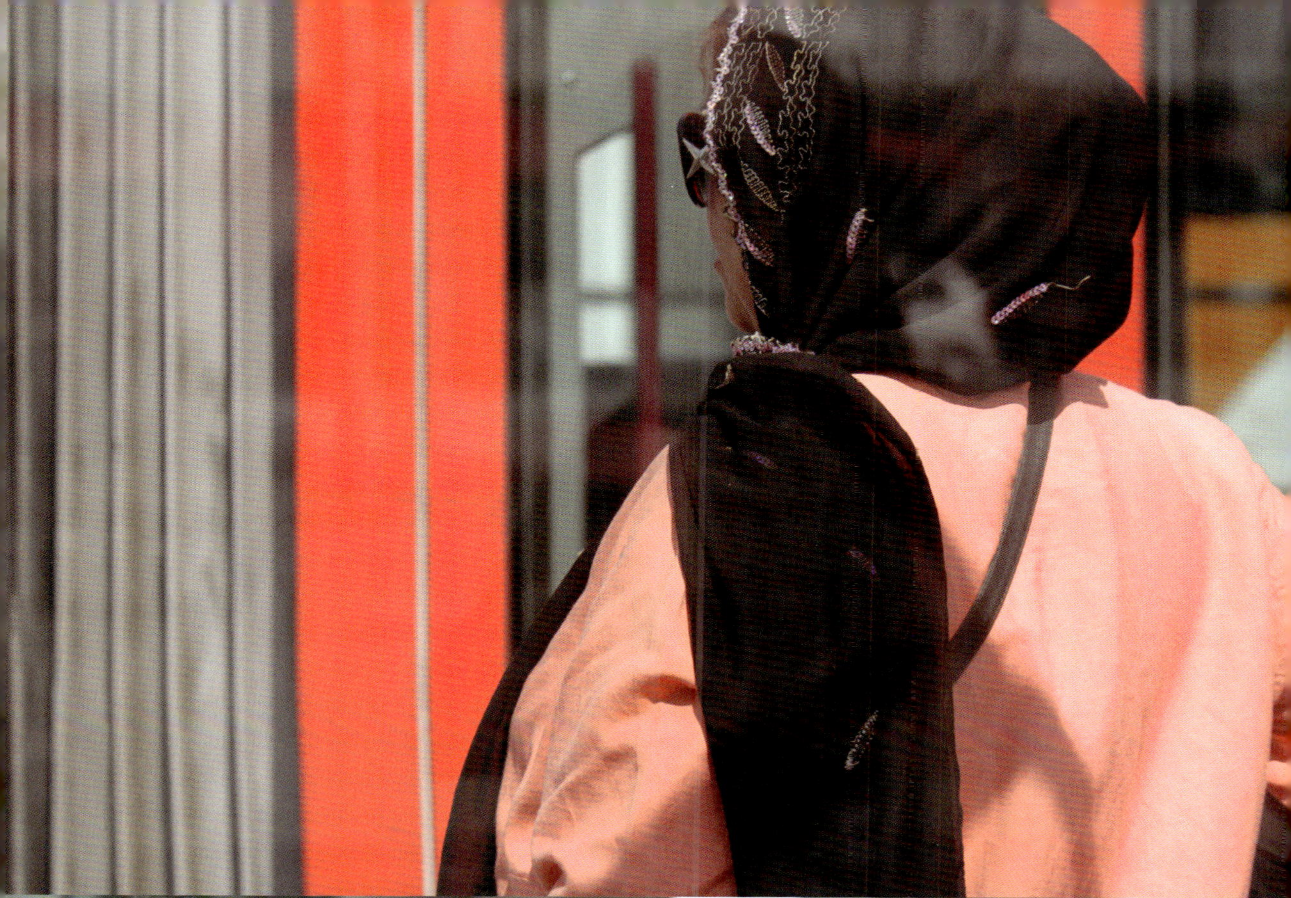

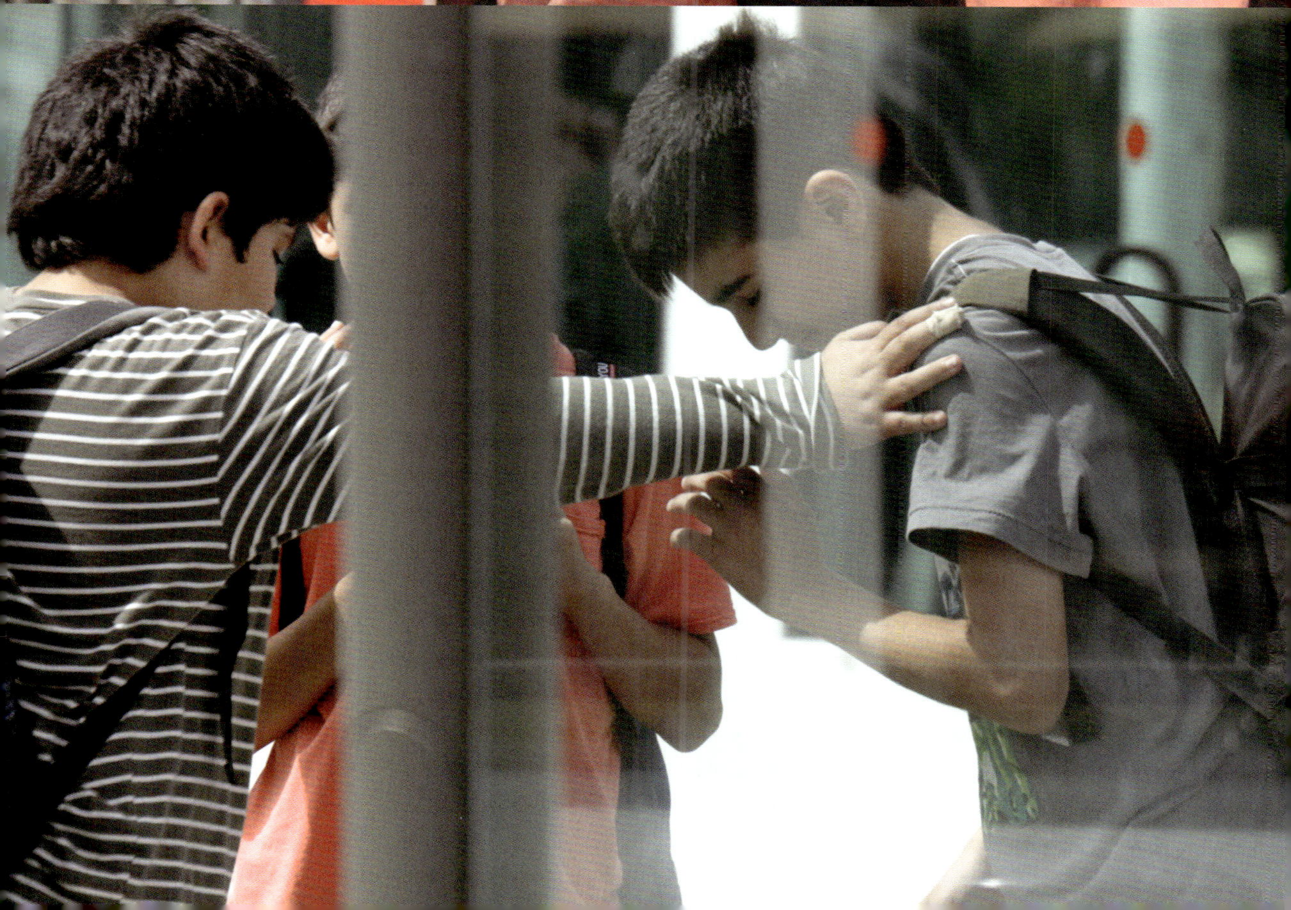

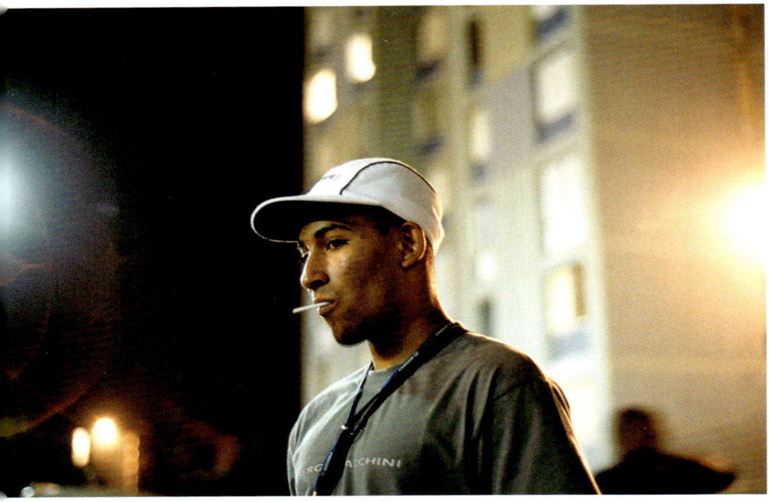

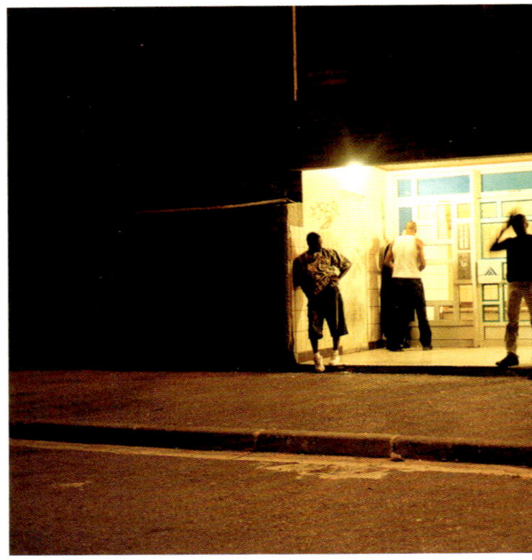

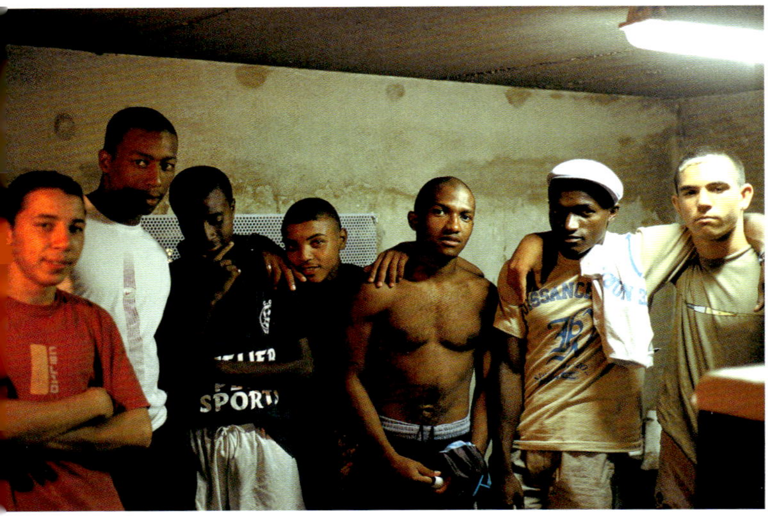

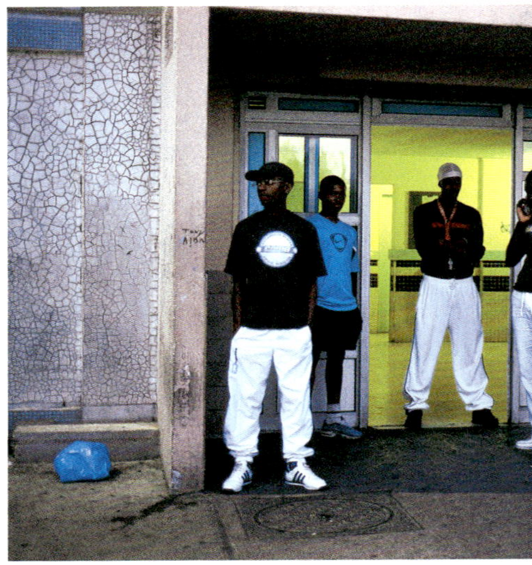

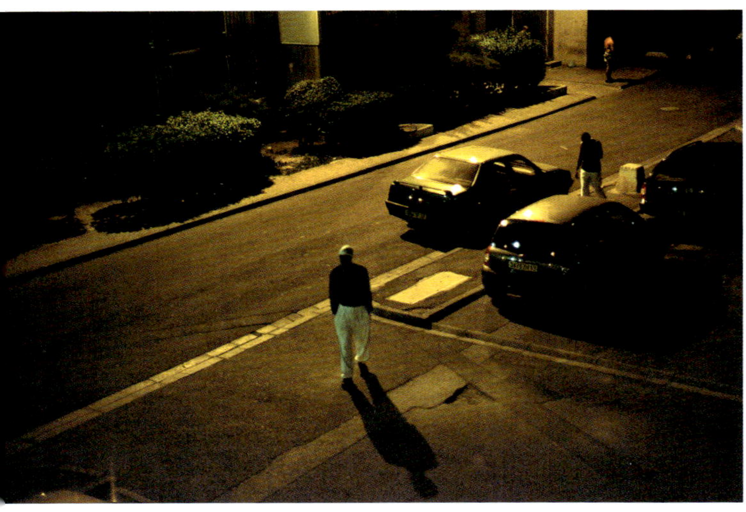

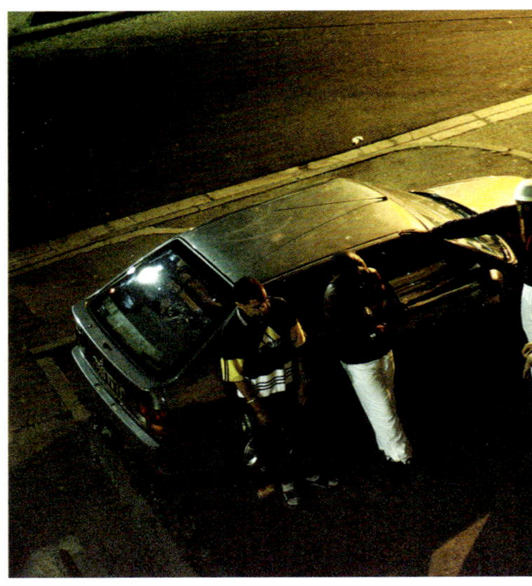

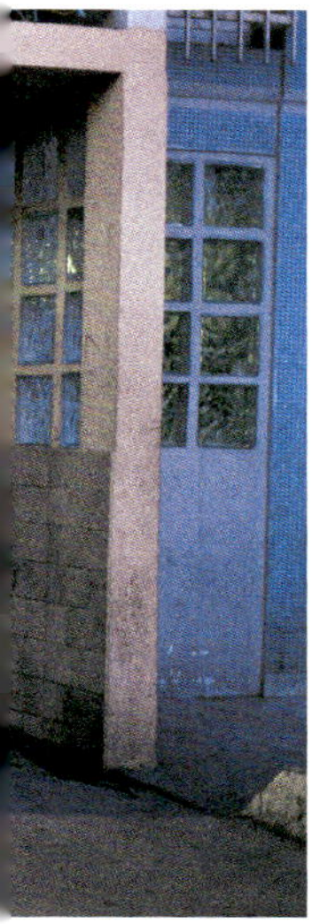

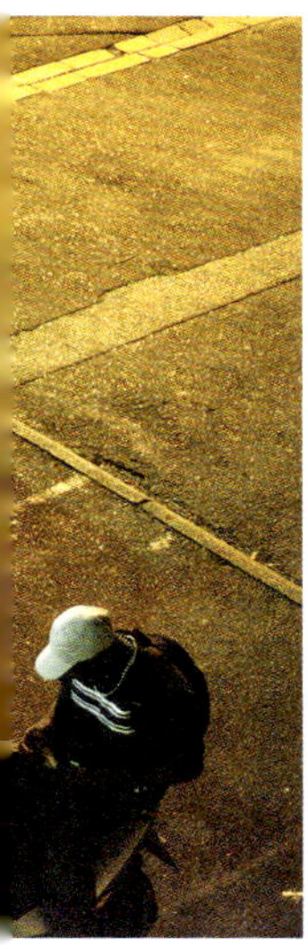

Vorige Seiten / previous pages:
Beat Streuli, Arbeitsmaterial / Working materials *Alter Messplatz Mannheim 07–11*, 2011 (Alter Messplatz, Mannheim)

Links / left: Tobias Zielony, *Abdilla*; *Entrée-1*; *Groupe 7; Entrée-2; Promeneur; Renault 19, Quartiers Nord,* 2003 (halle02 / Kunsthalle Heidelberg)

Grußwort

Für das Fotofestival Mannheim_Ludwigshafen_Heidelberg ziehen 3 Städte, 7 renommierte Ausstellungshäuser: die Kunsthalle und ZEPHYR der Reiss-Engelhorn-Museen in Mannheim, das Wilhelm-Hack-Museum und der Kunstverein in Ludwigshafen sowie der Kunstverein, die Sammlung Prinzhorn und die halle02 in Heidelberg mit dem Festivalveranstalter gemeinsam an einem Strang, um Deutschlands größtes kuratiertes Fotofestival zu realisieren.

Das Fotofestival Mannheim_Ludwigshafen_Heidelberg verbindet unsere 3 Städte und ihre renommierten Ausstellungshäuser auf vorbildliche Art und Weise und trägt auf kultureller Ebene zum Zusammenwachsen und -wirken der Metropolregion Rhein-Neckar bei. Wir sind gemeinsam der Überzeugung, dass das Fotofestival beispielgebend dafür ist, wie imagefördernd und identitätsstiftend sinnvolle Kooperationen benachbarter Städte für eine Region sein können.

Wir freuen uns die bereits 4. Ausgabe des Fotofestivals Mannheim_Ludwigshafen_Heidelberg *gemeinsam* präsentieren zu können.

Oberbürgermeister der Stadt Mannheim, Dr. Peter Kurz
Oberbürgermeisterin der Stadt Ludwigshafen am Rhein, Dr. Eva Lohse
Oberbürgermeister der Stadt Heidelberg, Dr. Eckart Würzner

Greetings

For the Fotofestival Mannheim_Ludwigshafen_Heidelberg, 3 cities and 7 renowned exhibition spaces are joining forces with the festival organizers to mount Germany's biggest curated photography festival: the Kunsthalle and ZEPHYR of the Reiss-Engelhorn-Museen Mannheim, the Wilhelm-Hack-Museum and Kunstverein in Ludwigshafen, and the Kunstverein, Sammlung Prinzhorn and halle02 / Kunsthalle Heidelberg in Heidelberg.

The Fotofestival Mannheim_Ludwigshafen_Heidelberg brings together our 3 cities and its preeminent exhibition venues in an exemplary manner in order to foster greater cohesiveness and concerted efforts at a cultural level in the Rhine-Neckar metropolitan region.

We are convinced that the Fotofestival constitutes a role model for how meaningful cooperative endeavors undertaken by neighboring cities can promote a region's image and lend it a greater sense of identity.

We are looking forward to presenting the fourth instalment of the Fotofestival Mannheim_Ludwigshafen_Heidelberg, *together*.

Lord Mayor of the City of Mannheim, Dr. Peter Kurz
Lady Mayor of the City of Ludwigshafen am Rhein, Dr. Eva Lohse
Lord Mayor of the City of Heidelberg, Dr. Eckart Würzner

Dank

Fotografie ist zu einer globalen Sprache geworden, die Menschen unabhängig von Alter oder kultureller Zugehörigkeit praktizieren und verstehen können. In dieser grundsätzlich lesbaren Sprache liegt aber auch ihre Herausforderung: Ihre Bedeutung kann sich je nach Standpunkt und Kontext des Betrachters verschieben.

Als Veranstalter des Fotofestivals Mannheim_Ludwigshafen_Heidelberg ist es uns ein Anliegen, Fotografie in Bedeutungszusammenhänge zu bringen, die für die Besucher des Festivals einen Mehrwert generieren. Unser internationales Festival hat den Anspruch, gewohnte Denk- und Sehmuster zu hinterfragen. Deshalb verfolgt das Fotofestival Mannheim_Ludwigshafen_Heidelberg ein klares Ausstellungskonzept: Wir laden wechselnde Kuratoren dazu ein, in den Ausstellungen spezifische Themen aus unterschiedlichen Perspektiven zu diskutieren.

Unser internationales Kuratorinnenteam, bestehend aus Katerina Gregos (GR / BE) und Solvej Helweg Ovesen (DK / DE), präsentiert mit dem Festivaltitel *The Eye is a Lonely Hunter: Images of Humankind* ein facettenreiches Bild der Menschheit in all der Vielfältigkeit unserer Zeit und führt in den Ausstellungen einen Diskurs über die Frage, wie Fotografie anthropologisches Wissen im heutigen Zeitalter vermitteln kann.

Hinter dem Fotofestival steht ein wachsendes, kulturelles Netzwerk, das die 3 Städte und ihre Kunstinstitutionen miteinander verbindet, und für 8 Wochen einen städte-übergreifenden Dialog entstehen lässt. Wir danken den 7 beteiligten Festivalinstitutionen sehr herzlich für wesentliche Impulse und ihre größtmögliche Unterstützung. Den Direktorinnen und Direktoren Barbara Auer, Wolfram Glatz, Johan Holten, Ulrike Lorenz, Thomas Röske, Susana Saez, Reinhard Spieler und Alfried Wieczorek gilt unser Dank. Für ihre unermüdliche Hilfe bei der Umsetzung möchten wir den Teams der Häuser danken: Thomas Köllhofer, Selini Andres, Petra Neff, Birgit Scheidecker und Lili Marocsik von der Kunsthalle Mannheim, Thomas Schirmböck, Marianne Aselmeier und Silvia Rückert von ZEPHYR der Reiss-Engelhorn-Museen Mannheim, Nina Gülicher, Udo Baur und Herbert Nolden vom Wilhelm-Hack-Museum, Stefanie Schubert vom Kunstverein Ludwigshafen, Friederike Schröder und Katja Arnold vom Heidelberger Kunstverein, Torsten Kappenberg und Gabi Tschudi von der Sammlung Prinzhorn, sowie Wolfram Glatz, Felix Grädler und ihrem Team der halle02 / Kunsthalle Heidelberg.

Die Ausstellungen wurden auf wie immer höchst professionelle Weise installiert. Wir danken den Hängeteams, die jedes Ausstellungssegment so aussehen lassen, wie es in der Organisation konzipiert wurde: Alexander Horn und André Wischnewski, Frank Hofacker, Markus Brehm und Arsen Kontus, Yvonne Vogel und Andrzej Naglowsky, Torsten Kappenberg sowie Michel Volkmer.

Durch die Unterstützung der beteiligten Häuser können wir ein umfangreiches Rahmenprogramm anbieten. Für kreative Ideen und interessante Veranstaltungen danken wir Dorothee Höfert, Theresia Kiefer, Stefanie Schubert und Friederike Schröder.

Nur mithilfe überzeugter Kooperationen kann Kultur auch in Zeiten der knappen Kulturetats zu einem lebendigen Austausch werden. All unseren Sponsoren, Förderern und Kooperationspartnern sind wir ebenfalls zu größtem Dank verpflichtet. Wir danken Klaus Philipp Seif, Friederike Reutter und Klaus Gasteiger von der BASF SE, Georg Müller und Christian Land von der MVV Energie AG, Thomas Fichtl und Claudia Cischek von der Heidelberger Druckmaschinen AG, Edmund Elsen und Katharina Bornkessel von der Stiftung Rheinland-Pfalz für Kultur, Peter Frankenberg und Hartwig Trinkaus von der Heinrich-Vetter-Stiftung, Pietro Soldini, Marianne Burki und Jelena Delic von Pro Helvetia, Thomas Golk von der Japan

Foundation, Jutta Ulmer-Straub und Harald Gall vom Ministerium für Wissenschaftliche Forschung und Kunst Baden-Württemberg, Friedolf Schiek vom Institut für Auslandsbeziehungen, Gitta Luiten, Marijn Veenhuijzen und Coby Reitsma von der Mondriaan Stichting, Rikke Björnböl von der Danish Arts Agency, Martin Kuon und Klaudia Marschner der Stiftungen Landesbank Baden-Württemberg, Kaspar von Mellenthin, Felix Zipse und Deborah Klein von myphotobook, Anne-Marie Croes und Hilde Lievens vom Flämischen Ministerium für Kultur, Jugend, Sport, Medien und Denkmalschutz, Petra Engesser und Martina Kopf der Verkehrsverbund Rhein-Neckar GmbH, Susann Becker und Anja Öffler von der Rhein-Neckar-Verkehr GmbH, Angelika Grabaum-Pertsch von der Daimler AG, Anne Charlotte Hauen vom Office for Contemporary Art Norway, Wolfgang Bielmeier und Stephanie Gläßer der GBG-Mannheimer Wohnungsbaugesellschaft mbH und Joachim Stumpp vom Klinikum Ludwigshafen. Michael Sieber und Regina Pfriem haben uns viele Türen geöffnet und wichtige Kontakte vermittelt.

Für anregenden Dialog und Austausch danken wir unseren Kooperationspartnern Gabriele Oßwald, Wolfgang Sautermeister und Tilo Schwarz von zeitraumexit e.V., Emeline Dufrennoy und Cécile Espitallier von La Chambre, Joachim Reck und Martin Klemmer von der EIDOTECH GmbH, Ditmar Schädel und Klaus Czerwinski von der Deutschen Gesellschaft für Photographie sowie Gerhard Rossbach und Corinna Hipp vom dpunkt Verlag. Für die Realisierung des Außenprojektes auf dem Alten Messplatz in Mannheim gilt unser ausgesprochener Dank Peter Bender von motorlab architekten. Ein besonderer Dank gilt auch unserer Grafikagentur raum mannheim mit Frank Hoffmann, der nicht nur das diesjährige Erscheinungsbild entwickelt, sondern auch die Ausstellungsgrafik konzipiert und umgesetzt hat.

Katerina Gregos und Solvej Helweg Ovesen haben großartige Ausstellungen mit hervorragenden Werken international renommierter Fotografinnen und Fotografen zusammengestellt. Ihre kuratorische Leistung sowie die hochrangigen Werke der am Festival beteiligten Fotografinnen und Fotografen geben dem Fotofestival Mannheim_Ludwigshafen_Heidelberg 2011 sein Profil und seinen unverwechselbaren Charakter. Ihnen gilt unser größter Dank.

Ganz besonders hervorzuheben ist das außerordentliche Engagement der 3 Städte Mannheim, Ludwigshafen und Heidelberg, die auch in finanziell schwierigen Zeiten nicht nachgelassen haben, das Fotofestival zu fördern und zu unterstützen. Ohne das große Engagement der 3 Städte wäre die Ausrichtung dieses Festivals nicht möglich.

Wir freuen uns auf ein bereicherndes Fotofestival, bei dem auch wir Veranstalter immer wieder neu von den vielschichtigen Ausdrucksweisen des fotografischen Mediums begeistert werden.

Der Vorstand des Fotofestivals Mannheim_Ludwigshafen_Heidelberg mit Dietrich Skibelski, Sabine Schirra, Hans-Martin Mumm und Michael Ebert sowie das Festivalteam mit Carolin Ellwanger, Sabine von Wussow und Heide Häusler

Acknowledgements

Photography has become a global language that people everywhere can speak and understand regardless of age or cultural affinity. But therein lies the challenge of this fundamentally legible language – the significance of any photograph depends on the point of view and the context of the beholder.

As the organisers of the Fotofestival Mannheim_Ludwigshafen_Heidelberg, we aim to place photography in meaningful contexts in order to enhance the experience of visitors to the festival. The purpose of our international festival is to question conventional modes of thinking and seeing. With this in mind, the Fotofestival Mannheim_Ludwigshafen_Heidelberg developed a clear exhibition concept and invited a series of curators to discuss specific exhibition themes from a range of different perspectives.

Under the title, *The Eye is a Lonely Hunter: Images of Humankind*, our international team of curators, headed by Katerina Gregos (GR / BE) and Solvej Helweg Ovesen (DK / DE), aims to present a multifaceted portrait of humanity in all the diversity of our time. The idea is also to stimulate discussion about the ability of photography to convey anthropological insights in today's world.

Behind the Fotofestival is a growing cultural network, linking together the three cities and their art institutions and allowing a cross-urban dialogue to unfold over a period of eight weeks. We would like to thank the seven institutions involved in the festival for the key impetus and outstanding support they have contributed to the event. Our particular thanks go to directors Barbara Auer, Wolfram Glatz, Johan Holten, Ulrike Lorenz, Thomas Röske, Susana Saez, Reinhard Spieler and Alfried Wieczorek. For their tireless efforts to make it all happen, we would also like to thank the individual teams involved: Thomas Köllhofer, Selini Andres, Petra Neff, Birgit Scheidecker and Lili Marocsik from the Kunsthalle Mannheim; Thomas Schirmböck, Marianne Aselmeier and Silvia Rückert from ZEPHYR of the Reiss-Engelhorn-Museen; Nina Gülicher, Udo Baur and Herbert Nolden from the Wilhelm-Hack-Museum; Stefanie Schubert from the Kunstverein Ludwigshafen; Friederike Schröder and Katja Arnold from the Heidelberger Kunstverein; Torsten Kappenberg and Gabi Tschudi from the Sammlung Prinzhorn; and Wolfram Glatz, Felix Grädler and their team at the halle02 / Kunsthalle in Heidelberg.

As always, the exhibitions have been installed to the highest professional standards. We would like to thank the installation teams, who have made every exhibition segment look exactly how it should be: Alexander Horn and André Wischnewski, Frank Hofacker, Markus Brehm and Arsen Kortus, Yvonne Vogel and Andrzej Naglowsky, Torsten Kappenberg and Michel Volkmer.

Thanks to the support of the art institutions involved, we are also able to offer a comprehensive supporting programme. We would like thank Dorothee Höfert, Theresia Kiefer, Stefanie Schubert and Friederike Schröder for their creative ideas and the fascinating events they have organised.

In this age of budgetary constraints, a lively cultural exchange is only possible with the help of several committed partners. A huge expression of thanks therefore goes to all our sponsors, supporters and collaborative partners. We would like to thank Klaus Philipp Seif, Friederike Reutter and Klaus Gasteiger from BASF SE; Georg Müller and Christian Land from MVV Energie AG; Thomas Fichtl and Claudia Cischek from Heidelberger Druckmaschinen AG; Edmund Elsen and Katharina Bornkessel from the Stiftung Rheinland-Pfalz für Kultur; Peter Frankenberg and Hartwig Trinkaus from the Heinrich-Vetter-Stiftung; Pietro Soldini, Marianne Burk and Jelena Delic from Pro Helvetia; Thomas Golk from the Japan Foundation; Jutta Ulmer-Straub and Harald Gall from the Baden-Württemberg Ministry of Science, Research and the Arts; Friedolf Schiek from the Institute for Foreign Relations; Gitta Luiten, Marijn Veenhuijzen and Coby Reitsma from the Mondriaan Stichting; Rikke Björnböl from the Danish Arts Agency, Martin Kuon and Klaudia Marschner from the Stiftungen Landesbank Baden-Württemberg; Kaspar von Mellenthin, Felix Zipse and Deborah Klein from myphotobook; Anne-Marie Croes and Hilde Lievens from the Flemish Ministry for Culture, Youth, Sport, Media and Historic Places; Petra Engesser and Martina Kopf from Verkehrsverbund Rhein-Neckar GmbH; Susann Becker and Anja Öffler from Rhein-Neckar-Verkehr GmbH; Angelika Grabaum-Pertsch from Daimler AG; Anne Charlotte Hauen from the Office for Contemporary Art Norway; Wolfgang Bielmeier and Stephanie Gläßer from GBG-Mannheimer Wohnungsbaugesellschaft mbH; and Joachim Stumpp from the Klinikum Ludwigshafen. Michael Sieber and Regina Pfriem opened many doors for us and helped up may contact with key stakeholders.

For the stimulating dialogue and exchange of ideas, we would like to thank our collaborative partners Gabriele Oßwald, Wolfgang Sautermeister and Tilo Schwarz from zeitraumexit e.V.; Emeline Dufrennoy and Cécile Espitallier from La Chambre; Joachim Reck and Martin Klemmer from EIDOTECH GmbH; Ditmar Schädel and Klaus Czerwinski from the Deutsche Gesellschaft für Photographie; and Gerhard Rossbach and Corinna Hipp from dpunkt Verlag. For his work in staging the open-air project on the Alter Messplatz in Mannheim our warm thanks go to Peter Bender of motorlab architekten. Special thanks are due to our graphic design agency, raum mannheim led by Frank Hoffmann, who not only developed the look of this year's festival but also designed and completed the exhibition graphics.

Katerina Gregos and Solvej Helweg Ovesen have put together a series of excellent exhibitions featuring outstanding works by internationally renowned photographers. Their curatorial skills and the impressive standard of works submitted by all the photographers involved are what give the Fotofestival Mannheim_Ludwigshafen_Heidelberg 2011 its high profile and unmis-takable character. We are enormously grateful to you both.

Special mention must be made of the extraordinary contribution of the three cities of Mannheim, Ludwigshafen and Heidelberg who, in these financially difficult times, did not shy away from backing and supporting the Fotofestival. Without the huge commitment of these three cities, the festival could not have been staged.

We look forward to a stimulating and inspiring Fotofestival, where even we as the organisers never cease to be amazed at the multifaceted, expressive power of the photographic medium.

Management Board of the Fotofestival Mannheim_Ludwigshafen_Heidelberg, Dietrich Skibelski, Sabine Schirra, Hans-Martin Mumm and Michael Ebert and the Festival team of Carolin Ellwanger, Sabine von Wussow and Heide Häusler

Einführung

Die 4. Ausgabe des Fotofestivals Mannheim_Ludwigshafen_Heidelberg trägt den Titel *The Eye is a Lonely Hunter: Images of Humankind*. Ihr Ansatz ist eine humanistische Sichtweise in der Tradition der dokumentarischen Fotografie, die in den letzten Jahren wieder an Bedeutung gewonnen hat. Das Festival präsentiert verschiedene fotografische, in der Schnittmenge zwischen dokumentarischer und künstlerischer Fotografie angesiedelte Herangehensweisen, die geprägt sind von einem feinen Gespür sowohl für starke visuelle Momente als auch für soziopolitische Zusammenhänge. Die Ausstellung spiegelt die erweiterten Grenzen des Mediums der Fotografie wider. Daher ist sowohl die „klassische" Fotografie vertreten als auch Installationen, Bildprojektionen, Filme und Videos. Das Festival beschäftigt sich mit der neuen und kritischen Art und Weise, wie Fotografie anthropologisches Wissen vermittelt. Von einer Vielzahl an geografischen Standpunkten aus gesehen, möchte es eine ausgewählte fotografische Erkundung zur Conditio humana zum Beginn des zweiten Jahrzehnts des 21. Jahrhunderts sein.

Unser Katalogbeitrag *The Eye is a Lonely Hunter: Images of Humankind* ist eine kuratorische Stellungnahme, die zum einen auf den historischen und theoretischen Hintergrund der Ausstellung eingeht und zum anderen die Position des Künstlers als Forscher auch in Bezug auf die Dokumentarfotografie, die visuelle Anthropologie und das Zeitgeschehen hinterfragt. Die 5 auf die jeweiligen Ausstellungsorte aufgeteilten Themenbereiche der Ausstellung („Das alltägliche Leben", „Affekt und Wirkung von Politik", „Ökologische Kreisläufe", „Rolle und Ritual" und „Lebenskreisläufe") werden ebenso wie die 3 Einzelpräsentationen von Beat Streuli, Roger Ballen und Tobias Zielony, als jeweils eigenständige Kapitel vorgestellt. Darüber hinaus haben wir TJ Demos mit seinem besonderen Interesse an fotografischen Medien und seiner Auseinandersetzung mit Kunst, Globalisierungsfragen sowie Post-Humanismus eingeladen, ein Essay zu unserem Katalog beizusteuern: "Photography's (Post) Humanist Interventions: Or, Can Photography Make the World More Liveable?" Die (post-)humanistische Interventionen der Fotografie oder: Kann Fotografie die Welt lebenswerter machen? Wir möchten allen teilnehmenden Künstlern herzlich danken, ohne deren Beiträge diese Ausstellung nicht möglich wäre. Insbesondere danken wir unserem großartigen Festivalteam: an erster Stelle der Geschäftsführerin des Fotofestivals Mannheim_Ludwigshafen_Heidelberg, Carolin Ellwanger, und der Ausstellungsleiterin, Heide Häusler, die unsere kuratorische Vision mit ganzem Herzen unterstützt haben und das Festival jedes Jahr einen Schritt weiterbringen; Heide Häusler für ihre zentrale Rolle in der Verwirklichung aller Ausstellungen und des Kataloges und ihrer Assistentin Julia Koch unter anderem für die Bildredaktion und die Betreuung der Multimedia-Installationen, Julia Mauga für Ihre Co-Organisation des Portfolio Reviews und die Mitarbeit am Rahmenprogramm, Seraphine Meya für die Koordination des Außenprojektes von Beat Streuli, Karoline Michaelis für ihre Mitarbeit im Bereich Marketing, Jonatan Ahlm Brenander für seine Kurztexte sowie Sabine von Wussow für ihre Administration und die Koordination des Portfolio Reviews als auch für ihre Hilfe, die sie uns und allen Künstlern während des gesamten Prozesses hat zukommen lassen; wir danken den Vorstandsmitgliedern des Fotofestivals Dietrich Skibelski (Vorsitzender), Sabine Schirra (stellvertretende Vorsitzende), Hans-Martin Mumm und Michael Ebert für ihre Loyalität, ihren Glauben an das Projekt und die uns entgegengebrachte Unterstützung; den beteiligten Kunstinstitutionen und ihren Direktoren – Ulrike Lorenz von der Kunsthalle Mannheim, Reinhard Spieler vom Wilhelm-Hack-Museum, Thomas Schirmböck von ZEPHYR der Reiss-Engelhorn-Museen, Barbara Auer vom Kunstverein Ludwigshafen, Johan Holten und Susana Sáez vom Heidelberger Kunstverein, Thomas Röske von der

Sammlung Prinzhorn sowie Wolfram Glatz und Felix Graedler von der halle02 / Kunsthalle Heidelberg – ebenso wie den jeweiligen Teams für ihre Offenheit, ihr Engagement, ihre Unterstützung und Gastfreundlichkeit; den beteiligten Städten und Bürgermeistern von Mannheim, Heidelberg und Ludwigshafen für ihre Zusammenarbeit; unseren Katalogdesignern Manuel Raeder und Manuel Goller und unserem Verlag Kehrer – besonders Klaus Kehrer – für diese wunderbare Publikation; unserem Hauptsponsor BASF SE für die durchgängige Unterstützung des Festivals, seine Großzügigkeit und das in unsere Ausstellung und unser Anliegen gesetzte Vertrauen; herzlich gedankt sei auch den Stiftungen, Galerien und Leihgebern, hier vor allem der DZ Bank Kunstsammlung, die die Realisierung von *The Eye is a Lonely Hunter: Images of Humankind* möglich gemacht haben.

Katerina Gregos & Solvej Helweg Ovesen
Kuratoren des 4. Fotofestivals Mannheim_Ludwigshafen_Heidelberg

Introduction

The fourth edition of the Fotofestival Mannheim_Ludwigshafen_Heidelberg bears the title *The Eye is a Lonely Hunter: Images of Humankind* and takes as its point of departure a humanist perspective in the tradition of documentary photography that has witnessed a resurgence in recent years. It showcases a variety of practices that are situated at the intersection between documentary and artistic photography, practices that are characterised by a strong sense of visuality but also a keen sense of socio-political awareness. The exhibition reflects the expanded boundaries of the medium and thus includes both 'classic' photography but also installations, slide projections, film and video. The festival focuses on the new and critical ways photography transports anthropological knowledge and aims to be a selective photographic survey of the human condition as we enter the second decade of the twenty-first century, seen from a plurality of geographical angles.

Our catalogue essay *The Eye is a Lonely Hunter: Images of Humankind* is a curatorial statement that elaborates the historical and theoretical background of the exhibition and the position of the artist as researcher also in relation to the field of documentary photography, visual anthropology and current affairs. The exhibition, which is separated into five thematic categories for each of the separate venues ('The Practice of Everyday Life', 'The Affect and Effect of Politics', 'Ecological Circuits', 'Role and Ritual', and 'Life Cycles') as well as three solo presentations by Beat Streuli, Roger Ballen and Tobias Zielony, are all introduced as separate chapters. Additionally we have invited TJ Demos, with his special interest in lens-based practices and research into art, the politics of globalisation and post-humanism, to contribute with his essay 'Photography's (Post) Humanist Interventions: Or, Can Photography Make the World More Liveable?'.

We would like to warmly thank all the participating artists, without whose contributions this exhibition would not be possible; the managing director of the Fotofestival Mannheim_Ludwigshafen_Heidelberg, Carolin Ellwanger, and the exhibition manager Heide Häusler for wholeheartedly and ambitiously supporting our curatorial vision and for bringing the Fotofestival to a new level with each edition; we would particularly like to thank Heide Häusler for her invaluable role in the realisation of all the exhibitions as well as the catalogue, and her assistant Julia Koch for overseeing the technical installations and image editing, Julia Mauga for the co-organization of the Portfolio Review and the Fringe program, Seraphine Meya for co-ordinating the project of Beat Streuli in public space, Karoline Michaelis for her assistance in promoting the Festival, Jonatan Ahlm Brenander for his text contributions, and Sabine von Wussow for her administrative organisation and Portfolio Review coordination, as well as assisting us and the artists throughout this process; Fotofestival board members Dietrich Skibelski (chairman), Sabine Schirra (vice chairman), Hans-Martin Mumm and Michael Ebert, for their loyalty, belief in the project and the support they have shown us; the participating art institutions and their directors – Ulrike Lorenz of the Kunsthalle Mannheim, Reinhard Spieler of the Wilhelm-Hack-Museum, Thomas Schirmböck of ZEPHYR of the Reiss-Engelhorn-Museen, Barbara Auer of Kunstverein Ludwigshafen, Johan Holten and Susana Sáez of Heidelberger Kunstverein, Thomas Röske of Sammlung Prinzhorn, and Wolfram Glatz and Felix Graedler of halle02 / Kunsthalle Heidelberg – as well as their respective teams, for their openness, engagement, assistance and hospitality; our catalogue designers Manuel Raeder and Manuel Goller and our publishers Kehrer, and particularly Klaus Kehrer, for this beautiful publication; our main sponsor BASF SE, for their continuous support of the festival and their generosity and trust in our exhibition and cause; as well as the foundations, galleries and lenders, here especially the DZ Bank Kunstsammlung, that have enabled the realisation of *The Eye is a Lonely Hunter: Images of Humankind*.

Katerina Gregos & Solvej Helweg Ovesen
Curators, 4. Fotofestival Mannheim_Ludwigshafen_Heidelberg

The Eye is a Lonely Hunter: Images of Humankind Eine Betrachtung der Conditio humana im Jahr 2011

Katerina Gregos & Solvej Helweg Ovesen

Das 4. Fotofestival ist eine fotografische Erkundung der *Conditio humana* zu Beginn des zweiten Jahrzehnts des 21. Jahrhunderts. Dabei werden Sichtweisen aus einer Vielzahl geografischer Standorte in Afrika, Südamerika, Europa und Asien präsentiert. Der Titel *The Eye is a Lonely Hunter: Images of Humankind* verweist auf die Position und das Wagnis des Fotografen sowie auf das Auge als einen „einsamen Jäger" nach einem besonderen Motiv. Dies soll unterstreichen, dass dokumentarische Vorgehensweisen, insbesondere der Moment der Auswahl und der Aufnahme – der „entscheidende Augenblick", wie der französische Fotograf Henri Cartier-Bresson, Vater des modernen Fotojournalismus, es nannte – auf Seiten des Fotografen zentrale politische Entscheidungen mit sich bringt. Der Name des diesjährigen Festivals ist inspiriert von dem Titel des Romans *The Heart is a Lonely Hunter* (1940) von Carson McCuller, die darin den Misshandelten, den Ausgegrenzten und den Vergessenen eine Stimme verleiht.

Was hat uns dazu bewogen, genau zu diesem Zeitpunkt, im Jahr 2011, eine künstlerische Betrachtung von Bildern der Menschheit vorzunehmen? Welche geschichtliche Motivation, welcher Kontext liegt diesem Schritt zugrunde? In den letzten Jahrzehnten sind universelle humanistische Werte in die Kritik geraten und oft hieß es, die Fotografie würde eher Lügen als die Wahrheit verbreiten. Genau vor einem Jahrzehnt, am 11. September 2001, stürzten die Zwillingstürme des World Trade Centers in New York in sich zusammen und das Rückgrat neoliberaler Weltmacht wurde erschüttert. Diese Entwicklung der Ereignisse hat strittige Themen in Bezug auf humanistische Werte verschärft – Fragen, wie sie auch in der Kunst immer wieder gestellt werden im Hinblick auf makro-politische Themen wie wirtschaftliche und ausbeuterische Kreisläufe, Imperialismus, Toleranz, ethnografisches „Anderssein", Redefreiheit, Selbstzensur, Zivilcourage, Unterdrückung und Marginalisierung von Frauen und Männern. Dies also bildet den Hintergrund unserer kuratorischen Motivation, alternative Bilder der Menschheit zu fordern, Bilder, die auf dokumentarischer Fotografie beruhen: Bilder, die es schaffen könnten, Persönlichkeiten in ihrer gesicherten Existenz und Laufbahn zu inspirieren und in eine andere Richtung zu lenken.

Anlässlich der Eröffnung des 4. Fotofestivals am Wochenende vom 9.–11. September präsentieren wir 57 Künstler aus 32 Ländern mit einer Auswahl von 700 Bildern und Kunstwerken, die beinahe ebenso viele Bilder der Menschheit beschreiben. Sie transportieren Erkenntnisse über inspirierende, kritische, mögliche und auch unmögliche Perspektiven eines fragmentierten Humanismus und berücksichtigen dabei den permanenten Spielraum des Anti-Humanismus. Die ausgestellten Arbeiten sind in 5 unterschiedliche Themenbereiche unterteilt, die für die Wirkungen und Affekte der makro-politischen Fragen unseres Jahrzehnts auf die Menschheit stehen. Sie werden als ein Gegendiskurs präsentiert und aus der subjektiven Position des Fotografen und des Betrachters heraus als Fallstudie gesehen.

Auf welche Weise wird die Untersuchung der *Conditio humana* im fotografischen Medium reflektiert? *The Eye is a Lonely Hunter: Images of Humankind* ist eine Ausstellung, die den *in situ*-Aspekt des Fotografen und des Fotografierten zum Zeitpunkt der Aufnahme mit einbezieht. Die subjektive Haltung der Menschen vor und hinter der Kamera sowie ihr persönliches Umfeld sind bei der Entstehung dieser Bilder häufig von zentraler Bedeutung. Das Auge als „einsamer Jäger" ist ein Auge, das nach der Besonderheit sucht, nach der Andersartigkeit und der Überraschung, nach Ausdrucksformen des Unsichtbaren und des Widersprüchlichen sowie nach Aspekten der Realität, die keine schlichten Erweiterungen des Selbst des Fotografen sind. Es sucht nach einem Bindeglied zur sichtbaren und unsichtbaren Welt, durch das Vorgehen und die Taktik des Fotografen ebenso wie die des Fotografierten. Über einen Zeitraum von eineinhalb Jahren hat das Kuratorenteam hinter dem 4. Fotofestival nach Möglichkeiten gesucht, wie Kunstwerke anthropologisches Wissen enthalten oder reflektieren können, das sich kolonialen Attitüden und normativen Werten widersetzt. Wir haben kritische Ansätze erkundet, um einen selbstgerechten westlichen Humanismus zu umgehen; unser Anliegen war es, eine umfassende Ausstellung zu realisieren, die die *Conditio humana* im Jahr 2011 in all ihrer Komplexität, Verschiedenheit und Unsicherheit aufzeigt.

Man könnte diesen neuen fotografischen Humanismus als einen Humanismus definieren, der sich auf unmittelbarere Weise engagiert, der die Verantwortlichkeiten und Problematiken anerkennt, die es mit sich bringt, wenn das „andere", das „Fremde", fotografisch festgehalten und repräsentiert wird, und der schließlich ein Hauptaugenmerk auf direkte Kommunikation, Interaktion und Vertrautheit legt – im Gegensatz zu „objektiver" Sozialanalyse oder „objektivem" Aktivismus. Diese Form engagierter Fotografie geht über das unmittelbare Einfangen eines Ereignisses und seiner Ursachen hinaus. Sie wendet sich einem Problem zu, auf das Richard Cross aufmerksam gemacht hat – ein Fotojournalist, der 1983 an der Grenze zwischen Honduras und Nicaragua getötet wurde. Er merkte an, dass Fotografen bei der Betrachtung von Dingen häufig sehr kurzsichtig seien und sich mehr für die unübersehbaren Symptome des Problems interessierten als für dessen Ursachen.[1]

Wie Cross aufzeigt, findet man in den Nachrichten und in der Bilderwelt der Mainstream-Medien kaum eine Selbstreflexion über das, was sich hinter den dramatischen Bildern der *Conditio humana* verbirgt und über die Rolle des Fotografen in einer solchen Situation – was aber nicht heißt, dass solche Bilder belanglos wären und nicht von anderen reflektiert werden könnten. Offenkundig gibt es zwischen den Absichten von Fotografen, Herausgebern und Auftraggebern von Nachrichten- und Medienbildern große Unterschiede. Und doch enthüllt jedes Foto, jedes Bild oder Dokument etwas über die Gesellschaft, die es verkörpert oder in der es entstand. Man denke beispielsweise an Modefotos in Frauenillustrierten. Stellen diese nicht ein hervorragendes Material für Kulturanthropologen dar, die etwa den Unterschied zwischen gesellschaftlichem Verhalten und Schönheitsidealen der 1950er-Jahre und heute untersuchen möchten? Zwar sind sie dafür nicht gemacht worden, dennoch können sie als Ausgangspunkt für Untersuchungen über die Ideale einer Gesellschaft dienen.

The Eye is a Lonely Hunter: Images of Humankind überdenkt die anthropologische Rolle der Fotografie und präsentiert sie als Teil eines kreativen Umgangs mit „*Selbst-andere*"-Dichotomien und dem Unterschied in postkolonialem Sinne. Fotografie nimmt hierbei Formen an, die entfremdet sind, abstrakt, surreal und eindringlich. So muss die Ausstellung des 4. Fotofestivals als ein ergänzender Freiraum für den anthropologischen und dokumentarischen Diskurs gesehen werden. Als Kuratorinnen haben wir uns um engagierte und talentierte Künstler und Fotografen bemüht, deren Bilder dokumentieren, wie sich Individuen (weniger *Völker*) den Herausforderungen des alltäglichen Lebens stellen. Der Fotograf leistet eine Art künstlerische Forschung in Ergänzung zu der Arbeit der Ethnografen, auf die wir im Kapitel „Der Künstler als Forscher" näher eingehen werden.

Künstlerische Fotografien können Einfluss haben auf die Art und Weise, wie Menschen die Welt sehen und darauf eingehen, ebenso wie anthropologische Fotografien auch. Darüber hinaus können sie sogar noch eindringlicher und evokativer sein als anthropologische Fotografien, die ja meist innerhalb des wissenschaftlichen

1 Richard Cross, „Photographers of the Vanguard", *News Photographer Magazine*, September 1981, neu abgedruckt in: „Photography and Propadanda" in: *Between the Eyes: Essays on Photography and Politics*, Aperture, New York 2005, S. 20.

Diskurses verbleiben, denn sie haben die Freiheit, Subjektivitäten und affektive Impulse aufzugreifen. Der Kunsthistoriker und Medientheoretiker Tom Gunning hat dazu gesagt, dass im Unterschied zu den Normen, die dem Wahrheitsanspruch des juristischen oder wissenschaftlichen Fotos zugrunde liegen, die Kunstfotografie ihre eigenen Regeln und Herangehensweisen schaffen und ihre Formen frei erkunden kann.[2]

Dies bildet den Hintergrund dafür, wie wir die Arbeiten dieser Ausstellung begutachtet, kategorisiert und arrangiert haben. Die Titel der einzelnen Bereiche, auf die wir später in einzelnen Kapiteln eingehen werden, sind „Das alltägliche Leben", „Affekt und Wirkung von Politik", „Ökologische Kreisläufe", „Rolle und Ritual" und „Lebenskreisläufe".

Die in der Ausstellung erkennbaren fotografischen Herangehensweisen, auf die sich die Untersuchung dieser Themen stützt, entstammen vorwiegend der dokumentarischen Tradition von Fotografie und Film: Fotojournalismus, Dokufiktion, anthropologische Fotografie, Schnappschüsse und Collagen aus Foto und Film; aber auch konstruierte, inszenierte Fotografie bleibt nicht außen vor, auch sie kann anthropologische Erkenntnisse und sogar essenzielle, in einem konstruierten Bild verschlüsselte Wahrheiten übermitteln. Die Traditionen der Porträt- und Landschaftsfotografie haben ebenso einen wichtigen Stellenwert in der Ausstellung und runden den Gesamteindruck der *Conditio humana* ab. Im Allgemeinen hatten wir bei unserer Arbeit eine weiter gefasste Vorstellung von Fotografie im Kopf, in der weniger ausschließlich formale Fragen als mehr der Inhalt selbst bei unseren Entscheidungen an erster Stelle standen, auch wenn wir gleichzeitig fotografische Positionen ausgewählt haben, die einen starken Sinn für das Visuelle aufweisen, zuweilen sogar ikonische Merkmale zeigen und zur Bearbeitung folgender Schlüsselfragen beitragen:

> Wie könnte ein Porträt der Menschheit im Jahr 2011 aussehen?
> Welchen wesentlichen Fragen und Herausforderungen steht die Menschheit heute gegenüber?
> Wie kümmern sich Menschen um ihresgleichen, wie erwecken sie Verständnis füreinander und wie wird dies durch das Medium Fotografie dokumentiert?
> Inwieweit lassen Fotografen und Fotografierte die Betrachter an ihrem Leben teilhaben?

Zur Beantwortung dieser spannenden Fragen haben wir uns auf die Suche gemacht nach künstlerischen Ausdrucksformen von Fotografie, Film und Video, die aus den Traditionen der dokumentarischen, ethnografischen und inszenierten Fotografie schöpfen sowie aus ihren Begegnungen mit Realität und Fiktion als erzählerische Mittel für Geschichten einerseits und Wahrheit andererseits. Wohl wissend, dass letztlich weder Kunst noch thematische Ausstellungen die Welt retten, wohl aber unser Verständnis von ihr beeinflussen können, würdigen wir die Tatsache, dass subjektives kritisches Denken einen Raum für empirische und theoretische Freiheit bietet, in der Wissen über Humanismus entstehen kann.

The Family of Man (Die Familie der Menschheit)

> „Fotografie hält die ganze Bandbreite der im menschlichen Gesicht eingeschriebenen Gefühle fest – die Schönheit von Erde und Himmel, die der Mensch geerbt hat; außerdem den Reichtum und die Konfusion, die der Mensch geschaffen hat. Sie ist ein unverzichtbares Werkzeug, will man den Menschen die Menschen erklären."[3]

The Eye is a Lonely Hunter: Images of Humankind ist auch eine kritische Reflexion über die Ausstellung *The Family of Man* (1955), ein Meilenstein der humanistischen Sichtweise in der Dokumentarfotografie des 20. Jahrhunderts. In vielerlei Hinsicht wird *The Eye is a Lonely Hunter* als

2 Tom Gunning, „What's the Point of an Index? Or, Faking Photographs", *Nordicom Review*, Band 5, Nr. 1/2, September 2004, S. 44.

3 Edward Steichen, *Time*, 7. April 1961.

Gegensatz zu jener Ausstellung präsentiert, ohne jedoch deren hohe Bedeutung abzustreiten. Zu der Zeit, als der Fotograf, Kurator und Museumsdirektor Edward Steichen (1879–1973) im Jahr 1955 seine äußerst erfolgreiche Ausstellung *The Family of Man* im Museum of Modern Art (MoMA) in New York realisierte, arbeitete er in einem Kontext, der völlig anders war, als das Umfeld, in dem sich Fotografen heute bewegen. Die in der Nachkriegszeit und zu Beginn des Kalten Krieges organisierte Ausstellung war Teil einer umfassenden Suche nach universellen humanistischen Werten und Perspektiven. Beispielsweise wurden diese Vorstellungen auch, auf eine andere Art, in der *documenta 1* bearbeitet, die 1955 in Kassel stattfand und von Arnold Bode initiiert worden war.[4] Steichen hat einmal gesagt, die Kunst um der Kunst willen sei tot, wenn sie überhaupt je gelebt hat. Ihm war demnach an den größeren existenziellen Fragen in der Kunst gelegen. Die Ausstellung *The Family of Man* war unterteilt in 37 archetypische beziehungsweise „universelle“ Themen wie Geburt und Tod, Familie, Bildung, Arbeit und Spiel, Krieg und Frieden und so weiter. Sie trat für die Vorstellung einer Universalität menschlicher Erfahrung ein und die Rolle der Fotografie bei ihrer Dokumentation; gleichzeitig spielte sie eine wichtige Rolle bei der Legitimierung des Mediums Fotografie als Kunst.

Zwar war die Ausstellung damals eine der populärsten und meist besuchten Fotoausstellungen aller Zeiten (als Wanderversion wurde sie in 38 Ländern auf 4 Kontinenten von mehr als 9 Millionen Menschen besucht), dennoch war sie auch deutlicher Kritik ausgesetzt – am bekanntesten ist die des französischen Philosophen Roland Barthes (1915–1980) in seinem Buch *Mythen des Alltags* (Mythologies, 1957). Seine Kritik richtete sich gegen die maßgebliche Aussage der Ausstellung, derzufolge die Menschen überall auf der Welt gleich seien, ungeachtet geografischer und kultureller Unterschiede. Problematisch war, dass Steichen viele der ausgestellten Bilder von lediglich 8 Fotoagenturen in New York bezogen hatte, obwohl für seine Ausstellung auch Fotografien eingesandt werden konnten – dadurch stammten die meisten Fotografen aus der westlichen Welt. Die Ausstellung stand für etwas, das man die Gemeinschaftlichkeit von Erfahrung nennen könnte, und sie machte eine Rhetorik globaler Universalität geltend, indem sie eine zuversichtliche Darstellung der universellen Familie der Menschheit präsentierte.[5]

Barthes Kritikpunkt war, dass die Ausstellung „das determinierende Gewicht der Geschichte“ aufhob und es vermied, historisch spezifische Fotografien mit einzubeziehen, Fotos, die einen Einblick in eben die sozialen, politischen und wirtschaftlichen Bedingungen boten, die dem Bild und dem jeweils dargestellten Motiv zugrunde lagen.[6] Barthes zeigte auf, dass, um diese Vorstellung einer universellen Erfahrung zu vermitteln, eine Dekontextualisierung vorgenommen worden war. Als Folge davon erschienen die Bilder in der Ausstellung beinahe abstrakt: sie waren Zeit und Ort enthoben, aus dem soziohistorischen Kontext gerissen und dann um spezifische, vermeintlich universelle Kategorien herum neu angeordnet worden. Da war kein Platz für geschichtliche Details, keine Andeutung der hinter der Situation liegenden Bedingungen, Besonderheiten und Konsequenzen. Barthes kritisierte sowohl diesen, wie er es nannte „doppeldeutigen Mythos von der menschlichen Gemeinschaft“, als auch Steichens klassischen humanistischen Ansatz, der, wie er behauptete, den Bereich der Erfahrung aus dem Fluss der Geschichte herausriss.[7]

Trotz Barthes fundierter Kritik sollte *The Family of Man* im Nachhinein auch re-kontextualisiert werden. Was aber manchmal auch vergessen wird, ist, dass Steichens Ausstellung nach Beendigung des Zweiten

4 Themenschwerpunkt der *documenta 1* war die *Entartete Kunst* als der Bereich der Tradition der abstrakten Malerei in der Modernen Kunst, die unter dem Nationalsozialismus abgelehnt wurde.

5 Roland Barthes, „The Great Family of Man“ (Die große Familie der Menschen) und „Myth as a Type of Speech“ (Der Mythos ist eine Aussage), *Mythologies*, englische Fassung, aus dem Französischen übersetzt von Annette Lavers, Jonathan Cape Ltd, London 1972, S.100–102, 109–110.

6 Barthes, *ibd.*

7 Barthes, *ibd.*

Weltkrieges das Anliegen hatte, einen allgemeinen Optimismus zum Ausdruck zu bringen, ein hoffnungsvolles Bild der Welt anstatt eines düsteren und fatalistischen Konzepts der Menschheit. Sein Anliegen war ein Appell an die menschliche Würde. Steichen wollte sich über all die bekannten, von Barthes aufgezählten Unterschiede hinwegsetzen – Hautfarbe, Rasse, Nationalität und wirtschaftliche Ungleichheiten. Barthes Argumente dienen dazu aufzuzeigen, dass Unterschiede entscheidend sind – aber so gerechtfertigt seine Kritik auf eine Weise gewesen sein mag, lässt er Steichens tiefere Motivation außer Acht. Steichen war zwar naiv, aber in gewisser Weise war es Barthes' Kritik auch. Steichen wollte die Ähnlichkeiten betonen und schlug eine beinahe tautologische Sichtweise vor: Menschen sind letzten Endes menschlich. Barthes hingegen wollte die Unterschiede zwischen den Menschen herausstellen. Im Grunde sprachen sie über unterschiedliche Dinge auf unterschiedlichen Ebenen. Am aufschlussreichsten ist vielleicht folgendes Zitat aus Barthes Kritik: „Dass das Kind unter guten oder schlechten Bedingungen geboren wird, dass es seine Mutter Schmerzen kostet oder nicht, dass es von Sterblichkeit betroffen wird oder nicht, dass es zu dieser oder jener Form der Zukunft Zugang hat, *davon* müssten die Ausstellungen zu uns sprechen, und nicht von einer ewigen Lyrik der Geburt."[8]

The Family of Man reflektierte und betonte eine sehr heitere Sicht der Menschheit; Steichens romantische Weltanschauung stimmte genau mit dem überein, was die Öffentlichkeit inmitten des Kalten Krieges hören und sehen wollte. Bezieht man diese allgemeine Stimmungslage mit ein, kann die akademische Kritik von *The Family of Man* auch als recht herablassend gegenüber den mehr als 9 Millionen Menschen eingestuft werden, die die Ausstellung gesehen haben, und deren Leben vielleicht doch in irgendeiner Weise davon berührt wurden. Durch Barthes Kritik werden sie als naiv, ungebildet oder voreingenommen beiseite geschoben. Im Gegensatz dazu hat sich Ariella Azoulay, Professorin für Visual Culture und Philosophie erst kürzlich zugunsten *The Family of Man* als einer visuellen Allgemeinen Erklärung der Menschenrechte ausgesprochen und liefert dadurch eine ganz andere Lesart des Themas. Ihrer Ansicht nach ist Barthes das meiste von dem entgangen, was die Fotografien in der Ausstellung zeigten; was der Autor behauptete zu sehen, waren soziale *Vorstellungen*. Die versteckte Ideologie, die er der Ausstellung zugeschrieben hat, war nichts anderes als Steichens ausdrückliche Intention beim Kuratieren. Anstatt die Fotos als deskriptive Statements mit universellem Anspruch zu lesen, regt Azoulay dazu an, sie als normative Statements zu lesen, die allgemeine Rechte beanspruchen. Kurz gesagt, sie schlägt vor, die Ausstellung als die erste visuelle Erklärung der Menschenrechte zu rekonstruieren.[9] Ein heutiger Gestaltungsansatz von *The Family of Man* müsste all diese Positionen berücksichtigen. Man könnte auch darüber diskutieren, dass wir an einem Punkt angelangt sind, an dem die Globalisierung, neue ökonomische Realitäten und kulturelle Homogenisierung uns dazu zwingen, trotz andauernder wirtschaftlicher und sozialer Ungleichheiten über ein gemeinschaftliches Dilemma nachzudenken.

The Eye is a Lonely Hunter unterscheidet sich in mehr als nur einer Hinsicht von *The Family of Man.* Zum einen werden die spezifischen Fallstudien und Themen von *The Eye is a Lonely Hunter* in einem sozialen Kontext präsentiert, während *The Family of Man* nach spezifischen Themen wie „Liebende", „Kinder", „Väter" und „Söhne", „Mütter" und „Töchter" oder abstrakteren Begriffen wie „Landwirtschaft", „Nahrung", „Arbeit" und ähnlichem aufgegliedert war. Außerdem besteht *The Eye is a Lonely Hunter* aus unterschiedlichen Subthemen, die versuchen, die gezeigten Fotos in einem sozialen, politischen, wirtschaftlichen und kulturellen Umfeld genau zu kontextualisieren. Während *The Family of Man* von Barthes – nicht zu Unrecht – ein gewisser tautologischer Ansatz vorgeworfen

8 Barthes, *ibd.;* zitiert nach der Übersetzung von Helmut Scheffel in: Roland Barthes, *Mythen des Alltags*, edition suhrkamp, Frankfurt a. M. 1964.

9 Ariella Azoulay, Vortrag auf dem Symposium *The Human Snapshot*, 2. Juli 2011, Luma Foundation, Arles, Frankreich.

wurde (Menschen sind menschlich letzten Endes), haben wir versucht, das allzu Offensichtliche zu vermeiden und einen eher verblüffenden, persönlichen Ansatz einzelner Fotografen zu präsentieren, von denen die meisten sich in dem Kontext, in dem sie arbeiten, gut auskennen und sich oft über Jahre in einem bestimmten Umfeld engagiert haben. Wir haben Fotografen aus der ganzen Welt ausgewählt, die von Dingen erzählen, die den Medien nicht immer passen, die Gegengeschichten liefern und wir haben sie dazu eingeladen, ihre eigene Kultur in einem fotografischen „Blick" zu präsentieren, der nicht auferlegt wird, sondern von innen heraus kommt.

In Asien, Amerika, Afrika und dem neuen Europa haben sich talentierte Fotografen auch in der Kunstszene einen Namen gemacht und sie arbeiten und stellen inzwischen auf internationaler Ebene aus. Wie sehen sie *The Family of Man* heute mit ihren Augen? Im 4. Fotofestival präsentieren diese Fotografen – ergänzend zu ihren Kollegen der westlichen Welt – unterschiedliche Weltsichten und Perspektiven womit sie sich des demokratischen Potenzials der Fotografie in erfrischender Weise bedienen, blicken auf existenzielle, spezifisch menschliche Situationen und auf das „andere". Zu einer Zeit, in der die Fotografie nicht mehr allein in den Händen der Menschen der Industrienationen liegt, liefern sie multi-ethnische Sichtweisen, behandeln dabei die Vorstellung vom Unterschied „von innen" heraus und entwickeln Gegendiskurse zum impliziten Imperialismus von *The Family of Man*.

Wir sind uns natürlich bewusst, dass es nicht möglich ist ein vollständiges Porträt der Menschheit zu zeigen; das wäre eine unmögliche Aufgabe, denn jede kuratierte Ausstellung ist – schon von ihrem Wesen her – selektiv. Was wir anstreben ist vielmehr eine breiter angelegte Darstellung aktueller, sich auf die *Conditio humana* und die menschlichen Erfahrungen auswirkenden Realitäten im Licht von postkolonialem Diskurs, Globalisierung, Multikulturalismus und geopolitischer, wirtschaftlicher und umweltbedingter Veränderungen. Während *The Family of Man* die verheerenden Auswirkungen des Zweiten Weltkriegs – beziehungsweise jede Andeutung von politischem Trauma, zivilem Konflikt oder Ungehorsam – zu leugnen schien, scheut unsere Ausstellung nicht vor negativen Utopien zurück und schließt sich nicht der Fiktion einer einzigen glücklichen Familie der Menschheit an.

Unsere Ausstellung ist weit entfernt von der idealen, harmonischen, weißen, heterosexuellen Präsentation, wie Steichen sie darbot; unsere Ausstellung würdigt vielmehr Alternativen zur weißen Mittelklasse, dem westlichen Ideal, indem sie das Anderssein und soziale Dissonanzen hervorhebt. Eines ist jedoch sicher: Wenn die Ausstellung *The Family of Man* heute erneut realisiert werden sollte, wäre sie aufgespalten, heterogen und widersprüchlich *und* es gäbe eine Gemeinsamkeit bestimmter Erfahrungen, eben weil die Welt kleiner wird und, für viele von uns, homogener.

Die Stimme des Bildes

The Eye is a Lonely Hunter: Images of Humankind richtet den Blick darauf, wie und warum Fotografie anthropologisches Wissen überbringt und jenen, die nicht gesehen oder gehört werden, eine Stimme verleiht. Die Ausstellung konzentriert sich auf die einzigartige Fähigkeit der Kamera, mit der Wirklichkeit umzugehen, Empathie zu erzeugen und spezifisch menschliche Gefühle zu erwecken. Die indexikalische Beziehung zwischen dem, was sich vor der Kamera befindet, was auf dem Bild gezeigt ist und der Geschichte, die damit dem Betrachter erzählt wird, ist eine der grundlegenden Untersuchungen der Ausstellung. Es geht dabei nicht unbedingt darum, ob dieses Bild wahr oder unwahr ist, obwohl es ein Ziel der Ausstellung ist, den potenziellen Wahrheitsanspruch der Fotografie wieder zur Geltung zu bringen. Jahrzehntelang wurde das Medium Fotografie sowohl in der bildenden Kunst als auch in den Massenmedien als bedeutungsleeres und manipulatives semiotisches Zeichen untersucht und dargestellt. Der Begriff der fotografischen Wahrheit kam auf den Prüfstand, und die Fähigkeit der Kamera, nicht nur zu inszenieren, sondern auch zu lügen, wurde deutlich. Und doch bietet die Fotografie etwas, das immer noch als aufklärerisch und nützlich gelten kann und darüber hinaus eine Form von Wissen als Gefühl oder Emotion erzeugt, das nach wie vor als wahrhaftig angesehen werden kann.

Roland Barthes beschreibt diesen Effekt als das fotografische *punctum*, ein Element, das die starre Oberfläche des Fotos wie ein Pfeil durchbohrt, die Banalität der Darstellung durchschneidet, das genau das aufrüttelt, was reglos hinter dem „Blick" liegt und beim Betrachter in Bezug auf die abgebildete spezifische Situation oder Person eine empathische Reaktion auslöst.[10] Das *punctum* ist dann eine Art subtiles *Jenseits* – so als würde das Bild über das, was es uns erlaubt zu sehen, hinaus eine Sehnsucht zum Ausdruck bringen. In seinem sehr nachdenklichen Beitrag für diesen Katalog spricht TJ Demos über den Begriff der Opazität. In diesem Sinne können wir Fotografie nicht nur im Hinblick auf das als wichtig betrachten, was sie abbildet, sondern auch, was sie außerhalb ihres Rahmens zu verstehen gibt, beziehungsweise was Barthes die unsichtbare Eigenschaft von Fotografie genannt hat, die wir ebenfalls nicht sehen können.[11] Bei der Betrachtung eines Bildes ist es also wichtig, sich überlegen oder vorstellen zu können, was außerhalb des Rahmens passieren könnte; nicht nur im Bild zu denken, sondern auch darüber hinaus.

Tom Gunning hat die Frage nach der Wahrheit in der Fotografie um einige wertvolle Einsichten ergänzt, indem er darauf aufmerksam macht, dass:

> „Der Apparat selbst weder lügen noch die Wahrheit sagen kann. Die für sich genommen sprachlose Fotografie ist darauf angewiesen, dass Menschen sich über sie oder für sie äußern. ... Sowohl historisch als auch institutionell muss das Foto, damit es die Wahrheit zum Ausdruck bringt, einer Reihe von Diskursen unterzogen werden, muss im Grunde zum unterstützenden Beleg für eine Aussage werden. Jeder der entweder die komplexe Geschichte kennt, durch die Fotografien bei Gerichtsverhandlungen als Beweismittel zugelassen wurden, oder weiß, welchen Prüfungen und Diskussionen sie unterzogen werden müssen, bevor sie in heutigen Verfahren diesen Status erlangen, muss erkennen, dass die Fotografie, um die Wahrheit zu berichten, in eine Behauptung integriert sein muss, die vielschichtigen – juristischen, rhetorischen und sogar wissenschaftlichen – Diskursregeln unterliegt."[12]

Darüber hinaus betont er die enge Wechselbeziehung zwischen Wahrheit und Fakten einerseits und konstruiertem Bild oder Täuschung andererseits, die als polare Gegensätze gelten können.

> „Als eine Kunstform war Fotografie nie solchen Restriktionen unterworfen hinsichtlich Sachlichkeit und Genauigkeit ... genau wie ein gefälschtes Bild darauf angewiesen ist, dass wir nach wie vor an die Verlässlichkeit von Bildern glauben, so ist ein spielerisches Bild, das sich vor unseren Augen dekonstruiert, auf unser Vertrauen in die Fähigkeit des Fotografen angewiesen, Objekte präzise zu zeigen."[13]

Gunning stellt die Vorstellung infrage, derzufolge Fotografien in erster Linie semiotisch funktionieren, als Zeichen also, die es zu dekodieren gilt. Er erkennt an, dass eine Fotografie indexikalisch funktionieren kann, postuliert aber, dass eine solche Eigenschaft zweitrangig ist, wenn es um die Fähigkeit der Fotografie geht, uns ein Bild der Welt vorzulegen – eine Position, der sich auch diese Ausstellung anschließt.

> „Bilder sind generell mehr als Zeichen und oftmals könnte man nur mit Mühe behaupten, dass sie sich auf irgendetwas anderes beziehen als auf sich selbst. Aber Fotografien scheinen auf eine seltsame Art und Weise aus sich

10 Roland Barthes, *Camera Lucida: Reflections on Photography*, Vintage Books, London 2000, S. 59.
11 Barthes, *ibd.*, S. 6.

12 Tom Gunning, „What's the Point of an Index? Or, Faking Photographs", S. 41.
13 Gunning, *ibd.*, S. 45.

heraus zu verweisen, und dies ist Teil der Begründung, dass der Index einen Teil der Kraft zu erklären scheint. Aber während Zeichen ihre Referenz auf eine Bedeutung reduzieren, würde ich behaupten, dass die Fotografie einen Zugang zu ihrem Motiv eröffnet, nicht als eine Bedeutung, sondern als eine Welt, vielfältig und komplex."[14]

Sogar Barthes selbst erkannte die „evidentielle Kraft" der Fotografie an, und dass die Kraft ihrer Aussage sich nicht auf das Objekt, sondern auf Zeit bezieht.[15]

Diese „evidentielle Kraft" hat vielleicht weniger mit Objektivität als mit Entscheidung zu tun, basierend auf dem Standpunkt des Fotografen. Man würde argumentieren, dass die Vorstellung von Wahrheit, die traditionell in der dokumentarischen Abbildung der Wirklichkeit liegen soll, auch in einer anderen, eher konstruierten Form der Fotografie existieren könnte, wo Tricks und Kunstgriffe den Vorrang vor der direkten Spiegelung der Realität haben. Und hier sollten wir vielleicht darüber nachdenken, dem Dämon der Ästhetisierung den Garaus zu machen, die oft als ideologisch suspekt betrachtet wird, weil sie möglicherweise den Verstand des Betrachters trüben könnte. So gesehen gibt es keine unverfälschte Form der Darstellung, selbst nicht in der Dokumentarfotografie, und zwar eben aufgrund der oben erwähnten Frage der Entscheidung. Angesichts der Beziehung zwischen Ethik, Ästhetik und Verantwortung möchten wir David Levi Strauss' Position zum Motiv anführen, die viel Stoff zum Nachdenken bietet:

„Die Vorstellung, dass, je veränderter oder ‚ästhetisierter' ein Bild ist, es umso weniger ‚authentisch' oder politisch wertvoll wird, muss ernstlich hinterfragt werden. Warum sollte Schönheit *nicht* zum Handeln auffordern können? ... Darstellen ist gleichbedeutend mit ästhetisieren – und das heißt verändern. Dies bietet große Spielräume für Entscheidungen und Möglichkeiten, dazu gehört aber nicht die Entscheidung, das Dargestellte *nicht* zu formen, zu verändern oder zu modifizieren. In der Praxis kann das nicht einfach ein Prozess sein. Dies gilt für die Fotografie genauso wie für andere Mittel der Darstellung. Das ist aber kein Grund, davor zurückzuschrecken. Ästhetik ist nicht objektiv und ist nicht auf quantitative wissenschaftliche Kriterien zu reduzieren. Quantität kann nur physikalische Phänomene messen und ist bei Ästhetik fehl am Platz, die häufig mit dem zu tun hat, was eben *nicht* vorhanden ist und durch die bloße Vorstellung Dinge entstehen lässt. Um für andere lesbar zu werden, müssen diese Vorstellungen kulturell und sozial enkodiert sein. Das ist Ästhetisierung."[16]

Insofern ist es ein interessanter Versuch, ein selektives „Porträt der Menschheit im Jahr 2011" zusammenzustellen, das einerseits ein Gegenstück zu dem 1955 gezeichneten Porträt der Menschheit ist und andererseits einen Vergleich dazu bietet. Aber auch für künftige Generationen kann dies von Interesse sein, damit diese später sehen können, wie wir uns 2011 sahen – so wie es für uns interessant ist, zu betrachten, wie wir uns 1955 sahen. Eine Fotografie ist sozusagen eine Art Guckloch der Zeit, durch das wir sehen können, wie Menschen, ihr Verhalten, ihre Kleidung und das, was sie besaßen, irgendwann einmal ausgesehen haben (meist eine sehr emotionsgeladene Angelegenheit).

Ohne den postmodernen Diskurs über die Fähigkeit der Kamera zu lügen, oder den Niedergang der fotografischen Wahrheit beiseite schieben zu wollen, bekräftigt die 4. Ausgabe des Fotofestivals die Fähigkeit der Fotografie, Zeugnis über die *Conditio humana* und die menschliche Erfahrung innerhalb realer sozialer und politischer Bedingungen abzulegen. Die ausgewählten Künstler setzen die Kraft der Fotografie dafür ein, das „Netz der Realität zu durchschneiden", um in den Worten Walter Benjamins zu sprechen, und vom Leben der Menschen zu erzählen – im Gegensatz zur Annäherung an die Fotografie als

14 Gunning, *ibd.*, S. 46.
15 Barthes, *Camera Lucida*, S. 89.
16 David Levi Strauss, „The Documentary Debate: Aesthetic or Anaesthetic?", *Between the Eyes: Essays on Photography and Politics*, Aperture, New York 2005, S. 9.

einem postmodernen Spiel mit Zeichen. Der Titel der Ausstellung unterstreicht diese Wertschätzung sozialen und kulturellen Engagements in der Fotografie, weshalb wir das folgende Kapitel dem Roman widmen, der uns zu diesem Titel inspiriert hat, *The Heart is a Lonely Hunter* von Carson McCuller.

The Heart is a Lonely Hunter

Titel und Konzept des 4. Fotofestivals *The Eye is a Lonely Hunter: Images of Humankind* schöpfen aus Carson McCullers' Roman *The Heart is a Lonely Hunter*, einem der meist gelesenen, übersetzten und geschätzten amerikanischen Romane des 20. Jahrhunderts. McCullers schrieb *The Heart is a Lonely Hunter* im Alter von nur 23 Jahren. Der Roman handelt von Menschen, die in den 1930er-Jahren ungehört am Rande der amerikanischen Gesellschaft leben, unter Rassismus und Armut leiden und nur wenig Aussicht auf eine bessere Zukunft haben. Eine Textilstadt in Georgia bildet den Schauplatz der Geschichte, in deren Mittelpunkt der taubstumme John Singer steht, der an einer Bar in einem Motel mit Menschen zusammentrifft, die ihre Probleme mit ihm teilen. Da ist Mick Kelly, ein mutiges und talentiertes Mädchen, das klassische Musik liebt und davon träumt, ein Klavier zu kaufen; Jake Blount, ein Trinker und Arbeiterführer; Biff Brannon, ein Beobachter und Besitzer eines Restaurants; und Dr. Benedict Copeland, ein idealistischer, afroamerikanischer Arzt. All diese Charaktere vertrauen sich Singer an und haben das Gefühl, er würde sie besser verstehen als irgendjemand sonst.

Im Zusammenhang mit dem diesjährigen 4. Fotofestival spricht der Roman eine wichtige Frage an: *Wie repräsentiert man die „Stimmlosen" in der Gesellschaft?* Das Buch beschreibt voller Poesie die Diskrepanz zwischen den beiden unterschiedlichen, aber häufig austauschbaren Fragen *Wer repräsentiert wen und warum?* und *Wer kann sich mit wem identifizieren und warum?* Die Identifizierung der Charaktere mit Singer ist eindeutig eine Projektion ihrer eigenen Bedürfnisse: Es findet keine echte Verständigung statt. Singer hört ihnen nur zu, weil es ihn von seiner eigenen Einsamkeit und seinen unerfüllten Sehnsüchten ablenkt – tatsächlich gibt es niemanden, der Singers eigene Bedürfnisse erkennt, und am Ende nimmt er sich das Leben. Singer schreibt in einem Brief an seinen einzigen Freund Spiros Antonopoulos:

> „Du erinnerst Dich wohl an die vier Menschen, von denen ich Dir erzählte, als ich bei Dir war... Alle vier sind sehr beschäftigt. Tatsächlich sie sind so beschäftigt, wie Du Dir's kaum vorstellen kannst. Ich meine nicht, dass sie Tag und Nacht beruflich arbeiten; sie beschäftigen sich in Gedanken mit so vielen Dingen, dass sie nicht zur Ruhe kommen ... Der Besitzer vom Café New York ist allerdings nicht so – der ist ganz anders ... Der ist ein Beobachter. Und alle haben irgendwas, was sie mehr lieben als Essen und Schlafen oder Wein und nette Gesellschaft. Daher sind sie auch immer so beschäftigt."[17]

Das entscheidende Dilemma in diesem Roman ist die Suche nach einer Art emotionalem Asyl für die Ideen und Hoffnungen der Charaktere. Die Ausstellung zeigt einen etwas anderen Blick, weil hier das Auge des Fotografen in der Rolle des einsamen Jägers die Sehnsucht nach Darstellung und den Wunsch, den Stimmlosen eine Stimme zu verleihen, ermöglicht. Hier sind das Herz und das Auge miteinander verbunden und mit sozialem und kulturellem Engagement in die Fotografie verstrickt. Die Ausstellung betont die Fähigkeit des Fotografen, emotionales Wissen zu transportieren und einen Blick und Sympathie für die Randerscheinungen der Gesellschaft in einer globalen Welt wachzurufen.
Die Fragen *Wer repräsentiert wen?* und *Wer identifiziert sich mit wem?* sind grundlegende Fragen. Wir haben Künstler und Fotografen aus der ganzen Welt eingeladen, die als interdisziplinäre Forscher tätig sind und einen Kontext repräsentieren, in dem sie, entweder für

17 McCullers, Carson *The Heart is a Lonely Hunter*, First Mariner Books Edition, Boston 2000, S.214 f. (zitiert nach der Übersetzung von Susanna Rademacher in: McCullers, Carson, *Das Herz ist ein einsamer Jäger*, Diogenes Verlag AG, Zürich 1974, S. 187 f.)

einen längeren Zeitraum oder ihr ganzes Leben lang, gelebt und gearbeitet haben. Wir wissen zwar zu schätzen, dass die globale Kunstwelt mit kurzen Arbeitsaufenthalten wichtige Türen für künstlerische Forschungsprojekte öffnet, für uns als Kuratorinnen ist es jedoch wichtig, Künstler vorzustellen, deren Arbeit zutiefst von der politischen, akademischen und journalistischen Genealogie ihrer Themen und Kontexte durchdrungen ist.

Der Künstler als Forscher

Die hier vorgestellten Künstler stellen häufig das Klischee vom „anderen" und vom „Selbst" infrage. Ihre engagierten Positionen sind vergleichbar mit der Situation von dokumentarisch oder ethnografisch arbeitenden Fotografen, die unter gefährlichen Bedingungen leben und arbeiten, um von noch undokumentierten oder unveröffentlichten Lebensweisen zu berichten. Im Licht des postkolonialen Diskurses werden westliche Perspektiven hinterfragt. Die Völker, die bis vor nicht allzu langer Zeit noch als „andere" dargestellt wurden, sind heute in der Lage, ihr eigenes fotografisches Selbstverständnis, ihre Identität und ihr Bild vom Westen zu vermitteln. Die Fotografie als Medium hat anthropologisch gesehen immer schon eine zentrale Rolle bei der Erschaffung eines kulturellen Selbstverständnisses und bei der Ausrichtung auf das der anderen gespielt. Wie der Titel dieser Ausstellung bereits erkennen lässt, sind die ausgestellten Kunstwerke losgelöst von der Aufmerksamkeit der Massen – der Fotograf ist in einsamer und unabhängiger Mission unterwegs (er führt keine Auftragsarbeit aus). Was das Auge sich auf seiner einsamen Jagd ersehnt, findet und denkt, ist vielmehr ein kontrastierender Diskurs zu der modernen Tradition normativer humanistischer Anthropologie. Es richtet sich stattdessen auf Existenzen oder geografische Phänomene, die unerwartet, surreal, marginalisiert, zurückgestoßen, außer Sichtweite sind.

An dieser Stelle kann es hilfreich sein, eine generelle Unterscheidung zwischen Anthropologie und Kunst in Bezug auf Forschung und Methode vorzunehmen, eine Unterscheidung, die lediglich theoretischer Natur, aber als Schema hilfreich ist. In *The Predicament of Culture – Twentieth-Century Ethnography, Literature, and Art* (1988) analysiert Professor James Clifford, wie Kunst, Literatur und Methoden des Sammelns und Ausstellens in Museen für Ethnografie Fiktionen des „anderen" schaffen. In dieser Tour de Force von Kunst und Anthropologie im Zeitalter der Globalisierung zeigt er sehr präzise Unterschiede in der Art und Weise auf, in der Anthropologen und Künstler Ethnografie im Laufe des letzten Jahrhunderts ausgeübt haben – die Anthropologen kommen aus einer humanistischen und dokumentarischen Tradition, die Künstler aus der *Aktivität* des „ethnografischen Surrealismus".

> „Anthropologischer Humanismus und ethnografischer Surrealismus müssen nicht als sich gegenseitig ausschließend betrachtet werden; sie können vielleicht am besten als Antinomien in einem vergänglichen, historischen und kulturellen Dilemma verstanden werden. Legt man den Gegensatz schematisch dar, beginnt der anthropologische Humanismus mit dem Verschiedenen und lässt es – durch Benennung, Klassifizierung, Beschreibung, Deutung – verständlich werden. Er macht vertraut. Im Gegensatz dazu greift eine ethnografische, surrealistische Praxis das Vertraute an und ruft einen Ausbruch der Andersartigkeit hervor – das Unerwartete."[18]

Kunsthistorische Beispiele für Vertreter des ethnografischen Surrealismus sind der Franzose André Breton (1896–1966) als Initiator des Surrealismus, und später dann Jean Rouch (1917–2004), der ethnografische Filmemacher und Begründer des Cinéma vérité. Die Künstler und Fotografen, die in der aktuellen Ausstellung zu sehen sind, betreiben ethnografische Forschung mit unterschiedlichen Ansätzen – einige neigen dazu, mit dem Andersartigen vertraut zu machen, aber viele inszenieren

18 Clifford, James, *The Predicament of Culture: Twentieth-Century Ethnography, Literature, and Art*, Harvard, Cambridge, Massachusetts 1999, S. 144 f.

das Gegenteil (nicht immer mit surrealistischen Ausdrucksmitteln). Beide Ansätze schaffen wichtige Inhalte, wenn es um die Darstellung der heutigen *Conditio humana* geht. Die ethische Kontingenz hingegen hängt aus unserer Sicht als Kuratorinnen immer davon ab, wie das Kunstwerk geschaffen und ausgestellt wird.

Es ist deshalb wichtig, einen Blick auf die reiche Vielfalt und Gegensätzlichkeit der unterschiedlichen künstlerischen und fotografischen Forschungsmethoden in der Ausstellung zu werfen. Der südafrikanische Fotograf Pieter Hugo untersuchte vor dem Hintergrund der Dokumentation und Darstellung sozialer Bedingungen und kultureller Identitäten die Tradition des Geschichtenerzählens in westafrikanischen „Nollywood"-Filmen und schuf Porträtfotos lokaler Charaktere, in denen sich die Mythen der schwarzen Hautfarbe widerspiegeln und Realität und Fiktion ineinander verwoben sind (die Reihe *Nollywood*, 2009). In der Serie *Today's Life and War* (2008) inszeniert die iranische Künstlerin Gohar Dashti Aufnahmen aus dem Alltag eines iranischen Paares auf dem Schauplatz des Krieges und lenkt den Blick auf die Fragilität der Intimität in Kriegsgebieten. Der kenianische Fotojournalist Boniface Mwangi dokumentiert in der Reihe *Post Election Violence* (2008) die Gewaltausbrüche zwischen den Volksstämmen, nachdem Präsident Mwai Kibaki sich mit einer manipulierten Wahl den Weg zur Macht erschlichen hatte.

Ausgehend von einem humanitären Standpunkt unternahm der dänische Fotograf Jacob Holdt 5 Jahre lang eine Reise als heimatloser Vagabund durch die afroamerikanische und weiße Unter-, Mittel- und Oberschicht-Gesellschaft Amerikas und erstellte mit seiner Canon Dial 35-2 eine umfangreiche Dokumentation, die er in einem Buch und einer Reihe von Lesungen vorstellte (die Reihe *American Pictures*, 1970–1975). Peggy Buth dokumentierte aus einer museumsbezogenen Perspektive und über einen Zeitraum von 5 Jahren den Wechsel der Ausstellungen und der Ausstellungsarchitektur im Königlichen Museum für Zentralafrika in Tervuren (in der Nähe von Brüssel), da das Museum bemüht war, seine Identität als Repräsentant einer Kolonialmacht zu rechtfertigen (die Reihe *Desire in Representation (Travelling through the Musée Royale)*, 2004–2009). Der kanadisch-holländische Dokumentarfotograf Paolo Woods hielt eines der größten imperialen Projekte unserer Zeit fest und folgte einigen der 500.000 Chinesen, die sich aufgemacht haben, Afrika durch den Aufbau einer Infrastruktur und die Erschließung von Ressourcen zu entwickeln und zu „erobern" (*Chinafrica*, 2007). Der chinesische Künstler Yang Yongliang befasst sich in seiner manipulierten Fotografie mit den überwältigenden und überaus schnell fortschreitenden Prozessen der Urbanisierung in China. Auf den ersten Blick sehen seine Bilder wie großformatige Gebirgslandschaften im traditionellen Stil der chinesischen *Shui-Mo*-Malerei und -Kalligrafie aus; bei näherem Hinsehen sind sie jedoch überwuchert von städtischer Infrastruktur und aus zahlreichen Fotos zusammengesetzt. Der deutsche Künstler Olaf Otto Becker dokumentiert Grönlands schmelzendes Eis und neue Flussformationen aus ins Meer abfließendem Schmelzwasser und präsentiert sie als erhabene Eislandschaften (*Above Zero*, Reihe *River 1*, 2008).

Dieses Eintauchen in aufreibende Situationen mit dem Ergebnis echter gelebter Erfahrung wird auch in der Arbeit von Geert Goiris deutlich, der für seine Fotos häufig gefährliche Reisen in die Wildnis unternimmt. Ein anders geartetes, jedoch ähnliches Engagement für einen bestimmten Schauplatz kann man bei Boris Mikhailovs beobachten. Er porträtiert Menschen auf der unhaltbaren Seite des post-sowjetischen Wirtschaftsbooms und fügt sich damit in die Tradition der sozial denkenden und handelnden Dokumentation und der subkulturellen Insider-Dokumentation ein, in der der Fotograf und sein Motiv in eine interaktive Beziehung eintreten. Auch Roger Ballens Fotos von Menschen am Rande der weißen Gesellschaft in Südafrika schöpfen aus der Verbindung zwischen Fotograf und Motiv. Taryn Simon verbrachte 2 Jahre mit Menschen, die zu Unrecht für Verbrechen, die sie nicht begangen hatten, verurteilt worden waren, im Gefängnis gesessen hatten und dann freigelassen wurden: Ihre Arbeit *The Innocents* (2002) untersucht die umstrittene Rolle der Fotografie in der Strafjustiz. Edward Burtynsky nimmt umfassende Nachforschungsprojekte in Angriff und beschäftigt sich mit Fragen des Industrialismus und des Post-Industrialismus, sich verändernden Produktionsmodellen, mit Umweltfragen und den Auswirkungen der Globalisierung sowie neoliberaler ökonomischer Vorgehensweisen. Er zeigt Fotoreihen, die vor allem auf eine serielle Darstellung Wert legen, um Wechsel, Ursache und Wirkung aufzuzeigen.

Als Abschluss dieser Abhandlung möchten wir über eine der kritischen und akademisch fundierten Stimmen nachdenken, die sich skeptisch zu der Frage, *wie* Kunst an der Anthropologie partizipieren kann, geäußert haben – gemeint ist der Kunstkritiker Hal Foster. In seinem Essay *The Artist as Ethnographer*, geht Foster auf James Clifford ein und betont, dass der Künstler, der eine Art „Quasi-Anthropologie" betreibt, die Wissenschaft der Anthropologie als eine Wissenschaft der „Alterität" schätzt.[19] Er argumentiert, dass es bei einer Begegnung des Künstlers mit dem anderen häufiger vorkommt, ein „Selbst-Othering" oder „Selbst-Fashioning" zu unternehmen, als seinem Motiv näher zu kommen (man muss sich auch die Frage stellen, ob das das Ziel ist?). Außerdem legt er dar, dass das mit einer derart idealistischen Intention entstandene Kunstwerk letzten Endes Gefahr läuft, von seinen Sponsoren als soziales Engagement zur Kenntnis genommen zu werden.[20] Das ist eine maßgebliche Kritik an der Rolle des Künstlers als Forscher und an seinem oder ihrem Bestreben, den anderen zu repräsentieren. Die Frage ist sowohl kulturpolitischer als auch rezeptionsästhetischer Natur: Wie wird das Publikum in die Ausstellung eingeführt? Liegt ein Schwerpunkt auf der Kommunikation oder steht der Sponsor im Mittelpunkt der Aufmerksamkeit? Was Foster jedoch außer Acht zu lassen scheint, ist die Tatsache, dass der Westen nicht länger den Rest repräsentiert, sondern von außen betrachtet wird und deshalb gezwungen ist, sich selbst zu betrachten. Zudem bietet das interdisziplinäre Betätigungsfeld der Kunst, und das ist ebenfalls von großer Bedeutung, häufig auch Fachleuten und „Wissensproduzenten" aus anderen akademischen Bereichen wie Archäologie, Geschichte, visueller Anthropologie, Politik, Geografie, Journalismus und Architektur ein Zuhause, und genau das zeigen wir in *The Eye is a Lonely Hunter: Images of Humankind*.

Wir hoffen, dass die Ausstellung ein neues ethisches Engagement für die Fotografie widerspiegelt, das die traditionellen Prämissen fotografischer Faktizität anerkennt und die Klippen des Stereotyps umgeht, die sich in der Vergangenheit gezeigt haben, wenn dokumentarische Praktiken ihre Motive versachlicht und in eine beklemmende „Wahrheit" gezwängt haben. Viele zeitgenössische Fotografen sind sich jetzt der Politik der Repräsentation und der Kommodifizierung ihres Blicks bewusst. Ihre Arbeiten werden im Rahmen des Fotofestivals die neue Definition der Fotografie und eine neue Wahrnehmung der Welt widerspiegeln.

19 Foster, Hal, *The Return of the Real–the Avant-Garde at the End of the Century*, chapter 10 *The Artist as Ethnographer*, An October Book, The MIT Press, Cambridge, Massachusetts, S. 303.
20 *ibd.*

The Eye is a Lonely Hunter: Images of Humankind On Depicting The Human Condition in 2011

Katerina Gregos & Solvej Helweg Ovesen

The 4th Fotofestival is a photographic survey of the human condition as we enter the second decade of the twenty-first century. The work here presents perspectives from geographically diverse locations in Africa, South America, Europe and Asia. The title *The Eye is a Lonely Hunter: Images of Humankind*, refers to the position and venture of the photographer and the eye as a 'lonely hunter' of a particular subject. That is to underline the fact that documentary practice, especially the moment of selecting and shooting – what the French photographer and father of modern photojournalism Henri Cartier-Bresson called the 'decisive moment' – entails core political decisions on the part of the photographer. The title of the festival is inspired by Carson McCuller's novel *The Heart is a Lonely Hunter* (1940), which gives voice to the mistreated, the rejected and the forgotten.

Why have we chosen to make an artistic survey of images of humankind at this point in time, in 2011? What is the historical motivation and context for such a move? In recent decades, universal humanist values have come under fire, and photography has been said to lie rather than tell the truth. Exactly a decade ago on 11 September 2001, the Twin Towers in New York collapsed, and the backbone of neo-liberal world power was jolted. This turn of events has exacerbated contentious issues surrounding humanist values – questions that are also prevalent in the arts in regards to macro-political issues of economic and exploitative circuits, imperialism, tolerance, ethnographic 'othering', freedom of speech, self-censorship, civic courage, suppression and marginalisation of women and men. This is the backdrop for our curatorial motivation to ask for alternative images of humankind founded in documentary photography: images that might divert and inspire identities in their grounded existence and becoming.

On the occasion of the opening weekend of the 4th Fotofestival (9–11 September 2011), we present 57 artists from 32 countries with a selection of 700 images and artworks that describe almost as many images of humankind. They transport knowledge about inspired, critical, possible, and impossible prospects of a fragmented humanism, and take into account the permanent leeway of anti-humanism. The images on display are divided into five different sub-themes marking the effects and affects on humankind of the macro-political questions of our decade. They are presented as a counter-discourse and seen from the subjective position of the photographer and viewer as case stories.

How is the exploration of the human condition reflected in the photographic medium? *The Eye is a Lonely Hunter: Images of Humankind* is an exhibition taking the *in situ* moment of the photographer and the photographed into account as a photograph is shot. The subjectivities of the persons behind and before the camera and their context are often central to the making of these images. The eye as a 'lonely hunter' is an eye that searches for particularity, difference, surprise, expressions of the invisible and the contradictory, and aspects of reality that are not mere extensions of the photographer's self. It searches for a connection to the visible and invisible world through the steps and the tactics of the photographer, but also of the photographed. Over a period of a year and a half, the curatorial team behind the 4th Fotofestival have sought ways in which artworks might contain or reflect upon anthropological knowledge that resists colonial attitudes and normative values. We have explored critical ways to bypass a self-righteous western humanism in order to make an extensive exhibition that portrays the human condition in 2011, inviting its complexity, difference and uncertainties.

We could define this new photographic humanism as one which is more directly engaged, acknowledges the responsibilities and problematics underlying the capturing of the 'other' and the politics of representation, and finally puts emphasis on direct communication, interaction and intimacy – as opposed to 'objective' social analysis or activism. This form of engaged photography goes beyond the instantaneous capturing of an event and its causes. It addresses a problem noticed by Richard Cross – a photojournalist who was killed on the Honduras / Nicaragua border in 1983 – who observed that 'photographers sometimes are very short-sighted in looking at causes. They are interested in the more dramatic symptoms of the problem, rather than the cause of the problem'[1].

As Cross points out, within mainstream news and media imagery there is very little self-reflection on causes of the dramatic images of the human condition, and the role of the photographer in that situation – but this does not mean that such images are of no value and cannot be reflected on by others. Evidently, there are large differences between the intentions of the photographers, editors and commissioners who create such news and media imagery. But any photograph, image or document reveals something about the society it represents or is made in. Take, for example, fashion photographs in women's magazines. Are they not wonderful material for an anthropologist who wants to study, let us say, the difference between societal behaviour and beauty ideals of the 1950s and today? While they were not made with that use in mind, they nevertheless can be and are used for as a platform for investigating a society's ideals.

The Eye is a Lonely Hunter: Images of Humankind critically reflects on the anthropological role of photography, and presents it as part of the creative negotiation of *self–other* dichotomies and difference in postcolonial terms. Photography here takes alienating, abstract, surreal, and penetrating forms. Thus the exhibition of the 4th Fotofestival must be seen as a complimentary space to anthropological and documentary discourse. As curators we have been looking for engaged and talented artists and photographers who generate images that document the way in which individuals (rather than *peoples*) engage with the challenges of everyday life. The photographer performs a kind of artistic research complimentary to that undertaken by ethnographers, which we will elaborate in the chapter 'The Artist as Researcher'.

Art photographs can change the way people see the world and respond to it, just as anthropological photographs might do. More importantly, they can be even more powerful and evocative than anthropological photographs, which mostly remain in the realm of scientific discourse, since they have a freedom to touch upon subjectivities and affective impulses. The art historian and media theorist Tom Gunning has stated that: 'In contrast to the protocols that enabled the truth claim of the legal or scientific photograph, art photography may create its own protocols and practices, free to explore its forms.'[2]

This is the background to how we have surveyed, categorised and arranged the work in this exhibition. The sub-themes, which we return to later in individual chapters, are entitled 'The Practice of Everyday Life', 'The Affect and Effect of Politics', 'Ecological Circuits', 'Role and Ritual', and 'Life Cycles'. The photographic traditions in the exhibition that support the exploration of these topics are mainly indebted to the documentary tradition in photography and film: photojournalism, docu-fiction, anthropological photography, snapshots, and photo- and film-collage, although they do not exclude constructed or staged photography which may also

1 Richard Cross 'Photographers of the Vanguard', *News Photographer Magazine*, September 1981, reprinted in 'Photography and Propadanda' in *Between the Eyes: Essays on Photography and Politics* (New York: Aperture, 2005), p. 20.

2 Tom Gunning 'What's the Point of an Index? Or, Faking Photographs', *Nordicom Review*, vol. 5, no.1/2 (September 2004), p.44.

transmit anthropological knowledge, and even essential truths encoded within a constructed image. The traditions of portrait and landscape photography also have an important presence in the exhibition and refine an overall impression of the human condition. In general, we have been working with an expanded idea of photography in mind, where content rather than exclusively formal questions have been at the forefront of our choices, though at the same time we have opted for photographic positions that have a strong sense of visuality, sometimes even an iconic quality and contribute to the processing of the following key questions:

> What would a portrait of humankind look like in the year 2011?
> What are some of the key issues and challenges facing humanity today?
> How do humans care for their kind and generate empathy between one another and how is this documented via the photographic medium?
> How do photographers and the photographed invite others inside their lives?

In order to answer these challenging questions, we have been looking for artistic photography, film and video that draws on the traditions of documentary, ethnographic and staged photography and their encounters with reality and fiction as means of storytelling and truth-telling. Aware that neither art nor thematic exhibitions at large can save the world, but can change our understandings of it, we acknowledge that subjective critical thinking offers a space of empirical and theoretical freedom and is a site for knowledge production on humanism.

The Family of Man

> 'Photography records the gamut of feelings written on the human face – the beauty of the earth and skies that man has inherited; and the wealth and confusion that man has created. It is a major force in explaining man to man.'[3]

3 Edward Steichen, *Time*, 7 April 1961.

The Eye is a Lonely Hunter: Images of Humankind is also a critical reflection on the exhibition 'The Family of Man' (1955), a milestone of the humanist perspective in documentary photography in the twentieth century. In many ways, *The Eye is a Lonely Hunter* is presented in contrast to that exhibition, even as it admits its importance. When the photographer, curator and museum director Edward Steichen (1879–1973) made his hugely successful 'The Family of Man' exhibition at The Museum of Modern Art (MoMA) in New York in 1955, he was working in a very different context to the one in which today's photographers operate. Organized in the aftermath of World War II and at the beginning of the Cold War, the exhibition was part of a larger quest for universal humanist values and perspectives. For example, these ideas were also played out, in a different manner, in the first documenta, *documenta 1*, held in Kassel in 1955, and organized by Arnold Bode.[4] Steichen is known to have said that 'art for art's sake is dead, if it ever lived'. He thus looked for the bigger existential questions in art. 'The Family of Man' was organized into 37 archetypal or 'universal' themes of birth and death, family, education, work, and play, war and peace, etc. The exhibition advocated the idea of the universality of human experience and photography's role in its documentation; it also played an important role in legitimating the medium of photography as art.

Although it was in its time one of the most popular and visited photographic exhibitions ever (touring to 38 countries in four continents and receiving more than nine million visitors) it subsequently received considerable critique – most prominently from the French philosopher Roland Barthes (1915–80) in his book *Mythologies* (1957) for the overriding proposition of the exhibition, which was that people are the same the world over, regardless of differences in geography and culture. Problematically, although also accepting submission of photographs

4 The thematic focus of *documenta 1* was *Entartete Kunst* (Degenerate Art), of the Modernist abstract painting tradition that was rejected during National Socialism.

for his exhibition, Steichen had sourced many of his images from just eight photo-journalist agencies in New York, and thus most photographers in the exhibition were from the western world. The exhibition advocated what can be called the commonality of experience and asserted a rhetoric of global universality, presenting a reassuring representation of the universal family of man.[5]

Barthes' critique was that the show suppressed 'the determining weight of History' and avoided the inclusion of 'historically specific' photographs, photographs that provided insight into the social, political or economic conditions that underlie the image and its depicted subject.[6] Barthes pinpointed the fact that in order to convey this idea of universal experience, a process of decontextualisation was implemented. As a result, the images in the exhibition appeared almost abstract: removed from time and place, disconnected from socio-historical context and then reorganised around specific supposedly universal categories. There was no room for historical detail, no mention of underlying conditions, specificities and consequences. Barthes criticized both what he called 'this ambiguous myth of the human community' and Steichen's classic humanist approach, which he argued removed the realm of experience from the flow of history.[7]

Despite Barthes' well-founded critique, it is important to also re-contextualise 'The Family of Man', with the benefit of historical hindsight. But what is also sometimes forgotten is that Steichen's exhibition wanted to express a general optimism after the end of World War II, to give a hopeful picture of the world instead of a bleak and fatalistic concept of mankind. His was a plea for human dignity. Steichen wanted to jump over all the known differences that Barthes mentioned – colour of skin, race, nationality and economic inequalities. Barthes' arguments are used to show that differences are decisive – but, however right Barthes' critique might have been in one sense, he does not take into account Steichen's deeper motivations. While Steichen was indeed naive, in a way so was Barthes' critique. Steichen wanted to stress the similarities, and indeed proposed an almost tautological point of view: humans are human after all. Barthes, meanwhile, wanted to highlight the differences between human beings. Fundamentally they were talking about different things on different levels. Most telling is perhaps the following quote from Barthes' critique: 'Whether or not the child is born with ease or difficulty, whether or not his birth causes suffering to his mother, whether or not he is threatened by a high mortality rate, whether or not such and such a type of future is open to him: this is what your exhibitions should be telling people, instead of an eternal lyricism of birth.'[8]

'The Family of Man' reflected and reinforced a very sunny vision of humanity; Steichen's romantic ideology perfectly coincided with what the public in the midst of the Cold War wanted to hear and see. If we take this public attitude into account, academic critiques of 'The Family of Man' can be seen as rather condescending towards the more than nine million people who saw it, and whose lives might have been touched by it in some way. Through Barthes' critique they are set aside as naïve, uneducated or biased. Ariella Azoulay, professor of visual culture and contemporary philosophy, more recently and by contrast, has argued in favour of 'The Family of Man' as a 'Visual Universal Declaration of Human Rights', thus providing another reading into the subject. She argues that Barthes missed most of what the photographs in the exhibition showed; what the author claimed to see were social *ideas*. The hidden ideology he ascribed to the exhibition was nothing more than Steichen's explicit intention in curating it. Instead of reading the photographs as descriptive statements with universal claims, Azoulay proposes

5 Roland Barthes 'The Great Family of Man' and 'Myth as a Type of Speech', *Mythologies*, trans. Annette Lavers (Jonathan Cape Ltd, 1972) pp.100–102, 109–110.
6 Barthes, ibid.
7 Barthes, ibid.

8 Barthes, ibid.

to read them as prescriptive statements claiming universal rights. In short, she proposes to reconstruct the exhibition as the first visual declaration of human rights.[9] A current formulation of 'The Family of Man' would have to take into consideration all these positions. One could also argue that we are at a point in time where globalisation, new economic realities and cultural homogenisation are now forcing us to increasingly consider a common predicament, despite continuing social and economic inequalities.

The Eye is a Lonely Hunter is different from 'The Family of Man' in more than one sense. Firstly the specific case stories and subjects of *The Eye is a Lonely Hunter* are presented in a social context, where 'The Family of Man' was ordered according to specific subjects, such as 'Lovers', 'Children', 'Fathers' and 'Sons', 'Mothers' and 'Daughters', or more abstract displays such as 'Agriculture', 'Eating', 'Labour', and the like. Furthermore, *The Eye is a Lonely Hunter* consists of different sub-themes, which precisely attempt to contextualise the photographs presented in a social, political, economic and cultural context. Where 'The Family of Man' was – not without reason – accused by Barthes of a certain tautological approach (humans are human after all) we have tried to avoid the all too obvious and present a more surprising personal approach by individual photographers, most of whom possess an in-depth knowledge or insight into the context they are working in, often engaging in a particular situation for years at a time. We chose photographers from all over the world, telling side-stories that don't always fit the media, that provide counter-narratives, and we invited them to present their own culture in a photographic 'gaze' that is not imposed, but comes from within.

In Asia, the Americas, Africa and all parts of the New Europe talented photographers have emerged also within the art scene, and they work and exhibit internationally. How does 'The Family of Man' look today through their eyes? In the 4th Fotofestival, these photographers – in addition to their western colleagues – present different worldviews and perspectives exploiting photography's democratic power in a refreshing way, looking at existential, uniquely human situations and on the 'other'. At a time when photography as a medium is no longer only in the hands of western man, they provide multi-ethnic perspectives, negotiating the idea of difference 'from within' and generating counter-discourses to the implicit imperialism of 'The Family of Man'.

We are of course aware that it is not possible to present a totalising portrait of humanity; that would be an impossible task, as any curated exhibition is selective, by its very nature. What we aim for, rather, is a broader representation of the current realities affecting the human condition and human experience in the light of postcolonial discourse, globalisation, multiculturalism, and geopolitical, economic and environmental shifts. Whereas 'The Family of Man' seemed in denial of the devastation of World War II – or any sense of political trauma, civil strife or disobedience – our exhibition does not shy away from dystopias, and does not subscribe to the fiction of a single happy family of man.

Also our exhibition is far from the ideal, harmonious, white, heterosexual presentation that Steichen fashioned; our exhibition rather acknowledges alternatives to the white middle class, western ideal, and highlights alterity and social discord. One thing is certain, however: if 'The Family of Man' were to be re-created today, it would be fractured, heterogeneous and contradictory *and* there would be a commonality of certain experience, precisely because the world is shrinking and becoming, for many of us, more homogeneous.

The Image Voice

The Eye is a Lonely Hunter: Images of Humankind focuses on how and why photography transports anthropological knowledge and gives voice to the unseen

9 Ariella Azoulay, lecture at the symposium *The Human Snapshot*, 2 July 2011, Luma Foundation, Arles, France.

or voiceless. The exhibition focuses on the camera's unique capacity to negotiate reality, generate empathy and evoke uniquely human sentiments. The indexical relationship between what is in front of the camera, what is imprinted on the image, and the story the image tells the viewer, is an essential element of investigation in the exhibition. The question is not necessarily whether this image is true or false, though the exhibition does seek to reinstate the potential truth claims of photography. For decades the medium of photography has been studied and represented as a free-floating and manipulative sign, both within the visual arts and the mass media. The notion of photographic truth has come under close scrutiny, and the camera's capacity to construct, even lie, has been exposed. However there are functions of photography that can still be seen as enlightening and useful, furthermore producing a form of knowledge as sentiment or emotion, which can still be seen as truthful.

Barthes describes this effect as the photographic *punctum*, which pierces the frozen surface of the photograph like an arrow, stings, and cuts through the banality of representation, subverts that which is inert under the 'gaze' and provokes an empathetic response in the viewer in relation to the specific situation or person depicted.[10] The punctum, then, is a kind of subtle *beyond* – as if the image launches desire beyond what it permits us to see. In his very thoughtful text in this catalogue TJ Demos talks about the notion of opacity. In that sense we may consider photography not only important in terms of what it represents or depicts, but also to what it infers outside its frame, or what Barthes has called the invisible property of photography, that which we also do not see.[11] In looking at a picture, therefore, it is important to be able to consider or to imagine what might be happening outside the frame, to think *outside* the image in addition to within it.

10 Roland Barthes, *Camera Lucida: Reflections on Photography* (London: Vintage Books, 2000), p.59.
11 Barthes, *ibid*, p.6.

Gunning has added some valuable insight into the question of truth in photography, pointing out that:

> 'The apparatus, in itself, can neither lie, nor tell the truth. Bereft of language, a photograph relies on people to say things about it or for it...Both historically and institutionally, in order to tell the truth, the photograph must be subjected to a series of discourses, become, in effect, the supporting evidence for a statement. Anyone who knows either the complex history by which photographs were granted evidentiary status in legal trial, or indeed the scrutiny and discussion to which they must be subjected before they are granted such status in contemporary trials must realize that in order to speak the truth the photograph must be integrated into a statement, subjected to complex rules of discourse – legal, rhetorical and even scientific.'[12]

Furthermore, he stresses the close interrelationship between truth and fact, and construction or fakery, both assumed to be polar opposites:

> 'As an art form photography has never been limited to any such restriction to the factual or accurate... just as a counterfeit image relies on us still believing in the reliability of images, a playful image that deconstructs itself before our eyes relies on our common investment in the photograph's ability to show objects accurately.'[13]

Gunning questions the notion that photographs function primarily semiotically, that is as signs to be decoded. He acknowledges that a photograph may function indexically but posits that such a capacity is secondary to a photograph's ability to present us with an image of the world – a position this exhibition also subscribes to.

> 'Pictures generally are more than signs, and frequently we would be hard pressed to claim they referred to anything other than themselves.

12 Gunning, ibid, p.41.
13 Gunning, ibid, p.45.

But photographs do seem to point beyond themselves in a curious manner, and this is part of the reason the index does seem to explain part of its power. But whereas signs reduce their reference to a signification, I would claim the photograph opens up a passageway to its subject, not as a signification but as a world, multiple and complex.'[14]

Even Barthes himself acknowledged the 'evidential force' of photography, and that the power of its testimony bears not on the object, but on time.[15]

This 'evidential force' perhaps has less to do with objectivity than choice, based on the photographer's point of view. We would argue that the notion of truth, which has traditionally been seen to reside in the documentary depiction of reality, may also exist in other forms of more constructed photography, where artifice takes precedence over the direct mirroring of reality. And here we should perhaps consider dispelling the demon of aestheticization, often considered ideologically suspect because it might anaesthetize the viewer. In this sense, there is no pure form of representation, even in documentary photography, precisely because of the question of choice mentioned above. In considering the relationship between ethics, aesthetics, and responsibility, we would like to posit David Levi Strauss' position on the subject, which offers much food for thought:

'The idea that the more transformed or 'aestheticized' an image is, the less 'authentic' or politically valuable it becomes, is one that needs to be seriously questioned. Why *can't* beauty be a call to action?...To represent is to aestheticize; that is to transform. It presents a vast field of choices but it does not include the choice *not* to transform, not to change or alter whatever is being represented. It cannot be a pure process, in practice. This goes for photography as much as for any other means of representation. But this is no reason to back away from the process. The aesthetic is not objective and is not reducible to quantitative scientific terms. Quantity can only measure physical phenomena, and is misapplied in aesthetics, which often deals with what is *not* there, imagining things into existence. To become legible to others, these imaginings must be culturally and socially encoded. That is aestheticization.'[16]

In that sense, an attempt to put together a selective 'portrait of mankind in 2011' is interesting as a counterpart to and in comparison with the portrait made of mankind in 1955. But it may also be interesting for future generations, in order to see how we saw ourselves in 2011 – just as it is interesting for us to see how we saw ourselves in 1955. A photograph is, so to speak, a kind of peephole in time through which we can see how people, their behaviour, clothes and possessions looked then (mostly a very emotionally charged enterprise).

While acknowledging the postmodern discourse of the camera's capacity to lie, and the demise of photographic truth the 4th edition of the Fotofestival argues for photography's capacity to bear witness to the human condition and to human experience within real social and political conditions. The selected artists harness the power of photography to 'penetrate reality's web', to borrow the words of Walter Benjamin, and tell of peoples' lives – as opposed to approaching photography as a post-modern play of signs. The title of the exhibition underlines this appreciation of social and cultural engagement in photography, which is why we dedicate the following chapter to the novel that inspired the title, Carson McCullers' *The Heart is a Lonely Hunter*.

14 Gunning, ibid, p.46.
15 Barthes, *Camera Lucida*, p.89.

16 David Levi Strauss, 'The Documentary Debate: Aesthetic or Anaesthetic?', *Between the Eyes: Essays on Photography and Politics* (New York: Aperture, 2005) p.9.

The Heart is a Lonely Hunter

The title and concept of the 4th Fotofestival *The Eye is a Lonely Hunter: Images of Humankind* draws from Carson McCullers' novel *The Heart is a Lonely Hunter*, one of the most read, translated and appreciated American novels of the twentieth century. McCullers wrote *The Heart is a Lonely Hunter* when she was just 23 years old. The novel examines the lives of voiceless and marginalized people in American society in the 1930s enduring racism, poverty and little prospect or opportunity. Set in a mill town in Georgia, the novel's main narrative concerns protagonist John Singer, a mute, and the people he encounters at a motel bar who share their struggles with him. There is Mick Kelly, a brave and talented young girl who loves classical music and dreams of buying a piano; Jake Blount, an alcoholic labour agitator; Biff Brannon, the observant owner of a diner; and Dr Benedict Copeland, an idealistic African-American doctor. All of these characters confide in Singer and feel that he understands them better than anybody else.

In relation to the 4th Fotofestival the novel touches upon an important question: *how to represent the 'voiceless' in society*? The book poetically describes the discrepancy between the two different but often interchanged questions of *who represents who and why?* and *who can identify with whom and why?* Clearly, the identification of the characters with Singer is a projection of their own needs: there's no real understanding. Singer only listens because it distracts him from his own loneliness and unfulfilled desires – indeed, nobody notices Singer's own needs, and, in the end he takes his own life. In a letter to his only friend Spiros Antonopoulos, Singer writes:

> 'You remember the four people I told you about when I was there... They are all very busy people. In fact they are so busy that it will be hard for you to picture them. I do not mean that they work at their jobs all day and night but that they have much business in their minds always that does not let them rest ... the New York Café owner is different ... He watches. The others all have something they hate. And they all have something they love more than eating or sleeping or wine or friendly company. That is why they are always so busy.'[17]

In the novel the crucial dilemma is seeking a kind of emotional asylum for the character's ideas and hopes. Somewhat differently, this exhibition addresses the eye of the photographer as a lonely hunter that accommodates the desire for representation and giving voice. Here, the heart and the eye are connected and implicated in photography with a social and cultural engagement. The exhibition emphasizes the photograph's capacity for transporting emotional knowledge and generating eyesight of and sympathy with the margins of society within a global society.

The questions of *who is representing whom?* and *who identifies with whom?* are essential ones. We have invited artists and photographers from all over the world who operate as interdisciplinary researchers, and who represent a context they have lived and worked within, either all their lives or on yearlong projects. Although we can appreciate that the global art world opens significant doors for artistic exploration through brief residencies, it is important to us as curators to present artists whose practice is deeply informed by the political, academic and journalistic genealogy of their topics and contexts.

The Artist as Researcher

The artists here often question the cliché of the 'other' and the 'self'. Their engaged positions parallel that of documentary or ethnographic photographers who live and work in hazardous situations in order to tell of undocumented or unpublicized ways of life. In the light of postcolonial discourse, western perspectives are being challenged. The peoples that were

17 Carson McCullers, *The Heart is a Lonely Hunter* (Boston: First Mariner Books Edition, 2000) pp.214–215.

until recently depicted as 'others', today have the ability to communicate their own photographic self-understanding and identity and their image of the west. Anthropologically, photography as a medium has always played a central role in creating a cultural self-understanding and orientation in that of others. As indicated in this exhibition's title, the photographs and artworks on display are extracted from the attention of the masses – the photographer is on a solitary and independent mission (not on a commission). What the eye desires, finds and thinks on its lonely hunt is, rather, a contrasting discourse to the modern tradition of normative humanist anthropology. Instead, it falls upon existences or geographies that are unexpected, surreal, marginalized, rejected, out of sight.

At this point it can be helpful to make a general distinction between anthropology and art in terms of research and method, which is merely a theoretical distinction, but useful as a schemata. Professor James Clifford's *The Predicament of Culture – Twentieth-Century Ethnography, Literature, and Art* (1988) analyses how art, literature, and methods of collecting and display in ethnographic museums create fictions of the 'other'. In this tour de force of art and anthropology in the era of globalisation, he pinpoints differences between the way anthropologists and artists have practised ethnography over the last century – the anthropologists coming from a humanist and documentary tradition and the artists from an 'activity' of 'Ethnographic Surrealism':

> 'Anthropological humanism and ethnographic surrealism need not be seen as mutually exclusive; they are perhaps best understood as antinomies set within a transient historical and cultural predicament. To state the contrast schematically, anthropological humanism begins with the different and renders it – through naming, classifying, describing, interpreting – comprehensible. It familiarizes. An ethnographic surrealist practise, by contrast, attacks the familiar, provoking the irruption of otherness – the unexpected.'[18]

Art historical examples of practitioners of ethnographic surrealism are the French André Breton (1896–1966), the initiator of Surrealism, and later Jean Rouch (1917–2004), the ethnographic filmmaker and founder of cinéma-vérité. There are different approaches to how ethnographic research is done amongst the exhibited artists and photographers in the exhibition today – some tend to familiarize, but many do the opposite (not always in a surrealist manner). Both approaches create important meanings when portraying the human condition today. Yet the ethical contingency, seen from our curatorial perspective, always depends on how the artwork is made, displaced and displayed.

It is therefore important to look at the broad variety and contrast of distinct artistic and photographic research methods in the exhibition. In terms of documenting and portraying social conditions and cultural identities, the South African photographer Pieter Hugo researched the storytelling tradition in West African 'Nollywood' films to make photographic portraits that reflect myths of blackness intertwining reality and fiction in his portraits of local characters (the *Nollywood series*, 2009). In the series *Today's Life and War* (2008), Iranian artist Gohar Dashti stages shots of an Iranian couple living out their domestic life in the field of war, drawing attention to the fragility of intimacy in war zones. In the series *Post Election Violence* (2008), Kenyan photojournalist Boniface Mwangi documented the post-election tribal violence as president Mwai Kibaki cheated his way to power in a rigged election.

From a humanitarian position Danish photographer Jacob Holdt undertook a five-year journey as a homeless vagrant through America's Afro-American and white under-, middle- and upper-class society, using his Canon Dial 35-2

18 James Clifford, *The Predicament of Culture: Twentieth-Century Ethnography, Literature, and Art* (Cambridge, Massachusetts: Harvard, 1999) p.144-145.

camera to make an extensive report that he presented in a book and a series of lectures (the *American Pictures* series, 1970–1975). From a museological perspective, Peggy Buth documented the changing displays and exhibition architecture in the Royal Museum for Central Africa in Tervuren (near Brussels) over a five-year period as the museum sought to rectify its identity as representing a colonial power (the *Desire in Representation (Travelling through the Musée Royale)* series, 2004–2009). The Canadian and Dutch documentary photographer Paolo Woods, documented one of the largest imperial projects of our times and followed some of the 500,000 Chinese who have set out to develop and 'conquer' Africa through building infrastructure and resources (*Chinafrica*, series, 2007). Chinese artist Yang Yongliang engages with the overwhelming and rapid processes of urbanisation in China in his manipulated photography. His images look like large-scale foggy mountain landscapes in the traditional style of Chinese 'Shui Mo' painting and calligraphy; at a closer look they are overgrown with urban infrastructure and composed from numerous photographs. German artist Olaf Otto Becker documents Greenland's melting ice and new river formations of water that now drain into the sea, presenting them as sublime icescapes (*Above Zero*, series, *River 1*, 2008).

This immersion into grueling situations resulting in real lived experience can also be traced in the work of Geert Goiris, who undertakes often perilous journeys into the wild in order to take his photographs. A different yet analoguous investment in a specific locale can be seen in Boris Mikhailov's portraits of people on the untenable side of the post-Soviet economic boom, which fits into the tradition of the socially-conscious documentary and the insider subcultural documentary where the photographer and the subject engages in an interactive relationship. Likewise, Roger Ballen's photographs of people living on the fringes of South African white society rely on a close connection between photographer and subject. Taryn Simon spent two years with individuals who were wrongly convicted, imprisoned, and then freed for crimes they did not commit: her work 'The Innocents' (2002) explores the debatable role of photography in the criminal justice system. Edward Burtynsky embarks on exhaustive investigative projects which delve deep into questions of industrialism and post-industrialism, shifting models of production, environmental issues and the effects of globalisation and neoliberal economic practices, presenting series of photographs that put an emphasis on seriality to indicate change, cause and effect.

As we draw this essay to a close, we would like to reflect on one of the critically and academically grounded voices to have expressed scepticism towards *how* art enters the field of anthropology – the art critic Hal Foster. In his essay 'The Artist as Ethnographer', Foster responds to James Clifford and stresses that the artist who performs a kind of 'quasi-anthropology' prizes the science of anthropology as a science of 'alterity'.[19] He argues that in the meeting between the artist and the other, it is more usual for the artist to undertake 'self-othering' or 'self-fashioning' than coming closer to his or her subject (one must also ask if that is the goal?). Furthermore, he states that the artwork made with such an idealistic intention, ultimately risks being 'recoded by its sponsors as social outreach'.[20] This is an important critique of the role of the artist as researcher, and his or her desire to represent the other. The question is both culture-political and reception-aesthetical: how is the audience introduced to the exhibition? Is that communication highlighted, or is the sponsor the centre of attention? Yet, what Foster seems to dismiss is that the west no longer represents the rest, but is being looked at and thus forced to look at itself. Furthermore, and also very importantly, the interdisciplinary field of art is often

19 Hal Foster, 'The Artist as Ethnographer', in *The Return of the Real: The Avant-Garde at the End of the Century* (Cambridge, Massachusetts: October Books / MIT Press) p.303.
20 Foster, ibid.

a home for practitioners and 'knowledge producers' from or informed by other academic fields such as archaeology, history, visual anthropology, politics, geography, journalism and architecture, which is what we show in *The Eye is a Lonely Hunter: Images of Humankind*.

We hope that the exhibition reflects a renewed ethical engagement with photography, which acknowledges traditional assumptions of photographic factuality, and avoids the pitfalls of stereotyping which have previously occurred when documentary practices objectified their subjects and grounded them in an oppressive 'truth'. Many contemporary photographers are now aware of the politics of representation and the commodification of the gaze, and their work in the Fotofestival will reflect this redefinition of the field and a new awareness of the world.

Die (post-)humanistische Interventionen der Fotografie oder: Kann Fotografie die Welt lebenswerter machen?
TJ Demos

Aufgrund der zahlreichen Ausstellungen zu Fotografie und Videokunst in den letzten 10 Jahren sind inzwischen viele von uns mit den ethisch-politischen Ambitionen der zeitgenössischen fotografischen Medien vertraut: auf sichtbare Konflikte als Ergebnis sozialer und politischer Ausgrenzung aufmerksam zu machen sowie kreative Alternativen für Gleichheit und globale Zugehörigkeit aufzuzeigen. Man betrachte zum Beispiel Edward Burtynskys Dokumentation der ökologischen Zerstörung auf den Ölfeldern in Kalifornien und Baku, die Darstellung der Armut und Obdachlosigkeit in Gujarat von Ravi Agarwal oder Guy Tillims Bildersprache des militärischen Konflikts im Kongo – alle Teilnehmer des zum vierten Mal stattfindenden Fotofestivals. Diese Künstler stehen beispielhaft für ein wichtiges Anliegen der zeitgenössischen Kunst: zur Bildung einer experimentellen und integrativen, demokratischen, öffentlichen Sphäre beizutragen und den sozialen Versäumnissen und politischen Manipulationen, wie sie in Regierungspropaganda und konsumorientierten Spektakeln zu finden sind, etwas entgegenzusetzen.
Dieses Anliegen stellt somit in gewisser Weise eine Fortsetzung des seit Langem bestehenden humanistischen Projekts, das die negativen Seiten von Nationalismus, gesellschaftlicher Ungleichheit und religiösen Gemeinden zu überwinden versucht, dar, indem es auf die Menschlichkeit der Allgemeinheit besteht und diesen Anspruch zur Universalität erhebt, um Missstände zu beseitigen und im Bereich der visuellen Kultur Wiedergutmachung zu leisten. Die Methoden dieser Künstler gehen auch über die Intention und das Engagement der sozialdokumentarischen Fotografie hinaus, wie sie von Zeitschriften und Fotobüchern aus der Mitte des 20. Jahrhunderts bekannt sind und nun seit etwa 20 Jahren in zunehmendem Maße auf den künstlerischen Kontext des Galerieraums übergreifen. Es ist gerade diese neuere, neohumanistische Formation, und insbesondere ihr Einzug in die zeitgenössische Kunst, die ich hier kritisch heranziehen möchte.

Ein wichtiger neuerer Beitrag zur Diskussion über Fotografie und Humanismus ist Ariella Azoulays Vorstellung des „Civil Contract of Photography", des Zivilpakts der Fotografie, in der sie den Aufbau einer inklusiven visuellen Kultur vorschlägt, die eine Plattform für die Einforderung von Rechten gegen nationale Ausgrenzung bietet (und man könnte die Ausgrenzung aus religiösen, gesellschaftlichen und ökologischen Gründen hinzufügen): „Gegen das politische System des Nationalstaats bereitete die Fotografie – zusammen mit anderen Medien, die die Voraussetzungen für die Globalisierung schufen – den Weg für eine Weltbürgerschaft: nicht die Angehörigkeit eines Staates, sondern eine wahrhaftige Bürgerschaft, möglicherweise mit dem Zivilpakt der Fotografie als ordnendem Rahmenwerk."[1]
Azoulay stützt ihre Argumentation auf den „Zivilpakt" der Fotografie, den sie als eine stillschweigende Übereinkunft der Betrachter von Fotografie versteht, die sich im Geist der modernen Menschenrechtsdiskussion entwickelt und bis zur Erklärung der Menschen- und Bürgerrechte der Französischen Revolution von 1789 (sowie der wichtigen Erklärung der Rechte der Frau und Bürgerin von Olympe de Gouges aus dem Jahr 1791) zurückgeht. Ihre moderne Entsprechung ist die Menschenrechtscharta der Vereinten Nationen vom 10. Dezember 1948 als Reaktion auf die Entmenschlichung durch die nationalistischen Ziele im Zweiten Weltkrieg, aber auch auf die politischen Teilungen infolge des aufkommenden Kalten Krieges.
Die Menschenrechte fanden – stärker als die nationalen Rechte – ihren visuellen Ausdruck in Zeichen setzenden Fotoprojekten der Nachkriegszeit wie etwa Edward Steichens Ausstellung *The Family of Man* (1955) und André Malraux' dreibändigem Werk *Le Musée imaginaire* (1952–1954). *The Family of Man* zitierte sowohl in der Ausstellung als auch in ihrem Katalog die

1 Ariella Azoulay, *The Civil Contract of Photography*, Zone, New York 2008, S. 134.

UN-Charta, und vor Kurzem hat Azoulay vorgeschlagen, die Ausstellung als eine „Visual Universal Declaration of Human Rights", eine Visuelle Allgemeine Erklärung der Menschenrechte, zu betrachten.[2]
Als einen weiteren Beitrag zum Zivilpakt der Fotografie zielt sie auf ihr heutiges kritisches humanistisches Potenzial ab, um der Entstehung von Ausnahmezuständen, in denen „nacktes Leben" von Staatsangehörigkeit unterschieden wird, entgegenzuwirken.[3] Azoulay und andere empfinden die Fotografie als ein privilegiertes Medium, da ihr System der Bildersprache eine direkte Verbindung zwischen Betrachter und Objekt darstellt, indem es einen ethisch-politischen Pakt allgemeiner Rechte anregt, der nationale Grenzen und Ausgrenzungen überwindet (beispielsweise ist die politische Unterscheidung zwischen israelischen „Staatsangehörigen" und palästinensischen „Einwohnern" eine dieser Ausgrenzungen, die es für Azouly anzufechten gilt). Für andere wiederum gebiert die Fotografie ein System der Empathie – ein seit Langem bestehendes Prinzip innerhalb der dokumentarischen Fotografie –, das im Namen einer allgemein empfundenen Menschlichkeit als Gegenmittel zu Gewalt und Unterdrückung verstanden wird und zur Allgemeingültigkeit der Menschenrechte überleitet.[4] Eine Fotografie, die die Sache der Menschenrechte voranbringt, besitzt daher das Potenzial, Leben erträglicher zu gestalten, da sie eine engagierte Bürgerschaft und empathische Betrachter heranbildet, die sich ausdrücklich für eine bessere Welt einsetzen wollen.

Humanistische Unterfangen wie *The Family of Man* sind jedoch aus einer Reihe von Gründen kritisiert worden. Zum Beispiel hat man auf die verborgenen Hierarchien hingewiesen, die den humanistischen Ansatz der Universalität Lügen strafen, da er normalerweise eine privilegierte weiße, männliche, heterosexuelle Normativität verrät. Kommentatoren haben auch darauf aufmerksam gemacht, wie die Philosophie des Humanismus im Westen artikuliert und global auf den Süden projiziert wurde, oft im Namen von abstrakten – aber wirtschaftlich und politisch motivierten – Konzepten für „Freiheit", „Modernisierung„ und „Kultur". Wie wir inzwischen wissen, handelt es sich dabei um Schlüsselbegriffe der philosophischen Rechtfertigung des Nachkriegskolonialismus und Neokolonialismus, dafür bestimmt, das „Primitive" in „Menschliches" umzuwandeln, wodurch sie die Grenzen des humanistischen Universalismus verraten, indem einige mehr Mensch sind als andere.[5]
Vertreter einer multikulturellen Gesellschaft setzten in den 1980er- und 1990er-Jahren ihre Angriffe auf den Eurozentrismus des Humanismus fort und stützten sich dabei auf die Quellen der poststrukturalistischen Kritik aus den 1960er- und 1970er-Jahren. Damals konfrontierten Kritiker wie Barthes, Foucault, Althusser, Deleuze und Derrida die Annahme einer subjektiven Autonomie mit einem Antihumanismus, der die determinierende Rolle subjektiver und sozialer Kräfte bemühte – für die Marxisten war dies die Marktwirtschaft, in der Psychoanalyse die psychische Struktur, für die Strukturalisten die historische

2 „Wir, die Menschen der Vereinten Nationen, sind entschlossen, nachfolgende Generationen von der Geisel des Krieges zu bewahren, die der Menschheit zu unseren Lebzeiten zweimal unsägliches Leid gebracht hat, und den Glauben in die fundamentalen Menschenrechte wieder zu beteuern sowie in die Würde und den Wert des Menschen, in die Gleichberechtigung von Mann und Frau und von allen Völkern, großen wie kleinen, ...", siehe Edward Steichen, *The Family of Man*, Museum of Modern Art, New York 1955, S. 184 f.
3 Ariella Azoulay, „The Family of Man as a Visual Universal Declaration of Human Rights", Grundsatzrede auf dem Symposium „The Human Snapshot", LUMA Foundation, Arles, Frankreich, 2.–3. Juli 2011.
4 Siehe beispielsweise Susie Linfield, „Photojournalism and Human Rights", in: *The Cruel Radiance: Photography and Political Violence*, University of Chicago Press, Chicago 2010. In ihrer Einleitung erklärt sie: „...wir können nicht zumindest nicht in sinnvoller oder realistischer Art und Weise über den Aufbau einer Welt mit Demokratie, Gerechtigkeit und Menschenrechten sprechen, ohne zuerst die Erfahrung ihrer Negation verstanden zu haben. Der Versuch, ein solches Verständnis zu erreichen, ist das, was ich mit ‚Empathie' meine, eine Qualität, auf die ich immer wieder zurückkomme; ohne sie geht die Politik der Menschenrechte ins Abstrakte, in romantischen Leichtsinn und Grausamkeit über." (S. XV).

5 Siehe zum Beispiel die Arbeit von Homi Bhabha und Gayatri Spivak, die die Rhetorik des liberalen Universalismus des 19. Jahrhunderts und der „Menschenrechte" zu Zeiten des Kolonialismus dekonstruierten und den Humanismus von einem postkolonialen Standpunkt aus kritisierten. Siehe auch die neuere Analyse der Paradoxien des aufgeklärten Universalismus während des Kolonialismus und der Sklaverei, in: Susan Buck-Morss, *Hegel, Haiti and Universal History*, University of Pittsburgh Press, Pittsburgh 2009.

und kulturelle Mediation von Sprache. Diese kritischen Betrachtungen wurden durch neuere Problematisierungen des Humanismus bis in das erste Jahrzehnt unseres Jahrhunderts fortgesetzt: Zum Beispiel haben Chantal Mouffe und Jacques Rancière dessen „postpolitische“ Annahme einer vereinten Sozialgemeinschaft (Menschheit) kritisiert, und Giorgio Agamben hat die „anthropologische Maschine“ dekonstruiert, das heißt ihre Basis, die für ihn funktioniert, um das Humane aus der Gegenüberstellung zum Inhumanen – mit oft blutigen Folgen – zu konstruieren. Für Immanuel Wallerstein ist die eigentliche Vorstellung von universalen menschlichen Werten nach wie vor ein Konzept des Westens, eine „Machtrhetorik“, derer sich mächtige westliche Regierungen bedienen, um schwächeren Staaten ihren Willen aufzuzwingen, in jüngerer Zeit hinter der moralisierenden Fassade der „Menschenrechte“.[6]

Das hat zur Folge, dass heute viele glauben, eine Rückkehr zum Humanismus sei keine Antwort auf die gegenwärtige Krise, sondern vielmehr ein Teil des Problems. Wie Matthew Calarco es formuliert: „Viele Posthumanisten nehmen an, dass Nihilismus und die größten politischen Katastrophen unseres Zeitalters eng mit genau dem Humanismus verbunden sind, der von Neohumanisten meistens als Lösung dieser Probleme angeboten wird.“[7]

Dass dieser jedoch für einige Theoretiker und Ausstellungsmacher nach wie vor attraktiv ist, beweist, wie stark das Vertrauen in das Erbe der Aufklärung und den modernen demokratischen Entwurf ist, der dem zeitgenössischen Humanismus zugrunde liegt. So vertrat zum Beispiel der verstorbene Literaturkritiker Edward Said einen von ihm sogenannten „vermittelnden Humanismus“, der in „Geschichte als beständigen agonistischen Prozess“ interveniert und „die nicht dokumentierte Zerrüttung von Exilierten ohne Wohnsitz und Obdach, Immigranten, umherziehenden oder gefangengenommenen Bevölkerungsgruppen“ aufdeckt, „für die es noch kein Dokument, keinen adäquaten Ausdruck gibt, um das zu ermessen, was sie erleben müssen.“[8] Er skizziert weiter, was in Wirklichkeit die Basis des modernen sozialdokumentarischen Konzepts ist: „Ich bin fest davon überzeugt, dass der Humanismus das Schweigen von umherziehenden, kaum überlebenden Gruppen beenden und ihre Welt der Erinnerung ans Tageslicht bringen muss, jene Art von Aussagen, die es nicht bis in die Nachrichten schafft ...“ Das war und ist schon immer das Leitmotiv von Kriegsfotografen und Dokumentatoren von Katastrophen seit der Erfindung der Fotografie.

Wenn heute einige glauben, dass die Fotografie diesen Entwurf eines vermittelnden Humanismus wiederbeleben könne, dann erschwert Agambens posthumanistische Kritik diesen Schritt zusätzlich und ist es allein schon deshalb wert, noch einmal auf seine These zurückzukommen – insbesondere, da sie sich auf 2 Hauptanliegen zeitgenössischer Fotografie und Videokunst bezieht, die auf diesem Fotofestival Thema sind: Menschenrechte und Ökologie. Die Lektüre von Agambens Buch *The Open* offenbart, dass diese beiden Bereiche nicht ohne Bezug zueinander stehen, da sich die gegensätzliche Logik des Humanismus sowohl der Trennung des politischen vom animalischen Leben bedient (und damit dem Missbrauch der Menschenrechte Vorschub leistet) als auch der Trennung von Mensch und Natur (und damit das Potenzial für Umweltkatastrophen erzeugt). Ein Ergebnis davon ist der heute immer häufiger anzutreffende „Ausnahmezustand“, der nach Agamben das Fundament für das moderne biopolitische Paradigma bildet, das heißt die Gouvernementalität von Leben.[9] Während der letzten Jahre sind in unserer Gesellschaft immer mehr Orte „inkludierter Ausschließung“ entstanden, Zonen legal angeordneten entpolitisierten Lebens, wie etwa Flüchtlingszentren und Militärgefängnisse. Neben dem Aufbau

6 Immanuel Wallerstein, *European Universalism: The Rhetorik of Power*, New Press, New York 2006.

7 Matthew Calarco, „Jamming the Anthropological Machine“, in: Steven DeCaroli und Matthew Calarco (Hg.), *On Agamben: Sovereignty and Life*, Stanford University Press, Stanford, Kalifornien, 2006.

8 Edward Said, *Humanism and Democratic Criticism*, Columbia University Press, New York 2004, S. 25 und 81.

9 Siehe Giorgio Agamben, *State of Exception*, übersetzt von Kevin Attell, University of Chicago Press, Chicago 2005.

eines zunehmenden Sicherheitsstaats wird die Bevölkerung weltweit durch die Sparpolitik mit ihren finanziellen Eingriffen in Gemeinschaftsgut (einschließlich der Kürzungen im Renten-, Erziehungs- und Gesundheitswesen) auf „nacktes Leben" reduziert.

Krisen in entfernten Regionen, insbesondere in „unterentwickelten" Staaten, begegnet man mit dem Rückgriff auf die Einforderung von Menschenrechten durch eine wachsende Schar von Nichtregierungsorganisationen. Sie definieren ein neues Zeitalter der Notstandssituationen, die von humanitären Katastrophen charakterisiert und von politisch-ökonomischen Erwägungen losgelöst sind.[10] Doch dieser Rückgriff hat sich als nicht sonderlich erfolgreich erwiesen. Während in der Praxis politische Rechte seit je an die Staatsbürgerschaft gekoppelt sind, mangelt es den Menschenrechten an einem institutionellen oder staatlichen Schutz- und Durchsetzungsmechanismus.[11] Theoretisch ist deshalb die Rückkehr zu der Vorstellung einer gemeinsamen Humanität mit dem Ziel, Ausgrenzungen abzuschaffen, von Anfang an gefährdet, da Humanität an sich eine Folge der anthropologischen Maschine ist, die stets über das Potenzial für die Entstehung von Hierarchien und Ausnahmen verfügt und damit auch von gewaltsamen Konsequenzen. Für manche Kritiker liegt die Antwort deshalb logischerweise nicht in der Erneuerung unseres Bekenntnisses zu den Menschenrechten, sondern eher darin, sich von der Idee der Humanität zu befreien sowie in der Erweiterung des Begriffs Humanismus.

Wie könnte man sich also von der Idee der Humanität befreien? Nach Agamben müsste man die anthropologische Maschine anhalten, indem man die Leere ihrer Aufspaltung in Mensch und Tier sowie in Mensch und Natur aufzeigt und „wir uns in diese Leere wagen".[12] Oder um es positiv auszudrücken: Eine Lebensform zu artikulieren, die von der Trennung zwischen Menschheit und Tierreich sowie zwischen politischem und biologischem Leben unabhängig ist – was die Aufgabe der „zukünftigen Gesellschaft" ist, eine Aufgabe, die es, wie Agamben einwendet, „größtenteils noch zu erfinden gilt".[13]

Natürlich könnte man sich dieser Aufforderung zur Aufgabe der Humanität widersetzen und stattdessen versuchen, zum nicht ausgeschöpften Potenzial demokratischer Politik und ihrer liberalen, humanistischen Ontologie zurückzukehren, indem man Spuren ihres aufklärerischen Vermächtnisses findet und rettet, um den Spielraum der Demokratie zu erweitern und ihre ethisch-politische Verpflichtung auch jenen zukommen zu lassen, die von ihren Normen ausgeschlossen sind. Man könnte sich sogar bemühen, demokratischen Humanismus mit der nicht-ausschließenden Basis Agambens zukünftiger Gesellschaft in Zusammenhang zu bringen, indem man eine progressive, reformerische Politik entwickelt, wie Said oder Chantal Mouffe es vorschlagen. Aber dann müsste man sich der Kritik stellen, dass der Humanismus bis jetzt zu genauso vielen Katastrophen inklusiver Ausschließung geführt habe, wie er erfolgreich überwunden hat. Hinzu kommt, dass die heutige westliche Politik, wenn überhaupt dann dafür bestimmt erscheint, die Intensivierung der biopolitischen Regulierung des Lebens fortzusetzen (insbesondere angesichts des drohenden Klimawandels und der immensen Flüchtlingsproblematik, die daraus entstehen wird), mit einer weiteren Aufspaltung in Staatsbürger und Migranten, Wohlhabenden und Armen, was, wie manche es nennen, zu einem globalen Apartheidsystem führt.[14] Doch vielleicht brauchen wir hier dieses philosophische Dilemma nicht zu lösen und zwischen

10 Siehe Craig Calhoun, „The Idea of Emergency: Humanitarian Action and Global (Dis)order", in: Didier Fassin und Mariella Pandolfi (Hg.), *Contemporary States of Emergency: The Politics of Military and Humanitarian Interventions*, Zone Books, New York 2010, S. 18–39.

11 Hierauf weist Agamben hin in: „Beyond Human Rights", in: *Means Without Ends: Notes on Politics*, University of Minnesota Press, Minneapolis 2000.

12 Giorgio Agamben, *The Open: Man and Animal*, übersetzt von Kevin Attell, Stanford University Press, Stanford 2004, S. 92.

13 Giorgio Agamben, *Homo Sacer: Sovereign Power and Bare Life*, übersetzt von Daniel Heller-Roazen, Stanford University Press, Stanford 1998, S. 3 und ders., *The Coming Community*, übersetzt von Michael Hardt, University of Minnesota Press, Minneapolis 1993

14 Siehe John Cavanagh et al. (Hg.), *Alternatives to Economic Globalization: A Better World is Possible: A Report of the International Forum on Globalization*, Berrett-Koehler, San Francisco, Kalifornien, 2002, S. 33.

den beiden Wegen zu wählen – viel eher können wir uns künstlerischen Ansätzen zuwenden, um zu sehen, wo sie uns hinbringen könnten.

Auf welche Art und Weise auch immer wir dieser Kritik am Humanismus begegnen, sie erlaubt uns, einige Probleme mit den Bildern der konventionellen dokumentarischen Darstellung von Leid zu erkennen – sei dies nun in den Medien oder im künstlerischen Kontext. Wenn die Fotografie in Notstandssituationen interveniert, arbeitet sie oft im Schulterschluss mit der Logik humanitärer Gesinnung. Das Problem ist, dass solche Vorgehensweisen dazu neigen, Krisen und die von ihnen betroffenen Personen zu entpolitisieren und zwar häufig aus Gründen, die im Mandat von Nichtregierungs- und UN-Organisationen liegen, nach dem Hilfe nicht politischen Akteuren, sondern den Opfern gewährt werden soll. Humanitäre Gesinnung will unmittelbar, direkt und ungeachtet der Identität oder politischen Orientierung der Opfer Leiden lindern, was die Betroffenen ihrer politischen Ansprüche beraubt und den größeren Kontext und die Gründe der Gewalt ignoriert. Man könnte sogar sagen, dass humanitäre Gesinnung nicht nur mit Opfern arbeitet, sondern auch eine Rolle bei ihrer *Hervorbringung* spielt, was die Teilung in biologisches und politisches Leben im Ausnahmezustand veranschaulicht.
Das Problem ist, dass die Bildung der Empathieaffekte in der dokumentarischen Darstellung eine falsche Nähe zwischen dem mitfühlenden Betrachter und dem gepeinigtem Opfer beabsichtigt, die, wie Kritiker anmerken, eher Schuld verringernd wirkt, als dass sie komplexe und strukturelle Problemlösungen bieten würde.[15] Die Situation gleicht der von humanitärer Hilfe, die oft nicht die notleidenden Opfer erreicht, sondern vielmehr den Fluss von finanziellen Mitteln aufrechterhält. Das Paradoxe an der humanitären Gesinnung ist, dass sie, statt einfach Leiden zu mildern, möglicherweise gleichzeitig das unterdrückende System, das dieses Leiden hervorbringt, unterstützt.[16] Tatsächlich sind mitfühlender Humanismus und humanitär begründeter Interventionismus kompliziert miteinander verflochten, insbesondere, da die emotionale Reaktion auf Sensationsfotojournalismus – sei dies aus Mitgefühl für hilflose Opfer oder aus Furcht vor Terrorgefahr – dazu neigt, humanitär begründete Einmischung zu unterstützen.[17] Notleidende „Mitmenschen" mit militärischer Unterstützung zu retten ist eines der vorrangigen Mittel, mit dem heute Intervention und Kriegseinsätze gerechtfertigt werden.

Einen ähnlichen Impuls verspürt man bei der Trennung von Mensch und Natur. Die desaströsen Folgen sind offensichtlich, wenn die Natur ohne Berücksichtigung des Langzeiteffektes auf die Ökosysteme des Menschen und der Natur zu einer ausbeutbaren Ressource für profitorientierte Unternehmungen wird. Doch wir treffen auf eine komplexere Herausforderung, wenn die gleiche Teilungsstruktur auf gut gemeinte Versuche, ein Naturreich zu schaffen, das geschützt oder wiederhergestellt werden will, angewandt wird. Denn das Ergebnis verweist die Natur in eine nichtkulturelle Zone organischer Reinheit zurück und erinnert beispielsweise an den mythopoetischen Ausgangspunkt, der der biologischen Umwelt von James Lovelocks Gaia-Hypothese zugrunde liegt – einem äußerst wichtigen Markstein in der Entwicklung der ökologischen Debatte der späten 1970er-Jahre –, nach der die Natur objektiviert in einer Ontologie endet, ohne Bezug zu sozialen, politischen und technologischen Prozessen.[18]
Das Problem ist, dass im Prinzip lobenswerte, umweltfreundliche Absichten in einer gefährlichen Entpolitisierung münden

15 Siehe beispielsweise die Kritik in den Schriften von Susan Sontag, Martha Rosler und Allan Sekula.

16 Siehe Linda Polman *The Crisis Caravan: What's Wrong with Humanitarian Aid?*, übersetzt von Liz Waters, Metropolitan, New York 2010 und Fiona Terry, *Condemned to Repeat? The Paradox of Humanitarian Action*, Cornell University Press, Ithaca 2002.

17 Wie Fassin und Pandolfi in ihrer Einleitung zu *State of Emergency* S. 16, schreiben: „Notstandssituationen ... haben immer affektbedingte Grundlagen, die sich von traditionellen Kriegssituationen vielleicht darin unterscheiden, dass die Gefühle, die hier zum Ausdruck kommen, vermutlich nicht nationalistischer Art sind, sondern als universalistisch dargestellt werden oder einfach als menschlich."

18 James Lovelock, *Gaia: A New Look at Life on Earth*, Oxford University Press, Oxford 1979.

können und genau die Objektivierung der Natur reproduzieren, die uns überhaupt erst in diese schwierige Situation gebracht hat. Der Politikgeograf Neil Smith beobachtet, dass „Natur und Gesellschaft in reziproker konzeptioneller Trägheit erstarren, wenn man sie voneinander trennt", da „das Postulieren einer fremden Natur die beispiellose Ausbeutung der Natur rational begründet und rechtfertigt ... (was) der ‚große Schwindel' ist, den der Kapitalismus, sowohl historisch als auch geografisch, verkörpert".[19]
Sind dagegen Natur und Gesellschaft miteinander verbunden, droht eine weitere Gefahr, die darin besteht, dass Leben zum Gegenstand der Biopolitik wird und die Umwelt als ultimative Domäne von Lebewesen zur Gewinnung von Wissen, Macht und Subjektivität dient. Wie der Politikwissenschaftler Timothy Luke argumentiert, geht mit der Expansion von internationalen Regulierungsgremien wie etwa der Weltkommission für Umwelt und Entwicklung der Vereinten Nationen die allmähliche Umgestaltung von Regierungen nach den Prioritäten einer „Umweltdisziplin" einher, indem auf „das Wissen und die Kompetenz von Umweltexperten und -bündnissen zurückgegriffen wird, um die Funktionstüchtigkeit aller biologischen Organismen und die Gesundheit ihres natürlichen Umfeldes zu kontrollieren."[20]
Ein Effekt solcher Umweltdisziplin ist, dass Soforthilfemaßnahmen erlassen werden, um demokratische Erwägungen zu umgehen und kritische Diskussionen über soziale Gerechtigkeit und Formen von Ungleichheit zwischen Nord und Süd zu ersticken. Stattdessen stellt die Dringlichkeit drohender ökologischer Desaster den Imperativ menschlichen Überlebens über alle politischen Erwägungen (und es überrascht daher keinesfalls, dass die G8-Staaten solche Dringlichkeit anwenden, um ihre eigenen, ökologisch unausgewogenen Umweltprogramme durchzuboxen, wie dies auf den letzten Konferenzen der UN-Vertragsstaaten geschah).[21] Hinzu kommt, dass disziplinarische Steuerungsmechanismen – wie etwa das Entwerfen von Sicherheitskonzepten gegen die Bedrohungen durch den Klimawandel, die Entwicklung von Anreizen für eine alternative Energiegewinnung sowie ökowirtschaftliche Verordnungen wie den Emissionsrechtehandel – meist direkt darauf ausgerichtet werden, zum Zwecke weiterer Ausbeutung, die Natur zu instrumentalisieren. Dies geschieht oft im Namen einer nachhaltigen Entwicklung, in der, den Anforderungen eines entstehenden Klimakapitalismus entsprechend, „Nachhaltigkeit" paradoxerweise die absolute Privilegierung des ökonomischen Wachstums meint.[22]

Angesichts dieser zugegebenermaßen beeindruckenden Herausforderungen stellt sich nun die Frage, auf was wir im Bereich der visuellen Kunst zurückgreifen können, um das Leben lebenswerter zu machen, also um mehr Demokratie, Gleichheit für alle und eine größere Nachhaltigkeit zu erreichen. Wie können diejenigen, die mit Bildern arbeiten, agieren, um die im Zusammenhang mit humanitär begründetem Interventionismus und antipolitischer Umweltdisziplin eindeutigen und gegenwärtigen Gefahren eines Neohumanismus zu vermeiden? Zum Abschluss möchte ich hier, im Rahmen des Fotofestivals und seiner Beiträge, zu einigen weiteren Fragen und vielleicht kreativen Lösungen anregen.

Von den Folgen zu den Ursachen

Wie wir gesehen haben, ist es wichtig, statt die Gründe und die Geschichte des Leids selbst als aller Erstes die Intention der dokumentarischen Fotografie zu hinterfragen, die Folgen von Konflikten festzuhalten, also das Leid anderer als Motiv für ein privilegiertes, mitfühlendes Publikum.
Auf welche Art und Weise könnte uns die Fotografie nun helfen zu verstehen, wie es dazu kommt, dass ein Teil der Menschheit

19 Neil Smith, „Forward", in: Nik Heynen et al. (Hg.), *In the Nature of Cities: Urban Political Ecology and the Politics of Urban Metabolism*, Routledge, London 2006, xiii f.
20 Timothy Luke, Environmentality as Green Governmentality, in: Éric Darier (Hg.), *Discourses of the Environment*, Blackwell, Oxford 1999, S. 146.

21 Siehe Alex Gourevitch, „Environmentalism – Long Live the Politics of Fear", *Public Culture*, Jg. 22, Heft 3, 2010, S. 411–424.
22 Siehe TJ Demos, „The Politics of Sustainability: Art and Ecology", in: Francesco Manacorda und Ariella Yedgar (Hg.), *Radical Nature: Art and Architecture for a Changing Planet, 1969–2009*, Barbican Art Gallery, London 2009, S. 17–30.

entpolitisiert wird, und wie andere Reaktionen als eine von Schuld befreiende Anteilnahme hervorgerufen werden können? Was ist mit der Komplizenschaft des Betrachters beim Versagen von Regierungen weltweit oder mit den Aktivitäten einer kapitalistischen Globalisierung? Wenn die mitfühlende Aufmerksamkeit für fotografierte Opfer militärischer Angriffe, Hungersnöte und Umweltzerstörung dazu neigt, die Unterstützung humanitär begründeter Intervention durch Umgehung politischer Erwägungen unkritisch zu untermauern, dann ist eine Alternative zur konventionellen Positionierung des Fotojournalismus in den Medien dringend notwendig.

Wir sehen in den Ausstellungen etliche Beiträge mit unterschiedlichen Annäherungen an eine solche anti-fotojournalistische, experimentelle Form der Fotografie – Beispiele, die auf den Verzicht eines sensationslüsternen Einsatzes der Fotografie hindeuten und damit die üblichen bildlichen Ausdrucksformen vermeiden, wie sie von Massenmedien präsentiert werden, beispielsweise das heroische Einbringen des Fotografen, die Konstruktion eines einzigartigen Events und Klischeebildes, die wahrheitsgetreue und objektive Darstellung von Realität sowie die Bezeugung schrecklicher Ereignisse und ihre Übermittlung an ein weit entferntes Publikum.[23]

Betrachten wir zum Beispiel Bruno Serralongues Bilder von den prekären und provisorischen Lebensbedingungen der Flüchtlinge an der französischen Grenze, die ganz bewusst nicht die „menschlich interessante" Geschichte in den Blickpunkt rücken, um so auf die realen Verhältnisse der Migranten aufmerksam zu machen. Oder nehmen wir Agarwals Bilder von Obdachlosen in Gujarat, die sich weigern, seine Protagonisten zu Opfern zu machen, und stattdessen würdige Formen von Überlebensstrategien und eines kreativen Alltags wiedergeben, selbst wenn sie parallel ein kritisches Bild von der ökonomischen Ungleichheit in Indien vermitteln. Genauso porträtiert Guy Tillim experimentelle Lebensformen in den urbanen Zentren des postkolonialen Südafrikas, indem er Lesarten aufzeigt, die sich klischeehaften Schilderungen widersetzen und dafür eher die ökonomischen Herausforderungen der Zeit nach der Apartheid offenbaren. Bedeutsamerweise handelt es sich bei diesen Projekten um oft umfangreich betextete Fotoserien, die Teil des sozialen Engagements der Fotografen sind und es aufgrund ihrer Bilderfolge ermöglichen, dass sich eine komplexe Geschichte entwickelt. Diese Projekte beabsichtigen weniger, eine Situation zu einem einzigen, spektakulären Bild zu verdichten, sondern lassen vielmehr eine Art pädagogische Ambition erkennen. Solche Bilder sind vielversprechend, nicht nur, weil sie das emotionale Potenzial der Fotografie ablehnen, sondern weil sie eine neue Strategie des Affekts anbieten, die das Problem eines Katastrophismus und nicht rationalen Interventionismus vermeidet.

Die Strategie des Affekts

Wenn sich das Bildsystem der Medien des Affekts bedient, um dadurch eine demokratische Debatte abzublocken, wie können wir dann einen neuen Umgang mit Affekten entwickeln, der soziale Gerechtigkeit, Gleichheit und politisches Engagement födert?[24] Und wie können wir dies bewerkstelligen, ohne Gefahr zu laufen, nur einen rationalen Diskurs zu führen – was angesichts der psychoanalytischen Erkenntnisse absolut unmöglich ist –, sondern vielmehr, um uns Affekte im Namen einer alternativen (oder antihegemonalen) Politik wieder adäquat anzueignen?

Betrachten wir die Bilder des kenianischen selbsternannten Fotoaktivisten Boniface Mwangi, der den Gewaltausbruch in seinem Land infolge der Wahlen von 2007 schildert, und der die Kamera dafür einsetzt, um, wie er selbst sagt, „Diktatoren zu stürzen, die Gesellschaft zu verändern und den Wandel zu beeinflussen"[25]. In Anbetracht seines

23 Siehe auch die vor Kurzem stattgefundene Ausstellung *Anti-Photojournalism*, kuratiert von Carles Guerra vom Virreina Centre de la Imatge in Barcelona, der das Konzept von Allan Sekula übernahm.

24 Brian Massumi beschreibt, wie Medien eine Regierungsfunktion übernommen haben, indem sie das neurophysiologische System der Betrachter über affektauslösende Stimuli beeinflussen. Siehe Brian Massumi, „Fear (The Spectrum Said)", in: *Positions*, 13. Jg., Heft 1, 2005.

25 Siehe seine Website: http://www.bonifacemwangi.com/bonnie/

Wunsches, Bilder solchen, durch Armut und militärische Unterdrückung hervorgerufenen Leids zu zeigen, stellt sich die Frage, ob wir als Betrachter für einen neuerfundenen Humanismus bereit sind, der auf der Komplexität unserer potenziellen Beziehungen und sogar unserer Solidarität mit den Ausgeschlossenen beharrt, wie Said betont. Oder: Was hat es mit der implizierten Herausforderung an den Präsentismus in der dokumentarischen Bilderwelt von Filmen wie dem von Sven Augustijnen und dem von Vincent Meessen auf sich, die beide die bis in unsere Gegenwart hineinreichenden Hinterlassenschaften des Kolonialismus erforschen? Augustijnen bedient sich ihrer in seinem Film *Spectres*, der Belgiens gewaltsame Intervention im Kongo während der Anfangsphase seiner Unabhängigkeit zu Beginn der 1960er-Jahre zum Thema hat, und konzentriert sich in ihm darauf, wie die Ermordung Lumumbas dargestellt und erstaunlicherweise von einem noch lebenden Beteiligten (Jacques Brassinne) heute gerechtfertigt wird. Meessens Film *Vita Nova* greift die komplexe Geschichte eines berühmten Bildes aus der Kolonialzeit auf. Es zeigt einen afrikanischen Jungen in Militäruniform, der vor etwas, was vermutlich eine französische Flagge ist, salutiert. Dieses Bild, das auf dem Titel von *Paris Match* erschien, war Gegenstand einer kritischen Analyse des französischen Literaturkritikers Roland Barthes, der es jedoch in seiner Autobiografie *Barthes par Barthes* unterlässt, sein Verhältnis zu seinem Großvater, Louis-Gustave Binger, zu diskutieren, der als Kolonialgouverneur die Elfenbeinküste an Frankreich „übergab".

Nach Ansicht des Kritikers Kobena Mercer rührt Meessens Darstellung der kolonialen Nachwirkungen im heutigen Burkina Faso zu Tränen – eine durch und durch *körperliche* Reaktion auf das emotionale Potenzial des Mediums Film, das jenseits von verbaler Sprache liegt.[26] So gesehen regen diese bewegenden Bilder – sowohl emotional einnehmend als auch politisch verändernd – zu einem alternativen Umgang mit Affekten gegenüber dominanten Formen mediatisierter Angst an, einen, der an eine postkolonialen Verpflichtung sozialer Gerechtigkeit anknüpft, selbst wenn wir noch immer kein ausreichend umfassendes und differenziertes Vokabular haben, um diesen zu definieren.

Politische Ökologie

Um dem Anthropozentrismus des Humanismus mit seiner gefährlichen Privilegierung der menschlichen gegenüber der nicht-menschlichen Umwelt etwas entgegenzusetzen, müssen wir Wege finden, die sozialen, wirtschaftlichen und technologischen Systeme miteinander zu verbinden, um für eine nachhaltige Zukunft Natur wieder begrifflich erfassbar zu machen (auch wenn sich eine solche Zukunft scheinbar täglich immer weiter vom Horizont des Möglichen entfernt). Eine seit Jahren bestehende theoretische Quelle hierfür ist Félix Guattaris ethisch-ästhetische Philosophie, nach der er empfiehlt, Ökologie als „transversal" zu begreifen, das heißt über miteinander verbundene subjektive, institutionelle und ökologische Bereiche.[27] Für ihn war es notwendig, Subjektivität unterschiedlich zu „produzieren", um sie einer „Re-Singularisation" – ein Begriff, den wir heute auf die Forderung nach Biodiversität anwenden könnten – zu- und von der gefährlichen industriellen Produktion von Homogenität wegzuführen.

In gewisser Weise wird diese Forderung in den Bildern von Burtynsks Darstellung der Massenproduktion in China negativ beantwortet oder auch in Geert Goiris' *Whiteout*-Serie, die die desorientierende Wahrnehmung hervorruft, wie sie in nicht-menschlichen Polarklimata auftritt, wo menschliche Technologie selbst bis in die unberührteste der unwirtlichen Umgebungen vorgedrungen ist. Nico Ilfoveanu wiederum zeigt in seinen chromatisch bearbeiteten Landschaften post-natürliche Szenerien. Mit diesen Beispielen besitzen wir ganz unterschiedliche Signale hinsichtlich der Sachlage einer menschen- und umweltfreundlichen Ökologie. Zwischen postindustrieller Homogenisierung und Lebensraumzerstörung zeichnen sie für

26 Siehe Kobena Mercers Text über Vincent Meessen, in: *Ars 11*, Kiasma Museum of Contemporary Art, Helsinki 2011.

27 Siehe Félix Guattari, *The Three Ecologies*, übersetzt von Ian Pindar und Paul Sutton, The Athlone Press, London 2000.

die Menschheit eine ungewisse Zukunft. Gleichwohl spricht die Mannigfaltigkeit solcher Ansätze dafür, sich durch ästhetische Ausdrucksweisen mit Ökologie zu befassen, da dies das Denken in Katastrophen vermeidet, was zu antipolitischen Vorgehensweisen führt, und es ablehnt, Ökologie zu einem wissenschaftlichen Diskurs zu degradieren. Dennoch, selbst hier müssen wir immer noch Widerstand leisten und dürfen nicht einer postpolitischen Vorstellung von Humanität oder bloßem Leben aufsitzen, nach der ein auf Konsens basierter Universalismus darin mündet, die Überlegungen zu ökologischer Gerechtigkeit in Bezug auf ökonomische und politische Ungleichheit zu ersetzen, wie etwa zwischen der Umweltpolitik des Nordens und der Forderung des Südens nach Schuldenerlass und Hilfe bei den Folgen des Klimawandels. Wenn sich der Humanismus den gespaltenen politischen Interessen der Nationen widersetzt, wie kann er dann einen Rahmen für Verhandlungen zwischen solch regionalen und hemisphärischen Gegensätzen bilden? Oder: Wie können wir eine posthumanistische Politik und Soziabilität aufbauen, die sowohl die Objektivierung der Natur als auch die Generalisierung der Menschheit vermeidet.

Veränderte Wahrnehmung

Wenn wir Subjektivität unterschiedlich produzieren müssen, dann können wir damit vielleicht anfangen, indem wir lernen, uns *anders* wahrzunehmen, sodass wir uns darüber selbst neu erfinden können. Dieser Grundgedanke könnte durch einen kreativ gestalteten Alltag, durch alternative Rollen und Rituale umgesetzt werden, wobei die Fotografie als ein Medium des kreativen Ausdrucks förderlich sein kann. Betrachten wir zum Beispiel Bani Abidis Bilder von Menschen in Pakistan während des Ramadan, die einen Raum zwischen der häuslichen und der öffentlichen Welt einnehmen; oder Pieter Hugos Werben für die skurril anmutenden Inszenierungen Nollywoods, wobei er fiktionale Charaktere aus der nigerianischen Filmindustrie in aus dem Zusammenhang herausgerissenen Alltagsszenen dokumentiert. Oder nehmen wir Ryan McGinleys Ausflug in die Welt von Heranwachsenden, der sowohl eine ästhetische Reise der subjektiven Erfindung als auch eine psychosexuelle der Entdeckung und Entfremdung zu erkennen gibt. Diese Bilder, so unterschiedlich sie auch sein mögen, streben nach Metaphern für Leben, das unterschiedlich gelebt werden will, und lehnen vielleicht sogar die Gemeinsamkeit von und die Erkennbarkeit des Menschen ab. Infolgedessen wird das Bild eher zu einem Raum der Vorstellungskraft als zu einer Dokumentation.

Alle diese oben kurz erwähnten unterschiedlichen Formen lehnen die Anschaulichkeit und Lesbarkeit von konventionellen Dokumentationsmethoden ab, sodass „wir" unsere Rolle als Betrachter oder sogar uns selbst als Teil einer allgemeinen Menschheit nicht mehr wiedererkennen. Diese Herangehensweise trägt zur Bildung einer Fotografie der Ursachen, der neuen Affekte, der politisierten Ökologie bei. Doch letztendlich können wir nicht einfach Bilder als Antworten auf soziale und politische Probleme betrachten, was Kunst auf eine Art mechanisierte Funktion reduzieren würde und Betrachter zu passiven Rezipienten ästhetischer Vorgaben. Vielmehr müssen wir aus Bildern das machen, was wir wollen, sie kritisch und kreativ in unsere eigenen sozialen, politischen und pädagogischen Handlungen integrieren und dadurch ihr Potenzial ausschöpfen. In diesem Sinne könnten – je nachdem, wie sich fotografische und auf Video basierende Praktiken über die Dokumentation hinaus und hin zu einer konstruktivistische Poetik bewegen – ästhetische Darstellungen einen Raum der Vorstellungskraft bieten, um neue Affekte von demokratischer politischer Beteilung, Gerechtigkeit und Gleichheit anzuregen. Solch ein Bestreben dürfte umso bestechender sein, wenn es die diverse Kritik am Humanismus mitberücksichtigt und auf dieser Basis innovative Vorschläge konstruiert.

Photography's (Post)Humanist Interventions: Or, Can Photography Make the World More Liveable?

TJ Demos

With numerous art exhibitions over the last decade featuring photography and video, many of us are now familiar with the ethico-political ambition of contemporary lens-based media: to render visible conflicts that are the results of social and political exclusions, and to provide creative alternatives for equality and global inclusivity. For example, consider Edward Burtynsky's documentation of ecological degradation in the oilfields of California and Baku; the portrayal of poverty and homelessness in Gujarat by Ravi Agarwal; or Guy Tillim's imagery of military conflict in the Congo – all participants in the fourth edition of the Fotofestival. These artists exemplify one powerful ambition of contemporary art: to contribute to the formation of an experimental and inclusive democratic public sphere and counter the social omissions and political manipulations found in governmental propaganda and consumerist spectacle.

As such, this ambition represents, in some ways, a continuation of the longstanding humanist project, which seeks to overcome the particularities of nationalism, corporate inequality, and religious communities, by insisting on the commonality of humanity, and using that claim to universality to file grievances and make reparations in the sphere of visual culture. Their practices also extend the concerns and commitments of social documentary, which have increasingly moved from the pages of magazines and photo-books (as in the mid twentieth century) to the artistic context of the gallery space in the last 20 years. It's this recent neo-humanist formation that I want to engage here critically, particularly its entrance into contemporary art.

An important recent contribution to the discourse around photography and humanism is Ariella Azoulay's notion of the 'civil contract of photography', according to which she proposes the construction of an inclusive visual culture that offers a platform for rights claims against national exclusions (and one could add religious, corporate, and environmental exclusions): 'Against the political order of the nation-state, photography – together with other media that created the conditions for globalization – paved the way for a universal citizenship: not a state, but a citizenry, a virtual citizenry, in potential, with the civil contract of photography as its organizing framework.'[1]

Azoulay bases her reasoning on photography's 'civil contract', which she sees as a tacit agreement among photography's viewers developing in the spirit of modern human rights discourse, going back to the French Revolution's 1789 Declaration of the Rights of Man and of the Citizen (as well as Olympe de Gouges' important 1791 Declaration of the Rights of Woman and the Female Citizen). Its modern edition is The Universal Declaration of Human Rights, adopted by the United Nations on December 10, 1948, which countered the dehumanization contained in the nationalist projects of World War II, as well as emerging Cold War political divisions.

The expression of *human* rights, rather than national ones, found its visual expression in signal photography projects of the postwar period such as Edward Steichen's exhibition 'The Family of Man' (1955) and André Malraux's three-volume catalogue *Le Musée imaginaire* (1952–1954). 'The Family of Man' cited the UN Charter in its exhibition and catalogue and recently Azoulay has proposed viewing the exhibition as a 'Visual Universal Declaration of Human Rights'.[2] As a further contribution to the civil contract of photography, she draws on its critical humanist potential today to counter the production of states of exception where 'mere life' is separated from citizenship.[3]

1 Ariella Azoulay, *The Civil Contract of Photography* (New York: Zone, 2008), p.134.

2 'We, the peoples of United Nations, Determined to save succeeding generations from the scourge of war, which twice in our lifetime has brought untold sorrow to mankind, and to reaffirm faith in fundamental human rights, in the dignity and worth of the human person, in the equal rights of men and women and of nations large and small...' See Edward Steichen, *The Family of Man* (New York: Museum of Modern Art, 1955), pp.184–185.

3 Ariella Azoulay, 'The Family of Man as a Visual Universal Declaration of Human Rights', Keynote address at the symposium 'The Human Snapshot', LUMA Foundation, Arles, France, 2–3 July, 2011.

For Azoulay and others, photography is a privileged medium in that its system of imagery presents a direct relation between viewer and subject, proposing an ethico-political contract of universal rights that transcends national bonds and exclusions (for instance, the political divisions between Israeli *citizens* and Palestinian *subjects* is one Azoulay means to contest). For others, photography creates a system of empathy – a longstanding documentary principle – which is understood to oppose violence and oppression in the name of a shared sense of humanity, opening onto the universality of human rights.[4] Photography that advances the cause of human rights thereby holds the potential to make life more liveable by creating an engaged citizenry, empathic viewers, who will ostensibly work for a better world.

Humanist undertakings such as 'The Family of Man', however, have been taken to task for a variety of reasons. Critics, for instance, have pointed out the hidden hierarchies belying humanism's construction of universality, which typically betrays a privileged white, male, heterosexual normativity. Commentators have also pointed out how the philosophy of humanism has been articulated in the west and projected onto the global south, often in the name of abstract – but economically and politically motivated – concepts of 'freedom', 'modernization' and 'civilization'. These are all key terms, as we now know, in the philosophical justification of postwar colonialism and neocolonialism, dedicated to transforming the 'primitive' into the 'human', and thus betraying the limitations of humanist universalism, for which some are more human than others.[5]

4 See, for instance, Susie Linfield, 'Photojournalism and Human Rights', in *The Cruel Radiance: Photography and Political Violence* (Chicago: University of Chicago Press, 2010). In her introduction she explains, '...we cannot talk—at least in meaningful or realistic ways—about building a world of democracy, justice, and human rights without first understanding the experience of their negation. The attempt to forge such an understanding is what I mean by 'empathy,' a value I repeatedly return to; without it, the politics of human rights devolve into abstraction, romantic foolishness, and cruelty.' (xv).

5 See the work of Homi Bhabha and Gayatri Spivak, for instance, who have deconstructed the rhetoric of nineteenth-century liberal universalism and the "rights of man" in the time of colonialism, and critiqued humanism from a postcolonial perspective. Also, see the recent analysis of the paradoxes of Enlightenment universalism during colonialism and slavery, in Susan Buck-Morss, *Hegel, Haiti and Universal History* (Pittsburgh: University of Pittsburgh Press, 2009).

Multiculturalists during the 1980s and 90s continued the attack on humanism's Eurocentrism, drawing on the resources of poststructuralist critiques of the 1960s and 70s. Then, critics such as Barthes, Foucault, Althusser, Deleuze, and Derrida countered the assumption of subjective autonomy with an antihumanism that stressed the determinative role of subjective and social forces – for Marxists, the market economy; for psychoanalysis, the psychic structure; for structuralists, the historical and cultural mediation of language. Those critical assessments have been expanded by more recent problematizations of humanism in the 2000s: for instance, Chantal Mouffe and Jacques Rancière have criticized its 'post-political' assumption of a unified social body (humanity); and Giorgio Agamben has deconstructed the 'anthropological machine' that is its basis, which for him functions to construct the human by opposing it to the non-human, often with bloody consequences. For Immanuel Wallerstein, the very notion of universal human values remains a western concept, a 'rhetoric of power' used by powerful western governments to enact their will on weaker states, most recently under the moralizing veneer of 'human rights'.[6] Consequently, today, many believe that a return to humanism is not the answer to present crises; rather it is part of the problem. As Matthew Calarco puts it, 'The assumption by many post-humanists is that nihilism and the major political catastrophes of our age are linked in a profound way with the very humanism typically offered by neo-humanists as a solution to these issues.'[7]

Still, its continued attractiveness for some theorists and exhibition makers is testimony to the belief in the Enlightenment heritage and the modern democratic project that stands behind contemporary

6 Immanuel Wallerstein, *European Universalism: The Rhetoric of Power* (New York: New Press, 2006).

7 Matthew Calarco, 'Jamming the Anthropological Machine,' in Steven DeCaroli and Matthew Calarco, eds., *On Agamben: Sovereignty and Life* (Stanford, CA.: Stanford University Press, 2006).

humanism. For instance, the late literary critic Edward Said supported what he termed an 'intercessive humanism' that intervenes in 'history as agonistic process still being made', and that exposes 'the undocumented turbulence of unsettled and unhoused exiles, immigrants, itinerant or captive populations for whom no document, no adequate expression yet exists to take account of what they go through.'[8] He goes on to sketch what is in fact the basis of the modern social documentary project: 'Humanism, I strongly believe must excavate the silences, the world of memory, of itinerant barely surviving groups, the kind of testimony that doesn't make it onto the reports...' Such has been the guiding principle of war photographers and documentarians of catastrophe since the very invention of photography.

If some believe today that photography can revive this project of an intercessive humanism, then Agamben's post-humanist criticism makes that move all the harder, and as such it's worth revisiting his argument further – particularly since it relates to two key concerns of contemporary photography and video that figure in the current Fotofestival: human rights and ecology. A reading of Agamben's book *The Open* reveals that these two categories are not unrelated, for humanism's oppositional logic operates by dividing both political life from animal life (creating the potential for human rights abuses), and humans from nature (creating the potential for environmental catastrophe). One result today is the proliferating 'state of exception' that, for Agamben, forms the basis of the modern biopolitical paradigm, meaning the governmentality of life.[9] In recent years spaces of 'included exclusions' – zones of legally prescribed depoliticized life, such as refugee centres and military 'black' sites – have expanded and become dispersed in contemporary society. In addition to the construction of a growing security state, financial onslaughts into the public commons (including cuts to pensions, education and health care) are reducing populations worldwide to 'mere life' via austerity measures.
Crises far away, particularly in 'underdeveloped' nations, have been met with the recourse to human rights claims by a growing class of NGOs, defining a new age of emergencies characterized by humanitarian catastrophes disconnected from politico-economic considerations.[10] Yet that recourse has been far from successful. Practically speaking, as political rights have historically been tied to citizenship, human rights lack an institutional or governmental framework for protection and enforcement.[11] Theoretically speaking, the return to the notion of a shared humanity to redress exclusions is therefore compromised from the start because humanity is itself an effect of the anthropological machine, where there is always the potential for the production of hierarchies and exceptions, and thus violent consequences. The answer for some critics, consequently, is not to renew our commitment to human rights, but rather to get rid of the concept of humanity, and by extension the concept of humanism.
What would it take to get rid of the concept of humanity? As Agamben suggests, it would mean stopping the anthropological machine by showing the emptiness of its separations – those between human and animal, and between human and nature – and to 'risk ourselves in this emptiness'.[12] Or to put it positively: to articulate a form of life independent from the divisions between humanity and animality, political and biological life – such is the task of the 'coming community', a task that, Agamben argues, remains 'largely to be invented'.[13]

8 Edward Said, *Humanism and Democratic Criticism* (New York: Columbia University Press, 2004), p.25 and 81.
9 See Giorgio Agamben, *State of Exception*, trans. Kevin Attell (Chicago: University of Chicago Press, 2005).

10 See Craig Calhoun, 'The Idea of Emergency: Humanitarian Action and Global (Dis)order', in *Contemporary States of Emergency: The Politics of Military and Humanitarian Interventions*, ed. Didier Fassin and Mariella Pandolfi (New York: Zone Books, 2010), p.18-39.
11 This point is made by Agamben in 'Beyond Human Rights', in *Means Without Ends: Notes on Politics* (Minneapolis: University of Minnesota Press, 2000).
12 Giorgio Agamben, *The Open: Man and Animal*, trans. Kevin Attell (Stanford: Stanford University Press, 2004), p.92.
13 Giorgio Agamben, *Homo Sacer: Sovereign Power and Bare Life*, trans. Daniel Heller-Roazen (Stanford, Stanford University Press, 1998), p.3; and Giorgio Agamben, *The Coming Community*, trans. Michael Hardt (Minneapolis: University of Minnesota Press, 1993).

Of course, one might resist this call to abandon humanity, and instead seek to return to the unrealized potential of democratic politics and its liberal humanist ontology, finding and retrieving moments from its Enlightenment legacy to expand democracy's scope and open its ethico-political commitment to those excluded from its norms. One might even try to bring democratic humanism into relation with the non-exclusionary basis of Agamben's coming community, building a progressive reformist politics, as Said or Mouffe have proposed. But to do so, one would have to confront the criticism that up until this point, humanism has led to as many catastrophes of inclusive exclusion as successful overcomings of such divisions. Moreover, contemporary politics in the west appears, if anything, destined to continue the intensification of the biopolitical regulation of life (especially given the threat of climate change and the massive refugee crisis it will generate), with further separations between citizens and migrants, wealthy and poor, which is leading to what some call a global system of apartheid.[14] Yet perhaps at this point, we don't need to resolve this philosophical quandary and choose between the two paths; rather, we can turn to artistic proposals to see where they might take us.

Whichever way we might answer these critiques of humanism, they do allow us to identify several problems with the conventional documentary images of suffering – whether in the corporate media or in the artistic context. When photography intervenes in states of emergency, it frequently works in tandem with the logic of humanitarianism. The problem is that such practices tend to depoliticize crises and the subjects caught within them, often for reasons owing to the mandates of NGOs and UN organizations, according to which aid is distributed not to political actors but to human victims. Humanitarianism aims to alleviate suffering with immediacy and a blindness toward the victim's identity or political orientation, which strips subjects of their political claims and ignores the larger context and causes of violence. One could even say that humanitarianism not only works with victims but plays a role in *producing* them, which exemplifies the division of biological life from political life in the state of exception.

The problem is that documentary's construction of the affects of empathy proposes a false proximity between the compassionate viewer and the anguished subject, which, as critics point out, works to alleviate guilt rather than provide solutions to problems that are complex and structural.[15] The situation is similar with humanitarian aid, which often does not reach victims in need, but rather perpetuates streams of funding. The paradox of humanitarianism is that instead of simply alleviating suffering, it may also sustain the oppressive systems that cause it.[16] In fact, compassionate humanism and humanitarian interventionism are intricately connected, especially in that the emotional response of sensationalized photojournalism – whether one of compassion for helpless victims, or of fear of threatening terrorism – tends to support humanitarian intervention.[17] To rescue fellow 'humans' in need with military assistance is one of the principal ways contemporary intervention and warfare are justified.

One perceives a similar impulse in the separation of humanity from nature. The disastrous effects are obvious when nature becomes an exploitable resource for profit-making activities without care for the long-term impact on human and natural ecosystems. Yet we encounter a more complex challenge when the same structure of separation finds its realization

14 See John Cavanagh et al., eds., *Alternatives to Economic Globalization: A Better World is Possible: A Report of the International Forum on Globalization* (San Francisco, CA: Berrett-Koehler, 2002), p.33.

15 See, for instance, the criticisms in the writings of Susan Sontag, Martha Rosler, and Allan Sekula.

16 See Linda Polman, *The Crisis Caravan: What's Wrong with Humanitarian Aid?*, trans. Liz Waters (New York: Metropolitan, 2010); and Fiona Terry, *Condemned to Repeat? The Paradox of Humanitarian Action* (Ithaca: Cornell University Press, 2002).

17 As Fassin and Pandolfi write in their introduction to *States of Emergency*, p.16: 'The states of emergency... are always based on affective foundations, which may be distinguished from traditional war situations in that the passions brought into play are supposedly not nationalist, but are presented as universalist—or simply as humanist.'

in well-intentioned attempts to construct a natural realm to be protected or restored. For the result relegates nature to a non-cultural zone of organic purity, recalling, for instance, the mythopoetic basis attributed to the biological environment in James Lovelock's 'Gaia' hypothesis – a crucial late-1970s marker in the development of ecological discourse – according to which nature ends up objectified as an ontology divorced from social, political and technological processes.[18]

The problem is that laudable environmentalist intentions can result in a dangerous depoliticization, reproducing the very objectification of nature that has got us into trouble in the first place. The political geographer Neil Smith observes that when 'sundered apart, nature and society die in reciprocal conceptual torpor', for 'the positing of an external nature rationalizes and justifies the unprecedented exploitation of nature... which is the "massive racket" that capitalism, historically and geographically, represents.'[19]

Alternately, if nature and society are connected, then a further danger presents itself in that life becomes subject to biopolitics, and the environment serves as the ultimate domain of being for the production of knowledge, power and subjectivity. As political scientist Timothy Luke argues, with the expansion of international regulatory bodies, such as the UN World Commission on Environment and Development, comes the gradual reshaping of government according to the priorities of 'enviro-discipline', referring to 'the authority of eco-knowledge, geo-powered forces to police the fitness of all biological organisms and the health of their natural environments.'[20]

One effect of such enviro-discipline is when emergency measures are declared so as to bypass democratic deliberation, shutting down critical debates about social justice and forms of inequality between the global north and south. Instead, the urgency of impending ecological disaster places the imperative of human survival above all political considerations (and it is not at all surprising that G8 countries use such urgency to force through their own economically biased environmental agendas, as at the recent COP meetings).[21] In addition, disciplinary modes of control – such as the conceptualizing of climate change threats in terms of security, developing alternative energy incentives and green economic imperatives like carbon trading – are typically directed toward instrumentalizing nature for the purpose of further exploitation. This is often done in the name of sustainable development, where, according to the demands of an emerging climate capitalism, 'sustainability' means – paradoxically – the privileging of economic growth above all else.[22]

Given these admittedly formidable challenges, what recourse do we have in the realm of visual culture to make life more liveable – meaning more democratic, egalitarian, and sustainable? How can those who work with images operate so as to avoid the clear and present dangers of neo-humanism, in relation to both humanitarian interventionism and antipolitical enviro-discipline? In the space that remains, I'll propose some further questions and possible creative solutions based on the framework of and inclusions in Fotofestival.

From Effects to Causes

First of all, as we've seen, it's important to question documentary's attachment to capturing the effects of conflicts – the pain of others as an object for a privileged, compassionate audience – instead of the causes and histories of suffering. How might photography help us comprehend how a depoliticized segment of humanity is produced, and how different responses than guilt-relieving compassion might be generated? What about the viewer's

18 James Lovelock, *Gaia: A New Look at Life on Earth* (Oxford: Oxford University Press, 1979).
19 Neil Smith, 'Forward', *In the Nature of Cities: Urban Political Ecology and the Politics of Urban Metabolism*, ed. Nik Heynen, et al. (London: Routledge, 2006), pp.xiii–xiv.
20 Timothy Luke, 'Environmentality as Green Governmentality', in *Discourses of the Environment*, ed. Éric Darier (Oxford: Blackwell, 1999), p.146.

21 See Alex Gourevitch, 'Environmentalism—Long Live the Politics of Fear,' *Public Culture* 22:3 (2010), pp.411–424.
22 See TJ Demos, 'The Politics of Sustainability: Art and Ecology', in *Radical Nature: Art and Architecture for a Changing Planet, 1969–2009*, ed. Francesco Manacorda and Ariella Yedgar (London: Barbican Art Gallery, 2009), pp.17–30.

complicity in the breakdown of global governance, or in the workings of capitalist globalization? If the compassionate regard for photographed victims suffering from military onslaught, famine, and environmental devastation tends to feed uncritically into the support for humanitarian intervention, bypassing political deliberation, then an alternative to the media's conventional positioning of photojournalism is urgently needed.

We see various approaches to such an anti-photojournalistic experimental modelling of photography in several examples from the show – examples that point toward a non-sensationalizing use of photography that avoids the common tropes of mainstream media presentations, such as the heroic positioning of the photographer, the construction of a singular event and iconic image, the truthful and objective portrayal of reality, and the bearing witness to terrible events and conveying them to faraway audiences.[23]

For instance, consider Bruno Serralongue's images of the precarious and temporary living conditions of refugees located on the border of France, which reject focusing on the 'human-interest' story in order to bring out the material circumstances of migrants. Or take Ravi Agarwal's images of homeless subjects in Gujarat that resist victimizing his subjects and instead portray dignified forms of creative everyday life and survival, even while bringing out a critical picture of economic inequality in India. Likewise, Guy Tillim portrays experimental forms of living in the urban centres of postcolonial South Africa, drawing out meanings that resist clichéd narratives and instead show the economic challenges that exist in the post-Apartheid era. Importantly, these projects are photographic series, often with extensive captioning, and embedded in the photographer's practice of social activism, which allow a complex story to develop over several images. Rather than attempting to condense a situation into a single spectacular image, these projects evince a kind of pedagogical engagement. Such images are promising not because they reject photography's emotional potential; rather, they suggest a new politics of affect that avoids the problem of catastrophism and non-rational interventionism.

The Politics of Affect

If the corporate media's image-system employs affect to block democratic debate, how can we invent a new regime of affect that supports social justice, equality and political engagement?[24] And how to do so not in favour of a purely rationalist discourse – clearly impossible, given the insights of psychoanalysis – but rather to re-appropriate affect in the name of an alternative (or counter-hegemonic) politics?

Consider the images of Kenyan self-styled photo-activist Boniface Mwangi, who pictures his country's descent into violence during the 2007 elections, employing the camera, as he claims, 'to bring down dictators, change society and influence change'.[25] Given his desire to share images of those suffering from poverty and military oppression, are we as viewers opened to a reinvented humanism insisting on the complexity of our potential relations and even solidarities with the excluded, as Said points out? Alternately, what of the implicit challenge to the presentism of documentary imagery in the films of Sven Augustijnen and Vincent Meessen, both of whom investigate legacies of colonialism that haunt our present. Augustijnen's film *Spectres* does so in relation to Belgium's violent intervention in the Congo during the early years of its independence in the early 1960s, focusing on how the assassination of Prime Minister Patrice Lumumba is represented and surprisingly justified by one surviving participant (Jacques Brassinne) today. Meessen's film *Vita Nova* takes up the complex history

23 See as well the recent exhibition *Anti-Photojournalism*, curated by Carles Guerra of Barcelona's Virreina Centre de la Imatge, which borrowed the concept from Allan Sekula.

24 Brian Massumi writes about how the media has assumed a governmental function by modulating viewers' neuro-physiological system via affective stimuli. See Brian Massumi, 'Fear (The Spectrum Said)', *Positions* 13:1 (2005).

25 See his website: http://www.bonifacemwangi.com/bonnie/

of French literary critic Roland Barthes' critical analysis of a famous colonial-era image of an African boy in military uniform saluting what is likely the French flag, which appeared on the cover of *Paris Match*, even while in his autobiography, *Barthes par Barthes*, the author failed to discuss his relation to his own colonist grandfather, Captain Louis-Gustave Binger, who 'gave' Côte d'Ivoire to France.

For the critic Kobena Mercer, Meessen's portrayal of the aftermath of colonialism in present-day Burkina Faso movingly provoked tears – a quintessential *bodily* response to film's affective realm that is beyond verbal language.[26] As such, these moving images – both emotionally engaging and politically transformational – propose an alternative regime of affects to dominant forms of mediatized fear, one that connects to a postcolonial debt of social justice, even if we still lack a vocabulary complex and subtle enough to define it.

Political Ecology

Against the anthropocentrism of humanism, with its dangerous privileging of the human above the non-human environment, we need to find ways to interconnect social, economic and technological systems in order to reconceptualize nature for a sustainable future (even as such a future seems to be receding daily from the horizon of the possible). One longstanding theoretical resource in this regard is Félix Guattari's ethico-aesthetic philosophy, according to which he proposed to comprehend ecology 'transversally', that is, via interconnected subjective, institutional and environmental registers.[27] For him, it was necessary to 'produce' subjectivity differently, to direct it toward 'resingularization' – a term we could relate today to the call for biodiversity – and away from the dangerous industrial production of homogeneity.

In some ways this call is answered negatively in the images of Edward Burtynsky's portrayal of mass production in China, or Geert Goiris' *Whiteout* series, which elicits the perceptual disorientation that occurs in non-human arctic climates, where human technology has invaded even the most pristine of inhospitable environments. Alternately, Nicu Ilfoveanu depicts post-natural scenes in his chromatically processed landscapes. With these examples, we have mixed signals in relation to the circumstances of human-environmental ecology. Between post-industrial homogenization and habitat destruction, they map an uncertain future for humanity.

The diversity of such approaches nonetheless speaks to the advantage of addressing ecology in aesthetic terms, in that it avoids the catastrophist thinking that leads to anti-political courses of action, and which refuses to relegate ecology to scientistic discourse. Still, even here we need to resist embracing a post-political notion of humanity, or bare life, according to which a consensus-based universalism ends up displacing the consideration of environmental justice in relation to economic and political inequality, for instance, between the global north's eco-politics and the south's demands for debt relief and assistance in adapting to climate change. If humanism opposes the divisions of national politics, how can it offer a framework to negotiate such regional and hemispheric antagonisms? Alternately, how can we configure a post-humanist politics and sociability that avoids both objectifying nature and generalizing humanity?

Misrecognition

If we need to produce subjectivity differently, then perhaps we can start by learning to *mis*recognize ourselves, so that we can reinvent ourselves anew. This imperative might be realized through a creative practice of everyday life, through alternative roles and rituals, which photography can facilitate as a medium of creative construction. Consider, for instance, Bani Abidi's images of people in Pakistan during Ramadan who inhabit a liminal space between domesticity and publicness; or Pieter Hugo's soliciting of bizarre dramatizations of Nollywood, whereby he documents fictional personas from the Nigerian

26 See Kobena Mercer's text on Vincent Messen in *Ars 11* (Helsinki: Kiasma Museum of Contemporary Art, 2011).
27 See Félix Guattari, *The Three Ecologies*, trans. Ian Pindar and Paul Sutton (London: The Athlone Press, 2000).

film industry in disjunctive scenes of everyday life. Or take Ryan McGinley's adolescent road trips, which suggest an aesthetic journey of subjective invention as much as a psycho-sexual one of discovery and estrangement. These images, however diverse, propose allegories for living life differently, and perhaps even reject the commonality and recognisability of the human. The image consequently becomes a space of imagination, less of documentation.

All of the diverse models considered briefly above reject the clarity and legibility of conventional documentary practice, so that 'we' no longer recognize our roles as viewers, or indeed ourselves as part of some generic humanity. Such work builds toward a photography of causes, of new affects, of politicized ecology. But ultimately we can't simply look to images as answers to social and political problems, which would reduce art to a kind of mechanized function, and viewers to passive recipients of aesthetic directives. Rather we must make of images what we will, integrating them critically and creatively into our own social, political, and pedagogical practices and thereby drawing out their potential. In this sense, aesthetic constructions – according to which photographic and video-based practices move beyond the documentary and into a constructivist poetics – might offer an imaginative space for proposing new affects of democratic political participation, justice and equality. Such an ambition will be all the more compelling if it considers the various critiques of humanism, building innovative proposals on that basis.

The Affect and Effect of Politics

S. / p. 2

Sven Augustijnen

Sven Augustijnens Arbeiten beschäftigen sich oft mit der Geschichte Belgiens, insbesondere mit der Zeit, als das Land unter König Leopold II. Kolonialmacht war und eines der gewalttätigsten Kapitel der europäischen Kolonialgeschichte schrieb. *Les Demoiselles de Bruxelles* (2008) besteht aus einer Fotoserie und einer Installation mit einer Szenerie aus Rattanstühlen, 2 Bananenstauden und einem Buch. Die Fotografien zeigen afrikanische Prostituierte in der Gegend der Avenue Louise in Brüssel (benannt nach Marie-Louise d'Orléans, der Mutter Leopolds II.), wie sie sich vor der Kamera theatralisch und verführerisch in Pose stellen. Diese Bilder sind im selben Rahmen neben Aufnahmen von Statuen, Monumenten und Gebäuden aus der kolonialen Phase platziert; Denkmäler und Orte der ehemaligen Administration, die in Beziehung zu Belgiens umstrittener kolonialer Vergangenheit im Kongo stehen, wie etwa die früheren Büros der Koloniallotterie sowie die königlichen Gärten. Besucher können im klischeehaft „exotischen" Leseraum auf einem Stuhl unter einer Bananenstaude die Publikation zur Installation zur Hand nehmen und Anekdoten aus dem Leben Leopolds lesen: über seine Liebe zum Essen, seine sexuellen Gelüste, seine Launenhaftigkeit und noch viele weiteren Details. *Les Demoiselles de Bruxelles* stellt einen Beitrag zu Brüssels kolonialer Vergangenheit dar und bedient sich dabei historischer Spuren, wie etwa Gebäuden, Monumenten und schriftlichen Überlieferungen. Dabei fungieren Prostituierte nach wie vor als ein lebender Beweis, dass die Geschichte immer noch im Körper des „anderen" nachhallt. Die Arbeiten rufen den Geist des Kolonialen durch das Körperliche wach: „Ein- und Auswirkung" der Politik in Fleisch und Blut. — KG
Sven Augustijnen wurde 1970 in Mechelen, Belgien, geboren. Er lebt und arbeitet in Brüssel, Belgien.

Sven Augustijnen's work has often revolved around the history of Belgium, with a special focus on its period as a colonial power under King Leopold II, one of the most violent chapters of European colonialism. *Les Demoiselles de Bruxelles* (2008) is a series of photographs and an installation of a staged environment with rattan chairs, two banana trees and a book. The photographs depict African prostitutes in the vicinity of Avenue Louise, Brussels (named in memory of Leopold II's mother, Marie-Louise d'Orléans), posing for the camera in theatrical, seductive postures. These images are juxtaposed, in the same frame, with statues, monuments, and buildings from the colonial period; memorials and ex-administrative spaces related to Belgium's contested colonial past in the Congo (such as the former offices of the Colonial Lottery and the King's gardens). Visitors can consult the publication that accompanies the installation by sitting in a chair under the banana tree in the clichéd 'exotic' reading room, and read stories from Leopold's life: his love of food, his sexual appetite, his petulance, and other details. *Les Demoiselles de Bruxelles* renders an account of Brussels' colonial past by way of historical traces, such as buildings, monuments, stories, in which the prostitutes still function as a living proof of that history that still resonates in the body of the 'other'. It raises the spectre of the colonial through the corporal: the 'affect' and 'effect' of politics in flesh and blood. — KG
Sven Augustijnen was born in 1970, in Mechelen, Belgium. He lives and works in Brussels, Belgium

www.augusteorts.be
www.janmot.com

Gohar Dashti

Gohar Dashti wurde kurz nach dem Sturz des Schahs und der islamischen Revolution von 1979 geboren und gehört einer Generation zeitgenössischer iranischer Künstler an, die uns das Bild eines neuen Iran vermitteln. Ihre Fotografien sind frei von westlichen Stereotypen über den Iran, gedenken aber den neueren historischen Traumata, dem Erbe der Gewalt und der Hinterlassenschaft des Krieges. Ihre Serie *Today's Life and War* (2008) zeigt ein junges Paar, das die gegenwärtig unsichere Zeit verkörpert. Die Szenen sind gestellt und der Schauplatz ist ein fiktives Schlachtfeld, auf dem das Paar seinen Alltagsbeschäftigungen nachgeht. Inmitten von Panzern, Waffen und anderer militärischer Ausrüstung sehen wir es in der Wüste zwischen Sandsäcken fernsehen, mit Soldaten im Hintergrund im Internet surfen, am Stacheldrahtzaun Wäsche

aufhängen, vor dem Kanonenrohr eines Panzers am Tisch essen und in einem Autowrack einen Geburtstag feiern. Die aufgrund der inhärenten Unvereinbarkeit völlig surreal anmutenden Situationen dieser Bilder symbolisieren die beständige – und überaus reale – Angst einer Generation, die sich an Zustände politischer Instabilität und die sich abzeichnende Bedrohung durch Gewalt und soziale Zerrüttung gewöhnt hat. Indem das Paar keinerlei Emotionen erkennen lässt – ihre Gesichter sind stets ausdruckslos –, strahlen sie eine Art Beharrlichkeit aus, eine Entschlossenheit, in dieser Zeit zu überleben, und deuten damit eine latent vorhandene Hoffnung auf Veränderung an. — KG
Gohar Dashti wurde 1980 in Ahvaz, Iran, geboren. Sie lebt und arbeitet in Berlin, Deutschland, und Teheran, Iran.

Gohar Dashti was born immediately after the fall of the Shah and the ensuing Islamic revolution in 1979 and is part of a generation of contemporary Iranian artists bringing a new Iran to our attention. Her photographs are devoid of western stereotypes of Iran, but mindful of recent historical traumas, the heritage of violence and legacy of war. Her series *Today's Life and War* (2008) features a young couple who symbolize current uncertain times. The photographs are staged, and take place in a fictionalized battlefield where daily activities take place. We see them in a desert amidst tanks, guns and other military equipment, watching television among sandbags, surfing on the Internet with soldiers in the background, hanging laundry on barbed wire, having dinner with the gun of a tank pointing at them, and celebrating a birthday in a wrecked car. While completely surreal because of the inherent contradiction in this situation, these images symbolize the constant – and very real – fear that exists amongst a generation of people that have grown used to situations of political instability and the looming threat of violence and social disruption. While the couple never betray any emotion – their faces remain expressionless and deadpan throughout – a sense of perseverance and determination to survive is evident, hinting at a latent hope for change. — KG
Gohar Dashti was born in 1980, in Ahvaz, Iran. She lives and works in Berlin, Germany and Tehran, Iran

www.kashyahildebrand.org

Fouad Elkoury

Fouad Elkoury verfügt über umfassende Kenntnisse und Erfahrungen, wenn es um die Schaffung von Bildern geht, die ein Porträt der *Conditio humana* in urbanem Umfeld von Gesellschaften liefern, die politischen Unruhen ausgesetzt sind. Neben seiner Arbeit als Fotograf und Filmemacher ist Elkoury Mitbegründer der Arab Image Foundation (einer gemeinnützigen Vereinigung, die sich dem Sammeln, Bewahren und dem Studium der Fotografie aus dem Nahen und Mittleren Osten, Nordafrika und der arabischen Diaspora widmet). In dieser Ausstellung zeigt er mehrere Werke, die sich über etwa 1 Jahrzehnt erstrecken und die Folgen der israelischen Invasion in Beirut im Jahr 1982 dokumentieren sowie die Nachwirkungen andauernder politischer Unruhen und des libanesischen Bürgerkriegs (1975–1990). Seine Bilder, sowohl Schwarz-Weiß- als auch Farbaufnahmen, richten den Blick auf den Alltag der in zerbombten, nicht mehr funktionsfähigen Häusern und Straßen lebenden Zivilbevölkerung und auch auf die Gebäude selbst. Jedes Bild offenbart eine andere Situation: der unsagbar traurige Blick eines älteren Mannes, der an einigen Gebäuden vorübergeht, von denen nichts als die äußere Hülle geblieben ist; eine sich sonnende Frau im verlassenen Sportstadion der Stadt, das erst wenige Stunden zuvor durch israelische Bomben zerstört wurde; ein junger Mann, der inmitten der Überreste einiger Gebäude mit einem Lächeln im Gesicht der Musik aus seinem Ghettoblaster lauscht; ein einzelner Mann auf einem Fahrrad, der ein Pferd mit sich führt; ein Blick über den weiten, desolaten Platz der Märtyrer im Zentrum Beiruts, wo ein einsamer Straßenhändler gedankenverloren an seinem Fahrrad lehnt – an wen auch sollte er seine Ware verkaufen? All diese Bilder belegen die Fähigkeit des Menschen, auch in schwierigsten Zeiten zu überleben und nicht aufzugeben. — SHO
Fouad Elkoury wurde 1952 in Paris, Frankreich, geboren. Er lebt und arbeitet in Paris, Frankreich, und Beirut, Libanon.

Fouad Elkoury has an extensive knowledge and experience of producing images portraying the human condition in urban setting of societies in the throes of political upheaval. As well as working as a photographer and filmmaker, Elkoury is a co-founder of The Arab Image Foundation (a non-profit association that collects, preserves and studies photographs from the Middle East, North Africa and the Arab diaspora). In this exhibition, he presents a body of work spanning a period of approximately a decade documenting the aftermath of the Israeli invasion of Beirut in 1982, as well as the after-effects of continuous political upheaval and the Lebanese civil war (1975-1990). The images, both in black-and-white and colour, focus on the everyday life of civilians living in and occupying bombed-out and dysfunctional streets and houses, as well as images of the architecture itself. Each image discloses a different situation: the infinitely sad look of an elderly man walking besides some shelled-out buildings; a woman sunbathing in the city's derelict sports stadium, demolished by Israeli bombardment just a few hours before; a smiling young man listening to his ghetto blaster standing amidst the remainders of some buildings; a lone man on a bicycle leading a horse; a view across the vast and desolate Martyrs' Square in central Beirut in which a single vendor leans absently against his bicycle - who is he going to sell his cakes to? These images appear as evidence of the ability of people to survive and carry on in the most turbulent times. — SHO

Fouad Elkoury was born in 1952 in Paris, France. He lives and works in Paris, France and Beirut, Lebanon

www.fouadelkoury.com

Panos Kokkinias

Panos Kokkinias´ Wirkungsbereich ist die inszenierte Fotografie. Alle seine Bilder sind sorgfältig arrangiert und komponiert, was seiner Arbeit eine beinahe filmische Wirkung verleiht. Seine Fotografien sind verwurzelt in der Realität oder in Situationen, die sich tatsächlich so ergeben könnten, dennoch beflügeln sie die Fantasie und eröffnen eine große Spannbreite an Interpretationsmöglichkeiten. Anlässlich des Fotofestivals hat Kokkinias für die einzelnen Themenbereiche der Ausstellung jeweils ein Bild angefertigt. Auf *Prespes* (2011) für „Affekt und Wirkung von Politik" sieht man ein Auto durch eine weite, prärieähnliche Landschaft fahren. Dahinter folgt eine Gruppe von Menschen, die voller Begeisterung griechische Flaggen schwenken. Offensichtlich soll hier etwas gefeiert werden, aber was? Oder könnte es dabei auch einen besorgniserregenderen Subtext geben? Die Euphorie der Gruppe könnte auch symptomatisch sein für die Art nationalistischer Gefühlsäußerungen beispielsweise nach einem gewonnen Fußball-Länderspiel oder für die zunehmenden - und sehr beunruhigenden - nationalistischen Tendenzen, die in jüngerer Zeit in ganz Europa festzustellen waren. Andererseits erinnert die Arbeit aber auch an ganz aktuelle Ereignisse und an vertraute Bilder in den Medien von verärgerten Griechen, die in Athen Protestfahnen schwenken, Gasmasken und Helme tragen und Molotowcocktails auf Polizisten werfen. *Prespes* (2011) erinnert uns auch an einen unvermeidlichen Nebeneffekt jeder politischen Entscheidung oder Handlung: Wo es Gewinner gibt, die einen politischen Sieg feiern, muss es auch Verlierer geben. Sie sind diejenigen, die in der Regel unsichtbar bleiben. In *Circle* (2011) für „Ökologische Kreisläufe" sieht man eine verlassene, karge Berglandschaft, fast ohne jegliche Vegetation. In der Bildmitte, kaum erkennbar, entdecken wir zwei kleine Figuren inmitten einer asphaltierten Straße in der Form eines Kreises; eine kreisrunde, vom Menschen in die Landschaft geprägte „Spur", die nirgendwohin führt. Bei näherer Betrachtung lässt sich ein alter Mann und ein Kleinkind ausmachen - wahrscheinlich ein Großvater mit seinem Enkel. Sie sind damit beschäftigt, eine kleine Zypresse zu pflanzen und zu gießen. Das Leben, in Form von Mensch und Pflanze, ist hier festgehalten, wie es gerade erst beginnt, gleichzeitig aber auch, wie es sich seinem Ende nähert. Das Pflanzen eines Baumes ist eine symbolische Geste zur Mahnung, wie wichtig es ist, sich auf die Natur zurückzubesinnen und für sie zu sorgen. Selbst in dieser unwirtlichen Umgebung existiert ein Versprechen auf die Zukunft und die Möglichkeit der Regeneration.

Aliki (2007), im Ausstellungssegment „Rolle und Ritual", zeigt eine Prostituierte und damit einen Berufsstand, der generell als das älteste Gewerbe der Welt gilt. Alle Elemente eines nicht offiziellen aber sehr bekannten Rituals sind gegenwärtig. Die Aufnahme lässt den Betrachter die Position eines potenziellen Kunden einnehmen, während das Mädchen durch ihre typische Fetischkleidung alle Zeichen ihres Gewerbes zur Schau stellt. Sie wartet bei Nacht in einer menschenleeren Unterführung, aber es scheinen keine Autos zu kommen. Das Bild

deutet das Ritual an, welches es zu verrichten gilt, aber in diesem eingefangenen Moment zeigt es nichts als die absolute Leere, Ruhe und Stille.
In *Theoni* (2011) für „Lebenskreisläufe" schauen wir aus einem kleinen Hof in einen Raum, in dem eine ältere Frau – höchstwahrscheinlich eine Großmutter – ein kleines Kind in ihren Armen hält. Diese Fotografie zeigt eine frappierende Ähnlichkeit zu dem Gemälde *Briefleserin in Blau* (ca. 1663–1664) des niederländischen Malers Vermeer, das eine offensichtlich junge, schwangere Frau zeigt, die einen Brief liest. Durch diesen „Kniff" kann Kokkinias auf mehr hinweisen, als eigentlich abgebildet ist: Er bedenkt das ungeborene Leben, das Vermeer beschreibt; die Zeit der Jugend ist in seiner Aufnahme durch das kleine Kind in den Armen der alten Frau repräsentiert; die Zeit der Reife ist durch die Ähnlichkeit zu der Schwangeren aus Vermeers Gemälde gegeben und schließlich wird das Alter durch die Frau symbolisiert, die das Kind trägt und die damit den Lebenskreislauf schließt.
Auf *Twenty Past Nine* (2011) für „Das alltägliche Leben" schauen wir vom Balkon eines ländlich gelegenen Hauses über eine geisterhaft angestrahlte nächtliche Szene, man sieht einige Bäume und eine schmale Straße, die zu in der Ferne liegenden Häusern führt. Ein bedrohlich dunkler Nachthimmel verstärkt die düstere Atmosphäre. Durch ein Fenster erkennt man eine spannungsgeladene Szene zwischen einem Paar, das in seiner hell erleuchteten Küche steht. Ihre Blicke sind nach innen gerichtet und sie scheinen in ihren eigenen Gedanken versunken zu sein. Ihr innerer Aufruhr durchdringt die dunkle nächtliche Atmosphäre. Haben sie gestritten? Sind sie mit ihrer Beziehung in einer Sackgasse angekommen? Wir bekommen gewisse dramatische Anhaltspunkte geboten – die Puzzleteile dieser Situation, die wie eine archetypische Szene eines häuslichen Dramas anmutet, müssen wir uns jedoch selbst zusammensetzen. — KG
Panos Kokkinias wurde 1965 in Athen, Griechenland, geboren. Er lebt und arbeitet in Athen, Griechenland.

Panos Kokkinias works in the field of staged photography. All his pictures are carefully composed and directed, as on the set of a movie production, lending all his work a dramatic cinematic quality. All of his works are rooted in reality, in real possible situations, which nevertheless enable leaps of the imagination and lay open a wide range of interpretive possibilities. For the Fotofestival, Kokkinias has created an image for each of the thematic categories of the exhibition.
In *Prespes* (2011), for 'The Affect and Effect of Politics', we see a car driving through a vast prairie like landscape. It is followed by a group of people, rapturously waving Greek flags. Clearly something has to be celebrated, but what? Or is there a more disturbing latent sub-text? The state of euphoria evoked could also be symptomatic of the kind of nationalistic outpourings that occur when a country has won a football game, for example or the increasing – and very disturbing – nationalistic tendencies that have sprung up all over Europe recently. *Prespes* also reminds us of one inevitable side effect of any political decision or action: if there are winners, celebrating some political victory, there must be losers too. Those are the ones who largely remain invisible.
In *Circle* (2011), for 'Ecological Circuits', we can see a deserted and barren mountainous landscape, with hardly any plant life. At the centre of the image we barely discern two tiny figures in the middle of a large circular concrete road, going nowhere but around itself. Upon closer inspection we are able to see an old man and a toddler – presumably a grandfather with his grandchild. In this stark and desolate landscape, they are planting and watering a small cypress tree. Even in this inhospitable environment there exists a promise for the future and the possibility of regeneration.
Aliki (2007), for 'Role and Ritual', depicts a practitioner of what is generally regarded as the oldest profession in the world. All the elements of an unofficial yet very well known ritual are present. The picture places the viewer in the position of the potential client, while the girl is clad with all the fetishistic clothing of her business. She waits in a deserted underpass by night, but no cars seem to be coming. The image intimates the ritual which is yet to be performed, but for this very arrested moment there is nothing but emptiness, silence, and stillness all around.
In *Theoni* (2011), for 'Life Cycles', we look

into a room from a small courtyard where an elderly woman – most possibly a grandmother – holds a young child in her arms. This photo bears uncanny resemblance to the painting *Woman Reading a Letter* (c.1663-1664), by the seventeenth-century Dutch painter Johannes Vermeer, which depicts a pregnant woman reading a letter. Through this 'trick' Kokkinias is able to suggest more than is actually depicted. He intimates the unborn life in the pregnant woman as seen by Vermeer; the period of youth in his own photograph is represented by the small child in the old woman's arms; the period of maturity is suggested by the pregnant woman in the Vermeer painting, and finally old age is pictured in his own photograph again, in the form of the woman carrying the child, thus completing the entire cycle of life. In his photo for 'The Practice of Everyday Life' we can see the balcony of a house in the countryside and we look into the spookily lit nocturnal countryside, with some trees and a small road bending away in the direction of some distant houses. A threatening dark night sky intensifies the gloomy atmosphere of the scene. Its *Twenty Past Nine* (2011) and through a window on the balcony we discern a scene of domestic tension and latent angst between a couple in their brightly lit kitchen. Their gazes are inwardly directed, they seem to be immersed in their own thoughts, yet their sense of internal turmoil permeates the dark nocturnal atmosphere. Did they have an argument? Have they reached an impasse in their relationship? We are offered certain dramatic clues, but left to piece together the puzzle of what looks like an archetypal scene of domestic drama on our own. – KG

Panos Kokkinias was born in 1965, in Athens, Greece. He lives and works in Athens, Greece

www.xippas.com

Boniface Mwangi

Boniface Mwangi ist Fotojournalist und Mitbegründer eines Fotostudios in Kenias Hauptstadt Nairobi. 2008 dokumentierte er die gewalttätigen Ausschreitungen in Kibera, dem größten Slum Nairobis, die nach der Wahl des Präsidenten Kibaki stattfanden. Bei diesen Wahlen, für die Millionen von Kenianern quer durch das Land gereist waren und stundenlang vor den Urnen angestanden haben, um ihre Stimme abzugeben, manipulierten beide Präsidentschaftskandidaten, Mwai Kibaki vom Volk der Kikuyu sowie Raila Amollo Odinga vom Volk der Luo, die Ergebnisse. Kibaki war darin erfolgreicher – und gewann. Nach der Wahl von Kibaki fürchteten die anderen Stämme (Kenias Bevölkerung besteht aus 48), dass ihre politischen Interessen nicht mehr vertreten würden. Mithilfe seines Assistenten Brian Emmanuel, der in Kibera lebt, dokumentierte Mwangi aus unmittelbarer Nähe den unter den Bürgern gewaltsam ausgetragenen Konflikt aus Sicht der Beteiligten. Als sich die verschiedenen ethnischen Gruppen gegenseitig mit Macheten, Steinen und Stöcken angriffen, wodurch es zu Verletzten, Toten und Verwüstungen kam, fotografierte Mwangi den Horror, wie das „Idealbild" von Demokratie immer mehr abhanden kam. Häuser wurden ausgeraubt und niedergebrannt, sodass viele Menschen obdachlos wurden. Diese Bilder dokumentieren die Entwicklung vom Beginn der Wahlkampagne bis zur eigentlichen Stimmabgabe, die Morde, Beerdigungen sowie die zahllosen Obdachlosen in ihren Schutzunterkünften. – SHO

Boniface Mwangi wurde 1985 in Nairobi, Kenia, geboren. Er lebt und arbeitet in Nairobi, Kenia.

Boniface Mwangi is a photojournalist and co-founder of a photographic studio in Nairobi, Kenya. In 2008 he documented the post-election violence that took place in the major slum area of Kibera, Nairobi, after the election of president Kibaki. Following elections in which millions of Kenyans travelled far and wide and queued for hours to cast their ballot, the two presidential candidates Mwai Kibaki (from the Kikuyu ethnic group) and Raila Amollo Odinga (from the Luo ethnic group) both manipulated the votes. Kibaki did so more – and won. When Kibaki was elected, the other tribes (Kenya is made up of 48 of these) feared that their political interests would not be taken into account. With the help of his assistant Brian Emmanuel (who lives in Kibera), Mwangi documented the violent civil conflict from within. As the different ethnic groups attacked each other with machetes, stones and sticks – causing injury, death and destruction – Mwangi photographed the horror as the 'ideal' of democracy faded further and further away. Houses were robbed and burnt, and many people became homeless. These images document the process from the start of the election campaign

through to the voting, the killings, burials, and the countless homeless sheltering in camps. — SHO
Boniface Mwangi was born in 1985 in Nairobi, Kenya. He lives and works in Nairobi, Kenya

www.bonifacemwangi.com

Bruno Serralongue

Bruno Serralongue erforscht und hinterfragt mithilfe von Fotografien die Methoden der Informationserzeugung und -verbreitung. Seine Arbeiten könnte man als unabhängige Dokumentarfotografie in sozialem und politischem Kontext bezeichnen. Im Gegensatz zum Mainstream-Fotojournalismus zieht Serralongue es vor, vom Standpunkt einer bestimmten sozialen Gruppe aus zu arbeiten. Und statt am Ereignis selbst, ist er mehr daran interessiert, wie eine Gruppe ein Ereignis erlebt. Er arbeitet unabhängig und ohne Presseausweis, organisiert seine Reisen selbst und benutzt eine sperrig auf Stativ montierte 4x5'' zusammenklappbare Laufbodenkamera, die ihn gewolltermaßen von Schnappschüssen abhält. *Calais* (2006-2008) ist eine Fotoserie aus Sangatte, einem Flüchtlingslager bei Calais in der Nähe des Eingangs zum Eurotunnel, der unterhalb des Ärmelkanals verläuft. Die französische Regierung löste 2002 das Lager zwar auf, aber illegale Immigranten benutzen den Ort immer noch als Ausgangspunkt, um eine Gelegenheit abzupassen, mit einem LKW nach Großbritannien überzusetzen. Die Fotografien zeigen zwischen Bäumen und Büschen versteckte, provisorisch aus Plastikplanen zusammengebaute Behausungen, an Ästen zum Trocknen aufgehängte Schlafsäcke sowie die Reste kleiner Lagerfeuer, an denen Essen zubereitet wurde. Da diese spontan entstandenen Siedlungen offenbar nicht mit unserer modernen „zivilisierten" Welt in Einklang zu bringen sind, machen sie auf eine der gravierendsten sozialen Wirklichkeiten unserer Tage aufmerksam: die Notlage von Migranten, die dem sozialen, ökonomischen oder politischen Elend zu entkommen versuchen, um andernorts ein besseres Leben zu finden. Die Folgen dieser Notlage werden hier nicht mittels Porträts von Individuen gezeigt, sondern durch die Enthüllung der Umstände, die diese Notlage in sehr realem und physischem Sinne mit sich bringt. — KG
Bruno Serralongue wurde 1968 in Chatellerault, Frankreich, geboren. Er lebt und arbeitet in Paris, Frankreich.

Bruno Serralongue researches and questions the procedures of production and diffusion of information by means of photographs. His work may be defined as socially and politically inspired independent documentary photography. In contradistinction to mainstream photo-journalism, Serralongue opts to work at the heart of a specific community, and is more interested in the way in which a community experiences an event than in the event itself. He works independently and without a press card, arranges his trips himself, and uses a cumbersome four-by-five-inch tripod-mounted folding camera that deliberately precludes him from taking casual snapshots. *Calais* (2006-2008) is a series of images made in Sangatte, an encampment for refugees in the neighbourhood of Calais, near the entrance to the Channel Tunnel. The French government closed the camp in 2002, but illegal immigrants continue to use the site as a base as they look for opportunities to board trucks heading for the UK. The photographs depict makeshift shelters made from plastic sheets hidden between trees and bushes, as well as sleeping bags hung in the shrubs to dry and remainders of little campfires used to prepare food. While these *ad hoc* settlements appear at odds with our modern 'civilized' world, they speak of one of today's gravest social realities: the plight of migrants as they attempt to escape conditions of social, economic or political hardship and find a better life elsewhere. The effects of this plight are registered here not in portraits of individuals, but through a revelation of the conditions this entails in very real, physical terms. — KG
Bruno Serralongue was born in 1968 in Chatellerault, France. He lives and works in Paris, France

www.brunoserralongue.com

Taryn Simon

The Innocents (2002) dokumentiert die Geschichte von Personen, die für Gewaltverbrechen, die sie nicht begangen hatten, im Gefängnis waren. Die Serie geht der Frage nach, ob Fotografie als glaubwürdiger Augenzeuge und Schiedsmann fungieren kann.
Der Hauptgrund für eine ungerechtfertigte Verurteilung ist eine falsche Identifizierung. Ein Opfer oder Augenzeuge identifiziert einen Tatverdächtigen aufgrund von

Fotografien und Gegenüberstellungen, derer man sich zur Rechtsdurchsetzung bedient. Diese Methode beruht auf der Annahme eines präzisen visuellen Gedächtnisses. Doch die Erinnerung von Augenzeugen kann sich unter dem Einfluss von Rasterbildern, Skizzen, Fahndungsfotos, Polaroids und Gegenüberstellungen verändern. Bei diesen Fällen lieferte die Fotografie der Strafverfolgung ein Instrument, das unschuldige Bürger zu Verbrechern machte. Fotografien unterstützten Polizisten, wenn es um die Identifizierung durch Augenzeugen ging, und halfen Staatsanwälten bei der Überführung der vermeintlichen Täter.
Simon fotografierte diese Männer an Orten, die für ihre unrechtmäßige Verurteilung von besonderer Bedeutung waren: am Schauplatz falscher Identifizierung, am Schauplatz der Festnahme, am Schauplatz des Verbrechens oder am Schauplatz des Alibis.
All diese Orte haben für die jeweiligen Personen widersprüchliche Bedeutungen. Der Schauplatz der Festnahme markiert den Anfangspunkt einer Realität, die sich auf Fiktion gründet. Der Schauplatz des Verbrechens ist willkürlich und entscheidend zugleich: Dieser Ort, an dem sie niemals gewesen waren, veränderte ihr Leben für immer. In diesen Fotografien setzt sich Simon mit dem Potenzial der Fotografie auseinander, die Grenzen zwischen Wahrheit und Fiktion zu verwischen – eine Ambiguität mit möglicherweise schwerwiegenden, ja sogar tödlichen Folgen.
Taryn Simon wurde 1975 in New York, USA, geboren. Sie lebt und arbeitet in New York, USA.

The Innocents, (2002) documents the stories of individuals who served time in prison for violent crimes they did not commit. At issue is the question of photography's function as a credible eyewitness and arbiter of justice.
The primary cause of wrongful conviction is mistaken identification. A victim or eyewitness identifies a suspected perpetrator through law enforcement's use of photographs and lineups. This procedure relies on the assumption of precise visual memory. But, through exposure to composite sketches, mugshots, Polaroids, and lineups, eyewitness memory can change. In the history of these cases, photography offered the criminal justice system a tool that transformed innocent citizens into criminals. Photographs assisted officers in obtaining eyewitness identifications and aided prosecutors in securing convictions.
Simon photographed these men at sites that had particular significance to their illegitimate conviction: the scene of misidentification, the scene of arrest, the scene of the crime or the scene of the alibi. All of these locations hold contradictory meanings for the subjects. The scene of arrest marks the starting point of a reality based in fiction. The scene of the crime is at once arbitrary and crucial: this place, to which they have never been, changed their lives forever. In these photographs Simon confronts photography's ability to blur truth and fiction – an ambiguity that can have severe, even lethal consequences.
Taryn Simon was born in 1975 in New York, USA. She lives and works in New York, USA

www.tarynsimon.com

Johan Spanner

Als ehemaliger UN-Blauhelmsoldat in den Jugoslawienkriegen (1991–1995) war er damals frustriert über die abwartende Haltung der internationalen Gemeinschaft zu intervenieren und, als dies schließlich geschah, über die Unfähigkeit der militärischen Präsenz. Im Irak verfolgte Spanner die Ereignisse von der Invasion 2003 bis 2009. Statt den Krieg zu mythologisieren, zeigen seine Fotografien präsentiert in „Affekt und Wirkung von Politik" die ihm eigene maßlose Absurdität. In einem Bild, *A suspected Mahdi Army militiaman is blindfolded in the street before being taken away by American forces. Baghdad, Iraq, 2005,* kauert ein Mann, dessen Gesicht mit einer Maske verbunden wurde, neben dem Lauf eines Maschinengewehrs. In seine Situation als festgenommener mutmaßlicher Täter eines geheimen Angriffs können sich die meisten von uns sicherlich nicht hineinversetzen. Das Bild berührt uns immer noch, drängt uns dazu, vielleicht nicht den Konflikt als Ganzes und im größeren Zusammenhang zu hinterfragen, sondern vielmehr seine individuellen Auswirkungen auf die Menschen. In der sehr unterschiedlichen Fotoserie und dem zugehörigen Video *Sworn Virgins** (2011) präsentiert in „Rolle und Ritual" hat Johan Spanner einige der letzten Vertreter einer 500 Jahre alten albanischen Tradition porträtiert: Patriarchen mit weisem Blick und tief gefurchten Händen in ihren Wohnzimmern oder vor ihren

kleinen Häusern auf dem Land. Einige lassen eine vornehme oder großväterliche Haltung erkennen, während andere mit gebeugtem Rücken von jahrelanger schwerer Arbeit gekennzeichnet sind. Doch diese albanischen Ältesten sind bei Weitem keine normalen Männer. Als Frauen geboren, ist ihnen allen ein eher ungewöhnlicher Weg in die Männerwelt gemein. Nach der Tradition gab es für Gemeinschaften, denen es an Männern mangelte, die den Vorstand bilden und damit die Sorge für sie hätten tragen können, einen Ausweg: Eine jungfräuliche Frau konnte die Pflichten und Rechte der Männer übernehmen. Von den Mitgliedern ihrer Gemeinschaft wurde diese jedoch nur dann akzeptiert, wenn sie neben dem Gelübde zur Jungfräulichkeit auch das soziale Verhalten und die praktischen Funktionen von Männern annahm. Heute sind die „eingeschworenen Jungfrauen" lebende Erinnerung an die unter außergewöhnlichen Umständen fließend ineinander übergehenden Geschlechterrollen selbst innerhalb zutiefst traditioneller Gesellschaften. — JAB
Johan Spanner wurde 1974 in Kopenhagen, Dänemark, geboren. Er lebt und arbeitet in Kopenhagen, Dänemark.

Having served as a UN peacekeeper during the Yugoslav wars (1991-1995), Johan Spanner became frustrated with the wait for international intervention and the impotence of the military presence when it finally arrived. In Iraq, Spanner became a photojournalist and followed the events from the invasion in 2003 until 2009. Instead of mythologizing the nature of war, his photographs displayed in 'The Affect and Effect of Politics' show its extreme absurdities. In one image *A suspected Mahdi Army militiaman is blindfolded in the street before being taken away by American forces. Baghdad, Iraq, 2005*, a man whose face is covered by a mask kneels besides the barrel of a machine gun. Arrested as the suspect of an undisclosed offence, the reality of his situation seems out of reach for most of us. The image still affects us, imploring us to question perhaps not the conflict in the grander scheme of things, but the specific effects it has on individuals.
In the essentially different series of photographic portraits and the related video *Sworn Virgins* (2011) shown in 'Role and Ritual' Spanner has portrayed some of the last bearers of a 500-year-old Albanian tradition. A group of aging patriarchs, with wise eyes and strong wrinkled hands pose in their small farmsteads. Some evince a gentlemanly or grandfather-like demeanor, while others' backs are bent from years of heavy labour. Yet these Albanian elders are far from ordinary men. Born female, all share a bond in their unusual passage into manhood. Traditionally, in order to care for their communities when men were lacking, a virginal woman could, as a last recourse, accept the privileges and responsibilities of men. Sworn to remain virgins, they would be accepted by their community only by adopting the social characteristics and practical functions of men. The sworn virgins are a living reminder of the fluctuation of gender-roles in exceptional circumstances, even within the most traditional of cultures. — JAB
Johan Spanner was born in 1974, in Copenhagen, Denmark. He lives and works in Copenhagen, Denmark

www.johanspanner.com

Guy Tillim

Guy Tillim ist ein ehemaliger Fotojournalist, der sich inzwischen der künstlerischen Fotografie widmet. In der Fotoserie *Avenue Patrice Lumumba* (2007-2008) schildert er, wie der Kolonialismus die Menschen und die Architektur der afrikanischen Staaten heute prägt. Patrice Lumumba (1925-1961) war der erste rechtmäßig gewählte Ministerpräsident (1960) der Demokratischen Republik Kongo, der nur 10 Wochen im Amt war, bevor er ermordet wurde. Bilder wie *Typing pool, Town Hall, Likasi, DR Congo* (2007) und *Administration building, Antsiranana, Madagascar* (2007) zeigen die Herausforderungen, mit denen sich neu entstehende Demokratien in Bezug auf Administration, Organisation und Kommunikation selbst heute noch konfrontiert sehen. Der Abbau von Bürokratie und postkolonialem Leben in Afrika ist das Thema dieser Serie mit Ansichten von etwas verschlafen und verstaubt wirkenden Innen- und Außenräumen, die eine Atmosphäre von Verlassenheit und Resignation vermitteln. Die Architektur (Büros und Wohnhäuser aus der Kolonialzeit) besteht aus Fassaden eines verblassten Idealismus, aus verkommenden Gespenstern. Die Gebäude in *Apartment building, Beira, Mozambique* (2007) und *Athénée Royal High School, Lumumbashi, DR*

Congo (2007) sind lebende Momente, Zeugnisse von Lumumbas modernistischen und nationalistischen Träumen für Afrika – einem utopistischen Konzept, das zwar nicht so realisiert werden konnte, wie es geplant war, das jedoch für die Zukunft mitberücksichtigt werden sollte. — SHO
Guy Tillim wurde 1962 in Johannesburg, Südafrika, geboren. Er lebt und arbeitet in Johannesburg, Südafrika.

Guy Tillim is a former photojournalist who has moved into the art context. In the photographic series *Avenue Patrice Lumumba* (2007-2008), he portrays the human affects and architectural effects of colonialism on African states today. Patrice Lumumba (1925-1961) was the Democratic Republic of Congo's first legally elected prime minister (1960), who governed for ten weeks until he was assassinated. Images such as *Typing pool, Town Hall, Likasi, DR Congo* (2007) and *Administration building, Antsiranana, Madagascar* (2007) depict the challenges faced by new democracies, even today, in terms of administration, organisation and communication. The decomposition of African bureaucracy and postcolonial life is the topic in this series of calm and dusty interiors and exteriors, where a feeling of abandon and resignation reigns. The architecture (offices and apartments built during colonial times) are facades of faded idealism, decaying ghosts. The buildings in *Apartment building, Beira, Mozambique* (2007) and *Athénée Royal High School, Lubumbashi, DR Congo* (2007) are living monuments, testimonies to Lumumba's modernist and nationalist dreams for Africa. It is a utopian idea, which came out differently than imagined, yet is important to bear in mind for the future. — SHO
Guy Tillim was born in 1962 in Johannesburg, South Africa. He lives and works in Johannesburg, South Africa

www.kuckei-kuckei.de

Paolo Woods

Paolo Woods macht fotografische Langzeitstudien, die sich zwar auf Nachrichten beziehen, aber nicht auf kurzlebige Medienthemen oder aktuelle Ereignisse. In seiner Serie *Chinafrica* (2007) in „Affekt und Wirkung von Politik" erforscht Woods die seit Kurzem stattfindende wirtschaftliche Eroberung des afrikanischen Kontinents durch China, die als eine Form von Neokolonialismus betrachtet werden kann. Auf der Suche nach Rohstoffen investieren die Chinesen seit einigen Jahren im großen Stil in Afrika. Als Folge davon haben sich chinesische Firmen und Unternehmer sowie etwa eine halbe Million chinesischer Immigranten in Afrika niedergelassen, um dort ein Vermögen zu verdienen. Woods dokumentiert große Industrieprojekte und kleinere Unternehmen, aber auch Händler, die in einigen der ärmsten Regionen der Welt arbeiten: Fabriken in Nigeria, Chinarestaurants und Karaokebars in Lagos, Staudammbau und Abholzung im Kongo, Kupfergewinnung in Sambia, Villen auf enteignetem Land in Brazzaville, Neubausiedlungen in Algerien sowie die Autobahnerschließung des gesamten Kontinents. Die Bilder sprechen von der Interaktion und dem oft gereizten Verhältnis zwischen Afrikanern und Chinesen: von Momenten unbeschwerter Heiterkeit bis zu spannungsgeladenen Szenen am Arbeitsplatz, wo die Bedingungen häufig hart und ausbeuterisch sind. Die Bilder von *Chinafrica* ergeben ein aufschlussreiches Porträt der ökonomischen Umwälzungen in einer globalisierten Welt und den daraus resultierenden menschlichen Beziehungen. Die andere Serie *Walk on My Eyes* (2005-2010) in „Das alltägliche Leben" entstand im Iran und nahm 5 Jahre in Anspruch. Woods wollte die iranische Gesellschaft erforschen und stellt die negativen Stereotypen, die man seit der islamischen Revolution mit dem Staat verbindet, durch Porträts von ganz gewöhnlichen Menschen infrage. Die Fotografien dieser Serie zeigen den Iran als einen Ort, an dem die Menschen ein normales Leben führen, Spaß haben und religiöse oder reformistische und liberale Ansichten hegen. Das Ergebnis ist oft amüsant, bewegend oder überraschend: Demonstranten der Grünen Revolution; Verkäufer mit Teppichen, deren Muster aus Bildern von nackten Frauen bestehen; wohlhabende Iraner in ihrer häuslichen Umgebung; eine Zahnärztin bei ihrer Arbeit; die Teheraner Schule für das Lachen (Teheran Laughing School). Diese Bilder zeugen von einer vielschichtigen menschlichen Gesellschaft und nicht von der homogenen Masse mit kollektiver Identität, als die sie das derzeitige Regime propagiert. — KG
Paolo Woods wurde am 1970 in Amsterdam, Niederlande, geboren. Zurzeit lebt er auf Haiti.

Paolo Woods engages in long-term photographic

research projects with a socio-political focus, that are news-related but not ephemeral media stories or 'hard news'. In the series *Chinafrica* (2007) presented in 'The Affect and Effect of Politics', Woods explores the recent economic conquest of the African continent by China, which can be considered a form of neo-colonialism. In recent years the Chinese have made massive investments in the African continent in search of coveted raw materials. As a result, Chinese companies and entrepreneurs and around half a million Chinese immigrants have moved to Africa to make their fortune. Woods documents large industrial projects and smaller businesses, as well as the merchants who work in some of the world's poorest countries: from factories in Nigeria, Chinese restaurants and karaoke bars in Lagos, dam building and timber exploitation in the Congo, copper extraction in Zambia, villas built on expropriated land in Brazzaville, new housing projects in Algeria, and highway constructions across the continent. The images speak of the interaction, and often strained relations between Africans and Chinese: from scenes of conviviality to scenes of tension in the workplace, where labour conditions are often harsh and exploitative. The images in *Chinafrica* are a telling portrait of economic shifts in a globalised world and the human relations they engender.
The other series *A Walk on My Eyes* (2005-2010) presented in 'The Practice of Everyday Life' was shot in Iran and took five years to complete. Woods set out to explore Iranian society and challenge the negative stereotypes associated with the state since the Islamic Revolution. The photographs in this series show Iran as a place where people lead normal lives, have fun and hold religious or reformist and liberal views. The results are often humorous, moving or unexpected: portraits of the Green Revolution reformist protestors; traders selling carpets adorned with images of naked women; affluent Iranians in their domestic settings; female professionals at work; and a school for laughter. These images bear testimony to a society that is complexly human and not the homogeneous mass the current regime propagates as a collective identity. — KG
Paolo Woods was born in 1970 in Amsterdam, the Netherlands. He currently lives in Haiti

www.paolowoods.net

Ecological Circuits S. / p. 28

Ravi Agarwal

Die umfangreichen Projekte des Fotografen und Umweltaktivisten Ravi Agarwals sind kraftvolle Kommentare zu den komplex vernetzten Strukturen unserer heutigen globalisierten Welt. Er stellt Fragen nach den Lebens- und Arbeitsbedingungen der Menschen in dem Teil von Indiens Wirtschaft, die der „informelle" Teil genannt wird, fragt nach den vielen, oft nicht sichtbaren Konsequenzen im Umgang mit der Natur und findet durch seine Arbeit zu seiner eigenen ökologischen Philosophie, die er „personal ecology" nennt. Der Ursprung des falschen und kurzsichtigen Umgangs mit dem Planeten sieht Agarwal bisweilen in der Trennung unseres „Selbst" von der Natur. Dass das Töten der Umwelt gleichbedeutend ist mit dem Selbstmord der Menschen, scheint vielen immer noch nicht klar.
Down and Out: Labouring under globalisation (1997–2000) entstand in Zusammenarbeit mit Jan Berman als Buchprojekt. Agarwal begleitete für dieses Projekt Leih- und Landarbeiter über einen Zeitraum von 2 ½ Jahren in der Gegend von Gujarat in der Nähe der Stadt Surat mit seiner Kamera. Auf dramatische Art und Weise sprechen die Bilder eine ambivalente Sprache: Die farbintensiven und ausdrucksstarken Bildwelten stehen in hartem Kontrast zu der Realität der Tagelöhner in der Textilindustrie, der Diamantenverarbeitung oder den Zuckermanufakturen und Baustellen aller Art.
Der *documenta11*-Teilnehmer Ravi Agarwal ist Gründer von Toxics Link, einer Plattform für nationalen Austausch über den Umgang mit Umweltgiften und ihren nachhaltigen Alternativen sowie Mitglied von Srishti, einer weiteren Umweltschutzassoziation. — HH
Ravi Agarwal wurde 1958 in New Delhi, Indien geboren. Er lebt und arbeitet in New Delhi, Indien.

Photographer and environmental activist Ravi Agarwal creates ambitious projects that form powerful commentaries on the intertwined structures of today's globalised world. He inquires into the conditions under which people live and work in India's informal economic sector, delving into the far-reaching and often unseen consequences for the natural environment, and ultimately arrives at his own environmental philosophy, which he dubs 'personal ecology'. Agarwal believes that our shortsighted handling of the planet stems from the way we separate our 'selves' from nature. His work underlines how many people don't realize that destroying our environment is tantamount to the collective suicide of humankind.
Down and Out: Labouring under Globalisation (1997–2000) is a book project Agarwal undertook in conjunction with Jan Berman. Agarwal photographed contract workers and peasant labourers in the Gujarat region near the city of Surat over a period of two and a half years. These images speak a dramatic, and yet ambivalent, language: the brightly

coloured and expressive imagery forms a harsh contrast to the quotidian reality of the day labourers in the textile industry, diamond processing plants, sugar factories and construction sites of every variety. Agarwal is the founder of Toxics Link, a platform for national information exchange on dealing with environmental toxins and finding sustainable alternatives. He is also a member of Srishti, another environmental association. — HH
Ravi Agarwal was born in 1958 in New Delhi, India. He lives and works in New Delhi, India

www.raviagarwal.com
www.toxicslink.org

Olaf Otto Becker

Der deutsche Landschaftsfotograf Olaf Otto Becker fliegt oft über Grönland nach Amerika, um eine der schlimmsten Folgen des Klimawandels zu dokumentieren: das Abschmelzen der Polarkappen. Aus der Luft waren ihm die blauen Wasserläufe aufgefallen, die sich tief in das vom Atlantik bis zum Nordpolarmeer ausdehnende Inlandeis eingeschnitten haben – kilometerlang dahinfließendes Schmelzwasser. Um diese Wasserläufe zu fotografieren, wagte sich Becker auf eine 450 Kilometer lange strapaziöse Trekkingtour durch diese unwirtliche Landschaft. In dieser Ausstellung präsentiert er aus einer Serie mit dem Titel *Above Zero* (2007–2008) 18 Fotografien von *River 1* (2008), einem dieser „Flüsse". Sie sind ein neueres Phänomen der Erderwärmung über 0 Grad Celcius in manchen Regionen Grönlands. Die Folgen dieser ökologischen Entwicklung sind auch an den Küsten Grönlands festzustellen, wo Eisblöcke in der Größe von kleinen Inseln abbrechen und dem offenen Meer zutreiben – ein Ereignis, das Becker in seiner Serie *Broken Line* (2003) festgehalten hat. Viele Forscher und Touristen reisen nach Grönland (an zugängliche und extra für diesen Zweck logistisch erschlossene Orte), um das Abschmelzen des Eises zu beobachten. Becker dokumentiert dieses neue globale Interesse als ein wichtiges Pendant zu ähnlichen Landschaftsveränderungen am Nordpol. — SHO
Olaf Otto Becker wurde 1959 in Lübeck-Travemünde, Deutschland, geboren. Er lebt und arbeitet in München, Deutschland.

German landscape photographer Olaf Otto Becker often flies over Greenland to America to document one of the most dramatic effects of climate change: the melting of the polar icecaps. From the air he has noticed deep blue rivers carved into the inland ice that run towards the Atlantic and Arctic oceans: countless kilometres of flowing water from melting ice blocks. In order to photograph these rivers, Becker ventured into this inhospitable landscape and trekked 450 km. In this exhibition, Becker presents 18 images from one particular river, *River 1* (2008) all of which form part of a series entitled *Above Zero* (2007–2008). The rivers are recent phenomena caused by the temperature rising above zero degrees in parts of Greenland. Part of the same ecological development recurs along Greenland's waterfronts, where ice blocks the size of small islands break off and float to the sea – an event portrayed by Becker in his series *Broken Line* (2003). Many researchers and tourists travel to Greenland (to accessible spots logistically arranged to suit the purpose) to observe the effects of the melting ice. Becker documents this new global concern as an important counterpart to similar landscape alterations at the North Pole. — SHO
Olaf Otto Becker was born in 1959 in Lübeck-Travemünde, Germany. He lives and works in Munich, Germany

www.olafottobecker.de

Edward Burtynsky

Edward Burtynskys Arbeit setzt sich eingehend mit dem Schicksal und der Zukunft unseres Planeten auseinander. Seine Fotografien zeigen auf, welchen Risiken und Schädigungen die Natur durch Industrialismus, Massenproduktion, urbanes Wachstum und die permanente Suche nach Ressourcen zur Befriedigung unserer nicht nachlassenden Bedürfnisse ausgesetzt ist. Er dokumentiert die Veränderungen der Umwelt durch menschliche Eingriffe in Bildern, die den Verlauf, die Ursachen und die Auswirkung davon ergründen. Burtynsky nennt seine Arbeit „a lament for the loss of nature at the hand of man" (ein Lamento für den Verlust der Natur durch die Hand des Menschen) und „a second look at the scale of what we call progress" (ein zweiter Blick auf die Dimension, die wir Fortschritt nennen). Er versucht, wie er selbst sagt, mithilfe seiner Bilder Millionen von Menschen zu überzeugen, sich am weltumspannenden Dialog der Nachhaltigkeit zu beteiligen. Seine Fotografien von Ölfeldern in Aserbaidschan, Abwrackwerften in Bangladesch, von Textil-, Schuh- und Handyfabriken in ganz China dokumentieren den Prozess von Produktion, Konsum und Verschwendung und zeigen ein trostloses Bild der Folgen menschlicher Gier in großem Maßstab. Seine vernarbten und desolaten Natur- und Stadtlandschaften sind einerseits faszinierend, andererseits aber unbestreitbar beängstigend, wirken einladend und abstoßend zur gleichen Zeit. Burtynskys Fotografien demonstrieren in einer unmissverständlichen Bildersprache, dass unser Lebensstil einen gesalzenen Preis fordert und dass Schönheit und biologische Vielfalt der Welt für immer verloren sein werden, wenn wir uns nicht selbst infrage stellen und weitreichende Veränderungen in Angriff nehmen. — KG
Edward Burtynsky wurde 1955 in Ontario, Kanada, geboren. Er lebt und arbeitet in Toronto, Kanada.

Edward Burtynsky's work is deeply engaged with the fate and future of our planet. His photographs depict how nature is threatened and damaged by industrialism, mass manufacturing, urban expansion, and the constant quest for resources to provide us with our incessant material needs. He documents the transformation of the environment by human intervention in series which examine process, cause and effect. Burtynsky calls his work 'a lament for the loss of nature at the hand of man' and 'a second look at the scale of what we call progress'. He uses his images to try to 'persuade millions of people to join in the global conversation on sustainability'. His photographs of oil fields in Azerbaijan, ship demolition sites in Bangladesh, textile mills, shoe manufacturers and mobile phone factories all over China document the process of production, consumption and waste, and present a bleak

picture of the consequences of human greed on a vast scale. His scarred and desolate natural or urban landscapes are beautiful on one level and indubitably alarming on another, being at once seductive and repulsive. Burtynsky's photographs demonstrate in an unequivocal pictorial language that our way of life has a steep price, and that the beauty and biodiversity of the world will be lost forever if we don't question ourselves and make important changes. — KG
Edward Burtynsky was born in 1955 in Toronto, Canada. He lives and works in Toronto, Canada

www.edwardburtynsky.com
www.galerie-roepke.de

Philippe Chancel

Ausgebildet in Wirtschaftswissenschaften und Journalismus, bewegt sich Philippe Chancel in seinen fotografischen Arbeiten am Schnittpunkt von Kunst, Dokumentation und Journalismus. In „Ökologische Kreisläufe" präsentiert Philippe Chancel Fotografien aus seiner Serie *Desert Spirit* (2007–2010), die die irreal wirkenden Wolkenkratzer und Wüstenlandschaften in den Vereinigten Arabischen Emiraten zeigen. Hier sehen Gebäude weniger wie Wohnhäuser für Menschen aus, sondern gleichen eher Macht demonstrierenden Monumenten der Ölindustrie. Aufgrund des heißen subtropischen Klimas und den Lebensgewohnheiten der Bevölkerung sind die Straßen und Strände Dubais weitgehend leer. Hochhäuser sind Trophäen-Gebäude, die fotografische Vorteile garantieren – Chancel hat sie ergriffen und zu den leeren Straßen der Wohnviertel in Kontrast gestellt. Die Arabische Halbinsel beherbergt eines der heute umstrittensten und größten architektonischen Utopia, bei dessen Umsetzung weder die Umwelt noch ökologische Nachhaltigkeit berücksichtig wurde, sondern allein der Profit der Ölindustrie im Vordergrund stand. Gibt es nun Ähnlichkeiten zwischen Dubais „Wüstentraum" und den modernistischen Architektur-Utopien im sozialen Wohnungsbau auf der ganzen Welt? Auch wenn die Visionen natürlich unterschiedlich motiviert sind, ist ihnen doch ein ähnlicher Mangel an Unbewohnbarkeit gemein.
Die Fotoserie *Arirang** (2006) ausgestellt in „Rolle und Ritual" dokumentiert die überdimensionierten Szenerien der Feierlichkeiten, bei denen Tausende von TurnerInnen das totalitäre Regime des verstorbenen Diktators Kim Il-sung und seines Sohns Kim Jong-il sowie die Arbeiterpartei und die Geschichte des kommunistischen Nordkoreas zelebrieren. In einem mit bis zu 150.000 Menschen besetzten Stadion führen gedrillte Kinder und Jugendliche perfekt einstudierte Choreografien auf. In diesem anthropozentrischen und populistischen Spektakel erscheint der Einzelne als farbiges „Pixel" in einem großen polychromen Gesamtbild. Diese nationalistischen bildhaften Formationen enthüllen die imaginäre Landschaft Nordkoreas: kitschig idyllische Huldigungen des ländlichen Lebens, der Macht des Militärs und der historischen Augenblicke seiner Politik des 20. Jahrhunderts. Auf der Arbeit von zahllosen, kollektiv disziplinierten Körpern und einer kontrollierten visuellen Darbietungsform basierend, stellt das Ritual auch die Existenz des menschlichen Individuums in Abrede. — SHO
Philippe Chancel wurde 1959 in Issy-les-Moulineaux, Frankreich, geboren. Er lebt und arbeitet in Paris, Frankreich.

* *Arirang* ist ein koreanisches Volkslied, das inoffiziell als Nationalhymne Gesamtkoreas gilt.

With a background in economics and journalism, Philippe Chancel creates photographic works that lie at the intersection of art, documentary and journalism. In 'Ecological Circuits' Chancel presents photographs from his series *Desert Spirit* (2007–2010) depicting the utopian-looking skyscrapers and sandscapes of the United Arab Emirates. Here, buildings look less like structures for people to live than monuments manifesting the power of oil. Due to the hot climate and local lifestyles, streets and beaches in Dubai are largely empty. High-rise buildings are trophies that guarantee photographic vantage, which Chancel has taken and contrasted with the empty street in the areas of private housing. The Arabian Peninsula is home to one of today's biggest and most problematic architectural utopias – a utopia built without any consideration of the environment or ecological sustainability and based on oil profits. Are there similarities between Dubai's 'desert dream' and the modernist architectural utopias of social housing blocks all over the world: differently motivated visions, of course, yet sharing a similar lack of inhabitability?
The photographic series *Arirang** (2006) in 'Role and Ritual' is a documentation of large-scale festival scenarios in which thousands of gymnasts in North Korea celebrate the totalitarian regime, the late Kim Il-sung and his son Kim Jong-il, the workers party, and the history of communist North Korea. At a stadium seating up to 150,000 people, well-trained youngsters perform perfectly executed choreographies. In this anthropocentric and populist spectacle, individuals appear as colourful image pixels in a grand overall picture. These nationalist visual formations reveal the North Korean imaginary landscape: kitsch idyllic celebrations of rural life, the power of the military and important moments in its twentieth-century political history. Based on the work of innumerable collectively disciplined bodies and the control of the visual appearance of spectacle, the ritual also denies individual human existence. — SHO
Philippe Chancel was born in 1959 in Issy-les-Moulineaux, France. He lives and works in Paris, France

* *Arirang* is a Korean folk song, sometimes considered the unofficial national anthem of Korea

www.philippechancel.com

Chen Chieh-Jen

Chen Chieh-Jens langsame, fesselnde Filme sind ohne Ton oder kommen mit einem Minimum an Geräuschen aus. Das macht sie nur noch eindrucksvoller, muss man sich doch voll und ganz auf das Bild konzentrieren. Chens Arbeit bewegt sich auf einem Terrain zwischen Fotografie und Film, mit dessen Hilfe er soziale, politische und historische Fragen beleuchtet, in denen es um an den Rand gedrängte und entrechtete Gemeinschaften in Taiwan

(sein Geburtsland) und woanders geht, während er gleichzeitig für eine Entschleunigung der Wahrnehmung eintritt. In seinem ohne Ton gedrehten Video *Factory* (2003) geht Chen auf die Verlagerung von Arbeitsmärkten und die sich verschiebenden Strukturen bei der industriellen Fertigung ein, die die Globalisierung durch ihre unablässige Suche nach immer billigeren Arbeitskräften und größeren Profiten mit sich bringt. Für die Produktion dieses Films, der in einer verlassenen Textilfabrik in Taiwan gedreht wurde, lud Chen einige der ehemaligen Textilarbeiterinnen ein, die bis zur Schließung dort gearbeitet hatten. In den Ruinen dieses jetzt gespenstischen Ortes, umgeben von damals zurückgebliebenen, nicht mehr benutzten Objekten, kehren die Frauen zurück an ihre Nähmaschinen – ein stummes Ritual ohne Ziel, ohne Zweck, ohne Zukunft, in dem die Zeit eingefroren zu sein scheint. Humankapital hat keine Geltung sobald es wirtschaftlich keinen Sinn mehr macht.
In *Lingchi – Echoes of a Historical Photograph* (2002) gezeigt in „Rolle und Ritual" nimmt der Künstler eine Neuinterpretation der chinesischen Geschichte vor, ausgehend von einem bekannten Dokumentarfoto aus dem Jahr 1905, das die letzte traditionelle, öffentliche, ritualistische Hinrichtung (*lingchi* bedeutet „Tod durch tausend Schnitte") im vormodernen China zeigt. Indem der Film die Beziehung zwischen Ritual, Religion, Politik, Folter, Erotik und Ästhetik aufzeigt und dabei die Frage nach kulturellem Relativismus und kolonialer Besitzergreifung sowie den gestörten Beziehungen zwischen Taiwan und China aufwirft, entwickelt er sich als qualvoll nüchterne Umschreibung der Geschichte an einem immer stärker traumatisierten menschlichen Körper. Das Werk hat seine Wurzeln in der Vergangenheit, lässt sich aber auch mit der aktuellen Situation in Taiwan in Verbindung bringen. Der gefolterte Mensch kann als Symbol für die zunehmenden Sorgen eines Landes im Sog der Globalisierung und Modernisierung gesehen und *lingchi* als eine Metapher für die vom Staat ausgeübte Gewalt gegen das Volk gelesen werden. — KG
Chen Chieh-Jen wurde 1960 in Taipeh, Taiwan, geboren. Er lebt und arbeitet in Taipeh, Taiwan.

Chen Chieh-Jen's slow-moving, immersive films are silent or have minimal sound, which makes them the more arresting, as one has to concentrate entirely on the image. Occupying a territory between photography and cinema, Chen's work examines the social, political, and historical issues relating to marginalized or disenfranchised communities in Taiwan (his place of birth) and beyond, while also arguing for the deceleration of perception. In his silent video *Factory* (2003) in 'Ecological Circuits', Chen explores the movement of labour markets and shifting patterns of industrial production in globalisation's incessant search for cheaper labour and larger profits. The film is shot in an abandoned garment factory in Taiwan, where Chen asked a group of women to revisit the derelict site they had been working in until it was closed. In the ruins of this now ghostly space, surrounded by abandoned disused objects, the women return to their sewing machines in a silent ritual with no purpose, no return, no future, where time seems to have frozen. Human capital becomes disposable when it no longer makes economic sense. In his other film *Lingchi – Echoes of a Historical Photograph* (2002) in 'Role and Ritual' the artist reinterprets Chinese history by taking as his point of departure an iconic twentieth-century documentary photograph from 1905 showing the last traditional, public, ritualistic execution (*lingchi* means 'death by a thousand cuts') in pre-modern China. Pinpointing the relationship between ritual, religion, politics, torture, eroticism and aesthetics, raising the question of cultural relativism and colonial appropriation, as well as Taiwan's troubled relationship with China, the film unfolds as a harrowingly literal rewriting of history on an increasingly traumatised human body. Today the tortured man can be seen as a symbol for the growing pains of a country in the throes of globalisation and modernization, and *lingchi* can be read as a metaphor for state-executed violence on the corpus of a people. — KG
Chen Chieh-Jen was born in 1960 in Taipei, Taiwan. He lives and works in Taipei, Taiwan.

Geert Goiris

Geert Goiris' fotografisches Werk widmet sich häufig Landschaften und geologischen Formationen, die sich seit Millionen von Jahren vermutlich nur wenig verändert haben. Er wagt sich oft in unbekanntes, karges oder unwirtliches Gelände ohne bestimmte geografische Charakteristika, um dessen wilde, ungezähmte Weiten zu erforschen sowie real und zugleich außerirdisch wirkende Bilder zusammenzutragen. Für seine Dia-Endlosprojektion *Whiteout* (2009–2010) nahm Goiris an einer Antarktisexpedition teil und begann, das gefährlich desorientierende meteorologische Phänomen des sogenannten White-Outs zu dokumentieren. Dieses kommt durch eine hohe Eiskristallkonzentration in der Luft zustande, wodurch die Landschaft in ein helles, weißes Licht getaucht wird: Boden und Himmel gehen dann scheinbar ohne Horizont ineinander über, Schatten sind nicht mehr erkennbar und nur dunkle Objekte können noch deutlich gesehen werden. Es entsteht der Eindruck, als befände man sich in einem riesigen, leeren Raum – ohne Begrenzung, Anfang oder Ende. Goiris dokumentiert die Expeditionsroute, die Wissenschaftler, die unter extremen Bedingungen in einer Forschungsstation leben und arbeiten, sowie die unwirtliche Umgebung (den Hauptakteur dieser Arbeiten). Er hebt die formalen Eigenschaften dieser puristischen, kargen und abstrakten Landschaft hervor, während er gleichzeitig schmerzlich daran erinnert, wie machtlos und klein der Mensch angesichts der Natur und ihrer Elemente ist. — KG
Geert Goiris wurde 1971 in Bornem, Belgien, geboren. Er lebt und arbeitet in Antwerpen, Belgien.

Geert Goiris' lens-based practice depicts landscapes and geological formations that probably have not altered much in millions of years. He often ventures into unknown, barren or hostile territory without a discernable geographical identity in order to explore its wild and untamed reaches, collecting images that appear at once real and alien. In order to make his looped slide projection *Whiteout* (2009–2010), Goiris joined an expedition to the Antarctic and set about

documenting this disorienting and dangerous meteorological phenomenon. Caused by high concentrations of ice crystals in the sky, whiteouts cloak the landscape in a bright white light: horizon disappears, no shadows are cast, and only dark objects may be seen clearly. The impression is that of being in a vast empty space, with no limits, beginning or end. Goiris documents the expedition's journey, the researchers who live and work at a research station under extreme conditions, and the hostile surrounding landscape (which is the protagonist in these works). He highlights the formal properties of this minimal, barren and abstract landscape while at the same time poignantly alluding to man's powerlessness and smallness in the face of nature and the elements. — KG
Geert Goiris was born in 1971 in Bornem, Belgium. He lives and works in Antwerp, Belgium

www.geertgoiris.info
www.catherinebastide.com

Nicu Ilfoveanu

Nicu Ilfoveanus *Steampunk Autochrome* (2004–2008) ist eine Serie, die postindustrielle Landschaften in Europa und der ehemaligen Sowjetunion zeigt. In diesen Bildern tauchen wie aus einem traumhaften Schleier Spuren einer Zivilisation in Form von allmählich verfallenden, aber nach wie vor monumental aufragenden Betonkonstruktionen auf. Obwohl viele dieser Gebäude kaum ein halbes Jahrhundert alt sind, wirkt ihre Gegenwart doch fast gespenstisch. Ähnlich den Bewegungsfotografien Eadweard Muybridges aus dem 19. Jahrhundert halten Ilfoveanus Arbeiten den Lauf der Zeit fest. Aber im Gegensatz zu dessen Konzeption der Sequenz – einer Serie sich entwickelnder, aufeinanderfolgender Ereignisse –, stellt *Steampunk Autochrome* die Zeit kumulierend dar. Die Vergangenheit erhebt auf alles um uns herum Anspruch. Selbst wenn die bestimmten Handlungsweisen und industriellen Unternehmungen zugrunde liegenden Absichten und Ideologien verloren gegangen sind, ihre Konsequenzen überziehen wie Narben die Landschaft: labyrinthartig ausgedehnte Städte oder abweisende Fabrikfassaden ragen am Horizont auf. In diesen Fotografien erscheint die Welt genauso anachronistisch wie die Technik, mit der sie aufgenommen wurde (einer Box-Kamera mit nur einer Blende und einer Belichtung). Das Ergebnis ist eine Bricolage aus dem Hypermodernen, das sich noch nicht eingestellt hat, und dem Archaischen, das seinen Abschluss noch nicht gefunden hat. Der Augenblick, in dem die Bilder der simplen Kamera entwickelt werden, ist der Moment, in dem Geschichte und Zukunft zu koexistieren scheinen, ineinander verwoben wie die Rauchschwaden verwandter Maschinen. — JAB
Nicu Ilfoveanu wurde 1975 in Pitesti, Rumänien, geboren. Er lebt und arbeitet in Bukarest, Rumänien.

Nicu Ilfoveanu's *Steampunk Autochrome* (2004–2008) is a series depicting post-industrial landscapes in several European and ex-Soviet cities. In these images fragmented traces of civilisation emerge as if from a dreamlike haze, in the form of slowly decaying yet still monumental high-rise concrete structures. Although many of these buildings are barely half a century old, their presence seems almost spectral. Much like the nineteenth-century photographer Eadweard Muybridge, Ilfoveanu bears witness to the passage of time. But unlike the former's conception of this as something sequential – a series of unfolding events – the *Steampunk Autochrome* series depicts time as cumulative. The past claims everything around us. Even if the ambitions or ideologies behind certain actions and industrial endeavours might be lost, their consequences still linger as scars on the landscape: labyrinthine urban sprawls or solemn factory facades protruding from the horizon. The world appears in these photographs as anachronistic as the technique that captured it (the photos are taken with a box camera with a single enclosed aperture and a single exposure.) The result is a bricolage of the hypermodern that has not yet begun and the archaic that has not yet reached its conclusion. The moment the images from Ilfoveanu's primitive camera are developed are the moment when history and the future seem to co-exist, intermingled like vapours from kindred machines. — JAB
Nicu Ilfoveanu was born in 1975 in Pitesti, Romania. He lives and works in Bucharest, Romania

www.ilfo.ro

Gulnara Kasmalieva & Muratbek Djumaliev

In ihrem Video und ihren fotografischen Arbeiten untersuchen Gulnara Kasmalieva und Muratbek Djumaliev den zerstörerischen Einfluss der ökonomischen, sozialen und politischen Unzufriedenheit innerhalb der kirgisischen Gesellschaft nach dem Niedergang des Kommunismus, wobei sie sich besonders auf die allgemeine Gleichgültigkeit gegenüber der Umwelt und der sich daraus resultierenden Katastrophen konzentrieren. Im Video *Spring* (2009) sprechen sie die zunehmenden Probleme im heutigen Kirgisistan an. Das Video wurde am Rand von Bishkek, ihrer Heimatstadt, aufgenommen, dem Schauplatz einer ungewöhnlichen Performance. Auf einer riesigen Müllhalde spielen 5 elegant gekleidete Streichmusiker *Der Frühling* aus Vivaldis Werk *Die vier Jahreszeiten* (1725). Die düsteren Farben des giftigen Schuttfeldes stehen in extremem Kontrast zum erhebenden Klang der Musik und den tadellos angezogenen Musikern. Die Szene verkörpert ein dramatisches Paradoxon: mit der Aufführung eines Stücks klassischer europäischer Kultur inmitten einer ökologischen Katastrophe konfrontiert zu sein. Ausdrucksvoll und lyrisch heben Kasmalieva und Djumaliev die schwierige Beziehung zwischen Mensch und Natur hervor sowie den schmerzlichen Überlebenskampf in Zeiten der Bedrängnis und machen dadurch auf den Skandal der vielen offenen Müllhalden in Kirgisistan aufmerksam. Gleichzeitig gelingt ihnen eine Art Wiedergutmachung, indem sie Kunst – in diesem Fall Musik – als ein Gegengift zu Gleichgültigkeit und der Wirklichkeit einer zerstörerischen dystopischen Gesellschaft einsetzen. — KG
Gulnara Kasmalieva (1960) und Muratbek Djumaliev (1965) wurden in Bishkek, Kirgisistan, geboren.
Sie leben und arbeiten in Bishkek, Kirgisistan.

In their video and photographic work Gulnara Kasmalieva and Muratbek Djumaliev examine the devastating effect of economic, social and political unrest on Kirghiz society following the fall of communism, concentrating on the general environmental neglect and catastrophe that has followed in its wake. In the video *Spring* (2009), they intimate the growing pains of modern Kyrgyzstan. The video was shot in the suburbs of Bishkek, their hometown, where an unusual performance is being staged. On top of an enormous garbage heap, five elegantly dressed string musicians play Vivaldi's 'Spring' from his opus *The Four Seasons* (1725). The mute colours of the poisonous expanse of debris contrasts starkly with the uplifting sound of the music and the impeccably dressed musicians. The scene bears witness to a dramatic paradox, one of being confronted with a scene of classical European culture performed amidst an ecological catastrophe. In an expressive and lyrical language, the artists highlight the troublesome relation between man and nature and the painful struggle for survival in times of distress, while addressing the scandal of the numerous open-air dumps found all over Kyrgyzstan. At the same time, they manage to articulate a sense of redemption through art – in this case music – as an antidote to neglect and the realities of a devastating dystopia. — KG
Gulnara Kasmalieva (1960) and Muratbek Djumaliev (1965) were born in Bishkek, Kyrgyzstan where they live and work

Panos Kokkinias S. / p. 201

Aglaia Konrad

Unser Bild von den Kulturen vergangener Zeiten nährt sich unter anderem aus der spezifischen Art und Weise ihrer architektonischen Hinterlassenschaften. Aus den steinernen Ausgrabungen und sichtbaren Reststrukturen lassen sich langsam ganze gesellschaftliche Zusammenhänge skizzieren und nachvollziehen.
Die österreichische Künstlerin Aglaia Konrad nähert sich mit analytischem, fast archäologischem Blick den urbanen Strukturen unserer heutigen Zivilisation und bringt die Ergebnisse ihrer Recherche als großformatiges Display an die Museumswände. Mit *Iconocopycity* (2011) breitet sich das ganze System der architektonischen Moderne und ihren stadtplanerischen Ideen vor unseren Augen aus – mitsamt aller Bedingungen und Konsequenzen für die moderne Gesellschaft.
Konrad betreibt keine klassische Architekturfotografie. Die Monotonie moderner Funktionsarchitektur und standardisierter Häuserblöcke wird in den All-Over-Panoramen der Künstlerin wie in einer Explosionszeichnung auseinander- und wieder zusammengesetzt. Details wechseln sich mit Gesamtansichten ab, Fotos vom Stadtraum sind durchsetzt mit Fotos von Architekturmodellen oder Szenen aus Filmen. Baustellen, Peripherien, Kreuzungen oder innerstädtische Highways sind unter ihren Motiven. Auf der Basis einer dokumentarischen Herangehensweise untersucht Konrad den Stadtraum als ein intensives Konglomerat aus Zeichen und Codes, aus Bewegung und Aktion, aus Repräsentation und Machtsymbolik. Ihr Metropolis'sches Wandtableaux ist eine alternative Kartografie, die die strukturellen Merkmale unserer heutigen Großstädte aufzeigt.
Aglaia Konrad wird in dieser Ausstellung mit dem Film *Concrete & Samples III – Carrara* (2010) eine weitere Arbeit zeigen. Aufgenommen in einem der bekanntesten Marmor-Steinbrüche der Welt im italienischen Carrara, wandert die Kamera meditativ die Schichten und Flächen des Natursteins ab, aus denen Künstler von Michelangelo bis zu Henry Moore ihre Werke schufen. In der sich ständig verändernden Landschaft lassen sich temporäre Architekturen erkennen, die Natur wird hier selbst zur Skulptur. — HH
Aglaia Konrad wurde 1960 in Salzburg, Österreich geboren. Sie lebt und arbeitet in Brüssel, Belgien.

We derive our notions of bygone civilizations from, among other things, the architecture they have left behind. Whole social fabrics can be gradually sketched out and reconstructed from archaeological excavations. Austrian artist Aglaia Konrad focuses her analytical, almost archaeological gaze on the urban structures of our own modern civilization, placing the results of her research onto museum walls as large-format displays. In *Iconocopycity* (2011), a wallpaper installation culled from her book *Iconocity* (2005), the whole panoply of architectural modernism and its urban planning ideas unfurls before our eyes. Konrad does not pursue classical architectural photography, but instead creates all-over panoramas that function like exploded drawings. Here, the monotony of modern functional architecture with its standardized housing blocks is picked apart and put back together: details alternate with general views; photographs of urban settings are interspersed with pictures of architectural models or movie scenes; repeated motifs include building sites, intersections and inner-city highways. Taking a documentary approach, Konrad investigates the city as a complex conglomeration of signs and codes, of movement and action, representation and the symbols of power. Her metropolitan wall tableaux form an alternative cartography of today's big cities. Konrad is also represented in the exhibition by her film *Concrete & Samples III – Carrara* (2010), which was shot at the eponymous marble quarry in Italy. Her camera meditatively scans up and down layers and surfaces of stone from which artists, from Michelangelo to Henry Moore, created their works. In this constantly changing landscape, temporary architectures can be discerned. Here, nature itself becomes sculpture. — HH
Aglaia Konrad was born in 1960 in Salzburg, Austria. She lives and works in Brussels, Belgium

www.augusteorts.be

Florian Maier-Aichen

Im Werk von Florian Maier-Aichen wird die Tradition der romantischen Landschaftsfotografie auf den Prüfstand gestellt und neu interpretiert, um die Art und Weise zu reflektieren, wie wir im 21. Jahrhundert die Welt erfahren. Indem Maier-Aichen das Genre der Landschaftsfotografie aufgreift, lässt er ihre Verknüpfung mit Umweltthemen, sowohl bezüglich der dokumentarischen als auch der malerischen Aussagekraft, wieder aufleben und rückt die Frage nach der fotografischen Authentizität ins Blickfeld. Dabei spricht er Aspekte der Globalisierung und unterschiedlichen

Wahrnehmungen an. Maier-Aichen fotografiert seine Motive – meist weite Landschaftsansichten – oft von unerwarteten Positionen aus und mietet dafür manchmal einen Hubschrauber, um aus der Luft Aufnahmen zu machen. Er unterzieht diese Bilder anschließend einer Bearbeitung, die auf einer Kombination aus analogen und digitalen Techniken basiert. Dabei verändert er geringfügig jedes Bild, um dessen visuelle Wirkung sowie den Aspekt des Unheimlichen in ihm zu verstärken. Seine Fotografien sind faktisch und fiktiv zugleich, bieten sowohl vertraute als auch eigenwillige Anblicke, lassen Orte wieder erkennen und wirken doch desorientierend. Sie sprechen von den Anfängen der Fotografie, ihrer Verwandtschaft zur Landschaft und Malerei und von den dramatischen Eingriffen in die Landschaft seit der Erfindung der Fotografie. *Untitled* (2011) etwa zeigt einen norwegischen Fjord inmitten eines gewaltigen Gebirgszugs mit einem riesigen, gerade ablegenden Kreuzfahrtsschiff – ausgeführt in artifiziell wirkenden, verwaschenen Grün- und Rosatönen. Einerseits sieht die Fotografie wie eine Ansichtspostkarte aus, ein Bild, das im Tourismus inflationär benutzt wurde und wird. Anderseits könnte es sich bei ihr um ein künstliches Konstrukt handeln, ein Modell oder ein Diorama in einem naturhistorischen Museum. Es ist dieses Weder-Noch, diese Unmöglichkeit, den Ort präzise zu lokalisieren, was Maier-Aichens Fotografien so bestechend macht. — KG
Florian Maier-Aichen wurde 1973 in Stuttgart, Deutschland, geboren. Er lebt und arbeitet in Los Angeles, USA, und Köln, Deutschland.

In the work of Florian Maier-Aichen the tradition of Romantic landscape photography is reviewed and reinterpreted in order to reflect our twenty-first century experience of the world. While appropriating the genre of landscape photography he renews its associations with environmental issues, documentary as well as painterly values, and also brings to the fore questions of photographic authenticity. In doing so he addresses issues of globalisation and modes of perception. Maier-Aichen often shoots his photographs – usually vast landscape vistas – from unexpected positions, sometimes hiring a helicopter in order to take his aerial views. He then manipulates his images using a combination of analogue and digital editing techniques, slightly altering each image in order to heighten its visual impact and sense of the uncanny. His photographs are at once factual and fictitious, familiar and bizarre, recognizable and disorienting. They speak of the advent of photography, its relationship to landscape and painting, and of dramatic interventions to the landscape made since photography's invention. *Untitled* (2011), for example, depicts a Norwegian fjord surrounded by an impressive mountain range, with a huge cruise ship that is just departing, rendered in artificial looking faded green and pink tones. On the one hand the photograph looks like a tourist picture postcard, an image used and reused to exhaustion; on the other hand it could be an artificial construct, a model, or a diorama in a natural history museum. It is this in-between state, this impossibility of pinpointing exact origins, that makes Maier-Aichen's photographs so intriguing. — KG
Florian Maier-Aichen was born in 1973 in Stuttgart, Germany. He lives and works in Los Angeles, USA, and Cologne, Germany.

www.baronianfrancey.com

Yang Yongliang

Von Weitem wirkt Yang Yongliangs 9 Meter lange Fotografie *Artificial Wonderland No. 1* (2010) wie eine friedliche Berglandschaft an einem leicht diesigen Tag. Bei näherer Betrachtung entdeckt man jedoch, dass die Berge mit Wolkenkratzern, Kränen, Stromleitungen, Fabriken und Industriesmog überzogen sind. Die Bergwelt scheint von Urbanität wie von einem sich ausbreitenden Virus heimgesucht worden zu sein. Dieses künstliche Wunderland ist China, ein Land, das sich mit atemberaubender Geschwindigkeit entwickelt, sei es nun in den Bereichen Wirtschaft, Politik, Gesellschaft und Industrie oder in Wissenschaft und Umwelt. Yongliangs Landschaft bezieht zu den ethischen und ökologischen Folgen dieses schnellen Wachstums Stellung. Ausgebildet in traditioneller chinesischer Malerei und Kalligrafie, nimmt der Künstler Rückgriff auf die Tradition der Landschaftsmalerei, in der Wasser und Berge ein harmonisches Bild ergeben. Im chinesischen Volksglauben werden Berge sowie die unversehrte Natur verehrt und seit je als Sujets in der Kunst gewürdigt. In *Artificial Wonderland No. 1* stellt Yongliang die Werte und die „Harmonie" der zeitgenössischen chinesischen Kultur infrage und wiederholt mithilfe des Mediums Fotografie die Geschichte von der Natur und dem menschlichen Eingriff im heutigen China. — SHO
Yang Yongliang wurde 1980 in Jiading, Schanghai, China, geboren. Er lebt und arbeitet in Schanghai, China.

From a distance Yang Yongliang's nine-metre-long photograph, *Artificial Wonderland No. 1* (2010) looks like a harmonious mountainous landscape on a slightly hazy day. Upon closer inspection, however, the mountains are covered with skyscrapers, cranes, power cables, factories and smog. Urbanism seems to have spread all over the mountains like a virus. This artificial wonderland is China: a country that is developing with dizzying speed in terms of the economy, politics, society, industry, science and the environment. Yang's landscape comments on the values and environmental consequences of such rapid growth. Having trained in traditional Chinese painting and calligraphy, Yang refers to the tradition of landscape painting in which water and mountains form a visual harmony. In Chinese religious beliefs, mountains and the unity of nature are worshiped, and are subjects traditionally celebrated in the arts. In *Artificial Wonderland No. 1* Yongliang questions the values and 'harmony' of contemporary Chinese culture, and uses the photographic medium to reiterate the story of nature and human intervention in China today. — SHO
Yang Yongliang was born in 1980 in Jiading, Shanghai, China. He lives and works in Shanghai, China

www.limnartgallery.com

Role and Ritual

S. / p. 56

Bani Abidi

In ihrer Foto-Serie *Karachi* (2009) zeigt Bani Abidi Menschen, die ihre privaten Beschäftigungen von ihren Wohnungen auf die Straße verlegt haben. Wir sehen eine Frau beim Schminken, einen Zeitung lesenden Mann sowie eine Frau am Bügelbrett. Die meisten drehen der Kamera den Rücken zu. Die Straßen sind leer, es ist kurz vor Sonnenuntergang. Was geschieht hier? Die Bildtitel beziehen sich auf die jeweils abgebildete Person, die Tageszeit und auf einen bestimmten Feiertag, wie zum Beispiel: *Jacky Mirza, 7:45 pm, 26 August 2008, Ramadan, Karachi.* Während des Ramadan enthalten sich Muslime vom Morgengrauen bis zum Sonnenuntergang des Essens und Trinkens sowie sexueller Kontakte. Abidi porträtiert einige von Karatschis religiösen Minderheiten (Hindus, Parsen und Christen) und „verbildlicht" deren Anwesenheit auf den Straßen zur Zeit des Ramadan, in der die fastende muslimische Bevölkerung eher in den Häusern bleibt. Abidi inszeniert und akzentuiert die immer wiederkehrenden Tätigkeiten des Alltags dieser Minderheiten im öffentlichen Raum. Sie bedient sich dabei eines Präsentationsmediums (die Fotografien sind in Leuchtkästen montiert), das die Präsenz dieser Menschen innerhalb des Bildraums noch zusätzlich betont. — SHO
Bani Abidi wurde 1971 in Karatschi, Pakistan, geboren. Sie lebt und arbeitet in Neu-Delhi, Indien, und Karatschi, Pakistan.

In her *Karachi* series (2009) Bani Abidi photographs individuals who have moved their private activity from their homes and onto the street. We see a woman putting on make-up, a man reading and a woman ironing. Most of the subjects have their back to the camera. The streets are empty and the sun is going down. What is going on? The title of each image refers to the person depicted and the hour of the day as well as a specific holiday: for example *Jacky Mirza, 7:45 pm, 26 August 2008, Ramadan, Karachi.* During Ramadan Muslims refrain from eating, drinking and sexual relations from dawn until sunset. Abidi portrays several religious minorities (Hindu, Parsi and Christian) in Karachi, Pakistan, and 'imagines' their presence in the streets during Ramadan; the fasting Muslims, by contrast, all gather inside. Abidi stages and emphasizes the continuous activity and life of these minorities in public space. The medium of presentation (her photographs are mounted on lightboxes) further reinforces their presence in photographic space. — SHO
Bani Abidi was born in 1971 in Karachi, Pakistan. She lives and works in New Delhi, India and Karachi, Pakistan

www.baniabidi.com

Said Atabekov

Said Atabekovs Werk beschäftigt sich mit der Geschichte Zentralasiens und Kasachstans, indem er die kommunistische Vergangenheit und andauernde islamische Kultur in den Fokus rückt. In der Zeit nach der Perestroika festigte Atabekov seine künstlerische Position als Begründer und Mitglied der nach wie vor existierenden Performancegruppe *Kyzyl Traktor* (Roter Traktor), Kasachstan, zu der auch Moldakul Narimbetov und Vitaly Simakov gehören. *Kyzyl Traktor* durchleuchtet die Archetypen der zentralasiatischen Kultur und des östlichen Mystizismus: Mythen, Religion, Natur, Schamanismus und pantheistische Rituale, wie sie auch heute noch in Kasachstan praktiziert werden. In der Fotoserie *The Way to Rome* von 2007 reist Atabekov durch Kasachstan und dokumentiert seine Landschaft, Menschen und Rituale: Frauen schieben in der Wüste einen liegengebliebenen UN-Wagen; alte Statuen sind mit Armeezubehör „dekoriert"; ein Mann trägt als Fruchtbarkeitsritual ein Mondsymbol über die Felder. Das Werk verweist auf Marco Polos Reise von Italien durch Zentralasien nach China und seine Rückkehr nach Rom. Diese berühmte Reise des 13. Jahrhunderts wurde zum Symbol für das erste Aufeinandertreffen von Ost und West und veranlasste als bedeutsames historisches Ereignis den Künstler dazu, es als Reflexion zur regionalen Geschichte aufzugreifen, beseelt von dem Wunsch, sie in einem weltumspannenden Zusammenhang zu verstehen. — SHO
Said Atabekov wurde 1965 in Bes Terek, Usbekistan, geboren. Er lebt und arbeitet in Shymkent, Kasachstan.

Said Atabekov's work explores the histories of central Asia and Kazakhstan through its communist past and ongoing Muslim culture. Atabekov consolidated his artistic position in the post-perestroika era as founder and part of the still existing artists' performance group *Kyzyl Traktor* (Red Tractor), Kazakhstan, together with Moldakul Narimbetov and Vitaly Simakov. *Kyzyl Traktor* critically examines the archetypes of central Asian culture and eastern mysticism: myth, religion, nature, shamanism and pantheistic rituals still practised today in Kazakhstan. In the photographic series *The Way to Rome*, (2007) Atabekov travelled through Kazakhstan and documented its landscape, people and rituals: women pushing a broken down United Nations car in the desert, ancient statues 'dressed' in army uniforms, and a man carrying a moon sign over the fields as a fertilising ritual. The work references Marco Polo's thirteenth-century journey from Italy through central Asia to China, and his return to Rome. This famous voyage came to symbolize the first encounter between the East and West and is a significant historical event to revisit for an artist reflecting on local history, with a desire to understand it in a worldwide perspective. — SHO
Said Atabekov was born in 1965 in Bes Terek, Uzbekistan. He lives and works in Shymkent, Kazakhstan

Peggy Buth

Mit *Desire in Representation (Travelling through the Musée Royale)* (2004–2009) untersucht Peggy Buth die Transformation von Belgiens Identität als ehemalige Kolonialmacht, wie sie das Königliche Museum für

Zentralafrika (KMZA) im belgischen Tervuren zum Ausdruck bringen möchte. In ihrer fotografischen Dokumentation über die Neuorganisation der Präsentation von Ausstellungsgegenständen strahlt der klassizistische Palast eine befremdende Leere und Vergänglichkeit aus. In diesen Bildern sind keine Besucher zu sehen, manchmal fehlen sogar die Exponate. Ohne Publikum und Ausstellungsbestand wirkt das Museum wie ein Rahmen, der darauf wartet, gefüllt zu werden. Büsten barbusiger schwarzer Frauen, Kolonialkarten und Kunsthandwerk afrikanischer Stämme treten als Fragmente eines Stücks auf, in dem es zu keinem Höhepunkt kommen kann. Objekte werden zu Requisiten und Bühnenkulissen, die das Museum als Stätte des Rituals einführt, als einen Ort inszenierter Präsentation und der Neupräsentation von Identitäten. Was als Objektiv gedacht war, durch das man das „andere" ergründen könnte, wird durch die Kamera zu einem Spiegel. Die fortwährende Neukonzipierung von Ausstellungsstücken und -räumen erscheint als eine nicht enden wollende Anstrengung: Die vom Museum repräsentierten Kulturen befinden sich – genauso wie die Ausstellungsstrategie – in ständiger Transformation. *Desire in Representation* offenbart die Sisyphus-Aufgabe von Museen, mit dem kontinuierlichen Fluss von sich weltweit immer wieder neu definierenden Identitäten Schritt zu halten. — JAB
Peggy Buth wurde 1971 in Berlin, Deutschland, geboren. Sie lebt und arbeitet in Berlin, Deutschland.

With *Desire in Representation (Travelling through the Musée Royale)* (2004–2009) Peggy Buth examines the transformation of Belgium's colonial identity as evinced by the Royal Museum for Central Africa, Tervuren, Belgium. Her photographic documentation of the re-arrangement of displays makes the neo-classical palace seem strangely vacant and transient. There are no visitors in these images; in some cases even the exhibits are also absent. Lacking both audience and permanent showpieces, the museum appears like a frame waiting to be filled. Busts of bare-breasted black women, colonial maps and tribal handicraft appear as fragments of a story that is unable to reach a culmination. Objects become props and set-designs establishing the museum as site of ritual, a place for ceremonies of presentation and the re-presentation of identities. What was meant as a lens through which one might examine the 'other' becomes, through the camera, a mirror. The perpetual re-design of exhibits and space appears as an endless toil: the cultures reflected by the museum are in constant transformation, as is the politics of display. *Desire in Representation* reveals the Sisyphean task of museums that try to keep up with the continuous flux of identities defined and re-defined throughout the world. — JAB
Peggy Buth was born in 1971 in Berlin, Germany. She lives and works in Berlin, Germany

www.klemms-berlin.com

Mariana Castillo Deball

Mariana Castillo Deball ist interessiert an der Frage, wie Archäologie Objekte und Vorstellungen einordnet und wie Künstler solche Dinge neu arrangieren, um landläufige Vorstellungen und Kategorien aufzubrechen. Aufgrund ihrer tiefen Verbindung zur Archäologie der aztekischen Ruinen, ihrer Mythologie und der Politik ihrer Aufarbeitung im heutigen Mexiko untersucht sie, wie derartige Schätze ausgegraben und über Tage offiziell archiviert werden. Die auf dem Festival präsentierte Diashow *There is a space later in time where you are just a memory* (2010) handelt von 2 mit dem aztekischen Menschenopferkult verbundenen mythischen Figuren und Gottheiten: Coatlicue (die Muttergöttin von Leben, Tod und Wiedergeburt) und ihre Tochter Coyolxauhqui (die Göttin des Mondes), beide dargestellt auf einem großen schildförmigen Steinrelief, das 1978 im Templo Mayor in Mexiko-Stadt gefunden wurde. Castillo Deball erzählt, wie Coyolxauhqui voller Empörung mithilfe ihrer Brüder – den Sternen – versuchte, ihre Mutter Coatlicue zu töten, als sie erfuhr, dass diese auf wundersame Weise geschwängert worden war. Glücklicherweise war Coatlicue schwanger mit der Sonne, die aus ihrem Leib sprang und sie schützte. Visuell präsentiert Castillo Deball die Geschichte unter Verwendung vergänglicher, keineswegs monumentaler Papierschnitte und Texte. Erst am Ende der Diashow sehen wir schließlich die Dokumentation der offiziellen Offenlegung des mythologischen Steinreliefs. Auf diese Weise werden Blick und Aufmerksamkeit des Betrachters von der politischen und materiellen Enträtselung eines „neuen" Reliefs für das Museum verschoben hin zu Inhalt und Zeitlosigkeit des dem Steinrelief zugrunde liegenden, ziemlich aggressiven aztekischen Mythos. — SHO
Mariana Castillo Deball wurde 1975 in Mexiko-Stadt, Mexiko, geboren. Sie lebt und arbeitet in Berlin, Deutschland.

Mariana Castillo Deball is interested in how the science of archeology orders objects and ideas and how artists re-order such things in order to disrupt commonly-held ideas and categories. Deeply connected to the archeology of Aztec ruins, their mythology, and the politics of their unraveling in contemporary Mexico, she researches how these treasures are dug up and officially received above ground. The slideshow presented in the exhibition, *There is a space later in time where you are just a memory* (2010), takes as its point of departure two mythical figures and deities connected to the Aztec cult of human sacrifice: Coatlicue (the mother of life, death and rebirth) and her daughter, Coyolxauhqui (the goddess of the moon), who are both represented in a grand circular stone relief that was found at Templo Mayor in Mexico City in 1978. Deball recounts how, when Coatlicue became mysteriously pregnant, her infuriated daughter Coyolxauhqui attempted to murder her mother with the help of her celestial brothers, the stars. Luckily, Coatlicue was pregnant with the sun, which jumped out of her womb to protect her. Visually Deball presents the story with the use of ephemeral and anti-monumental paper cutouts and text. Only at the end of the slideshow do we finally see the documentation of the official unraveling of the mythological stone relief. In this way the viewers' attention and focus is shifted from the political and material unraveling of a 'new' relief for the museum to the content and timelessness of a rather abrasive Aztec myth, which motivated the existence of the stone relief. — SHO

Mariana Castillo Deball was born in 1975 in Mexico City, Mexico. She lives and works in Berlin, Germany

www.barbarawien.de

Philippe Chancel S. / p. 210

Chen Chieh-Jen S. / p. 210

Hasan & Husain Essop

Die Fotografien der Zwillingsbrüder Hasan & Husain Essop untersuchen die Rolle des Mannes in der Gesellschaft, insbesondere die Stellung, die muslimische Männer in säkularen Gesellschaften einnehmen möchten. Eines ihrer wichtigsten Anliegen ist dabei die gespaltene Identität junger Muslime in Kapstadt, Südafrika. *Garden of Earthly Delights* (2007) zeigt zum Beispiel einen Mann im Anzug, der in einem Garten von stehenden Muslimen umringt allein auf dem Boden sitzend meditiert. Das Bild reflektiert, wie spirituelles Leben und der Pfad zu den „earthly delights" (irdischen Freuden) miteinander verbunden sind. Die Arbeiten der Künstler stellen oft inszenierte Ereignisse dar, in denen der Machismo zum Ausdruck kommt: in *Pit Bull Fight* (2007) hetzen islamisch und westlich gekleidete Männer ihre Hunde aufeinander; in *Pennsylvanians* (2008) hat sich Hasan Essop mit einem farbenprächtigen Kostüm, wie es normalerweise von einer berüchtigten Kapstadter Gang getragen wird, herausgeputzt. Es werden rituelle Gesten der Einbeziehung und Ausgrenzung, der Hierarchien unter Männern, aber auch Augenblicke friedlicher Koexistenz vorgeführt. Bedeutsamerweise treten Hasan & Husain Essop in ihren Bildern immer als Teil der Inszenierung auf. Die Spannung zwischen sich und dem „anderen" ist in ihren Arbeiten evident – sie gehen der Frage nach, wie sich männliche Identität in und zwischen der westlichen und der islamischen Welt darstellt. — SHO
Hasan & Husain Essop wurden 1985 in Kapstadt, Südafrika, geboren. Sie leben und arbeiten in Kapstadt, Südafrika.

The photographs of twin brothers Hasan & Husain Essop explore the role of the male subject in society, and particularly the position that Muslim men seek in secular society. One of their main concerns is the split identity assumed by young Muslims living in Cape Town, South Africa. *Garden of Earthly Delights* (2007), for example, features a man dressed in a business suit who sits down alone and meditates in the middle of a group of standing Muslims in a garden. The image is a reflection on how spiritual life and the path to the 'earthly delights' are connected. The artists' works often feature staged moments of machismo: in *Pit Bull Fight* (2007) young men dressed in Muslim and western clothes set their dogs against each other; in *Pennsylvanians* (2008) Hasan Essop dresses up in a colourful costume typically worn by a feared group of gangsters in Cape Town. Ritual gestures of inclusion and exclusion, of hierarchies between men, but also moments of peaceful coexistence are enacted. Importantly, the Essops appear and pose in all their images. The tension between self and 'other' is evident in the work, which asks how male identity is performed in and between the western and Muslim worlds. — SHO
Hasan & Husain Essop were born in 1985 in Cape Town, South Africa. They live and work in Cape Town, South Africa

www.goodman-gallery.com

Peter Funch

Der Fundus an Großstadtmythen der Menschheitsgeschichte ist groß. Von Babel hören wir, wenn wir dem Phänomen einer Gleichzeitigkeit verschiedener Kulturen begegnen. Die Stadt ertrank in einem nicht enden wollenden Stimmengewirr verschiedenster Sprachen. Sind wir wirklich alle so verschieden? In seiner Serie *Babel Tales* (2006–2010) eröffnet uns der dänische Fotojournalist Peter Funch, einen fast kaleidoskopartigen Blick auf das urbane Treiben unserer heutigen Großstädte. Funch fotografierte über einen längeren Zeitraum von den gleichen, festen Standorten aus die vorbeiziehenden oder wartenden Passanten. In einem nächsten Schritt filterte er nun die Akteure seiner Fotos heraus, die scheinbar in ähnlicher Pose oder gleicher Beschäftigung an exakt derselben Stelle zu sehen waren und fügte diese am Computer zu einem Bild zusammen. Die Konfrontation ihrer unbewussten Haltungen und Handlungen in einer quasi-fotografischen Gleichzeitigkeit führt zu wahnwitzigen Tableaus vermeintlicher Großstadtindividuen. Die auf diese Weise zusammengebrachten Menschen bilden Choreografien des Alltäglichen und erzeugen vor dem Auge des Betrachters das laut lärmende Echo einer Conditio humana im Jahre 2011, das die Titel der einzelnen Werke verstärken: *Informing Informers* (2006), *Observing Observers* (2007), *Following Followers* (2007) Funch entlarvt den Aktionsradius des Menschen in dieser Serie als tautologisches Prinzip. In diesem Perpetuum mobile müssen wir uns den Menschen als glücklichen Menschen vorstellen. — HH
Peter Funch wurde 1974 in Dänemark geboren. Er lebt und arbeitet in Kopenhagen, Dänemark und New York, USA.

Over the course of history, humankind has amassed a huge fund of big city myths. When we encounter the phenomenon of the co-existence of different cultures, we tend to speak of Babel: the city that drowned in a cacophony of diverse languages. Are we really so different? In his series *Babel Tales* (2006–2010) Danish photojournalist Peter Funch opens up an almost kaleidoscopic vista onto the comings-and-goings of today's major metropolises. Funch took up a fixed position in each city, from where he shot, over an extended period of time, all the people who passed by or lingered in front of his camera. He then edited the photographs with a computer, filtering out individuals who had appeared in exactly the same spot in a similar pose or going about the same activity, and compiled them into a new image. The juxtaposition of their unconscious postures and actions in a quasi-photographic simultaneity yields ludicrous tableaux of supposedly urbane individuals. Brought together in this way, the figures perform choreographies of everyday life, generating before the viewer's eyes a raucous echo of the human condition. Funch exposes the radius of action of human beings in this series as a tautological principle, as is evinced by the works' titles: *Informing Informers* (2006), *Observing Observers* (2007), *Following Followers* (2007). We must imagine them, caught up, as they are in this *perpetuum mobile*, as happy people. — HH

Peter Funch was born in 1974 in a small town in Denmark. He lives and works in Copenhagen, Denmark and New York, USA

www.peterfunch.com

Igor Grubic

Der Performancekünstler Igor Grubic entwickelt individualisierte „Befreiungsrituale", die er erstmals an öffentlichen Plätzen in Kroatien aufgeführt und dokumentiert hat. Die Installation *366 Liberation Rituals* (2008) ist eine Zusammenstellung von Fotografien dieser Rituale, die als subtiler Ausdruck einer politischen Haltung gegen Konservatismus, Nationalismus und Liberalismus im heutigen Kroatien betrachtet werden können. Indem der Künstler diese von ihm selbst entwickelten Rituale über den Zeitraum eines Jahres aufführte, wird seine eigene demokratische Position im öffentlichen Raum sichtbar. Jedes Ritual trägt einen bezeichnenden Titel: In *Scarves and Monuments* (2008) verbindet Grubic Statuen der antifaschistischen Bewegung den Mund mit roten Halstüchern, um auf den Einfluss des kulturellen und politischen Erbes in der Gegenwart hinzuweisen und um die historischen Positionen der durch diese Monumente repräsentierten Arbeiter und Denker in der heutigen Gesellschaft zu beleben. *Monument of Flowers* (2008) war ein ähnliches Ritual, in dem der Künstler an einem Ort, an dem Skinheads einen Homosexuellen töteten, Blumen niederlegte und eine Skulptur zu Ehren von im Krieg gegen die Naziherrschaft gefallenen Kämpfern mit Blumen schmückte. In *Small contemplative actions* (2008) rasierte er sich einen anarchistischen Stern in die wie bei einem Mönch kurz geschorenen Haare und exponierte sich so in verschiedenen Umgebungen und Situationen, dass eine Symbolik des Gegensatzes sowie gute „fotografische Möglichkeiten" entstanden: in einer katholischen Kirche, an einem leeren Swimmingpool und am Eingang zu einer Burg. — SHO

Als Teil der Zusammenarbeit zwischen dem 4. Fotofestival Mannheim_Ludwigshafen_Heidelberg und dem Performancefestival *Wunder der Prärie* im Ausstellungs- und Performance-Zentrum zeitraumexit, Mannheim (vom 5–17 September 2011) wird Grubic eine Reihe von Performances zu *366 Liberation Rituals* aufführen.

Igor Grubic wurde 1969 in Zagreb, Kroatien, geboren. Er lebt und arbeitet in Zagreb, Kroatien.

Performance artist Igor Grubic has conceived of a series of individualised 'liberation rituals', which he initially realised and documented in public spaces in Croatia. The installation *366 Liberation Rituals* (2008) is a constellation of photographs centred on Grubic's self-invented rituals, which can be seen as micro-political stances confronting conservatism, nationalism, and liberalism in Croatia today. Performing these rituals over the period of a year, the artist demarked his own democratic position within the public space. Each ritual has its own indicative title: in *Scarves and Monuments* (2008), Grubic placed red scarves over the mouths of monuments to the anti-fascist movement to highlight the impact of the cultural and political heritage in the present, and to activate the historical positions of workers and thinkers represented in the statues in today's society. *Monument of Flowers* (2008), was a similar ritual in which the artist placed flowers on a spot where skinheads killed a gay man, and on a sculpture that pays tribute to fallen fighters resisting the Nazis in World War II. In *Small contemplative actions* (2008), he shaved his hair like a monk, leaving only the shape of an anarchist star, and placed himself in different situations that clash symbolically and create good 'photo opportunities': in a Catholic church, in front of an empty swimming pool, and at the entrance to a castle. — SHO

Grubic will present a series of performances referring to the *366 Liberation Rituals* as part of a collaboration between the 4. Fotofestival Mannheim_Ludwigshafen_Heidelberg and the performance festival *Wunder der Prärie* realised at the performance and exhibition space *Zeitraum Exit*, Mannheim, 5–17 September 2011.

Igor Grubic was born in 1969 in Zagreb, Croatia. He lives and works in Zagreb, Croatia

www.artvehicle.com/feature/23

Pieter Hugo

In Pieter Hugos Porträtserie *Nollywood* (2008–2009) werden Aspekte des Alltagslebens in Nigeria zusammen mit fiktionalen Elementen zu einer Reihe von surrealen Szenarien zusammengeführt. Hugo präsentiert eine Neuinszenierung von Charakterdarstellern aus Nollywood, Nigerias billig produzierender aber boomender Filmindustrie, die, in Anspielung auf Indiens Bollywood benannt, inzwischen die drittgrößte der Welt ist. Hier werden in nur einer Woche Blockbusterfilme voller Dramatik und Leidenschaft produziert: Die Laienschauspieler werden live gecastet, gedreht wird an realen Schauplätzen. Oft erzählt der Film eine Geschichte aus dem Leben der jeweiligen Schauspieler, gemixt mit Unterhaltung und Themen wie Hexerei, Korruption und Prostitution. Von diesen Filmen inspiriert, ließ Pieter Hugo ein Team aus Schauspielern für seine extrem stilisierten, überspitzten und theatralischen Bilder Modell stehen. In *Escort Kama. Enugu, Nigeria* (2008) und *Chigozie Nechi. Enugu, Nigeria* (2009) tragen beide Schauspieler Theatermasken als Teil des stark erotisch aufgeladenen Bildinhalts. In *Emeka Uzzi* (2009) verkleidet Hugo einen Schauspieler tiefgründig-originell als

Coca-Cola trinkenden Neandertaler und verkörpert dadurch die gegensätzlichen stereotypen Darstellungen eines unterentwickelten Afrikas zusammen mit dem Sinnbild des Kapitalismus und der Globalisierung. Hugo greift in seinen Arbeiten nicht nur die Fantasiewelt Nollywoods auf, sondern erkundet in ihnen auch die sozialen Verhältnisse in Westafrika – und lässt dabei dem Betrachter genügend Raum, sich ein eigenes Bild von der dortigen Lebenswirklichkeit zu machen. *Steven Amoako, Wild Honey Collector, Techiman District, Ghana* (2005) ist Teil einer weiteren Serie mit dem Titel *Portraits (Wild Honey Collector)* und zeigt, wie der Titel bereits sagt, einen Wildhonigsammler. Den Kopf mit einer Plastiktüte und die Hände mit Blättern vor Bienen und Rauch geschützt, wirkt sein Anblick grotesk und fremdartig und doch gleichzeitig vollkommen natürlich. — SHO
Pieter Hugo wurde 1976 in Johannesburg, Südafrika, geboren. Er lebt und arbeitet in Kapstadt, Südafrika.

In Pieter Hugos' *Nollywood* portrait series (2008–2009) aspects of everyday life in Nigeria as well as fictional elements are conflated in a series of surrealist scenarios. Hugo presents a restaging of characters from Nigeria's cheap yet growing film industry, Nollywood (a play on India's Bollywood), which is third largest in the word. Here, overdramatic blockbuster films are made in just one week with live casting and rapid shooting of local actors in real locations. Often the films recount the actors' own stories, including tales of witchcraft, bribery, comedy and prostitution. Inspired by these films, Pieter Hugo hired a team of actors to pose for his highly stylized, exaggerated and theatrical images. In *Escort Kama. Enugu, Nigeria* (2008) and *Chigozie Nechi. Enugu, Nigeria* (2009) both actors wear theatrical masks as part of the strong erotic current in the pictures. In *Emeka Uzzi* (2009) Hugo humorously dresses up an actor as a Neanderthal drinking Coca Cola, thus epitomising the contrasting stereotypical projections of primitive life in Africa with the symbol of capitalism and globalisation. Hugo's work not only imitates the Nollywood imaginary, but also investigates the social conditions in West Africa leaving the viewer space to imagine the reality of life there. *Steven Amoako, Wild Honey Collector, Techiman District, Ghana* (2005), part of another series entitled *Portraits (Wild Honey Collector)* is (as the title indicates) a wild honey collector. Covering, as he does, his head with a plastic bag and his hands with leaves as protection from the bees and smoke, his image appears at once bizarre, alien, and entirely natural. — SHO
Pieter Hugo was born in 1976 in Johannesburg, South Africa. He lives and works in Cape Town, South Africa

www.pieterhugo.com

Panos Kokkinias S. / p. 201

Vincent Meessen

Ausgangspunkt für Vincent Meessens Film *Vita Nova* (2009) ist ein bekanntes Titelblatt der französischen Illustrierten *Paris Match* von 1955. Das Titelbild zeigt einen salutierenden schwarzen Jungen in französischer Uniform; im Vorspann des Artikels wird berichtet, dass dies der „kleine Diouf" sei, der „mit seinen Kameraden aus Ouagadougou gekommen ist ... um das fantastische Spektakel zu eröffnen, das die französische Armee in dieser Woche im Palais des Sports präsentieren wird". Ausgehend von diesem Cover für den Beginn seines Films begibt sich Meessen auf die Suche nach Diouf, dem Jungen in Uniform, die in eine aufwendige Geschichte eingebettet wird, in der auch die Schriften von Roland Barthes eingeflochten werden – jenes Autors, der in seinem Werk *Mythen des Alltags* (Mythologies, 1957) eine scharfe semantische Kritik zu diesem Foto verfasst hatte. Der Film spricht die Frage der Darstellung des „anderen" an, die Umschreibung von Geschichte und die Verfälschung von Identität. Unter Zuhilfenahme einer Vielzahl von Archiven, Wochenschauen aus den 1950er-Jahren und seines eigenen, in Afrika erstellten Filmmaterials entwickelt Meessen eine parallele und aktualisierte Geschichte, die die Schreckgespenster von Kolonialismus und Fotografie heraufbeschwört. Durch diesen Rückgriff auf umfangreiches Material aus den 1950er-Jahren füllt der Film auch die autobiografische Geschichte einer anderen Figur mit Leben: die von Roland Barthes selbst. Meessen belebt den Geist des Schriftstellers neu und lässt ihn im Film in der Gestalt eines Schwarzen wiederauferstehen. Mit diesem Film verknüpft Meessen Vergangenheit und Gegenwart, Fakten und Fiktion, das Persönliche und das Politische, indem er aufzeigt, wie geschichtliche Ereignisse sich auf Individuen im Laufe der Zeit auswirken. — KG
Vincent Meessen wurde 1971 in Baltimore, USA, geboren. Er lebt und arbeitet in Brüssel, Belgien.

Vincent Meessen's film *Vita Nova* (2009) takes as its point of departure an iconic front page of the French magazine *Paris Match*, from 1955. The cover image is of a young soldier shown in the act of saluting; the standfirst informs readers that this is 'Small Diouf', who has 'come from Ouagadougou with his comrades … to open the fantastic spectacle that the French Army presents this week at the Palais des Sports'. Taking this cover as his cue, Meessen embarks on a search for Diouf the young soldier, weaving it with an elaborate narrative involving the writings of Roland Barthes – the author who wrote a piercing semantic critique of this image in his book *Mythologies* (1957). The film raises issues of the representation of the 'other', the rewriting of history, and the fabrication of identity. Using newsreels from the 1950s and his own footage shot in Africa, Meessen creates a parallel and updated story, which raises the spectres of colonialism and photography. Employing a variety of archives and diverse source material, the film also gives life to the autobiographical story of another character: Roland Barthes himself. Meessen resuscitates the spectre of the author, who returns in the film reincarnated as a black man. With this film, Meessen connects past and present, fact and fiction, the personal and the political, pointing to how

historical events affect individuals over the course of time. — KG
Vincent Meessen was born in 1971 in Baltimore, USA. He lives and works in Brussels, Belgium

www.normal.be

Kirstine Roepstorff

Kirstine Roepstorff eignet sich aus Büchern, Zeitungen, Zeitschriften und von Tapeten Abbildungen und Fotografien an, indem sie diese und ihren Bildgehalt zu Collagen und Wandarbeiten aus Papier neu arrangiert. Mithilfe einer Reihe von selbst entwickelten Archetypen erforscht sie in ihrer Arbeit die Strategien von Repräsentation. Von der deutschen Dadaistin Hannah Höch (1889–1978), einer Pionierin der Fotomontage und wegweisenden Feministin, inspiriert, hat Roepstorff eine auf die Collage basierende Praktik entwickelt, mit der sie die Unterdrückungsmechanismen innerhalb der Gesellschaft entschieden kritisiert. Höch wies in ihren Fotomontagen darauf hin, dass Frauen in der Gesellschaft oft nur wie Puppen behandelt würden. Diese Kritik liegt auch Roepstorffs *The Six Realms (Including the Summer of Discontent)* von 2007 zugrunde, einem collagierten Tableau bestehend aus der vergrößerten Schwarz-Weiß-Fotokopie einer Fotografie tanzender osteuropäischer Frauen aus den 1950er-Jahren. Roepstorff geht jedoch noch einen Schritt weiter: Indem sie die Silhouetten der Frauen mit Papierausschnitten und -streifen dekoriert, die verschiedene Aspekte aus deren Leben erkennen lassen, unterstreicht sie, wie die Bewegung der Frauen als bemächtigender Marsch gelesen werden kann. Roepstorff erläutert, dass sich diese Collage mit der physischen „Erdung" von Menschen beschäftigt, zwischen deren Ansichten und Meinungen zwar Welten liegen können, die aber durch das kollektive Ritual des Tanzes miteinander verbunden sind. Die Collage ist beeinflusst von der buddhistischen Vorstellung der 6 Daseinsbereiche, in die man hineingeboren wurde und im nächsten Leben wieder hineingeboren wird. Manche von ihnen sind angenehm, andere dagegen nicht. — SHO
Kirstine Roepstorff wurde 1972 in Kopenhagen, Dänemark, geboren. Sie lebt und arbeitet in Berlin, Deutschland.

Kirstine Roepstorff appropriates photographic images from books, newspapers, magazines and wallpaper, and rearranges them and their visual imaginary in her collages and paper murals. Her work explores the politics of representation through an array of archetypes invented by the artist. Inspired by the German Dada artist, Hannah Höch (1889–1978) (one of the pioneers of photo-collage and an innovative feminist), Roepstorff has developed a collage-based practice that is highly critical of repressive mechanisms in society. In her collages, Höch pointed out that women in society were often treated as mere puppets. This critique also underlies Roepstorff's *The Six Realms (Including the Summer of Discontent)* (2007), a collage panel consisting of an enlarged black and white photocopy of a photograph from the 1950s of dancing Eastern European women. Roepstorff goes further: by decorating their silhouetted forms with paper cut-outs and strips that indicate various aspects of their lives, she emphasises how their movement can be regarded as an empowered march. Roepstorff states that this collage is concerned with the physical 'grounding' of people whose thoughts and minds may be worlds apart but who are united through the collective ritual of dance. The collage draws from the Buddhist notion of the six reams of existence one is born and re-born into – some more pleasant than others. — SHO
Kirstine Roepstorff was born in 1972 in Copenhagen, Denmark. She lives and works in Berlin, Germany

www.christinawilson.net

Jeremy Shaw

Als Künstler, DJ und Musikproduzent untersucht Jeremy Shaw mithilfe der Medien Video, Fotografie und Installation bestimmte Tanz- und Transzendenzrituale der zeitgenössischen Subkultur. Die daraus entstandenen Arbeiten erscheinen häufig in Gestalt wissenschaftlicher Experimente. Für *Transcendental Capacities (Electronic Dance Music Grid – 1978– 2001)* (2011) präsentiert in „Rolle und Ritual" benutzte Shaw eine Kirlian-Kamera, um die physische Wirkung, die eine bestimmte zeitgenössische elektronische Musik auf eine Person hat, zu dokumentieren und arrangierte 45 dieser Polaroidbilder in einer Vitrine. Von jeder Person wurde ein Finger fotografiert, um dessen energetische „Aura" während des Hörens eines bestimmten Musikstücks festzuhalten. Jedes Polaroid bildet daher die Reaktion des Zeigefingers der jeweiligen Person auf die verschiedenen vertrauten Rhythmen und Songs ab. In dem Video *DMT* (2004) als Teil von „Lebenskreisläufe" präsentiert Shaw ein Experiment, in dem mehrere Personen kurz nach einem DMT-Trip interviewt werden. DMT (N-Dimethyltryptamin) ist eine Droge, die geraucht beim Konsumenten eine kurze, aber intensive Veränderung des visuellen Erlebens hervorruft. Häufig geschieht dies in Form einer Vision von einem Hyperraum, dem Hören fremdartiger Töne und einem physischen Schütteln, gefolgt vom Sehen farbenkräftiger Muster. Shaw interviewte über 30 Personen unmittelbar nach einem Trip und befragte sie dabei nach ihren Wahrnehmungen jenseits des bekannten Raum-, Zeit- und Körpergefühls. Das Video zeigt uns die Gesichter der Teilnehmer während ihres Trips in Nahaufnahme, und es wird deutlich, dass die hier erfassten, sehr unterschiedlichen Erfahrungen eng mit ihre Persönlichkeit und Psyche verbunden sind. Doch statt subkulturelle Phänomene zu individualisieren, stellt Shaw sie vielmehr generalisierend und seriell dar. Als ob er empirisches Material für eine breiter angelegte Studie über unsichtbare Empfindungen, Erinnerungen und chemische Übertragungen sammeln würde, die Menschen mit bestimmten Songs und pop- oder subkulturellen Ritualen erfahren und verbinden. — SHO
Jeremy Shaw wurde 1977 in Vancouver, Kanada, geboren. Er lebt und arbeitet in Berlin, Deutschland, und Vancouver, Kanada.

Artist, DJ and music producer Jeremy Shaw explores specific dance and transcendence rituals in contemporary subcultures through the media of video, photography and installation. The resulting works often appear in the guise of scientific experiments. *In Transcendental Capacities (Electronic Dance Music Grid – 1978–2001)* (2011) displayed in 'Role and Ritual' Shaw used the Kirlian Aura Camera to document the physical impression that specific contemporary electronic tunes have on a particular person, and has arranged 45 of these Polaroids in a vitrine. Each person's finger is photographed to record its energy 'aura' as they listen to a specific piece of music. Each Polaroid therefore represents the individual's indexical reaction to the various well-known beats and songs. In the video *DMT* (2004) as part of 'Life Cycles', Shaw presents an experiment in which several people are interviewed shortly after experiencing a DMT trip. DMT (N-dimethyltryptamine) is a drug that users smoke, giving a strong but brief audiovisual experience. Often, this takes the form of a vision of a hyperspace, alien sounds and physically shaking – followed by a vision of strongly coloured patterns. Shaw interviewed more than 30 people immediately after a trip, asking each subject about his or her out-of-body, out-of-time, out-of-space experiences. In the video we see close-up studies of the participants' faces recorded during their trips, and realize that their experiences are strongly related to the participants' personas and psychological makeup. Rather than individualising subcultural phenomena, Shaw serialises or generalises them. It is as if he is collecting empirical material for a broader study of invisible sentiments, memories, and chemical transmissions that people experience and connect with certain songs and pop or subcultural rituals. — SHO
Jeremy Shaw was born in 1977 in Vancouver, Canada. He lives and works in Berlin, Germany and Vancouver, Canada

www.jeremyshaw.net

Johan Spanner S. / p. 205

Clemens von Wedemeyer

Mit *Found Footage* (von: *Die vierte Wand*) (2008–2010) präsentiert Clemens von Wedemeyer Film, Video und ein Interview als Teile seiner Ausstellung *Die Vierte Wand* (Barbican 2009). Hier nimmt er Bezug auf den „ersten Kontakt" der Tasaday, einer ethnischen Gruppe im Regenwald der philippinischen Insel Mindanao, mit westlichen Forschern im Jahr 1971. Die Wissenschaftler glaubten, sie hätten einen von jeglicher Zivilisation „unberührten" Stamm entdeckt. Diese Annahme wurde angezweifelt, als ein Journalist 15 Jahre später die Tasaday erneut besuchte und vermutet wurde, dass diese die ganze Zeit über im westlichen Lebensstil in Häusern eines benachbarten Dorfs gelebt hatten. Bedienten die Tasaday bei ihrer „Entdeckung" 1971 nur das Bild vom primitiven Leben, wie man es sich im Westen vorstellt? Welche Rolle kommen Film und Fotografie bei solchen Erkundigungen zu? Der Film *Found Footage* (2008–2009) ist Teil der Installation und besteht aus vom Künstler zusammengestelltem, aufgefundenem Filmmaterial aus den Fernsehberichten über die Forscher und deren ersten Kontakt mit den Tasaday und offenbart, wie die Entdeckung dirigiert und Falschheit konstruiert wurde. *Intro* (2009) ist ein Kurzfilm mit einer Darstellerin aus einem von Wedemeyer inszenierten Theaterstück aus *Die Vierte Wand.* Der Titel bezieht sich auf die gedachte Trennungslinie zwischen der Bühne und dem Publikum im Theater. Sie ermöglicht den Besuchern, das, was sie auf der Bühne sehen, für wahr zu halten, und den Schauspielern, das Publikum während ihres Auftritts zu ignorieren. Die Installation bringt die Theatralik der Medien und die Selbstinszenierung der Tasaday zur Sprache. — SHO
Clemens von Wedemeyer wurde 1974 in Göttingen, Deutschland, geboren. Er lebt und arbeitet in Berlin, Deutschland.

In *Found Footage* (from: *The Fourth Wall*) (2010) Clemens von Wedemeyer presents film, photography, and an interview as parts of his exhibition 'The Fourth Wall' (Barbican, 2009). Here he takes point of departure in the 'first contact' between the Philippine ethnic group, the Tasaday, and western explorers in the rainforests of Mindanao, Philippines, in 1971. The explorers believed they had discovered a tribe 'untouched' by civilisation. This assumption was called into question when a journalist again visited the Tasaday 15 years later and it transpired that they had lived a western lifestyle in houses in a neighbouring village all along. Were the Tasadays only enacting a western image of primitive living when 'discovered' in 1971? What is the role of film and photography in such investigations? The film that is part of the installation, *Found Footage*, consists of the artist's compilation of found footage from explorers' TV reports of first contacts and discloses how the imaginary of western discovery is constructed. *Intro* (2008) is a short film that presents one female character from Wedemeyer's recent restaging of the Tasaday encounter as part of *The Fourth Wall.* The title refers to the imagined division between the stage and the audience in the theatre, which enables audiences to believe that what they see on stage is real, and actors to ignore the audience as they act. The installation touches upon the theatricality of the media and the self-staging of the Tasaday tribe. — SHO
Clemens von Wedemeyer was born in 1974 in Göttingen, Germany. He lives and works in Berlin, Germany

www.antifilm.de

Life Cycles S. / p. 88

Mac Adams

Auf der Fotografie *Parallel Lives, Bones* (1999) ist ein auf einem Heulager gebettetes menschliches Skelett auf einem Glastisch zu sehen. Sonderbarerweise wirft es

einen völlig unerwarteten Schatten: den eines Hundes, der unter dem Tisch einen Knochen frisst. Mac Adams schildert hier mit minimalen Mitteln einen Kreislauf der Vernichtung – Jagen, Füttern und den gnadenlosen Lauf der Zeit. Versiert im Herstellen von einprägsamen Illusionen in Film und Bildhauerei sowie dichten liter-arischen Darstellungen, bewegt sich Adams innerhalb der Tradition der konstruierten narrativen Fotografie. Die Serie *Parallel Lives* (1999) besteht aus Stillleben mit Äpfeln, Trauben, gefalteten Servietten, Heubündeln, Kerzen, Steinen und Knochen auf Glas-tischen, deren losgelöste Schattenrisse an Tiere, Jäger und Räuber erinnern. Die Fotografien machen die verrottenden Arrangements des Künstlers und ihre Schatten unsterblich – einen Geist, der nur für den kurzen Augenblick existierte, in dem er von einer bestimmten Perspektive aus fotografiert wurde. Technisch gesehen bedingen Stillleben und Schattenriss einander, denn beide sind von den selben Materialien, Raum und Licht, ab hängig. Doch als Bilder stehen sie jeweils für sich. In Adams Fotografien entwickelt sich der Sinngehalt aus der Leerstelle zwischen Objekten, Bildern und Projektionen – zwischen dem, was wir sehen, und dem, was wir wissen. — SHO
Mac Adams wurde 1942 in Wales, Großbritannien, geboren. Er lebt und arbeitet in New Jersey, USA, und New York, USA.

In the photograph *Parallel Lives, Bones* (1999) a human skeleton is arranged on a bed of hay on a transparent table. Oddly, it casts a shadow of a completely different set-up: a dog eating a bone under the table. Here Mac Adams describes a cycle of annihilation – hunting, feeding and the merciless passage of time – with minimal means. Adept at creating memorable cinematic and sculptural illusions and terse literary narratives, Adams operates within the tradition of constructed, narrative photography. The series *Parallel Lives* (1999) consists of still lifes of apples, grapes, folded serviettes, bundles of hay, candles, stones and skeleton bones on glass tables whose detached silhouettes resemble animals, hunters and predators. The photographs immortalise the artist's decaying arrangement and its shadow – a spectre that existed for a just a brief moment as it was photographed from a particular perspective. Technically, the still life and the silhouette are interdependent (they both rely on the same material, space and light), but they are nevertheless disjunctive as images. In Adams' photographs meaning evolves from the void between objects, images and projections – between what we see and what we know. — SHO
Mac Adams was born in 1943 in Wales, UK. He lives and works in New Jersey and New York, USA

www.macadamsstudio.com

Köken Ergun

In seiner 3-Kanal-Videoinstallation *Wedding* (2009) verwendet Köken Ergun Material von mehr als 40 türkischen Hochzeitsfeiern in Berlin. Das Ergebnis ist eine verwirrende Bilderflut: eine Braut, die sich in einem Beauty-salon für die Hochzeit schönmachen lässt; ein von tobenden Kindern umringter Mann, der im Freudentaumel Dollarscheine in die Luft wirft; ernst dreinblickende Männer beim peniblen Zählen der Geldscheine, die das Paar als Geschenk erhalten hat. Bei dieser spontan Zusammenkunft von selbsternannten Bankangestellten, die die Übersicht darüber verlieren, was von wem gegeben wurde, scheinen romantische Idealvorstellungen von Liebe keinen Platz zu haben. Indem die Installation verschiedene Hochzeitsfeiern zeigt, geht sie über die Darstellung eines speziellen Ereignisses hinaus. Sie ist vielmehr die Dokumentation einer im Exil lebenden Gemeinde, die ihre Identität neu inszeniert, die Dokumentation eines kollektiven Aktes kultureller Selbstdefinition. Da jedes Gemeinschaftsereignis sowohl eine Innen- als auch eine Außenansicht erzeugt, wird uns die Gelegenheit zu 2 gegensätzlichen Perspektiven geboten: dem immanenten oder dem exoterischen Blickwinkel. Das Auge des Erzählers scheint hier die Position des „Insiders" einzunehmen. Da *Wedding* jedoch von Teilnehmern dieser Feiern aufgenommen wurde, wirkt der kritische Blick dieser Arbeit nie herablassend oder exotisierend. — JAB
Köken Ergun wurde 1976 in Istanbul, Türkei, geboren. Er lebt und arbeitet in Berlin, Deutschland.

In his three-channel video projection *Wedding* (2009) Körken Ergun uses material recorded at over 40 different Turkish wedding ceremonies held in Berlin. The result is a bewildering flow of images: a bride is being prepared for the ceremony in a beauty parlour; a man in a state of exhilaration throws dollar-bills in the air while surrounded by ecstatic children; a row of austere-looking men keep close count on donations made to the couple. Romantic

ideals of love seem to have no place with this informal assembly of impromptu bank clerks, who lose track of what was given and by whom. Since the film depicts several celebrations, it becomes more than an account of a specific event. It is the documentation of an exiled community re-enacting its identity, a collective act of cultural self-definition. As every communal event creates an inside as well as an outside, we are offered the possibility of two conflicting gazes: the intrinsic or the exoteric. Here, the eye of the narrator seems to be on the inside. Because *Wedding* was recorded by participants in these ceremonies, its critical gaze never seems condescending or exoticizing. – JAB
Köken Ergun was born in 1976 in Istanbul, Turkey. He lives and works in Berlin, Germany

kokenergunwritings.blogspot.com

Simon Fujiwara

Die Installation *Before the Fall* (2010) besteht aus einem altmodischen Campingtisch mit darauf arrangierten Essensresten, schmutzigem Besteck, Fotografien und vom Künstler geschriebenen Texten. Die eine Seite der Tischplatte ist mit FKK-Fotos von 1936 belegt, während auf der anderen Farbreproduktionen von Gemälden zu sehen sind, die Adam und Eva vor und nach dem Sündenfall zeigen. Jede Tischseite besitzt eine eigene Aussage zu Nacktheit und Unschuld. Fujiwaras Arbeit wird oft mit autobiografischer Konnotation präsentiert und ist durchzogen von verborgener und offenkundiger Homoerotik. *Before the Fall* gibt eine Begebenheit aus dem Leben des Künstlers wieder und beschreibt, wie seine Eltern auf einer Urlaubsreise nach Deutschland mit ihm versehentlich in einem FKK-Zeltlager gelandet sind. In dem zur Installation gehörenden Text schildert Fujiwara diese Erfahrung: „Deutschland war berühmt für seine Freikörperkultur, aber als Brite hatte ich noch nie zuvor einen nackten Menschen gesehen. Natürlich konnte ich damals nicht wissen, dass dies ein Anblick war, nach dem ich mich in den kommenden Jahren immer und immer wieder sehnen würde." *Before the Fall* ist eine Installation, die den Augenblick des Erwachens erforscht, den Moment, in dem man sich seiner sexuellen Attraktivität bewusst wird. – SHO
Simon Fujiwara wurde 1982 in London, Großbritannien, geboren. Er lebt und arbeitet in Berlin, Deutschland.

Before the Fall (2010) consists of an installation of leftover food, dirty cutlery, photographs and texts written by the artist, arranged on top of an old-fashioned camping table. On one side of the table there are images from an FKK (a nudist camp in Germany) taken in 1936, and on the other there are colour reproductions of paintings depicting Adam and Eve before and after the Fall. Each side of the table has its own narrative regarding nudity and innocence. Fujiwara's work is often presented in an autobiographical register, and is shot through with clandestine and overt homoeroticism. *Before the Fall* features a personal anecdote describing how, on a holiday trip to Germany, Fujiwara's parents accidentally took him to a nudist camp. In a text that forms part of the work, Fujiwara describes this experience: 'Germany was famous for its nudism, but being British, I had never seen a naked man before and so I could not have known that it was a sight I would crave again and again in the coming years.' *Before the Fall* is an installation that explores the moment of awakening when one discovers one's own feelings of sexual attraction. – SHO
Simon Fujiwara was born in 1982 in London, UK. He lives and works in Berlin, Germany

www.neuealtebruecke.com

Agnès Geoffray

In Agnès Geoffrays Serie *Les suspendus* (2010–2011) wird die Doppeldeutigkeit des Titels – „The Hanged" (Die Erhängten) wie auch „The Suspended" (Die Hängenden) – durch die an ein Diptychon erinnernde Präsentation reflektiert. Sowohl aus Bildern der Künstlerin als auch aus gefundenen Fotografien bestehend, eröffnen diese Arbeiten einen Raum für Imagination und Fiktion. Das Potenzial des Bildes liegt in seiner Fähigkeit, verschiedene Assoziationen heraufzubeschwören. Schönheit und Zerbrechlichkeit koexistieren neben einer unterschwelligen Andeutung von Sterblichkeit oder Gewalttätigkeit. Ein vergrößerter und unscharfer Schnappschuss von Eva Braun in einbeiniger Ballettposition an einem Seeufer *(Braun Eva)* ist in unmittelbarer Nähe zu einer kleinformatigen Fotografie platziert, die einen toten, an einer Pfote aufgehängten Nerz *(Vanité)* zeigt. Hinter dieser augenfälligen Darstellung kann eine tiefgründigere Bedeutungsebene ausgemacht werden, die sich auf das bekanntermaßen kurze Leben

Eva Brauns und das ähnliche Schicksal des Nerzes bezieht – beide sind dem Untergang geweiht. Ein weiteres eindrucksvolles Beispiel ist die Gegenüberstellung der großformatigen Fotografie einer verwelkenden Lilie *(Nature morte)* und der kleinformatigen eines mit dem Kopf nach unten hängenden, offenbar toten Mannes, der in einem Stacheldrahtzaun gefangen ist *(En suspense)*. Auf formaler Ebene lässt sich eine gewisse Ähnlichkeit zwischen den Gliedmaßen des hängenden Mannes und den halb abgebrochenen Blütenstielen der Lilie erkennen. Auf einer tieferen Bedeutungsebene wird man jedoch an den beunruhigenden Unterschied zwischen natürlichem Verfall und einem von Menschenhand herbeigeführten Tod erinnert. *Les suspendus* ruft uns im Grunde genommen unsere eigene Verwundbarkeit und die Endlichkeit unseres Lebens ins Gedächtnis, aber auch den Schwebezustand unserer Existenz, mit dem wir als menschliche Wesen im Laufe unseres Lebens häufig konfrontiert werden. — KG
Agnès Geoffray wurde 1973 in St. Chamond, Frankreich, geboren. Sie lebt und arbeitet in Brüssel, Belgien, und Paris, Frankreich.

In Agnès Geoffray's series *Les suspendus* (2010–2011) the *double entendre* of the title (*The Hanged* as well as *The Suspended*) is reflected in its diptych-like presentation. Consisting of both images shot by the artist and found photographs, these works open up a space for the imagination and fiction. The potency of the image lies in its capacity to conjure multiple associations. Beauty and fragility co-exist with a latent sense of mortality or violence. An enlarged and blurred snapshot of Eva Braun standing in a ballet pose on one leg on the shore of a lake (entitled *Braun Eva*), is hung next to a small photograph of a dead mink, which hangs from its paw (*Vanité*). Behind this conspicuous feature, a more profound meaning can be traced, related to our knowledge of the short life of Eva Braun and the similar fate of the mink, both doomed. Another striking example is the confrontation between the large photograph of a dying lily (*Nature morte*) and a small one of a seemingly dead man hanging upside down, trapped in barbed wire (*En suspense*). On a formal level one can notice a certain resemblance between the posture of the limbs of the hanging man and the half broken stems of the lily. On a deeper level, one is reminded of the disconcerting contrast between natural decay and manmade death. Ultimately, *Les suspendus* reminds us of our vulnerability and the finitude of our own individual lives, as well as the state of existential 'suspension' – those in-between states – we are often confronted with as human beings during our lives. — KG
Agnès Geoffray was born in 1973 in St. Chamond, France. She lives and works in Brussels, Belgium and Paris, France

www.agnesgeoffray.com

Jacob Holdt

Jacob Holdt reiste Anfang der 1970er-Jahre in die USA und lebte dort einige Jahre als Vagabund, angewiesen auf die Hilfsbereitschaft Fremder, die ihm Essen und Unterkunft gaben. Holdts Schnappschüsse von Paaren und Bilder von betenden Menschen gehören zu einer umfangreichen Fotodokumentation über die extreme Armut und Ungerechtigkeit, die er innerhalb der amerikanischen Gesellschaft beobachtet hat, *American Pictures* (1970–1975). Die sich umarmenden Paare mit ihren liebevollen Blicken und Zärtlichkeiten stehen in starkem Kontrast zu den oft schonungslos offenen und erschreckenden Diskriminierungsszenen, die Holdt andernorts aufgenommen hat. Durch seine Philosophie der totalen Bejahung (also möglichst alles zu akzeptieren, was ihm angeboten wurde), brachte Holdt sich häufig selbst in die Gefahr, Schmerz und Armut am eigenen Leib zu erleben – was ansonsten in sicherer Entfernung auf der anderen Seite des Objektivs geblieben wäre. Durch diese Art der Identifikation werden die Bilder, obgleich sie in ihrer Intimität spektakulär sind, niemals zu effekthascherischen Anblicken oder gleiten ins Exotisierende oder Spekulative ab. Befreit vom moralisierenden Blick, porträtiert Holdt diese Szenen und Menschen ohne aufdringlich oder ästhetisierend distanziert zu werden. In seinen Bildern liegt eine Schönheit und Wahrheit, die für Fotografen reserviert ist, denen es auf die eine oder andere Weise gelingt, die Linse der Kamera zu „durch-brechen". — JAB
Jacob Holdt wurde 1947 in Kopenhagen, Dänemark, geboren. Er lebt und arbeitet in Kopenhagen, Dänemark.

Jacob Holdt moved from Denmark to the USA in the early 1970s and came to spend several years there as a vagrant relying on the kindness of strangers for food and shelter. Holdt's snapshots of couples and images of people praying are part of a vast

photographic documentation of the extreme poverty and injustice he witnessed in American society, *American Pictures* (1970–1975). The couples embracing, exchanging looks of tenderness and loving caresses are in stark contrast to the often gritty and horrific scenes of discrimination Holdt has elsewhere portrayed. Through a philosophy of complete affirmation, that is of trying to accept everything that was offered him, Holdt often put himself in danger, partaking in the pain and poverty that would have otherwise stayed safely on the other side of the lens. Through this empathy the pictures, though spectacular in their intimacy never become spectacles neither do they lapse into the exoticizing or speculative. Freed from a moralizing gaze, Holdt portrays these scenes and people without becoming intrusive or aesthetically distanced. His images hold a beauty and truth reserved for photographers who, in one way or another, manage to 'break through' the camera's lens. — JAB
Jacob Holdt was born in 1947 in Copenhagen, Denmark. He lives and works in Copenhagen, Denmark

www.american-pictures.com

Rinko Kawauchi

Rinko Kawauchi erkundet in ihren Arbeiten Familienepisoden, zwischenmenschliche Beziehungen, die Natur und den Kreislauf des Lebens. Ihre Arbeit ist von einer außergewöhnlichen Intimität und einer ganz besonderen Feinheit geprägt, die ihr durch einfühlsame Kompositionen, ein besonderes Verständnis von Oberflächenstrukturen und Detailansichten gelingt, die in weichen Pastellfarben gehalten sind. Indem sie zarte, vergängliche Bilder ihrer eigenen Familie ebenso wie von Pflanzen, Blüten, Tieren und Landschaften einfängt, spricht ihre Arbeit von Leben und Tod, der Jugend und dem Altern sowie der Vergänglichkeit der Zeit. *Aila* (2004; abgeleitet vom Türkischen *aile*, „Familie"), präsentiert in „Lebenskreisläufe", ist eine Bilderreihe, die das Leben in all seinen Abschnitten zeigt. Die vorwiegend in der Natur aufgenommenen Fotografien zelebrieren deren faszinierende Vielfalt und Schönheit in schlichten, unaufdringlichen und doch zutiefst einfühlsamen und lyrischen Bildern, die uns dennoch stets an die Endlichkeit alles Lebendigen erinnern. Von einem Margeritenfeld vor tiefblauem Himmel oder der Großaufnahme eines Schmetterlingsflügels bis zur Geburt eines Fohlens oder einer Reihe geschlachteter Hühner mit über dem Hackklotz hängenden Köpfen – Kawauchis Kamera hält das Leben in all seiner atemberaubenden Vielfalt fest und betont dabei die Wunder der Natur ebenso wie ihre unvermeidbaren Tragödien. Kawauchis Arbeit übermittelt eine Sicht auf die Welt, in der Schönheit ein Gegenmittel für die Gewissheit von Verfall und Sterblichkeit liefert. Ihre Diaprojektion *Cui Cui* (2005) in „Das alltägliche Leben", an der sie 13 Jahre arbeitete, besteht aus einer ganzen Reihe solcher Fotografien. Diese Präsentation bietet einen intimen Einblick in Kawauchis eigene Familie und deren tägliche Rituale: von Familientreffen und einer Hochzeit über den Tod des Großvaters sowie einer Geburt bis hin zu Gartenarbeit oder dem Auftragen von Speisen auf einen Esstisch und zwischendrin immer wieder atemberaubende Blütenbilder und faszinierende Details wie Blattadern in Großaufnahme. Kawauchi lenkt die Aufmerksamkeit des Betrachters auf die Verletzlichkeit und Vergänglichkeit unseres Lebens und der Natur. Und sie zollt der rings um uns verborgenen Schönheit Tribut, ebenso wie den zwischenmenschlichen Beziehungen, die uns am meisten bedeuten. — KG
Rinko Kawauchi wurde 1972 in Shiga, Japan, geboren. Sie lebt und arbeitet in Tokio, Japan.

Rinko Kawauchi's work explores family episodes, human relations, nature and the cycle of life. Her work is characterised by an extraordinary intimacy and delicacy, achieved through sensitive compositions, careful attention to texture and detail rendered in soft pastel colours. Capturing fragile, transient images of her own family members as well as of plants, flowers, animals and landscapes, her work speaks of life, death, youth, aging and the passing of time. *Aila* (2004) (from the Turkish word *aile* meaning 'family') presented in 'Life Cycles' is a photographic series that depicts life in all its stages. Consisting primarily of images of nature, *Aila* celebrates its fascinating diversity and beauty in understated, profoundly sensitive and lyrical images that nevertheless constantly remind us of the finite nature of all living things. From a field of daisies against a clear blue sky or a close-up of the wings of a butterfly, to the birth of a colt or a row of slaughtered chickens with their heads hanging over the chopping block, Kawauchi's camera captures life in all its breathtaking diversity, highlighting the miracles of nature and its inevitable tragedies. Her work conveys a view of the

world in which beauty provides an antidote to the certainties of entropy and mortality. Her slide projection *Cui Cui* (2005) in 'The Practise of Everyday Life', which took 13 years to complete, is composed of a series of photographs. The work provides an intimate insight into Kawauchi's own family and their daily rituals: from family gatherings, a wedding, the death of a grandfather, and a new birth, to the practice of gardening or the laying of a table with food, while at the same time being interspersed with breathtaking images of flowers in bloom or ravishing details such as a close-up of the veins of a leaf. Kawauchi draws the viewer's attention to the fragility and ephemeral nature of our lives and the natural world, and pays tribute to the beauty that lies hidden all around us and the human relationships that matter to us most. – KG
Rinko Kawauchi was born in 1972 in Shiga, Japan. She lives and works in Tokyo, Japan

www.priskapasquer.de

Panos Kokkinias S. / p. 201

Heta Kuchka

Wie nah kann man dem Tod kommen? Die phänomenologisch dokumentarische Perspektive der Videoarbeit Heta Kuchkas sucht ihn zwischen dem konkreten Mobiliar von Sarg und Leichenwagen als reales Ereignis. Die finnische Künstlerin begleitet 2 Mitarbeiter eines Bestattungsunternehmens bei ihren täglichen Aufgaben. Gefasst erzählen die beiden von ihren Begegnungen mit dem Tod und stellen dabei in routinierter Betrachtung Fragen nach der Art von sozialen Bindungen in Großstädten und nach unserem Umgang mit dem Lebensende. Trotz dieses narrativen Charakters der Arbeit erzählt *Tuomo & Paavo* (2008) keine Geschichte. Das Video ist vielmehr eine gedankliche Betrachtung, eine Assoziationskette vor der Folie des Ortes, an dem man dem Tod nah zu sein scheint, wobei er tatsächlich niemals wirklich zu sehen ist. Heta Kuchkas Auseinandersetzung mit dem Tod, wie auch andere ihrer autobiografisch motivierten Werke sind intensive, persönliche Recherchen, in denen die Künstlerin mit dokumentarischer Neugierde den Schnittstellen in den Kreisläufen des Lebens nachstellt. Dabei involviert sie sich oft monatelang in das Geschehen, verlässt Städte und bereist Länder, die Aufschluss über ihr Leben geben könnten. Ihre Befragungen dokumentieren den Versuch einer Selbstverortung, befragen das Subjekt und seine Verankerung in sozialen Zusammenhängen. – HH
Heta Kuchka wurde 1974 in Helsinki, Finnland, geboren. Sie lebt und arbeitet in Helsinki, Finnland.

How close can we come to death without actually dying? In her documentary-style video works, Heta Kuchka adopts a phenomenological perspective and seeks an answer amidst the concrete accoutrements of funeral rites: the coffin and hearse. In *Tuomo & Paavo* (2008) the Finnish artist accompanied two funeral home workers as they carried out their daily work. Calmly, the two describe their encounters with death and muse about the present-day quality of social ties in our big cities and how we deal with mortality. Despite the narrative character of the work, it does not tell a story. The video is instead a contemplative scrutiny, a chain of associations against the foil of a place where we seem to be so close to death and yet where it can never actually be seen. Kuchka's exploration of the theme of death, like her other autobiographically motivated works, is based on intensive personal research in which the artist stalks the crossroads of life cycles with documentary curiosity. In the process, she often becomes deeply involved with her subjects for months at a time, leaving cities and journeying through countries that might provide clues to her own life.
Her investigations document an attempt to localize her own existence, inquiring into the status of the subject and his or her anchoring in social contexts. – HH.
Heta Kuchka was born in 1974 in Helsinki, Finland. She lives and works in Helsinki, Finland

www.hetakuchka.org

Ryan McGinley

Ryan McGinleys fotografisches Lustspiel kokettiert mit der Anziehungskraft unschuldig anmutender Freizügigkeit. Seine häufig überbelichteten oder in warmen Farben strahlenden Sequenzen erinnern an zufällige Schnappschüsse und lassen den Betrachter an intimen Momenten teilhaben: *Hanna (Blonde Meadow)* (2009) deren Silhouette sich hinter den hohen Grashalmen einer Sommerwiese verbirgt; *Marlon and Rebecca* (2007–2008) in fallengelassener Selbstversunkenheit. *Jakes (Jakes Falling Cut Chest)* (2009) zerkratzte Brust, bei deren Anblick das filigran utopische Idealbild bricht. Handelt

es sich um harmlose Spuren vom Spiel in der Natur oder um äußere Zeichen innerer Verletzungen? McGinley inszeniert adoleszente, meist androgyne nackte Körper vor idealer Naturkulisse: „schwebend", springend, flüchtig. Eine Faszination für die Fotografie von Nan Goldin scheint erkennbar , die in den 1980er-Jahren in eindringlichen Porträts ihr Zusammenleben und -lieben innerhalb ihres Freundeskreises dokumentierte und eine Welt zwischen Glamour und Selbstzerstörung auffächerte. McGinley jedoch konstruiert Situationen, in denen er ein rein unbeschwertes Lebensgefühl finden und festhalten kann. Quer durch Amerikas weite Landschaft reist er mit Freunden, überlässt sich und seine Protagonisten einem fotografischen Abenteuer, das sich aus sich selbst heraus entwickelt. McGinley erschafft zeitlose Traumbilder von harmloser Leichtigkeit, die unsere stets gehegte Sehnsucht nach Momentverlorenheit bedienen, das Idol Jugend feiern und die Euphorie des absoluten Freiheitsgefühls auf den Betrachter überspringen lassen. – CE
Ryan McGinley wurde 1977 in Ramsay, New Jersey, USA, geboren. Er lebt und arbeitet in New York, USA

Ryan McGinley's work revolves around the theme of youth, flirting with the appeal of innocent-looking permissiveness. Often overexposed or rendered in warm, radiant tones, his sequences of photos are reminiscent of candid snapshots, allowing the viewer to share in intimate moments: a glimpse of *Hanna (Blonde Meadow)* (2009), whose silhouette plays hide-and-seek behind the tall grasses of a summery meadow, and of *Marlon and Rebecca* (2007-08) who stand in self-absorbed rapture. McGinley stages scenes using models with adolescent, usually androgynous and naked bodies that appear to float or fall in front of idyllic natural backdrops. This filigree world is ruptured when we notice *Jake's Falling Cut Chest* (2009). Are his wounds harmless traces of playing outdoors in nature, or external signs of an inner wound? Even though there is an evident fascination here with the photographs of Nan Goldin, who documented in her vivid 1980s portraits her life and loves amidst a circle of friends caught between glamour and self-destruction, McGinley focuses instead on dramatizing carefree scenes. He sets off across America's vast countryside, abandoning himself and his protagonists to a photographic adventure that develops all on its own. McGinley creates timeless images of light-hearted reverie that cater to our constant yearning to lose ourselves in the moment. His photographs celebrate our idolization of youth and sweep us up in the feeling of freedom invoked by a choreographed euphoria. – CE
Ryan McGinley was born in 1977 in Ramsay, New Jersey, USA. He lives and works in New York, USA

www.ryanmcginley.com

Barbara Metselaar Berthold

Barbara Metselaar Bertholds horizontales Fotoraster, ein Tableau mit dem Titel *The Tall Tale of Freewill* (2011), zeigt eine Mischung neuer und älterer Bilder von Ost-Berlin zu DDR-Zeiten und heute. Das Tableau umfasst Porträts, Party-Schnappschüsse und urbane Landschaften der 1970er-Jahre (aus der Reihe *Still Dreaming*), 80er-Jahre (*Being fed up*), 90er-Jahre (*Escaping in mind*) und heute (*make-or-brake* und *keep on walking*). Die Fotos in den ersten 3 Reihen stammen aus den 1980er-Jahren, als die Berliner Mauer noch stand; die der letzten beiden Reihen hingegen entstanden nach dem Mauerfall. In den einzelnen Spalten sieht man jeweils dieselben Personen und dieselbe Umgebung, durch Zeitsprünge voneinander getrennt. Diese Zeitsprünge lassen die Positionen auf beiden Seiten, die ja eher durch Zeit als durch geografische Gegebenheiten getrennt sind, entfremdet wirken. Auf jene, die erst nach der Wiedervereinigung zur Welt kamen und auch auf alle, die nie auf direkte Weise von der Mauer betroffen waren, mag das wie eine absurde Fabel wirken, modifiziert durch die Secondhand-Erzählungen der Belletristik und den nüchternen Rationalisierungen der Historisierung. Die Zeit hat die jungen Berliner hinter der Mauer verändert, ebenso wie sie die Stadt verändert hat, die einst durch sie geteilt war. Seit dem Abriss der Mauer entsteht eine neue Landschaft mit ihren eigenen Absurditäten und Schranken. Eine Landschaft der Gentrifizierung, der sozialen Trennung und der Kommerzialisierung. Die Gesellschaft ist zwar einem ständigen Wandel unterworfen, aber Barbara Metselaar Bertholds Fotografien sind die lebenden Beweise für eine Beständigkeit innerhalb dieses fließenden Wandels. Der Kampf um eine alltägliche Existenz scheint eine Strategie zu sein, um Prinzipien der Trennung hinter sich zu lassen. – JAB

Barbara Metselaar Berthold wurde 1951 in Pleißa, Deutschland, geboren. Sie lebt und arbeitet in Berlin, Deutschland.

Barbara Metselaar Berthold's horizontal grid of photographs, a tableau, entitled *The Tall Tale of Freewill* (2011), which features a mix of new and existing images of East Berlin during DDR times and today. The tableau includes portraits, snapshots from parties and urban landscapes in the 1970s (from the series *Still Dreaming*), 80s (*Being fed up*), 90s (*Escaping in mind*) and today (*make-or-break* and *keep on walking*). The photographs in the first three rows are from the 1980s, when the Berlin Wall was still standing; the last two rows were shot after its fall. In the individual columns, we observe the same persons and environments, set apart by leaps in time. These leaps make the positions on either side seem estranged, separated as they are by time rather than geography. For those born after the unification and all those never directly affected by the Wall, it might seem an absurd fable, transformed through the second-hand recounts of popular fiction and the sober rationalizations of historicization. Time has transformed the young Berliners behind the Wall, just as it transformed the city it once divided. Since it was dismantled, a new landscape has been drawn with absurdities and barriers of its own. It is a landscape of gentrification, segregation and commercialization. Although society transmutes and is transmuted, Barbara Metselaar Berthold's photographs are the living documents of a constant state within this flux. The struggle for an everyday existence seems to be a strategy for transcending principles of separation. — JAB
Barbara Metselaar Berthold was born in 1951 in Pleißa, Germany. She lives and works in Berlin, Germany

Boris Mikhailov

Der ukrainische Fotograf Boris Mikhailov eröffnet einen Blick in die Krankenakte seines Landes: Mit schonungslosem Blick porträtiert er Obdachlose vor den verdreckten Kulissen des kleinstädtischen Milieus seiner Heimatstadt Charkiw als Mitträger der großen politischen Umstellungen der ehemaligen Sowjetunion. Mit dem Zusammenbruch der UdSSR begann das Wirtschafts- und Gesellschaftssystem des Landes zu kippen. Was Mikhailov auf den Fotos der Serie *Case History* (1997–1999) zeigt, sind die in Schieflage geratenen Randfiguren der post-kommunistischen Gesellschaft, für die es keinerlei Halten mehr gibt. Insgesamt umfasst das Projekt rund 500 Fotografien, die zwischen 1997–1999 entstanden sind. Um den Menschen seiner Bilder so nahe zu kommen, hat Mikhailov einige Zeit mit ihnen verbracht. Er hat sich in das Leben und die Bedingungen der Straße eingefunden und Junge und Alte, Kinder und Jugendliche in ihrem Alltag festgehalten.
Boris Mikhailov's fotografische Position in der Subkategorie „Lebenskreisläufe" steht in der Tradition sozialdokumentarischer Fotografie, auch wenn der Fotograf seine Motive bisweilen bewusst in Szene setzt. Die entblößten und randalierten Körper wurden ihm mitunter gegen ein kleines Honorar gezeigt. Diese Inszenierung konfrontiert den Betrachter mit einer Nacktheit in mehrfachen Sinne: Die entblößte Körperlichkeit ist ein Symbol für die Hilflosigkeit gegenüber einem im Wandel begriffenen System, es ist die nackte Wirklichkeit vor dem Hintergrund einer radikalen Abwesenheit politischer, sozialer und persönlicher Perspektiven. — HH
Boris Mikhailov wurde 1938 in Charkiw, ehemalige Sowjetunion, geboren. Er lebt in Kharkov, Ukraine und Berlin, Deutschland.

Ukrainian photographer Boris Mikhailov allows us to see the hidden or overt desuetude that has beset his country. With an unsparing gaze he portrays homeless people against the dirty backdrop of the small-town milieu in his hometown of Kharkov as casualties of the great wave of political change that swept over the former Soviet Union in the 1990s. With the collapse of the USSR, the economic and social system in the Ukraine began to crumble. In his photographic series *Case History* (1997–1999) Mikhailov captures the fringe figures of post-Communist society, people whose lives were thrown off track and who have never regained their equilibrium. The project encompasses some 500 photographs. Mikhailov spent considerable time with his subjects in order to get this close to them. He got wrapped up in life on the streets, snapping photographs of young and old, children and youth as they went about their daily routines.
Mikhailov's photographic position in the subcategory of 'Life Cycles' stands in the tradition of social documentary photography, even if he sometimes stages his images. The sitters in some cases revealed their bared and ravaged bodies to him for a small fee. The dramatization of the fates in these pictures

confronts the viewer with nakedness in multiple respects: the naked body as a symbol of the helplessness of its owner in the face of a system in flux, and also representing naked reality in the radical absence of political, social or personal prospects. — HH
Boris Mikhailov was born in 1938 in Kharkov, Ukraine. He lives and works in Kharkov, Ukraine and Berlin, Germany

www.suzanne-tarasieve.com

Torbjørn Rødland

In Torbjørn Rødlands Fotografien treten immer wieder Sinnbilder des Todes auf. Die Flammen um die schwarz werdenden Schädel während der Einäscherung, der vollkommene Frieden, den die Urne ausstrahlt, die stumm duldende, archaisch anmutende Kiefer, die von Flechten erdrückt wird – sie alle legen eine bestimmte Lesart nahe. Zwischen Form und Inhalt scheint es einen engen Zusammenhang zu geben, ähnlich dem zwischen populärer und kommerzieller Fotografie. Doch hinter dem, was vielleicht als Plattitüde mit bitter-süßem Nachgeschmack aufgefasst werden könnte, verbirgt sich etwas von Belang. Unbeeindruckt von provozierenden Banalitäten spürt Rødland der irrationalen Sehnsucht nach, die uns selbst in gut beleuchteten Landschaften heimsucht. Sein Blick richtet sich auf die Möglichkeiten, die ein mythischer Inhalt bietet, wo immer er zu finden ist. Im Gegensatz zu Fotografien, die eine kommerzielle oder auch eine andere Botschaft vermitteln sollen, bezeichnet Rødland seine Arbeiten als im Freudschen Sinne pervers: zwischen Freude und Umsetzung gibt es keinerlei Zusammenhang. Da viele Betrachter auf die Sprache der Konsumwelt und der Nützlichkeit konditioniert sind, könnte das Vokabular seines visuellen Diskurses als fremdartig empfunden werden. Was auf den ersten Blick als Verstoß gegen dieses Prinzip erscheinen könnte, ist vielleicht eine Notwendigkeit, um sowohl die flüchtigen als auch die vergänglichen Aspekte der Welt zu erkennen. — JAB
Torbjørn Rødland wurde 1970 in Stavanger, Norwegen, geboren. Er lebt und arbeitet in Los Angeles, USA.

In Torbjørn Rødland's photographs, symbols of death are reiterated in his series *Burning Skull* (2008–2010) where we can see the flames around blackening skulls in the process of being cremated, suggesting indexical readings. There seems to be an intimate closeness between form and content, resembling that of popular and commercial photography. But under what might be understood as platitudes and their sickly sweet aftertaste, something of importance is hiding. Undaunted by provoking banalities, Rødland explores the irrational longing that haunts us even within well-lit landscapes. His eye is attracted to the possibilities of mythical content, wherever it might be found. In contrast to photographs that are utilized to convey a message, commercially or otherwise, Rødland's photographs are self-admittedly perverse in the Freudian sense: there is no correlation between pleasure and production. Conditioned as many viewers are to the language of products and utility, the vocabulary of his visual discourse might seem alien. What might at first be transgressive of this principle is perhaps a necessity for seeing both the ephemeral and the transitory aspects of the world. — JAB
Torbjørn Rødland was born in 1970 in Stavanger, Norway. He lives and works in Los Angeles, USA

www.rodland.net

Jeremy Shaw S. / p. 220

Fiona Tan

Die international renommierte Künstlerin Fiona Tan arbeitet mit den Medien Film und Fotografie, indem sie sowohl ihre eigenen Bilder erschafft, als auch gefundenes Material neu zusammensetzt. In *Vox Populi, Tokyo* (2007) collagiert Fiona Tan Fotografien aus persönlichen und privaten Familienalben zu einem großformatigen Wandtableau: Aufnahmen des alltäglichen Lebens: von Kindern, Freunden, der Familie; Gruppenporträts von Arbeitskollegen, entstanden bei besonderen Anlässen oder private Reise- und Ferienerinnerungen. Die aus 305 Einzelbildern bestehende fotografische Installation ist Teil einer Serie, die sie in verschiedenen Ländern und Orten dieser Welt wie Norwegen (2004), Sydney (2006) oder der Schweiz (2010) realisiert hat. Mit *Vox Populi, Tokyo* (2007) zeigt sie eine facettenreiche Collage, die den Fluss des Lebens zu archivieren sucht und die in ihrer Zusammenschau ein Porträt der japanischen Gesellschaft formt. In die Kategorien „Portraits", „Home" und „Nature" gruppiert, werden familiäre Muster, kulturelle Rollen und Codes, die die individuelle Existenz im Kontext ihrer

Umwelt verorten, erkennbar. Das verbindende Element der verschiedenen Werkserien ist eine kontinuierliche Auseinandersetzung mit dem Thema Identität und die Befragung individueller und gesellschaftlicher Konditionierung. — CE
Fiona Tan wurde 1966 in Indonesien geboren. Sie lebt und arbeitet in Amsterdam, Niederlanden.

Internationally acclaimed artist Fiona Tan works in the media of film and photography, creating her own imagery or redeploying found material. In *Vox Populi, Tokyo* (2007), Tan has created a large-format wall tableau consisting of images collected from personal and private family photo albums that features pictures of everyday life – children, friends and family, colleagues at work, special occasions, private travel and holidays. The photographic installation, which is made up of 305 individual images, is part of a series that she has made in different cities and countries including Norway (2004), Sydney (2006) and, more recently, Switzerland (2010). In *Vox Populi, Tokyo* (2007), she presents a diverse collage of images that attempt to archive the flow of life and time spread out before us, forming, when taken together, a portrait of Japanese society. Grouped into the categories 'Portraits', 'Home' and 'Nature', the photographs manifest familiar patterns: cultural roles and codes that localize each individual existence within the context of his or her surroundings. Linking the works is a continuous exploration of the theme of identity, along with an inquiry into individual and social conditioning. — CE
Fiona Tan was born in 1966 in Indonesia. She lives and works in Amsterdam, the Netherlands

www.fionatan.nl
www.frithstreetgallery.com

The Practice of Everyday Life S. / p. 114

Sofia Burchardi & Plamen Bontchev

Wir nähern uns gerade einem Generationenwandel: Kinder werden in eine Welt hineingeboren, in der Virtuelles und Reales scheinbar ineinander übergehen. Diejenigen von uns, die die Welt, so wie sie vorher war, kannten, sind über diese drohende Verschmelzung von Online- und Offline-Existenzen vielleicht irritiert. In *Alone Together* (2011) drücken Sofia Burchardi und Plamen Bontchev die widersprüchlichen Erwartungen an ein sich neu formulierendes Zeitalter aus, in dem Grenzen verschwimmen und sich auflösen. Anhand einer Reihe von Interviews mit Personen, die sich dafür im Internet auf eine Anzeige gemeldet hatten, haben die Künstler die Gewohnheiten im Umgang mit Computer und Internet untersucht. Sie sind insbesondere der Frage nachgegangen, inwiefern die Aussicht, beständig „verkabelt" zu sein, Identitäts- und Bewusstseinsfindungen beeinflusst. Die Befragten scheinen gespalten zu sein: Sie projizieren sich in eine virtuelle Welt, von der ihre Körper losgelöst sind und ausgeschlossen bleiben. Ihre verschiedenen leibhaftigen Bilder sind zu einem einzigen Linsenrasterbild verschmolzen. Mit dieser Technik lassen sich sogenannte Wackelbilder herstellen, die je nach Blickwinkel des Betrachters ein anderes Bild ergeben. Will der Betrachter individuelle Gesichtszüge ausmachen, muss er eine bestimmte Position einnehmen und bewegungslos in ihr verharren – andernfalls geht das Bild nahtlos von einem Gesicht in ein anderes über. In diesem Gruppenporträt blenden sich die Interviewten in zahllosen Variationen ein und aus. Wir nehmen sie vielleicht so wahr, wie wir uns online wahrnehmen – scheinbar unserer leiblichen Existenz entbunden und dadurch frei, Verhaltensweisen und Identitäten ohne Konsequenzen zu wechseln. — JAB
Plamen Bontchev wurde 1980 in Burgas, Bulgarien, geboren. Er lebt und arbeitet in Berlin, Deutschland.
Sofia Burchardi wurde 1981 in Kopenhagen, Dänemark, geboren. Sie lebt und arbeitet in Berlin, Deutschland.

We are approaching a generational shift in which children now are born into a world where the virtual and the actual seem to merge. Those of us who knew the world that preceded this might find ourselves bewildered by this impending conflation of online and offline existence. In *Alone Together* (2011) Sofia Burchardi and Plamen Bontchev express the conflicting expectations of an emerging age in which borders blur and dissolve. Through a series of interviews conducted with people they got into contact with through an internet ad, they have researched attitudes on computer and internet usage, how the prospect of being constantly 'wired' affects conceptions of identity and consciousness. The interviewees appear split: they project themselves out into a virtual world from which their bodies remain absent and detached. Their diverse corporal images are merged together in a single lenticular photograph. This technique makes images appear moving or transforming, changing with the vantage-point of the viewer. In order to ascertain any individual features the observer needs to position himself in an exact location and stay completely still, as the image otherwise will shift seamlessly from one face to another. In this group portrait, the interviewees blend in and out of innumerable possibilities. We find them as we may find ourselves online, seemingly disengaged from our corporal existence and thus free to change attitudes and identities without consequence. — JAB
Plamen Bontchev was born in 1980 in Burgas, Bulgaria. He lives and works in Berlin, Germany.
Sofia Burchardi was born in 1981 in Copenhagen, Denmark. She lives and works in Berlin, Germany

Marie-José Burki

Die Zeit steht still. Man hört klassische Musik. Nach einem reichhaltigen, opulenten Mahl, nach all dem Essen und Trinken, wurde viel geredet (aber vielleicht war das gar nicht so viel). Die Konversation versiegt, die Menschen halten inne,

die Luft stagniert – abgesehen vom aufsteigenden Rauch einer Zigarette. Dies ist die Atmosphäre in Marie José Burkis Film *De nos jours (dedans)* von 2004, der ein Stillleben aus Essen und Getränken auf einer Tafel inmitten einer luxuriösen Umgebung in den Blickpunkt rückt: übrig gebliebene Koteletts, gebratenes Huhn, Fisch mit Gräten, gebackene Zwiebeln, leere Weinflaschen, Zigarettenschachteln und einige gut situierte Gäste mittleren Alters. Ihre Haltung erweckt den Anschein, als ob sie in ihrer Handlung angehalten worden wären, und das, obwohl der Film selbst weiterläuft. Die Szenerie ist in Naheinstellung gedreht, die Kamera umkreist den Tisch und die Gesichter – eines ist immer noch hinter einer venezianischen Maske verborgen – und gibt dem Betrachter einen fragmentierten, aber sehr persönlichen Eindruck von der schläfrigen Stimmung der ausklingenden Party. Formal gesehen, bewegt sich der Film mit seiner langsamen Kameraführung, seinen Stillleben, Nahaufnahmen und den eingefrorenen Bewegungen der Gäste zwischen Fotografie und bewegten Bildern. Die Spannung zwischen den filmischen und fotografischen Einstellungen, zwischen dem Zustand des Wünschens und dem der Befriedigung, öffnet Raum und Zeit für ein Nachsinnen über die Dinnerparty als eine hedonistische Praxis im Alltagsleben der westlichen Mittel- und Oberschicht. — SHO
Marie José Burki wurde 1961 in Biel, Schweiz, geboren. Sie lebt und arbeitet in Brüssel, Belgien.

Time stands still. Classical music is playing. In the after hour of a rich and luxurious dinner, after eating and drinking, much has been said (and perhaps that was not even a lot). The conversation, the people and the air are motionless – apart from the fresh smoke drifting from an after-dinner cigarette. This is the atmosphere of Marie José Burki's film *De nos jours (dedans)* (2004), which zooms in on a still life of food and drink on a dinner table in an affluent setting: leftover ribs, roast chicken, fish with exposed bones, baked onions, empty wine bottles, cigarette boxes and a set of middle class, middle-aged guests. They pose as if their act has stopped, even as the film itself continues. The setting is filmed in close-up, the camera circulating the table and the faces – one still wearing a Venetian masque – giving the viewer a fragmented, yet intimate impression of the dormant mood of the party leftovers. Formally, this film locates itself between still and moving images, with its slow camera movement, still lifes, close-ups, and the frozen poses of the dinner guests. The tension between the filmic and photographic tenses, between the states of desire and satisfaction, opens a space and time for meditation on the dinner party as a hedonist practice of everyday life in western middle- and upper-class society. — SHO
Marie José Burki was born in 1961 in Biel, Switzerland. She lives and works in Brussels, Belgium

www.mjburki.be

Peter Funch S. / p. 217

Alexandros Georgiou

Alexandros Georgious Arbeiten drehen sich um ein ernsthaftes Bemühen, die eigene Persönlichkeit und Identität zu artikulieren, indem er wie ein Forscher des 21. Jahrhunderts die Welt erkundet und dabei seine persönlichen Erfahrungen akribisch genau aufzeichnet. Beinahe alles, auf das er beim Reisen stößt, kann Gegenstand seines Interesses sein: von der landschaftlichen Panoramasicht bis zum kleinsten Detail direkt vor seinen Augen. Für die Serie *Varanasi* (2009), die Teil der Serie *Without my Own Vehicle* ist, reiste Georgiou von Athen über die Türkei, den Iran und Pakistan bis nach Varanasi (auch als Benares bekannt) am Westufer des Ganges im indischen Bundesstaat Uttar Pradesh – ausschließlich mit öffentlichen Verkehrsmitteln. Er verbrachte das gesamte Jahr 2009 in Varanasi und machte seinen Aufenthalt dort zum Teil seines umfangreichen Forschungsprojektes über verschiedene Aspekte des Alltags und die individuellen täglichen Überlebensstrategien. Seine Reiseerfahrungen dokumentierte er mithilfe einfacher visueller Materialien: Fotografien einer billigen Digitalkamera, handgezeichneten und -kolorierten Fotokopien dieser Fotografien, Notizen und selbst gemachten Ansichtskarten. Diese Postkarten mit Fotografien von Varanasi schickte er Sammlern und Freunden – Menschen, die ihn während seiner Reisen unterstützten. Seine Texte auf der Rückseite geben Einblick in seine Gedankenwelt, vermitteln aber auch gleichzeitig ein Bild der einfachen und bescheidenen Alltagswirklichkeit der Menschen, denen er begegnet ist, und lassen vermuten, dass es eine Menge von ihnen zu lernen gibt. — KG
Alexandros Georgiou wurde 1972 in Athen, Griechenland, geboren. Er lebt und arbeitet in Athen, Griechenland.

Alexandros Georgiou's works revolve around a sincere endeavour to articulate his own personality and identity by meticulously recording his private experiences as he scours the world like a twenty-first century explorer. His subject matter can be almost anything he stumbles on while travelling: from broad landscape views to the tiniest details in front of his eyes. For the series *Varanasi* (2009) (part of the series *Without my Own Vehicle*), he travelled from Athens through Turkey, Iran and Pakistan to Varanasi (also known as Benares), on the west bank of the River Ganges in Uttar Pradesh, India, using public transportation only. He spent the entire year of 2009 in Varanasi as part of his general research project into diverse aspects of quotidian practices and daily personal survival strategies. He recorded his travel experiences in the form of modest visual material: photographs made with a cheap digital camera, hand-drawn and hand-coloured photocopies of these, notes, and hand-made picture postcards. He sent these postcards, which include photographs of Varanasi, to collectors and friends – people who supported him during his travels. His texts, written on their backside, give insight into his thoughts, as well as the modest or humble daily realities and practices of the peoples he encounters, and infers there is a lot to be learnt from them. — KG
Alexandros Georgiou was born in 1972 in Athens, Greece. He lives and works in Athens, Greece

www.koroneougallery.com

Francesco Giusti

Die in der Serie *Sapologie* (2009) porträtierten Herren gehören einer subkulturellen Bewegung in der Republik Kongo an: Als Sapeurs eifern sie bis zur äußersten Perfektion dem Archetypus des europäischen Dandys nach. Ihre Bezeichnung leitet sich vom Akronym von „Société des Ambianceurs et des Personnes Élégantes" (Gesellschaft für Unterhalter und elegante Menschen) ab sowie vom französischen Verb „se saper" (sich anziehen). Einerseits könnte man dieses Phänomen als Ausdruck einer offenbar nicht aufzuhaltenden Ausweitung der westlichen Konsumkultur verstehen. Andererseits legen die farbenprächtigen Fotografien Francesco Giustis eine andere Lesart nahe: Die extravaganten Posen und Selbststilisierungen der Sapeurs in den staubigen Straßen Brazzavilles stehen in starkem Kontrast zu der allgegenwärtigen Armut. Tatsächlich sind die Sapeurs nicht so betucht, wie sie in ihren teuren französischen und italienischen Anzügen den Anschein erwecken. Vielmehr sind sie dazu gezwungen, Gelegenheitsarbeiten anzunehmen oder manchmal sogar ihre Anzüge zu verleihen, um über die Runden zu kommen. Auf der Straße eignen sie sich eine verlorengegangene aristokratische Haltung an: Sie verbreiten durch eine Großzügigkeit, die an Selbstinszenierung grenzt, und bewusst adaptierte Grazie und Eleganz einen kulturellen Wert jenseits des Alltäglichen – luxuriöse Schönheit. Mit dieser Dokumentation über die Sapeurs, die sich der Darstellung von Verschwendung hingeben, verdeutlicht Giusti, dass überschäumende Lebensfreude überall zu finden ist. — JAB
Francesco Giusti wurde 1969 in Lecco, Italien, geboren. Er lebt und arbeitet in Mailand, Italien.

The gentlemen portrayed in the series *Sapologie* (2009) are part of a Congolese subculture of *sapeurs*: men who seemingly emulate the archetype of European dandyism to uncanny perfection. Their name comes from the acronym Société des Ambianceurs et des Personnes Élegantes (Society for Atmosphere Setters and Elegant People) as well as the verb 'se saper' – to dress up. On one level, this phenomenon might be understood as a sign of the seemingly unstoppable expansion of western consumer culture. But the vibrant photographs of Francesco Giusti suggest another reading. The flamboyant posing and self-styling of the *sapeurs* on the dusty streets of Brazzaville is in stark contrast to the surrounding poverty. Indeed, the *sapeurs* aren't necessarily as well-to-do as they might appear (dressed as they are in expensive French and Italian fashions), but are rather men who are forced to make ends meet by taking odd jobs and sometimes even renting out their suits. On the streets, they adopt a lost aristocratic practice: spreading surplus value in culture – luxurious beauty – through a generosity bordering on self-spectacle, as well as a conscious adoption of grace and elegance. Through his documentation of the *sapeurs*' dignified performance of excess, Giusti reveals that exuberance can be found anywhere. — JAB
Francesco Giusti was born in 1969 in Lecco, Italy. He lives and works in Milan, Italy

www.francescogiusti.com

Cao Guimarães

Cao Guimarães möchte lieber die in einfachen und banalen Dingen verborgene Poesie sichtbar machen, statt Objekte nur zu dokumentieren oder zu kommentieren. Er besitzt einen Blick für das Unerwartete, das in eigentümlichen Handlungen von Menschen liegt. Guimarães' Fotoserie *Gambiarras* (seit 2001 fortlaufend) ist überwiegend von der Spontaneität, Kreativität, Lebendigkeit und dem situativen Einfallsreichtum im Alltagsleben der Brasilianer inspiriert. Seine Fotografien erkunden, wie Menschen durch Individualisieren und Improvisieren ihre alltägliche Umgebung zu „ihrer eigenen" machen, indem sie die Dinge um sie herum und die sie ständig im Gebrauch haben, verändern, modifizieren und verbessern. *Gambiarras* zeigt diese Art der Anpassung sehr anschaulich: „gambiarra" ist ein populärer brasilianischer Ausdruck und bedeutet so viel wie „zum Funktionieren bringen" oder „kaputte Gegenstände improvisierend zu reparieren" oder auch „für normale Alltagsprobleme ungewöhnliche Lösungen zu finden". Guimarães hält „gambiarra" für Philosophie, Religion und Kunst in einem und für eine Möglichkeit „einen kleinen, dünnen Ast zu entdecken, wenn man gerade in den Abgrund zu fallen droht". Die Serie nahm 2001 als work in progress ihren Anfang und besteht nun aus einem Archiv mit über 100 Fotografien. Sie stellen einen Tribut an die menschliche Kreativität dar, mit den unterschiedlichsten Problemen zurechtzukommen: Der abgerissene Träger eines BHs wird mit einer Büroklammer befestigt, eine CD zum Lampenschirm umfunktioniert und das Gewicht eines Würfels hält eine Plattenspielernadel in der Rille. Neben einer Art anthropologischer Untersuchung der menschlichen Erfindungsgabe bei der Entwicklung von Überlebensstrategien für den Alltag ist *Gambiarras* auch eine Anerkennung simpler Erfindungen sowie des Humors angesichts schwieriger Umstände und fehlender Mittel. — KG
Cao Guimarães wurde 1965 in Belo Horizonte, Brasilien, geboren. Er lebt und arbeitet in Belo Horizonte, Brasilien.

Cao Guimarães is interested in uncovering the poetry hidden in modest or banal subject matter, rather than simply documenting or commenting on it. He has a keen eye for the unexpected in people's most idiosyncratic actions. Guimarães' photographic series *Gambiarras* (2001–ongoing) is primarily inspired by the spontaneity, creativity, *ad hoc* inventiveness and liveliness of everyday Brazilian life. His photographs investigate how people, through individualizing and improvising their quotidian world, 'make it their own' by altering, modifying or improving the things surrounding them in their daily routine. *Gambiarras* is a clear example of this way of working: *gambiarra* is a popular Brazilian expression meaning to 'make do', or fix broken utensils and objects in an improvised way, as well as finding unusual solutions for usual daily problems. In Guimarães' own words *gambiarra* is philosophy, religion and art alike, and a way of "finding the tiny little branch when you're falling into the abyss". The series started in 2001 as a work in progress, and now consists of an archive of more than 100 photographs that exists as a tribute to human creativity in

tackling multifarious problems: fixing the broken strap of a bra with a paperclip, using a CD as a lamp shade and the weight of a die to keep the needle of a gramophone in the groove. Apart from a kind of anthropological research into human inventiveness in devising survival strategies for daily life, *Gambiarras* is a tribute to modest invention and humour in the face of hardship and lack of means. — KG
Cao Guimarães was born in Belo Horizonte, Brazil, in 1965, where he lives and works.

www.xippas.com

Jacob Holdt S. / p. 224

Rinko Kawauchi S. / p. 225

Panos Kokkinias S. / p. 201

Tris Vonna-Michell

Tris Vonna-Michell ist ein Geschichtenerzähler und ein Performer, der auch mit fotografischem Material arbeitet. Wesentlicher Bestandteil seiner Arbeit ist die Gestaltung von Dia- und Soundinstallationen. Den Künstler zeichnet eine große Leidenschaft für das Medium Dia und die dazugehörigen Projektoren aus, ein taktiles Lowtech-Medium. Seine Kunstwerke nehmen die Form des gesprochenen Wortes an (live oder aufgezeichnet), begleitet von Diashows. In eindringlichem Rhythmus, inspiriert durch die Konkrete Poesie, spricht Vonna-Michell wie ein hypnotisierendes zeitgenössisches Orakel, greift dabei zurück auf die bei Stadtspaziergängen gesammelten Impressionen und setzt subjektive persönliche und allgemein bekannte Erzählungen neu zusammen. In seinen Berichten geht es um die urbane Geschichte von Städten wie Detroit und Berlin – um Orte, Ereignisse und ihre Entstehung –, nicht selten lässt er sich dabei leiten oder auch unterbrechen durch ein Abgleiten in seine eigenen Assoziationen und Erinnerungen an seine Kindheit im englischen Essex. Als Erweiterung zu seinen urbanen Betrachtungen hat Vonna-Michell ein neues Werk geschaffen, *endless tapes* (2011), mit Bildern, die der Künstler in Ludwigshafen, Mannheim und Heidelberg aufgenommen hat. Während seines Besuchs in der Region ließ sich Vonna-Michell faszinieren vom Mannheimer Straßennetz und dem Industriehafen, der Friesenheimer Insel und der Architektur in Ludwigshafen. Diese neue Dia-Installation zieht den Betrachter mit regionalen Geschichten in ihren Bann, präsentiert in einem abgewandelten Fluss aus Zeit, Raum und Materialität. — SHO
Tris Vonna-Michell wurde 1982 in Southend-on-Sea, England, geboren. Er lebt und arbeitet in London, England, und Stockholm, Schweden.

Tris Vonna-Michell is a storyteller and a performer who also works with photographic images. An integral part of his practice is the production of slide and sound installations. The artist has a great passion for the low-tech and tactile medium of slides and the projectors that go with it. His artworks take the form of spoken word performances (live or recorded) accompanied by slideshows. With an insistent rhythm inspired by concrete poetry, and drawing on impressions gathered on urban walks, Vonna-Michell speaks as a mesmerising contemporary oracle re-ordering subjective personal and public narratives. The stories he tells are of the urban history of places such as Detroit and Berlin – of places, events and their creation – often guided or interrupted by lapses into his own associations and childhood memories growing up in Essex, UK. Expanding his urban research, Vonna-Michell has created a new work *endless tapes* (2011), with images shot by the artist in Ludwigshafen, Mannheim and Heidelberg. Visiting the area, Vonna-Michell became fascinated by the street grid and the industrial harbour in Mannheim, Friesenheimer Island, and the architecture of Ludwigshafen. This new slide installation envelopes the viewer with local histories, presented in an altered flow of time, space and materiality. — SHO
Tris Vonna-Michell was born in 1982 in Southend-on-Sea, UK. He lives and works in London, UK, and Stockholm, Sweden

www.janmot.com
www.capitainpetzel.de

Paolo Woods S. / p. 207

Solo Presentations

ROGER BALLEN
Sammlung Prinzhorn, Heidelberg, S. / p. 136

Roger Ballens Ausgangspunkt für seine Arbeit ist soziologischer und anthropologischer Art und rückt die Entrechteten, Marginalisierten sowie das Abseitige in den Fokus. Ballen wurde durch seine eindringlichen Schwarz-Weiß-Fotografien von Menschen am Rande der weißen Gesellschaft Südafrikas bekannt. Seine Motive sind in düsteren, schäbigen häuslichen Umgebungen inszeniert und resultieren in kraftvollen, aufwühlenden und verstörenden Bildern, die über Voyeurismus hinausgehen und sich in den Bereich der Affekte vorwagen. Seine Serie *Outland* (1987–2000), deren Vollendung beinahe 20 Jahre in Anspruch nahm, umfasst einige der fesselndsten und bestechendsten Dokumente menschlichen Lebens im Südafrika des ausgehenden 20. Jahrhunderts. *Outland* zeigt das Leben der entlegenen und armen, weißen Bevölkerung auf dem Land (in den „dorps“ oder kleinen Dörfern), die mit dem Ende der Apartheit jegliche Privilegien verlor und viele von den Menschen in einer Art Schockstarre zurückließ. Es sind tief bewegende Bilder: Eingefroren zwischen dokumentarischer und konstruierter Darstellung, zwischen Theater und Wirklichkeit, machen sie die harte Realität der Menschen des weißen Südafrikas deutlich, von Außenseitern, die durch das soziale Netz gefallen sind. Die Bilder von *Shadow Chamber* (2001–2004) aus dem ersten Jahrzehnt dieses Jahrhunderts sind sogar noch aufwühlender. Sie zeigen entfremdete, psychisch gestörte Menschen in schmuddeligen Räumen, manchmal zusammen mit ihren Haustieren, die ebenso verhaltensgestört und verwirrt wirken wie ihre Besitzer. Diese

Fotografien erfassen mit großem Einfühlungsvermögen den Alltag von Menschen, die beinahe völlig außerhalb der Gesellschaft leben: ein vielsagendes und bildmächtiges psychologisches Dokument über das nackte Leben. — KG
Roger Ballen wurde 1950 in New York, USA, geboren. Er lebt und arbeitet in Johannesburg, Südafrika.

Roger Ballen's point of departure is sociological and anthropological, with a focus on the disenfranchised, the marginalised and the peripheral. He has become known for his piercing black-and-white photographs of people living on the fringes of South African white society. His subjects are staged in gloomy and shabby domestic settings, resulting in powerful, disturbing and alienating pictures, which transcend voyeurism and venture into the territory of the affective. His series *Outland*, which took almost 20 years to complete, consists of some of the most arresting and piercing documents of human life of the latter part of the twentieth century in South Africa. *Outland* captures the life of the isolated and poor rural white population (in the dorps or small villages), who lost any privileges they had with the end of the apartheid and left many in a psychological state of shock. These images are haunting: frozen between documentary and constructed narratives, theatre and reality, they represent the crude realities of the inhabitants of white South Africa, outsiders who fell through the social net. The images in *Shadow Chamber*, from the first decade of this century, are even more haunting. They picture estranged, psychologically shaken people in grubby rooms, sometimes accompanied by pets who appear as maladjusted and confused as their owners. These photographs capture with great empathy the daily life of people living almost entirely outside of society: a telling and intense psychological document of bare life. — KG
Roger Ballen was born in 1950 in New York, USA. He lives and works in Johannesburg, South Africa

www.rogerballen.com
www.gagosian.com

BEAT STREULI
Alter Messplatz
Mannheim, S. / p. 140

Beat Streuli wurde bekannt für seine Porträts von anonymen Passanten, die er über die Jahre in den Großstädten der Welt, von Sydney und Tokio über Athen, London und New York, aber auch in kleineren Städten fotografiert hat. Ethnologische oder kulturelle Hintergründe und Differenzen der Passanten treten zugunsten einer phänomenologischen Betrachtung ihrer beiläufigen Handlungen und Körpergesten in den Hintergrund. Die Repetition menschlicher Formen entwickelt sich zu einer meditativen Befragung einer Conditio humana. Beat Streuli wird eine ortsspezifische Arbeit für das 4. Fotofestival entwickeln. Auf dem Alten Messplatz in Mannheim wird eine diagonal zum Platz laufende Fotopalisade entstehen, die Mannheimer Passanten in Großaufnahme zeigt. Für die Aufnahmen wird Streuli im Juli in der Stadt – und vor allem auch auf dem Messplatz selbst – unterwegs sein und fotografieren. Die in Mannheim geplante Präsentation auf großformatigen Plakatwänden bricht den musealen Ausstellungskontext des Festivals auf und bringt die Fotos an den Ort ihrer Entstehung zurück. Die Passanten werden mit dem Darstellungsformat und den Repräsentationsmechanismen einer Werbefläche konfrontiert. Damit ergänzt Streuli den Fragenkatalog des Ausstellungskonzeptes um die Frage nach der Verortung des Menschen in einer konsumistischen Gesellschaft. — HH
Beat Streuli wurde 1957 in Altdorf, Schweiz, geboren. Er lebt in Zürich, Schweiz, Düsseldorf, Deutschland und Brüssel, Belgien.

Beat Streuli has become internationally known for his portraits of anonymous passers-by that he has taken over a period of years in the major cities of the world, from Sydney and Tokyo to Athens, London and New York, but also in smaller cities. Ethnic and cultural backgrounds and differences take backstage here to a phenomenological examination of people's incidental actions and gestures. The repetition of human forms develops into a meditative inquiry into the human condition.
Streuli has developed a site-specific installation for the 4th Fotofestival. On the south side of Mannheim's Der Alte Messplatz, beside the old train station, a photographic palisade featuring huge close-ups of passers-by in Mannheim, occupies a long stretch of this urban space of transit. Streuli spent time in July in Mannheim to take these pictures – especially on the Messplatz itself.
The presentation of the images on large-format billboards breaks with the festival's context as museum exhibition and brings the photographs back to the place where they originated. People passing by the installation will be confronted with an image format and representation mechanisms they are familiar with from advertising. To the list of issues addressed in the exhibition concept, Streuli hence adds the question of where to localize the human being in a consumption-oriented society. — HH
Beat Streuli was born in 1957 in Altdorf, Switzerland. He lives and works between Zurich, Switzerland, Dusseldorf, Germany and Brussels, Belgium

www.beatstreuli.com

TOBIAS ZIELONY
halle02 / Kunsthalle Heidelberg, S. / p. 144

Seit mehr als 10 Jahren beobachtet und dokumentiert Zielony das nächtliche Leben in den Vorstädten in Deutschland, Polen, Kanada, den USA, Frankreich und Italien. Seine Aufnahmen zeigen Jugendliche, wie sie sich an Tankstellen, Parkplätzen und verlassenen Wohnsiedlungen herumtreiben. Sowohl die Serie *Quartiers Nord* (2003) als auch die Serie *Vele* (2009–2010) widmen sich der bedrückenden Architektur und den schwierigen sozialen Verhältnissen. *Quartiers Nord* besteht aus einer Serie mit 9 Fotografien über den Norden Marseilles, wo die Bevölkerung überwiegend algerisch ist oder aus anderen nordwestafrikanischen Ländern kommt. Die Serie *Vele* umfasst 17 Fotografien unterschiedlichen Formats über einen Sozialbaukomplex im Norden Neapels. Le Vele, der Name der Siedlung, bedeutet „Die Segel" und mutet optimistisch an, doch sie wurde noch vor der Fertigstellung von Familien der Mafia besetzt und ist heute zum Drogenumschlageplatz der Stadt geworden. Zielony hat die überdimensionierte, aber außergewöhnliche Architektur aus Beton und Metall nachts aufgenommen – mit seinen endlosen Korridoren und verstellten Aussichten ist sie zu einer visuellen Metapher für das soziale Leben des Anwesen geworden. Zielony zielt darauf ab, das Herz eines urbanen Ortes und seine Bedeutung für einen Jugendlichen einzufangen. Überall auf der Welt wird die lokale Jugendkultur von der globalen Kultur – Film, Mode, Drogen und Musik – inspiriert, die, als „Styles" adaptiert, dem Ausdruck der eigenen Identität dient. Und genau diese Aspekte kommen zum Vorschein, wenn die Jugend fotografiert wird. — SHO
Tobias Zielony wurde 1973 in Wuppertal, Deutschland, geboren. Er lebt und arbeitet in Berlin, Deutschland.

For over a decade Zielony has observed and documented the nocturnal life of suburban Germany, Poland, Canada, USA, France and Italy. His images depict youths hanging out and posing in petrol stations, car parks and deserted social housing estates. The series *Quartiers Nord* (2003) and *Vele* (2009–2010) both deal with the alienating architectures and social relations. *Quartiers Nord* consists of a series of nine photographs taken in the northern part of Marseille, where the population is largely Algerian or North West African. *Vele* is a series of 17 images in various sizes from a social housing complex in the north of Naples. *Le Vele* is the name of the complex and optimistically means 'The Sails', but was squatted by Mafia families before the building was finished and nowadays has become the drug-dealing centre of the city. Zielony has recorded the bombastic yet fantastical architecture of concrete and metal at night, with its vast passageways and blocked perspectives becoming a visual metaphor for the estate's social life. Zielony aims to capture the heart of an urban site and what it means to a youngster. Local youth cultures all around the world share the fact that they are inspired by global culture – film, fashion, drugs and music – which are adapted as 'styles' of representation of identity, and it is these aspects that are apparent when the youth are photographed. — SHO
Tobias Zielony was born in 1973, in Wuppertal, Germany. He lives and works in Berlin, Germany

www.tobiaszielony.de

Werkverzeichnis / List of Exhibited Works

Wenn nicht anders genannt, sind alle Werke Courtesy der Künstler. / Unless otherwise specified, all works are courtesy the artist.

Bani Abidi
Karachi Series – 1, 2009
6 Duratrans in Leuchtkästen / in lightboxes
je / each 50.8 x 76.2 cm
Courtesy der Künstler und / the artist and Green Cardamom

Mac Adams
Parallel Lives, 1999
4 C-Prints
je / each 76 x 76 cm,
74 x 101 cm
Courtesy gb agency, Paris

Ravi Agarwal
Down and Out: Labouring under Globalisation, 1997–2000
13 C-Prints auf / on Alu Dibond
je / each 76 x 50 cm

Said Atabekov
Way to Rome, 2007
12 C-Prints
je / each 50 x 65 cm
Courtesy: Impronte Contemporary Art, Mailand / Milan

Sven Augustijnen
Les Demoiselles de Bruxelles. Recueil d'articles, 2008
Buch und 29 Lambda-Prints in 10 Bronzerahmen verschiedener Größe / a book and 29 Lambda-Prints in 10 brass frames of various sizes
Privatsammlung / private collection, London

Roger Ballen
Outland, 1987–2000
24 Selen getonte Silberabzüge / Selenium toned silver prints
je / each 40 x 40 cm
Courtesy der Künstler und / the artist and Gagosian Gallery

Shadow Chamber, 2001–2004
9 Selen getonte Silberabzüge / Selenium toned silver prints
je / each 40 x 40 cm
Courtesy der Künstler und / the artist and Gagosian Gallery

Boarder, 2005, aus der Serie / from the series *Boarding house*
1 Selen getonter Silberabzug / Selenium toned silver print
40 x 40 cm
Courtesy der Künstler und / the artist and Gagosian Gallery

Olaf Otto Becker
River 01, 2007
18 C-Prints
je / each 40 x 50 cm

A measuring station being anchored deeper in the ice because of melting, 2008
C-Print
111 x 133 cm

River 2 Position 1, 2008
C-Print
111 x 133 cm

River 2 Position 2, 2008
C-Print
111 x 133 cm

Tryptichon Illulissat Icefjord, 2003
3 C-Prints
je / each 156 x 128 cm (gerahmt / framed)

Sofia Burchardi & Plamen Bontchev
Alone Together, 2011
Vitrine mit 8 Pigment Prints / vitrine with 8 pigment prints
je / each 30 x 40 cm
1 Achtphasen Lenticular Porträt / eight-phase lenticular portrait
110 x 160 cm

Marie José Burki
De nos jours (dedans), 2004
Video, Farbe, Ton / video, colour, sound
10:18 min.
Courtesy Galerie Baronian Francey, Brüssel / Brussels

Edward Burtynsky
Manufacturing #16, Bird Mobile, Ningbo Province, China, 2005
C-Print
68.58 x 86.36 cm

Manufacturing #11, Youngor Textiles, Ningbo, Zhejiang Province, China, 2005
C-Print
68.6 x 86.4 cm

Manufacturing #8, Textile Mill, Xiaoxing, Zhejiang Province, China, 2005
C-Print
99.06 x 124.46 cm

Manufacturing #6a & #6b, Hongqingting Shoe Factory, Wenzhou, Zhejiang, China (Diptychon / diptych), 2004
C-Print
je / each 99.06 x 124.46 cm

Nickel Tailings #37, Sudbury, Ontario, 1996
C-Print
101.6 x 152.4 cm

Oil Fields #18, McKittrick, California, 2003
C-Print
101.6 x 127 cm

Oil Refineries #2, Oakville, Ontario, 1999
C-Print
101.6 x 127 cm

Old Factories #4, 2005
C-Print
68.6 x 86.4 cm

Shanghai City Panorama, Shanghai, China, 2005
C-Print
66.7 x 152.4 cm

Shipbreaking #5, Chittagong, Bangladesh, 2000
C-Print
101.6 x 127 cm

Shipbreaking #5, Chittagong, Bangladesh, 2001
C-Print
68.6 x 86.4 cm

Shipyard #12, Qili Port, Zhejiang Province, China, 2004
C-Print
124.5 x 99.1 cm

Socar oil Fields #4, Baku, Azerbaijan, 2006
C-Print
68.6 x 86.4 cm

Socar Oil Fields #6, Baku, Azerbaijan, 2006
C-Print
61 x 94 cm

Socar Oil Fields #1a & 1b, Baku, Azerbaijan, 2006
C-Print
je / each 101.6 x 152.4 cm

Alle Arbeiten / all images Courtesy Galerie Stefan Röpke, Köln / Cologne

Peggy Buth
Desire in Representation (Travelling through the Musée Royale), 2004–2009
70-teilige Serie / Series of 70 photographs
Archivprint gerahmt / archival print, framed
je / each 46 x 32 cm
Courtesy die Künstlerin / the artist und / and Klemm's, Berlin

Mariana Castillo Deball
There Is a Space Later in Time Where You Are Just a Memory, 2010
Video, S/W / b&w, ohne Ton / silent
7 min.
Courtesy die Künstlerin / the artist und / and Galerie Barbara Wien Wilma Luckatsch, Berlin

Philippe Chancel
Arirang #1, #2, #3, #4, 2005
4 Inkjet Prints auf / on Hahnemühle Fine Art Paper
je / each 150 x 90 cm
Courtesy der Künstler / the artist und / and Galerie Philippe Chaume, Paris

Desert Spirit, 2007–2010
4 Inkjet Prints auf / on Hahnemühle Fine Art Paper
je / each 80 x 60 cm
courtesy der Künstler / the artist und / and Galerie Philippe Chaume, Paris

Chen Chieh-jen
Factory, 2003
Einkanal-Videoinstallation / Single-channel video installation
Super 16mm übertragen auf / transferred to DVD, Farbe / colour, ohne Ton / silent
31:09 min.

Lingchi – Echoes of a Historical Photograph, 2002
Einkanal-Videoinstallation / Single-channel video installation
Super 16mm übertragen auf / transferred to DVD, S/W / b&w, Ton / sound
21:04 min.

Gohar Dashti
Today's life and war, 2008
8 C-Prints
je / each 120 x 90 cm

Fouad Elkoury
Armenian Photo / Civil War, Beirut 1982
C-Print auf / on Alu-Dibond
50 x 75 cm

Cité sportive / Civil War, Beirut July 15, 1982
C-Print auf / on Alu-Dibond
75 x 50 cm

Sabra and Shatila / Civil War, Beirut 1982
C-Print auf / on Alu-Dibond
90 x 135 cm

Rue de Damas / Beirut City Centre, Beirut 1991
C-Print auf / on Alu-Dibond
100 x 125 cm

Place des Martyrs / Beirut City Centre, Beirut 1991
C-Print auf / on Alu-Dibond
50 x 62.5 cm

The Flag / Beirut City Centre, Beirut 1991
C-Print auf / on Alu-Dibond
80 x 100 cm

Jeu de dupes / Traces of War, Beirut 1995
C-Print auf / on Alu-Dibond
50 x 75 cm

Köken Ergun
Wedding, 2007–2008
Dreikanal-Videoinstallation / Three

channel video installation. Farbe / Colour. Ton / sound
12 min.

Hasan & Husain Essop
Garden of Earthly Delights, 2007
Lightjet C-Print auf / on Fuji Crystal Archive Paper
84 x 118 cm

Pit-bull Fight, 2007
Lightjet C-Print auf / on Fuji Crystal Archive Paper
84 x 118 cm

Suguud, Closest to God, 2007
Lightjet C-Print auf / on Fuji Crystal Archive Paper
84 x 118 cm

Off to the North Pole, 2008
Lightjet C-Print auf / on Fuji Crystal Archive Paper
70 x 123 cm

Kavali, 2008
Lightjet C-Print auf / on Fuji Crystal Archive Paper
84 x 118 cm

Pennsylvanians, 2008
Lightjet C-Print auf / on Fuji Crystal Archive Paper
84 x 118 cm

Pit-bull Training, 2008
Lightjet C-Print auf / on Fuji Crystal Archive Paper
70 x 123 cm

Fast Food, 2008
Lightjet C-Print auf / on Fuji Crystal Archive Paper
70 x 123 cm

Alle Arbeiten / All images Courtesy die Künstler / the artists und / and Goodman Gallery, Südafrika / South Africa

Simon Fujiwara
Before the Fall, 2011
Campingtisch, Landkarte, Fotografien, Texttafeln, Campingzubehör / Camping table, map, photographs, text on card, camping ephemera
80 x 100 x 150 cm
Courtesy Privatsammlung / Private Collection, Italien / Italy

Peter Funch
Babel Tales, 2006–2010
C-Print auf / on Alu-Dibond
je / each 58 x 129 cm
Courtesy der Künstler / the artist und / and V1 Gallery, Kopenhagen / Copenhagen

Agnès Geoffray
Les suspendus, 2010–2011
8 Fine Art Prints
verschiedene Größen / different sizes

Alexandros Georgiou
Without my own vehicle, Varanasi, 2009–2010
Fotografien mit Mischtechnik bearbeitet / mixed media processed photographs
verschiedene Größen / different sizes
© der Künstler / the artist, Courtesy of Eleni Koroneou Gallery, Athen / Athens

Francesco Giusti
Sapologie, 2009
8 Digital Colour Prints auf / on Alu-Dibond
je / each 100 x 100 cm

Geert Goiris
Whiteout, 2008–2011
Diaprojektion von 50 Dias / Slideshow of about 50 chromes
je / each 6 x 7 cm
Courtesy Galerie Art: Concept, Paris

Igor Grubić
366 Liberation Rituals, 2008–2009
23 C-Prints, je / each 20 x 30 cm
15 C-Prints, je / each 30 x 45 cm
7 C-Prints, je / each 50 x 70 cm

Cao Guimarães
Gambiarras, 2000–2011
8 C-Prints je / each 45 x 58.5 cm
2 C-Prints je / each 58.5 x 45 cm
2 C-Prints je /each 64.5 x 98.5 cm

Alle Arbeiten / all images © Cao Guimarães
Courtesy der Künstler / the artist und / and Xippas Gallery, Paris & Athen / Athens

Jacob Holdt
American Pictures, 1970–1975
13 Lambda-Prints auf / on Alu-Dibond
je / each 53.6 x 73.7 cm und / and 139.4 x 191.7 cm

Pieter Hugo
Nollywood, 2008-2009
6 C-Prints
je / each 102 x 102 cm
© der Künstler / the artist, Courtesy STEVENSON, Kapstadt /Cape Town / Johannesburg und / and Yossi Milo, New York

Wild Honey Collectors, 2005
2 C-Prints
je / each 82 x 82 cm
© der Künstler / the artist, Courtesy STEVENSON, Kapstadt / Cape Town / Johannesburg und / and Yossi Milo, New York

Nicu Ilfoveanu
Steampunk Autochrome, 2004–2008
16 Ultragiclée Prints / Digigraphie® certified
je / each 68 x 102 cm und / and 94 x 140 cm

Gulnara Kasmalieva & Muratbek Djumaliev
Spring, 2009
Video, Farbe / colour, Ton / sound
12:42 min.

Rinko Kawauchi
Aila, 2004
C-Print auf / on Alu Dibond
je / each 101 x 101 cm
Courtesy Galerie Priska Pasqeur, Köln / Cologne

Cui Cui, 2005
Diaprojektion auf / Slideshow on DVD, Farbe / colour, Ton / sound
Courtesy Galerie Priska Pasqeur, Köln / Cologne

Panos Kokkinias
Circle, 2010
C-Print
120 x 157 cm

Twenty Past Nine, 2010
C-Print
120 x 162 cm

Prespes, 2009
C-Print
120 x 194 cm

Thecni, 2006
C-Print
158 x 120cm

Aliki, 2007
C-Print
120 x 177cm

Alle Arbeiten / all images courtesy der Künstler / the artist und / and Xippas Gallery, Paris & Athen / Athens

Aglaia Konrad
Iconocopycity, 2011
Wandtapete / Wallpaper
ca. 500 x 600 cm

Concrete & Samples III - Carrara, 2010
16mm auf / on DVD, Farbe / colour, ohne Ton / silent
19:23 min.
Courtesy Aglaia Konrad, Galerie Nadia Vilenne, Liège, Galerie Michael Wiesehöfer, Köln / Cologne

Heta Kuchka
Tuomo & Paavo, 2009
Video, Farbe / colour, Ton / sound
28 min.

Florian Maier-Aichen
Untitled, 2011
C-Print
217.8 x 278.1 cm gerahmt / framed

Untitled, 2011
C-Print
211.5 x 186.1 cm gerahmt / framed

Östersjön I, 2011
C-Print
163.8 x 127.6 cm gerahmt / framed

Untitled, 2011
C-Print
218.4 x 156.2 cm gerahmt / framed

Alle Arbeiten / all images Courtesy der Künstler / the artist und / and Blum & Poe, Los Angeles, 303 Gallery, New York, Gagosian Gallery, London, und / and Baronian Francey, Brüssel / Brussels

Ryan McGinley
Road Trips, 2007–2009
4 C-Prints aus der Serie / from the series
verschiedene Größen / different sizes
Courtesy The Breeder, Athen / Athens und / and Team Gallery, New York

Blue Moon, 2009
Aus der Serie / from the series *Road trips*
C-Print
Privatsammlung / Private Collection, Athen / Athens; Courtesy The Breeder, Athen / Athens und / and Team Gallery, New York

Vincent Meessen
Vita Nova, 2009
Video übertragen auf Hard Disk / video transfered on hard disk,
Farbe / colour, Ton / sound
26 min.

Fac Dissimile, 2010
Druckwerke, 1. Edition, 10.000 Freiexemplare / printed matter, first edition, 10.000 free copies
Koproduziert von / Co-produced by Fotofestival, De Brakke Grond, Kiasma Museum, und / and Espace Khiasma
ca. 100 x 80 x 60 cm

Barbara Metselaar Berthold
The Tall Tale of Freewill, 1978–2011
Block von 25 Fotos / tableau consisting of 25 photographs
10 C-Prints
15 S/W-Prints / b&w prints
je / each 45 x 30 cm

Boris Mikhailov
Case History, 1997
3 C-Prints
je / each 175 x 121 cm
Privatsammlung / Private Collection, Courtesy Galerie Suzanne Tarasieve, Paris

Boniface Mwangi
Kenya Post Election Violence, 2007–2008
28 C-Prints auf / on Alu-Dibond
je / each 30 x 45 cm

Torbjørn Rødland
Burning Skull no. 1, no. 2, no. 4, 2008–2010
3 C-Prints auf / on Alu-Dibond
je / each 55 x 70 cm
Courtesy der Künstler / the artist und / and Nils Stærk, Kopenhagen / Copenhagen

Kirstine Roepstorff
The Six Realms, 2007
Collage, Mischtechnik / Collage mixed media
332 x 584 cm
Courtesy Galleri Christina Wilson, Copenhagen

Bruno Serralongue
Calais, 2006–2008
7 Ilfochromes auf Alu-Dibond hinter Plexiglas / 7 Ilfochrome on Alu-Dibond with Plexiglas
verschiedene Größen / different sizes
Courtesy Air de Paris, Paris

Jeremy Shaw
Transcendental Capacities (Electronic Dance Music Grid – 1978 – 2001), 2011
45 Kirlian Polaroids in einer Holz/Metalvitrine / 45 Kirlian Polaroid photographs in wood and metal vitrine
137.2 x 71.1 x 106.7 cm

DMT, 2005
Video, Farbe / colour, Ton / sound
95:27 min.
Courtesy der Künstler / the artist und / and Blanket Contemporary, Vancouver

Taryn Simon
The Innocents, 2002
9 C-Prints
je / each 123.5 x 159 cm
DZ BANK (Kunstsammlung)

Johan Spanner
Sworn Virgins, 2009
10 Inkjet Prints
je / each 50 x 60 cm

Iraq Series, 2003–2009
6 Inkjet Prints
je / each 70 x 100 cm

Beat Streuli
Alter Messplatz Mannheim 07–11, 2011
Fototapete auf Sperrholz / Wallpaper on plywood
3.5 m x 70 m
Courtesy der Künstler / the artist und / and Galerie Eva Presenhuber, Zürich / Zurich

Fiona Tan
Vox Populi Tokyo, 2007
305 C-Prints individuell gerahmt / individual framed, als fotografische Installation / as photographic installation
je / each 13 x 18 cm
Gesamtgröße / over all size
850 x 230 cm
Courtesy die Künstlerin / of the artist und / and Frith Street Gallery, London

Guy Tillim
Avenue Patrice Lumumba, 2007/2008
10 Archivabzüge auf handgeschöpftem Papier aus Baumwollfasern / Archival pigment inks on cotton rag paper
je / each 91.5 x 131.5 cm und / and 49.7 x 71.4 cm
DZ BANK (Kunstsammlung)

Tris Vonna-Michell
endless tapes, 2011
Ortsspezifische Multimedia Installation / Site specific mixed media installation

Clemens von Wedemeyer
Found Footage (von: Die vierte Wand), 2008–2009
Video, Fotografie, 16mm, Installation / Video, photography, 16mm, installation
verschiedene Größen / different sizes

Paolo Woods
Walk on my Eyes, 2004–2009 (released 2010)
5 C-Prints aus der Serie / from the series
je / each 90 x 90cm

Chinafrica, 2007
5 C-Prints aus der Serie / from the series
je / each 90 x 90 cm

Yang Yongliang
Artificial Wonderland No. 1, 2010
Wandtapete / Wallpaper
169 x 900 cm

Tobias Zielony
Quartiers Nord, 2003
8 C-Prints aus der Serie / from the series
verschiedene Größen / dimensions variable
Alle Bilder / all images courtesy der Künstler / the artist und / and KOW BERLIN, Berlin

Vele, 2010
9 C-Prints aus der Serie / from the series
verschiedene Größen / dimensions variable
Alle Bilder / all images courtesy der Künstler / the artist und / and KOW BERLIN, Berlin

Diese Publikation erscheint anlässlich des Festivals / This catalogue is published on the occasion of the festival *The Eye is a Lonely Hunter: Images of Humankind*

4. Fotofestival Mannheim_ Ludwigshafen_Heidelberg
09. September – 06. November 2011

Herausgegeben von / Edited by

Katerina Gregos, Solvej Helweg Ovesen und dem / and Fotofestival Mannheim_ Ludwigshafen_Heidelberg e.V.

mit Texten von / with Texts by
Jonatan Ahlm Brenander (JAB)
Carolin Ellwanger (CE)
Katerina Gregos (KG)
Heide Häusler (HH)
TJ Demos
Solvej Helweg Ovesen (SHO)

Katalog Gestaltung von / Catalogue Design by
Manuel Raeder und / and Manuel Goller

Veranstalter des Festivals ist das Fotofestival Mannheim_Ludwigshafen_ Heidelberg e.V. Die 3 beteiligten Städte Mannheim, Ludwigshafen, Heidelberg sind im Vorstand vertreten. / The producer of the festival is Fotofestival Mannheim_Ludwigshafen_Heidelberg e.V. The three participating cities, Mannheim, Ludwigshafen and Heidelberg, are represented in the festival Board:

Vorstand / Board
Dietrich Skibelski, Sabine Schirra, Hans-Martin Mumm, Michael Ebert

Ausstellungen / Exhibitions

Konzeption und künstlerische Leitung des Festivals / Conception and Artistic Directors of the festival
Katerina Gregos, Solvej Helweg Ovesen

Geschäftsführung und Festivalmanagement / Managing Director and Festival Management
Carolin Ellwanger

Ausstellungsleitung / Exhibition management
Heide Häusler

Geschäftsstelle / Office Manager
Sabine von Wussow

Assistentin Ausstellungsorganisation / Assistant to exhibition co-ordination
Julia Koch

Praktikantinnen / Interns
Jonatan Ahlm Brenander, Julia Mauga, Seraphine Meya, Karoline Michaelis

Ausstellungsaufbau / Installation
Yvonne Vogel, Andrzej Naglowsky, Torsten Kappenberg, Frank Hofacker, Markus Brehm, Michael Volkmer, Alexander Horn, Andrej Wischnewski, Team halle02.

Ausstellungstechnik / AV equipment and technical installation
Eidotech: Joachim Reck und / and Martin Klemmer

In-situ-Projekt in Kooperation mit motorlab-Architekten / in situ project In cooperation with motorlab-Architekten

Akquise und Kooperationen / Acquisition and Cooperations
Carolin Ellwanger

Pressearbeit / Public relations
Goldmann PR in Zusammenarbeit mit / in conjunction with
Carolin Ellwanger, Seraphine Meya

Marketing / Marketing
Carolin Ellwanger, Karoline Michaelis

Gestaltung / Print design
Raum Mannheim

Website
Code Poetry

Portfolio-Review

Organisation / Organisation
Sabine von Wussow, Julia Mauga

Beteiligte Ausstellungs-institutionen / Collaborating Institutions / Exhibition Venues

Kunsthalle Mannheim
Ulrike Lorenz, Thomas Köllhofer, Selini Andres, Petra Neff, Dorothee Höfert, Birgit Scheidecker

ZEPHYR der Reiss-Engelhorn-Museen
Alfried Wieczorek, Thomas Schirmböck, Marianne Aselmeier, Silvia Rückert

Wilhelm-Hack-Museum, Ludwigshafen
Reinhard Spieler, Nina Gülicher, Herbert Nolden, Udo Baur

Kunstverein Ludwigshafen
Barbara Auer, Stefanie Schubert, Yvonne Vogel

Heidelberger Kunstverein
Susana Saez, Friederike Schröder, Katja Arnold, Yvonne Vogel

Sammlung Prinzhorn
Thomas Röske, Torsten Kappenberg, Liane Wendt

halle02 / Kunsthalle Heidelberg
Wolfram Glatz, Felix Grädler

Katalog / Catalogue

Konzeption und Gestaltung des Katalogs / Catalogue concept and design
Manuel Raeder und / and Manuel Goller

Verantwortliche Redaktion Inhalt / Content Editors
Katerina Gregos, Solvej Helweg Ovesen

Redaktion / Editing
Katerina Gregos (Englisch / English)
Heide Häusler (Deutsch / German)

Bildredaktion / Photo editors
Julia Koch / Katerina Gregos

Lektorat / Copyediting
Colin Perry (Englisch / English)
Nicole Hoffmann (Deutsch / German)

Übersetzungen / Translations
aus dem Deutschen / from German:
Jennifer Taylor
aus dem Englischen / from English:
Angelika Franz, Claudia Theis-Passaro

Bildbearbeitung / Image processing
Kehrer Design Heidelberg: Jürgen Hofmann, Patrick Horn

Gesamtherstellung / Production
Kehrer Design Heidelberg

Fotonachweise / Photo credits
© Air de Paris, Paris: S. / p. 14–15
Courtesy der Künstler / the artist und / and Blanket Contemporary, Vancouver: S. / p. 82–83, 109
Photo(s) © Edward Burtynsky, courtesy Galerie Stefan Röpke, Köln / Cologne / Nicholas Metivier Gallery, Toronto: S. / p. 36–37
Courtesy der Künstler / the artist und / and Blum & Poe, Los Angeles, 303 Gallery, New York, Gagosian Gallery, London und / and Baronian Francey, Brüssel / Brussels: S. / p. 50–51
Courtesy die Künstlerin / the artist und / and Frith Street Gallery, London: S. / p. 112–113
Courtesy der Künstler / the artist und / and Gagosian Gallery: S. / p. 136–139
Courtesy Galerie Baronian_Francey, Brüssel / Brussels: S. / p. 120–121
Courtesy die Künstlerin / the artist, Foto / photo: Galerie Nadja Vilenne, Liège S. / p. 47
Courtesy der Künstler / the artist und / and Galerie Philippe Chaume, Paris: S. / p. 38–39, 68–69
Courtesy der Künstler / the artist und / and Galerie Suzanne Tarasieve, Paris: S. / p. 106–107
Courtesy der Künstler / the artist and Galerie Xippas, Paris / Athen / Athens: S. / p. 11, 44, 78, 100
Courtesy die Künstlerin / the artist und / and Galerie Barbara Wien Wilma Lukatsch, Berlin, : S. / p. 67
Courtesy Galleri Christina Wilson, Kopenhagen / Copenhagen, Photo: Anders Sune Berg: S. / p. 80–81
Courtesy Galerie Priska Pasqeur, Köln: S. / p. 100–131

Courtesy gb agency, Paris: S. / p. 92
Courtesy die Künstler / the artists und / and Goodman Gallery, Südafrika / South Africa: S. / p. 71
Courtesy Green Cardamom, London: S. / p. 60–61
Courtesy die Künstlerin / the artist und / and Klemm's, Berlin: S. / p. 64–65
Courtesy Kuckei + Kuckei, Berlin und / and STEVENSON Gallery, Kapstadt / Cape Town: S. / p. 24–25
© der Künstler / the artist, courtesy Eleni Koroneou Gallery, Athen / Athens: S. / p. 124–125
Courtesy der Künstler / the artist und / and Nils Stærk, Kopenhagen / Copenhagen: S. / p. 108
Courtesy Impronte Contemporary Art, Mailand / Milan: S. / p. 62–63
Courtesy Tobias Zielony und / and KOW BERLIN, Berlin: S. / p. 144–145
Courtesy Privatsammlung / Private Collection, Italien / Italy: S. / p. 94–95
© der Künstler / the artist, courtesy The Breeder, Athen / Athens und / and Team Gallery, New York: S. / p. 102–103
Courtesy V1 Gallery, Kopenhagen / Copenhagen: S. / p. 122–123, 72–73
© der Künstler / the artist, courtesy Galerie Art: Concept, Paris: S. / p. 41
Photo: Alexander Koch, © VG Bild Kunst: S. / p. 87
Photo: Hugo Muñoz: S. / p. 87
© der Künstler / the artist, courtesy STEVENSON, Kapstadt / Cape Town / Johannesburg und / and Yossi Milo, New York: S. / p. 66–67
© der Künstler / the artist, courtesy Gagosian Gallery: S. / p. 16–19

Alle übrigen Aufnahmen stammen von den Künstlern. / All other photographs are courtesy of the artists.

Bibliografische Information der Deutschen Nationalbibliothek
Die deutsche Nationalbibliothek verzeichnet diese Publikation in der Deutschen Nationalbiografie; detaillierte bibliografische Daten sind im Internet unter http://dnb.d-nb.de abrufbar. /
Bibliographical information published by the Deutsche Nationalbibliothek
The Deutsche Nationalbibliothek lists this publication in the Deutsche Nationalbiografie; detailed bibliographical data is available on the Internet at http://dnb.d-nb.de.

ISBN 978-3-86828-240-5

Kehrer Heidelberg Berlin
www.kehrerverlag.com

Das 4. Fotofestival Mannheim_Ludwigshafen_Heidelberg ist ein Großprojekt der Kulturvision 2015. Wir danken all unseren Sponsoren und Partnern für ihre großzügige Unterstützung. / The 4. Fotofestival Mannheim_Ludwigshafen_Heidelberg is a major project of Kulturvision 2015. For their support, we wish to express our heartfelt thanks to all our sponsors, patrons, constant partners and to the exhibition venues participating in this project:

Unser Premiumsponsor / Our Premium Sponsor

BASF
The Chemical Company

Unser Hauptsponsor / Our Main Sponsor

MVV Energie

Unsere Förderer / Our Patrons

STADTMANNHEIM² · Stadt Ludwigshafen am Rhein · Stadt Heidelberg · Metropolregion Rhein-Neckar · FESTIVALREGION RHEIN-NECKAR

Weitere Partner / Further Partners

HEIDELBERG · Stiftung Rheinland-Pfalz für Kultur · Heinrich-Vetter-Stiftung · schweizer kulturstiftung prohelvetia · Baden-Württemberg · JAPANFOUNDATION · ifa Gefördert durch das Institut für Auslandsbeziehungen aus Mitteln der Kulturabteilung des Auswärtigen Amtes · Mondriaan Stichting (Mondriaan Foundation) · STATENS KUNSTRÅD DANISH ARTS COUNCIL · LBBW Stiftungen Landesbank Baden-Württemberg · myphotobook · With the support of the Flemish authorities · OCA Office for Contemporary Art Norway · VRN Verkehrsverbund Rhein-Neckar · rnv · GBGMANNHEIM²

Kooperationspartner / Co-Operation Partners

zeitraumexit · LA CHAMBRE · dpunkt.verlag · MOTOR LAB/AR CHITEK TEN///. · DGPh Deutsche Gesellschaft für Photographie e.V. · EIDOTECH www.eidotech.com · DZ BANK [KUNSTSAMMLUNG]

Medienpartner / Media Partners

Camera Austria · monopol Magazin für Kunst und Leben

4. Fotofestival Mannheim Ludwigshafen Heidelberg

BANI ABIDI
MAC ADAMS
RAVI AGARWAL
SAID ATABEKOV
SVEN AUGUSTIJNEN
ROGER BALLEN
OLAF OTTO BECKER
SOFIA BURCHARDI &
PLAMEN BONTCHEV
MARIE JOSE BURKI
EDWARD BURTYNSKY
PEGGY BUTH
MARIANA CASTILLO DEBALL
PHILIPPE CHANCEL
CHEN CHIEH-JEN
GOHAR DASHTI
FOUAD ELKOURY
KÖKEN ERGUN
HASAN & HUSAIN ESSOP
SIMON FUJIWARA
PETER FUNCH
AGNES GEOFFRAY
ALEXANDROS GEORGIOU
FRANCESCO GIUSTI
GEERT GOIRIS
IGOR GRUBIC
CAO GUIMARÃES
JACOB HOLDT
PIETER HUGO
NICU ILFOVEANU
GULNARA KASMALIEVA &
MURATBEK DJUMALIEV
RINKO KAWAUCHI
PANOS KOKKINIAS
AGLAIA KONRAD
HETA KUCHKA
FLORIAN MAIER-AICHEN
RYAN MCGINLEY
VINCENT MEESSEN
BARBARA METSELAAR BERTHOLD
BORIS MIKHAILOV
BONIFACE MWANGI
TORBJØRN RØDLAND
KIRSTINE ROEPSTORFF
BRUNO SERRALONGUE
JEREMY SHAW
TARYN SIMON
JOHAN SPANNER
BEAT STREULI
FIONA TAN
GUY TILLIM
CLEMENS VON WEDEMEYER
TRIS VONNA-MICHELL
PAOLO WOODS
YANG YONGLIANG
TOBIAS ZIELONY

Cover: Fouad Elkoury, *Jeu de dupes / Traces of War Beirut 1995;* Beat Streuli, Arbeitsmaterial / Working material *Alter Messplatz Mannheim 07-11*, 2011; Roger Ballen, *Children's Bedroom Wall*, 2000; Cao Guimarães, *Gambiarras #86*, 2008; Philippe Chancel, *Ghost city*, aus der Serie / from the series *Desert Spirit*, 2007–2010; Rinko Kawauchi, *Untitled*, aus der Serie / from the series *Cui Cui*, 2005; Ravi Agarwal, *Kite string making, Surat, India*, aus der Serie / from the series *Down and Out*, 1997–2000; Fiona Tan, *Vox Populi, Tokyo*, 2007; Boniface Mwangi, *Kenya Post Election Violence*, 2007–2008; Alexandros Georgiou, *Shiva under Kali's foot*, 2010, aus der Serie / from the series *Without my own vehicle, Varanasi*, 2009–2010; Jacob Holdt, "Paternal love on the 12th floor in the slum. Chicago, IL" aus / from *American Pictures*, 1970–1975

Back cover: Francesco Giusti, *BONGA BONGA - Republic of the Congo - Pointe-Noire*, aus der Serie / from the series *Sapologie*, 2009; Ryan McGinley, *Marlon and Rebecca* aus der Serie / from the series *Road Trips*, 2009; Pieter Hugo, *Steven Amoako, Wild Honey Collector, Techiman District, Ghana*, 2005; Clemens von Wedemeyer, Standbild aus /video still from *Found Footage*, als Teil von / as part from *The Fourth Wall*, 2009; Said Atabekov, aus der Serie / from the series *Way to Rome*, 2007; Olaf Otto Becker, *River 1, Position 1*, 2007; Peggy Buth, *Desire in Representation (Travelling through the Musée Royale)*, 2004-2009; Florian Maier-Aichen, *Untitled*, 2011

KEHRER